KU-574-425

WITHDRAWN

LIVERPOOL JMU LIBRARY

3 1111 01145 9607

CHILDHOOD

CHILDHOOD

Critical Concepts in Sociology

Edited by Chris Jenks

Volume III

Routledge
Taylor & Francis Group

LONDON AND NEW YORK

First published 2005
by Routledge
2 Park Square, Milton Park, Abingdon, Oxon, OX14 4RN

Simultaneously published in the USA and Canada
by Routledge
270 Madison Avenue, New York, NY 100016-0602

Routledge is an imprint of the Taylor & Francis Group

Editorial matter and selection © 2005 Chris Jenks; individual
owners retain copyright in their own material

Typeset in 10/12pt Times by Graphicraft Limited, Hong Kong
Printed and bound in Great Britain by
MPG Books Ltd, Bodmin, Cornwall

All rights reserved. No part of this book may be reprinted or
reproduced or utilised in any form or by any electronic,
mechanical, or other means, now known or hereafter
invented, including photocopying and recording, or in any
information storage or retrieval system, without permission in
writing from the publishers.

British Library Cataloguing in Publication Data
A catalogue record for this book is available from the British Library

Library of Congress Cataloging in Publication Data
A catalog record for this book has been requested

ISBN 0-415-34024-1 (Set)
ISBN 0-415-34027-6 (Volume III)

Publisher's Note
References within each chapter are as they appear in the original complete work

CONTENTS

CONTENTS

ACKNOWLEDGEMENTS

Volume III

The publishers would like to thank the following for permission to reprint their material:

Taylor & Francis Books for permission to reprint Erica Burman, 'Discourses of the Child', in *Deconstructing Developmental Psychology*, (London: Routledge, 1994), pp. 48–64.

Taylor & Francis Books for permission to reprint Erica Burman, 'Morality and the Goals of Development', in *Deconstructing Developmental Psychology*, (London: Routledge, 1994), pp. 177–189.

Free Association Books Ltd., for permission to reprint Nikolas Rose, 'The Young Citizen' in *Governing the Soul*, (New York: Routledge, 1990), pp. 87–97.

Taylor & Francis Books for permission to reprint Matthew Speier, 'The Everyday World of the Child', in J. Douglas, ed., *Understanding Everyday Life*, (London: RKP, 1970), pp. 74–82.

Northwestern University Press for permission to reprint Maurice Merleau-Ponty, 'The Child's Relations with Others', in *The Primacy of Perception*, (Evanston, Illinois: Northwestern University Press, 1964), pp. 107–119.

University of Southern Denmark for permission to reprint Valerie Walkerdine, 'Safety and Danger: Childhood, Sexuality and Space at the End of the Millennium', in *Research in Childhood: Sociology, Culture and History*, (Denmark: University of Southern Denmark, 2000), pp. 197–212.

Stewart Asquith, 'When Children Kill Children: The Search for Justice', *Childhood*, 3, 1, 1996, pp. 99–116. (Copyright © Sage, 1996) Reproduced by permission of Sage Publications Ltd.

Joann Conrad, 'Lost Innocent and Sacrificial Delegate: The JonBenet Ramsey Murder', *Childhood*, 6, 3, 1999, pp. 313–355. (Copyright © Sage, 1999) Reproduced by permission of Sage Publications Ltd.

Jenni Harden, 'There's No Place Like Home: The Public/Private Distinction in Children's Theorizing of Risk and Safety', *Childhood*, 7, 1, 2000, pp. 43–59. (Copyright © Sage, 2000) Reproduced by permission of Sage Publications Ltd.

James Garbarino and Claire Bedard, 'Spiritual Challenges to Children Facing Violent Trauma', *CHILDHOOD*, 3 4, 1996, pp. 467–478. (Copyright © Sage, 1996) Reproduced by permission of Sage Publications Ltd.

Ulrich Beck, extracts from *Risk Society: Towards a New Modernity*, (London: Sage Publications, 1992), pp. 106–119. (Copyright © Sage, 1992) Reproduced by permission of Sage Publications Ltd. and Ulrich Beck.

Taylor & Francis Books for permission to reprint Karl Mannheim, 'The Problem of Generations', in *Essays in the Sociology of Knowledge*, (London: RKP, 1927), pp. 98–110.

University of Southern Denmark for permission to reprint Leena Alanen, 'Childhood as Generational Condition: Towards a Relational Theory of Childhood', in *Research in Childhood: Sociology, Culture and History*, (Denmark: University of Southern Denmark, 2000), pp. 11–30.

Taylor & Francis Books for permission to reprint Margaret O'Brien, Pam Alldred and Deborah Jones, 'Children's Constructons of Family and Kinship', in J. Brannan and M. O'Brien, eds., *Children and Families: Research and Policy*, (London: Falmer Press, 1996), pp. 84–100.

Disclaimer

The publishers have made every effort to contact authors/copyright holders of works reprinted in *Childhood: Critical Concepts in Sociology*. This has not been possible in every case, however, and we would welcome correspondence from those individuals/companies whom we have been unable to trace.

Part 7

DEVELOPMENT, GOVERNANCE AND EMERGENCE

43

GENETIC EPISTEMOLOGY

Jean Piaget

Source: *Genetic Epistemology*, New York: W. W. Norton & Company Inc., 1971, pp. 1–19.

Genetic epistemology attempts to explain knowledge, and in particular scientific knowledge, on the basis of its history, its sociogenesis, and especially the psychological origins of the notions and operations upon which it is based. These notions and operations are drawn in large part from common sense, so that their origins can shed light on their significance as knowledge of a somewhat higher level. But genetic epistemology also takes into account, wherever possible, formalization—in particular, logical formalizations applied to equilibrated thought structures and in certain cases to transformations from one level to another in the development of thought.

The description that I have given of the nature of genetic epistemology runs into a major problem, namely, the traditional philosophical view of epistemology. For many philosophers and epistemologists, epistemology is the study of knowledge as it exists at the present moment; it is the analysis of knowledge for its own sake and within its own framework without regard for its development. For these persons, tracing the development of ideas or the development of operations may be of interest to historians or to psychologists but is of no direct concern to epistemologists. This is the major objection to the discipline of genetic epistemology, which I have outlined here.

But it seems to me that we can make the following reply to this objection. Scientific knowledge is in perpetual evolution; it finds itself changed from one day to the next. As a result, we cannot say that on the one hand there is the history of knowledge, and on the other its current state today, as if its current state were somehow definitive or even stable. The current state of knowledge is a moment in history, changing just as rapidly as the state of knowledge in the past has ever changed and, in many instances, more rapidly. Scientific thought, then, is not momentary; it is not a static instance; it is a process. More specifically, it is a process of continual construction and reorganization. This is true in almost every branch of scientific investigation. I should like to cite just one or two examples.

The first example, which is almost taken for granted, concerns the area of contemporary physics or, more specifically, microphysics, where the state of knowledge changes from month to month and certainly alters significantly within the course of a year. These changes often take place even within the work of a single author who transforms his view of his subject matter during the course of his career. Let us take as a specific instance Louis de Broglie in Paris. A few years ago de Broglie adhered to Niels Bohr's view of indeterminism. He believed with the Copenhagen school that, behind the indeterminism of microphysical events, one could find no determinism, that indeterminism was a very deep reality and that one could even demonstrate the reasons for the necessity of this indeterminism. Well, as it happens, new facts caused de Broglie to change his mind, so that now he maintains the very opposite point of view. So here is one example of transformation in scientific thinking, not over several successive generations but within the career of one creative man of science. Let us take another example from the area of mathematics. A few years ago the Bourbaki group of mathematicians attempted to isolate the fundamental structures of all mathematics. They established three mother structures: an algebraic structure, a structure of ordering, and a topological structure, on which the structuralist school of mathematics came to be based, and which was seen as the foundation of all mathematical structures, from which all others were derived. This effort of theirs, which was so fruitful, has now been undermined to some extent or at least changed since McLaine and Eilenberg developed the notion of categories, that is, sets of elements taken together, with the set of all functions defined on them. As a result, today part of the Bourbaki group is no longer orthodox but is taking into account the more recent notion of categories. So here is another, rather fundamental area of scientific thinking that changed very rapidly.

Let me repeat once again that we cannot say that on the one hand there is the history of scientific thinking, and on the other the body of scientific thought as it is today; there is simply a continual transformation, a continual reorganization. And this fact seems to me to imply that historical and psychological factors in these changes are of interest in our attempt to understand the nature of scientific knowledge.[1]

I should like to give one or two examples of areas in which the genesis of contemporary scientific ideas can be understood better in the light of psychological or sociological factors. The first one is Cantor's development of set theory. Cantor developed this theory on the basis of a very fundamental operation, that of one-to-one correspondence. More specifically, by establishing a one-to-one correspondence between the series of whole numbers and the series of even numbers, we obtain a number that is neither a whole number nor an even number but is the first transfinite cardinal number, *aleph zero*. This very elementary operation of one-to-one correspondence, then, enabled Cantor to go beyond the finite number series, which was the only one in use up until his time. Now it is interesting to ask where this operation of one-to-one correspondence came from. Cantor did not invent it, in the sense that one invents a radically new construction. He found it in his own thinking; it had already been a part of his mental equipment long before he even turned to mathematics, because the most elementary sort of sociological or psychological observation reveals that one-to-one correspondence is a primitive operation. In all sorts of early societies it is the basis for economic exchange, and in small children we find its roots even before the level of concrete operations. The next question that arises is, what is the nature of this very elementary operation of one-to-one correspondence? And right away we are led to a related question: what is the relationship of one-to-one correspondence to the development of the notion of natural numbers? Does the very widespread presence of the operation of one-to-one correspondence justify the thesis of Russell and Whitehead that number is the class of equivalent classes (equivalent in the sense of one-to-one correspondence among the members of the classes)? Or are the actual numbers based on some other operations in addition to one-to-one correspondence? This is a question that we shall examine in more detail later. It is one very striking instance in which a knowledge of the psychological foundations of a notion has implications for the epistemological understanding of this notion. In studying the development of the notion of number in children we can see whether or not it is based simply on the notion of classes of equivalent classes or whether some other operation is also involved.

I should like to go on now to a second example and to raise the following question: how is it that Einstein was able to give a new operational definition of simultaneity at a distance? How was he able to criticize the Newtonian notion of universal time without giving rise to a deep crisis within physics? Of course his critique had its roots in experimental findings, such as the Michaeloson-Morley experiment—that goes without saying. Nonetheless, if this redefinition of the possibility of events to be simultaneous at great distances from each other went against the grain of our logic, there would have been a considerable crisis within physics. We would have had to accept one of two possibilities: either the physical world is not rational, or else human reason is impotent—incapable of grasping external reality. Well, in fact nothing of this sort happened. There was no such upheaval. A few metaphysicians (I apologize to the philosophers present) such as Bergson or Maritain were appalled by this revolution in physics, but for the most part and among scientists themselves it was not a very drastic crisis. Why in fact was it not a crisis? It was not a crisis because simultaneity is not a primitive notion. It is not a primitive concept, and it is not even a primitive perception. I shall go into this subject further later on, but at the moment I should just like to state that our experimental findings have shown that human beings do not perceive simultaneity with any precision. If we look at two objects moving at different speeds, and they stop at the same time, we do not have an adequate perception that they stopped at the same time. Similarly, when children do not have a very exact idea of what simultaneity is, they do not conceive of it independently of the speed at which objects are traveling. Simultaneity, then, is not a primitive intuition; it is an intellectual construction.

Long before Einstein, Henri Poincaré did a great deal of work in analyzing the notion of simultaneity and revealing its complexities. His studies took him, in fact, almost to the threshold of discovering relativity. Now if we read his essays on this subject, which, by the way, are all the more interesting when considered in the light of Einstein's later work, we see that his reflections were based almost entirely on psychological arguments. Later on I shall show that the notion of time and the notion of simultaneity are based on the notion of speed, which is a more primitive intuition. So there are all sorts of reasons, psychological reasons, that can explain why the crisis brought about by relativity theory was not a fatal one for physics. Rather, it was readjusting, and one can find the psychological routes for this readjustment as well as the experimental and logical basis. In point of fact, Einstein himself recognized the relevance of psychological factors, and when I had the good chance to meet him for the first time in 1928, he suggested to me that is would be of interest to study the origins in children of notions of time and in particular of notions of simultaneity.

What I have said so far may suggest that it can be helpful to make use of psychological data when we are considering the nature of knowledge. I should like now to say that it is more than helpful; it is indispensable. In fact, all epistemologists refer to psychological factors in their analyses, but for the most part their references to psychology are speculative and are not based on psychological research. I am convinced that all epistemology brings up factual problems as well as formal ones, and once factual problems are encountered, psychological findings become relevant and should be taken into account. The unfortunate thing for psychology is that everybody thinks of himself as a psychologist. This is not true for the field of physics, or for the field of philosophy, but it is unfortunately true for psychology. Every man considers himself a psychologist. As a result, when an epistemologist needs to call on some psychological aspect, he does not refer to psychological research and he does not consult psychologists; he depends on his own reflections. He puts together certain ideas and relationships within his own thinking, in his personal attempt to resolve the psychological problem that has arisen. I should like to cite some instances in epistemology where psychological findings can be pertinent, even though they may seem at first sight far removed from the problem.

My first example concerns the school of logical positivism. Logical positivists have never taken psychology into account in their epistemology, but they affirm that logical beings and mathematical beings are nothing but linguistic structures. That is, when we are doing logic or mathematics, we are simply using general syntax, general semantics, or general pragmatics in the sense of Morris, being in this case a rule of the uses of language in general. The position in general is that logical and mathematical reality is derived from language. Logic and mathematics are nothing but specialized linguistic structures. Now here it becomes pertinent to examine factual findings. We can look to see whether there is any logical behavior in children before language develops. We can look to see whether the coordinations of their actions reveal a logic of classes, reveal an ordered system, reveal correspondence structures. If indeed we find logical structures in the coordinations of actions in small children even before the development of language, we are not in a position to say that these logical structures are derived from language. This is a question of fact and should be approached not by speculation but by an experimental methodology with its objective findings.

The first principle of genetic epistemology, then, is this—to take psychology seriously. Taking psychology seriously means that, when a question of psychological fact arises, psychological research should be consulted instead of trying to invent a solution through private speculation.

It is worthwhile pointing out, by the way, that in the field of linguistics itself, since the golden days of logical positivism, the theoretical position has been reversed. Bloomfield in his time adhered completely to the view of the logical positivists, to this linguistic view of logic. But currently, as you know, Chomsky maintains the opposite position. Chomsky asserts, not that logic is based on and derived from language, but, on the contrary, that language is based on logic, on reason, and he even considers this reason to be innate. He is perhaps going too far in maintaining that it is innate; this is once again a question to be decided by referring to facts, to research. It is another problem for the field of psychology to determine. Between the rationalism that Chomsky is defending nowadays (according to which language is based on reason, which is thought to be innate in man) and the linguistic view of the positivists (according to which logic is simply a linguistic convention), there is a whole selection of possible solutions, and the choice among these solutions must be made on the basis of fact, that is, on the basis of psychological research. The problems cannot be resolved by speculation.

I do not want to give the impression that genetic epistemology is based exclusively on psychology. On the contrary, logical formalization is absolutely essential every time that we can carry out some formalization; every time that we come upon some completed structure in the course of the development of thought, we make an effort, with the collaboration of logicians or of specialists within the field that we are considering, to formalize this structure. Our hypothesis is that there will be a correspondence between the psychological formation on the one hand, and the formalization on the other hand. But although we recognize the importance of formalization in epistemology, we also realize that formalization cannot be sufficient by itself. We have been attempting to point out areas in which psychological experimentation is indispensable to shed light on certain epistemological problems, but even on its own grounds there are a number of reasons why formalization can never be sufficient by itself. I should like to discuss three of these reasons.

The first reason is that there are many different logics, and not just a single logic. This means that no single logic is strong enough to support the total construction of human knowledge. But it also means that, when all the different logics are taken together, they are not sufficiently coherent with one another to serve as the foundation for human knowledge. Any one logic, then, is too weak, but all the logics taken together are too rich to enable logic to form a single value basis for knowledge. That is the first reason why formalization alone is not sufficient.

The second reason is found in Gödel's theorem. It is the fact that there are limits to formalization. Any consistent system sufficiently rich to contain elementary arithmetic cannot prove its own consistency. So the following questions arise: logic is a formalization, an axiomatization of something, but of what exactly? What does logic formalize? This is a considerable problem. There are even two problems here. Any axiomatic system contains the undemonstrable propositions or the axioms, at the outset, from which the other propositions can be demonstrated, and also the undefinable, fundamental notions on the basis of which the other notions can be defined. Now in the case of logic what lies underneath the undemonstrable axioms and the undefinable notions? This is the problem of structuralism in logic, and it is a problem that shows the inadequacy of formalization as the fundamental basis. It shows the necessity for considering thought itself as well as considering axiomatized logical systems, since it is from human thought that the logical systems develop and remain still intuitive.

The third reason why formalization is not enough is that epistemology sets out to explain knowledge as it actually is within the areas of science, and this knowledge is, in fact not purely formal: there are other aspects to it. In this context I should like to quote a logician friend of mine, the late Evert W. Beth. For a very long time he was a strong adversary of psychology in general and the introduction of psychological observations into the field of epistemology, and by that token an adversary of my own work, since my work was based on psychology. Nonetheless, in the interests of an intellectual confrontation, Beth did us the honor of coming to one of our symposia on genetic epistemology and looking more closely at the questions that were concerning us. At the end of the symposium he agreed to co-author with me, in spite of his fear of psychologists, a work that we called *Mathematical and Psychological Epistemology*. This has appeared in French and is being translated into English. In his conclusion to this volume, Beth wrote as follows: "The problem of epistemology is to explain how real human thought is capable of producing scientific knowledge. In order to do that we must establish a certain coordination between logic and psychology." This declaration does not suggest that psychology ought to interfere directly in logic—that is of course not true—but it does maintain that in epistemology both logic and psychology should be taken into account, since it is important to deal with both the formal aspects and the empirical aspects of human knowledge.

So, in sum, genetic epistemology deals with both the formation and the meaning of knowledge. We can formulate our problem in the following terms: by what means does the human mind go from a state of less sufficient knowledge to a state of higher knowledge? The decision of what is lower or less adequate knowledge, and what is higher knowledge, has of course formal and normative aspects. It is not up to psychologists to determine whether or not a certain state of knowledge is superior to another state. That decision is one for logicians or for specialists within a given realm of science. For instance, in the area of physics, it is up to physicists to decide whether or not a given theory shows some progress over another theory. Our problem, from the point of view of psychology and from the point of view of genetic epistemology, is to explain how the transition is made from a lower level of knowledge to a level that is judged to be higher. The nature of these transitions is a factual question. The transitions are historical or psychological or sometimes even biological, as I shall attempt to show later.

The fundamental hypothesis of genetic epistemology is that there is a parallelism between the progress made in the logical and rational organization of knowledge and the corresponding formative psychological processes. Well, now, if that is our hypothesis, what will be our field of study? Of course the most fruitful, most obvious field of study would be reconstituting human history—the history of human thinking in prehistoric man. Unfortunately, we are not very well informed about the psychology of Neanderthal man or about the psychology of *Homo siniensis* of Teilhard de Chardin. Since this field of biogenesis is not available to us, we shall do as biologists do and turn to ontogenesis. Nothing could be more accessible to study than the ontogenesis of these notions. There are children all around us. It is with children that we have the best chance of studying the development of logical knowledge, mathematical knowledge, physical knowledge, and so forth. These are the things that I shall discuss later in the book.

So much for the introduction to this field of study. I should like now to turn to some specifics and to start with the development of logical structures in children. I shall begin by making a distinction between two aspects of thinking that are different, although complementary. One is the figurative aspect, and the other I call the operative aspect. The figurative aspect is an imitation of states taken as momentary and static. In the cognitive area the figurative functions are, above all, perception imitation, and mental imagery, which is in fact interiorized imitation. The operative aspect of thought deals not with states but with transformations from one state to another. For instance, it includes actions themselves, which transform objects or states, and it also includes the intellectual operations, which are essentially systems of transformation. They are actions that are comparable to other actions but are reversible, that is, they can be carried out in both directions (this means that the results of action A can be eliminated by another action B, its inverse: the product of A with B leading to the identity operation, leaving the state unchanged) and are capable of being interiorized; they can be carried out through representation and not through actually being acted out. Now, the figurative aspects are always subordinated to the operative aspects. Any state can be understood only as the result of certain transformations or as the point of departure for other transformations. In other words, to my way of thinking the essential aspect of thought is its operative and not its figurative aspect.

To express the same idea in still another way, I think that human knowledge is essentially active. To know is to assimilate reality into systems of transformations. To know is to transform reality in order to understand how a certain state is brought about. By virtue of this point of view, I find myself opposed to the view of knowledge as a copy, a passive copy, of reality. In point of fact, this notion is based on a vicious circle: in order to make a copy we have to know the model that we are copying, but according to this theory of knowledge the only way to know the model is by copying it, until we are caught in a circle, unable ever to know whether our copy of the model is like the model or not. To my way of thinking, knowing an object does not mean copying it—it means acting upon it. It means constructing systems of transformations that can be carried out on or with this object. Knowing reality means constructing systems of transformations that correspond, more or less adequately, to reality. They are more or less isomorphic to transformations of reality. The transformational structures of which knowledge consists are not copies of the transformations in reality; they are simply possible isomorphic models among which experience can enable us to choose. Knowledge, then, is a system of transformations that become progressively adequate.

It is agreed that logical and mathematical structures are abstract, whereas physical knowledge—the knowledge based on experience in general—is concrete. But let us ask what logical and mathematical knowledge is abstracted from. There are two possibilities. The first is that, when we act upon an object, our knowledge is derived from the object itself. This is the point of view of empiricism in general, and it is valid in the case of experimental or empirical knowledge for the most part. But there is a second possibility: when we are acting upon an object, we can also take into account the action itself, or operation if you will, since the transformation can be carried out mentally. In this hypothesis the abstraction is drawn not from the object that is acted upon, but from the action itself. It seems to me that this is the basis of logical and mathematical abstraction.

In cases involving the physical world the abstraction is abstraction from the objects themselves. A child, for instance, can heft objects in his hands and realize that they have different weights—that usually big things weigh more than little ones, but that sometimes little things weigh more than big ones. All this he finds out experientially, and his knowledge is abstracted from the objects themselves. But I should like to give an example, just as primitive as that one, in which knowledge is abstracted from actions, from the coordination of actions, and not from objects. This example, one we have studied quite thoroughly with many children, was first suggested to me by a mathematician friend who quoted it as the point of departure of his interest in mathematics. When he was a small child, he was counting pebbles one day; he lined them up in a row, counted them from left to right, and got ten. Then, just for fun, he counted them from right to left to see what number he would get, and was astonished that he got ten again. He put the pebbles in a circle and counted them, and once again there were ten. He went around the circle in the other way and got ten again. And no matter how he put the pebbles down, when he counted them, the number came to ten. He discovered here what is known in mathematics as commutativity, that is, the sum is independent of the order. But how did he discover this? Is this commutativity a property of the pebbles? It is true that the pebbles, as it were, let him arrange them in various ways; he could not have done the same thing with drops of water. So in this sense there was a physical aspect to his knowledge. But the order was not in the pebbles; it was he, the subject, who put the pebbles in a line and then in a circle. Moreover, the sum was not in the pebbles themselves; it was he who united them. The knowledge that this future mathematician discovered that day was drawn, then, not from the physical properties of the pebbles, but from the actions that he carried out on the pebbles. This knowledge is what I call logical mathematical knowledge and not physical knowledge.

The first type of abstraction from objects I shall refer to as simple abstraction, but the second type I shall call reflective abstraction, using this term in a double sense. "Reflective" here has at least two meanings in the psychological field, in addition to the one it has in physics. In its physical sense reflection refers to such a phenomenon as the reflection of a beam of light off one surface onto another surface. In a first psychological sense abstraction is the transposition from one hierarchical level to another level (for instance, from the level of action to the level of operation). In a second psychological sense reflection refers to the mental process of reflection, that is, at the level of thought a reorganization takes place.

I should like now to make a distinction between two types of actions. On the one hand, there are individual actions such as throwing, pushing, touching, rubbing. It is these individual actions that give rise most of the time to abstraction from objects. This is the simple type of abstraction that I mentioned above. Reflective abstraction, however, is based not on individual actions but on coordinated actions. Actions can be coordinated in a number of different ways. They can be joined together, for instance; we can call this an additive coordination. Or they can succeed each other in a temporal order; we can call this an ordinal or a sequential coordination. There is a before and an after, for instance, in organizing actions to attain a goal when certain actions are essential as means to attainment for this goal. Another type of coordination among actions is setting up a correspondence between one action and another. A fourth form is the establishment of intersections among actions. Now all these forms of coordinations have parallels in logical structures, and it is such coordination at the level of action that seems to me to be the basis of logical structures as they develop later in thought. This, in fact, is our hypothesis: that the roots of logical thought are not to be found in language alone, even though language coordinations are important, but are to be found more generally in the coordination of actions, which are the basis of reflective abstraction. For the sake of completeness, we might add that naturally the distinction between individual actions and coordinated ones is only a gradual and not a sharply discontinuous one. Even pushing, touching, or rubbing has a simple type of organization of smaller subactions.

This is only the beginning of a regressive analysis that could go much further. In genetic epistemology, as in developmental psychology, too, there is never an absolute beginning. We can never get back to the point where we can say, "Here is the very beginning of logical structures." As soon as we start talking about the general coordination of actions, we are going to find ourselves, of course, going even further back into the area of biology. We immediately get into the realm of the coordinations within the nervous system and the neuron network, as discussed by McCulloch and Pitts. And then, if we look for the roots of the logic of the nervous system as discussed by these workers, we have to go back a step further. We find more basic organic coordinations. If we go further still into the realm of comparative biology, we find structures of inclusion ordering correspondence everywhere. I do not intend to go into biology; I just want to carry this regressive analysis back to its beginnings in psychology and to emphasize again that the formation of logical and mathematical structures in human thinking cannot be explained by language alone, but has its roots in the general coordination of actions.

Note

1 Another opinion, often quoted in philosophical circles, is that the theory of knowledge studies essentially the question of the validity of science, the criteria of this validity and its justification. If we accept this viewpoint, it is then argued that the study of science *as it is*, as a fact, is fundamentally irrelevant. Genetic epistemology, as we see it, reflects most decidedly this separation of norm and fact, of valuation and description. We believe that, to the contrary, only in the real development of the sciences can we discover the implicit values and norms that guide, inspire, and regulate them. Any other attitude, it seems to us, reduces to the rather arbitrary imposition on knowledge of the personal views of an isolated observer. This we want to avoid.

44

DEVELOPMENTAL PSYCHOLOGY AND THE STUDY OF CHILDHOOD

Valerie Walkerdine

Source: M. J. Kehily, ed., *An Introduction to Childhood Studies*, Buckingham: Open University Press, 2004, pp. 96–107.

Introduction

Over the last decade or so there has been a sea change in the study of childhood. Work coming from sociology and cultural studies (James and Prout 1997; Buckingham 2000; Lee 2001; Castenada 2002) has been quite rightly critical of the place of developmental psychology in producing explanations of children as potential subjects, whose presence is understood only in terms of their place on a path towards becoming an adult. Instead, current sociological approaches stress the importance of understanding how child subjects are produced in the present and of blurring the line between childhood as an unfinished and adulthood as a finished state (Lee 2001). It would seem from this work that sociology has displaced the psychological study of children altogether and so I want to raise some issues about how we might think about the place of psychology in the understanding of childhood and also to raise concerns about the apparent solving of a problem of psychology by shifting explanations to the other pole of individual-society dualism – sociology (Henriques *et al.* 1998).

The place of psychology in accounts of childhood

As many commentators point out, psychology has had a central place in understanding childhood. While many point to the importance of the beginning of compulsory schooling in Europe for explaining the emergence of concern about childhood as a separate state, as has been demonstrated elsewhere (Walkerdine 1984; Rose 1985), psychology has had a central role to play since its emergence at the end of the nineteenth century. This section will briefly set out the emergence of developmental psychology as part of the

13

scientific study of children. I will argue that the idea of development assumes a rational, civilized adult as its end-point. The criticisms by sociologists of the idea of the child as a potential adult derive from developmental psychology's concern with a path towards an end-point. Since the idea of development has come to appear so commonplace and normal, it is difficult to imagine how a psychological approach to childhood could be different. I will argue that sociological studies of childhood have a tendency towards dualism – that is, they still maintain a separation between something called sociology and something called psychology and have a tendency to want to explain childhood sociologically, which has two effects. The first is to leave no room for a discussion of the 'psychological' and the other is to get rid of developmental psychology only to replace it with a set of hard 'facts' derived, for example, from cognitive neuroscience. This problem, present in a number of sociological accounts (Lee 2001) leaves no place for either a reworking of psychology nor for moving beyond dualism. I want therefore to ask what place psychology might have and what a post-developmental approach to childhood might actually look like.

The emergence of developmental psychology as the study of childhood

Many have pointed to the importance of the rise of science from the seventeenth century for understanding the emergence of psychology as a science (Venn 1984). Using a Foucaultian framework, we can be clear that developmental psychology was made possible by what Foucault calls certain 'conditions of possibility' (Foucault 1979). That is, certain historical conditions make the emergence of developmental psychology seem natural and inevitable. What we need to think about is what could produce this effect? What needs to be understood is that this idea of studying children scientifically was a new idea. As Ariès ([1960] 1986) and other historians tell us, the idea of childhood as a separate state is a modern one. Ariès puts forward a convincing case that up until the eighteenth century children were regarded simply as small adults, and he analyses in particular Velasquez's, painting, *Las Meninas*, to demonstrate that the children in the painting are represented as miniature adults. These royal children were already betrothed at an early age. Among the lower orders, children also routinely worked alongside adults and were often used specifically for jobs which adults could not do – the chimney sweep in the story *Peter Pan* being perhaps the most obvious British example (a story written at a time when there was an outcry about child labour). In particular, industrialization brought with it a move away from a rural life in which small people were integrated into farming and village life, to factories which regularly employed children. As we know, in many parts of the world, child labour is still not only common but an important source of income for families. It is generally accepted that what brought about the idea of childhood as something separate was the emergeuce of popular and then compulsory schooling (Walkerdine 1984), established in Britain around 1880. What were the conditions which made a national system of education seem important? While child labour was important, the poverty of the 'working classes' brought with it crime. Jones and Williamson (1979) argue that schooling was set out as the solution to two national problems: crime and pauperism (that is, becoming a burden on the state by being poor and needing poor relief). It was argued that these two conditions were moral issues, produced by the habits and life of the poor. Schooling would allow children to learn to read the Bible and therefore to lead a more moral life. Jones and Williamson said: 'the deterioration in moral character was related to a deterioration in the religious character of the population and the political threat which this posed' (1979: 67).

It was the political threat that would be abated by teaching children correct moral values through the inculcation of good habits, rather than ending poverty. Crime and pauperism in this analysis are taken to be produced by certain qualities, habits, which could be changed. This idea of habits fits absolutely with what emerged within psychology as accounts of conditioning. As Rose (1985) argues, it was a 'happy accident' that psychology had the tools to hand! Science was used to develop a system of scientific schooling in which good habits could be taught. The monitorial schools were the prime example of this. But these schools were soon found to be wanting as children would 'recite the Lord's prayer for a half penny' (Jones and Williamson 1979: 88). It is at this point that childhood as a separate aspect of psychology could be taken to enter the stage. If habits were not enough, what had to be understood and regulated was something about the specific *nature* of children. It needs to be said here that the focus of this concern was the children of the masses. The male children of the wealthy were already being educated and had been educated in schools for many hundreds of years, or had been given private tutors. These children were being equipped to enter a life of wealth, government and leadership. So, the nature that concerns us is the nature of the masses, the poor, those likely to produce the 'disturbances of the social order' (Hamilton 1981: 2). It is common to refer here to the schools set up by industrialist Robert Owen as part of his Scottish mills. Owen looked to the French Revolution for a model of progress and beyond that to the work of Rousseau. As the historian Stewart says, 'Owen's educational principles could almost be summed up as Rousseauism applied to working-class children' (1972: 35). It was the achievement of rationality that was Owen's concern, a rationality which was at the heart of liberal government. That is, an understanding of liberal government as operating without overt coercion through a process of rational decision making. To take part in this government, the masses had to be rational (or failing that, at least be reasonable). The issue then became one of how to produce rational adults out of a mob, mass or herd, an issue which was at the heart of concerns within a number of emerging branches of psychology, such as social psychology and psychoanalysis. The search for the nature of children became an attempt to understand how to produce rational adults through education. Rousseau's concept of nature, however, was one taken out of French courtly life – the nature of shepherds and shepherdesses, not of poor peasants. Rousseau produced a fictional account of the education according to nature of two prototypical children, Emile and Sophie. To understand how this concept of nature came to stand for the 'nature of the child' we need to make reference to other debates about nature that were merging in other scientific domains. Nikolas Rose (1985) makes clear that the concept of animal versus human nature was a centre-point of post-Enlightenment thinking. He gives the example of the Wild Boy of Aveyron: a boy, named Victor, who was found in the eighteenth century in the woods in Aveyron in France, apparently having been brought up by animals. His education, to be turned from a human animal into a civilized and rational being, was seen as a test of whether human animals could become, through education, rational and civilized human beings capable of being part of liberal government. The civilizing project therefore was to take those Others – human animals, dangerous classes, savages and other colonial subjects, and turn them into rational, civilized human beings. Castenada (2002) argues that the nature of the Other was understood through an evolutionary account. The nature of those Others was simply lower down the evolutionary chain – the issue was, could they be brought up further by an education that worked with and not against their nature? For this to work, it was necessary to know what that nature was. What is significant for the story of childhood is that evolution, a science which became well-known with Darwin's work on the evolution of species, argued that human nature is not a simple bedrock but has been formed by a process of evolution – that is, of change and adaptation to an environment over long periods of prehistorical time. Darwin extended his study of evolution to the idea of ontogeny (the evolution of the species-being) copying or recapitulating phylogeny (the evolution of the species). To this end he studied his infant son (Darwin 1887). The idea of studying children in terms of an evolutionary process took off around this time, with child study societies being established around Britain. If human nature was understood as a process of evolutionary adaptation which was copied by the species-being it is not hard to understand that the evolutionary idea could be taken to relate to Others (lower classes, colonial peoples, savages, women) who were seen as lower down the evolutionary scale, and children, who were doing their own process of evolving as species-beings. Childhood in this way became a developmental process in which adaptation to the environment was understood as a natural stage-wise progression towards a rational and civilized adulthood, which was to be the basis for liberal government. Of course, the environment could be such as to inhibit full development, which kept those Others lower down the evolutionary scale.

What I have been at pains to establish then is that the idea of development is a historically specific one, which has a particular place in government in Foucault's sense. It is not natural or inevitable as a way of understanding what we have come to call childhood. Indeed, the natural itself is a very specific reading of the relation of a biology, understood evolutionarily, to a psychology. Of course it would be possible to argue that what studies in evolution demonstrated was an advance on what we knew before and so we now know scientifically that childhood is a distinct state which follows a stage-wise progression towards adulthood. My argument here is that this approach ignores the historical specificity of the introduction of the idea of development. That specific history demonstrates not a simple path of progress towards greater knowledge but a political project of liberalism which drew on scientific studies for its rationale. In this analysis, the production of the rational subject for liberalism is central (Henriques *et al.* 1998).

Childhood and developmental psychology

We have seen why a developmental account of childhood was established and we have understood its setting – the school – as the site in which the correctly developing child on a path to rationality is to be produced. Within developmental accounts there are classically aspects of human nature and those of an environment, with the human nature gradually changing and adapting to the environment. The best-known exponent of this approach is Jean Piaget. Piaget's approach to development could be described as the archetype of developmental theories in that it assumes a developmental approach to rationality or intelligence, produced out of the adaptation of structures of thinking to the structure of the physical world. Through a series of ingenious experiments, Piaget attempted to demonstrate the evolution or successive adaptation of structures of reasoning until they attained adult rationality. What we need to understand here is the status of the 'truths' supplied by this approach. When we see a child being able successfully to accomplish a Piagetian task, such as conservation of liquids, it looks like the theory must be valid and true. But there is no such necessary relation between the accomplishment of this task and something called development. The task itself is part of a theoretical framework which makes certain assumptions about the nature of mind, childhood, evolution, a pregiven subject changed through adaptation to a physical world etc. None of these things is given a priori at all. What Foucault's work allows us to understand is that the truths of Piaget's and other claims about development are not timeless and universal scientific verities but are produced at a specific historical moment as an effect of power. That is, the concerns about the production of the rational individual and the setting out of a naturalistic developmental sequence to achieve that, as well as the whole way the idea of development is put forward, are part of technologies of population management, which themselves are an aspect of how power works (Henriques *et al.* 1998). Thus, this approach is not relative – it does not say that there are a number of truths about development, all of which might have validity. Rather, it is the centrality of the relation of knowledge and power which allows us to understand how and why these particular claims to truth become enshrined as fact at any particular moment.

This is missed by many new sociological approaches to childhood, which stress a move to active childhood. The issue is rather to understand that childhood is always produced as an object in relation to power. Thus, there can be no timeless truth, sociological or psychological, about childhood. There can rather be understandings of how childhood is produced at any one time and place and an imperative to understand what kinds of childhoods we want to produce, if indeed we want childhood at all. For example, developmental psychology understands children's thinking as becoming more and more like that of adults. It figures therefore that children's thinking is assumed to be different from adult thinking and that this difference is understood as a deficiency, a natural deficiency that will be put right as the child grows up. This position is described by James and Prout (1997) as seeing children as 'human becomings' rather than human beings. However, Lee (2001) understands this position as in some ways 'throwing out the baby with the bath-water' in the sense that children are in need of supplementation. Lee asks 'how does the "being" child change if that change is not thought of as the supplementation of a natural lack? What could "growing up" mean once we have distanced ourselves from the dominant frameworks' account of socialization and development?' (Lee 2001: 54). Of course, we can also argue that supplementation and lack define aspects of that so-called stable state of adulthood. After all, old people (for example) often need supplementation as they get older. Indeed, we can understand the definition of adulthood as a stable state of being, and indeed equally as a definition of childhood as unstable, as a product of power. That is, liberal government is dependent on a notion of rights and responsibilities carried out by rational, stable beings. Any instability is often understood as childlike and as developmentally regressive. Whereas, we could understand adulthood as an unstable state too, with a fictional stability produced in the practices in which adulthood is defined and accomplished.

The other important issue to remember is that childhood as defined in terms of economic dependency on adults, access to schooling etc., is, in fact, still the norm for only a minority of the world's children. Children in many countries routinely work, and, as we know, multinationals like Nike are very dependent upon inexpensive child labour. In that sense, the modern western conception of the child exists, as Castenada (2002) argues, in circuits of exchange between the First World and the Third. In this case, for example, the situation of prosperity for adults and children in the West is directly produced by the exploitation of children in the Third World. There is no figure of the child who stands outside such circuits of exchange. In this case, the story of the developing child does something more than universalize human becomingness. It also means that we can only see the relation of exploitation between the First World and the Third as one in which Third-World children are being denied a childhood or are underdeveloped. If the First-World child exists, in a sense, at the expense of the Third, the complex economic relationality is being lost in the developmental explanation.

However, in relation to the western present, arguments have been made that globalization and neo-liberalism have produced a situation which has extended education and therefore childhood dependence well into the twenties, a period which would previously have been considered adult. Similarly, low pay and casual work have produced a situation in which people are not able to afford to leave the parental home until they are into their twenties and thirties. Lee (2001) understands this historical shift in the West as blurring the lines between adulthood and childhood and there-fore presenting childhood as a shifting state. Buckingham (2000) argues that after Postman's (1983) announcement of the 'end of childhood' because of television's access to 'adult' programmes, children in the West have considerable economic power, being a prime market, even if it is their parents who actually buy the goods. These arguments, taken together, suggest a historical shift in which childhood and adulthood, being and becoming, are no longer clear and distinct categories in the West, though for many adult and child Others, they have never been distinct.

Doing childhood differently

Given these arguments, developmental psychology has to be understood as a powerful technology of the social, which itself inscribes and catches up children and adults. However, as we have seen following arguments put forward by Lee and others about the present historical shifts, the economic and social position of both children and adults is changing, allowing the conditions of emergence for new regimes of power/knowledge and modes of population management. Within this context, we can rethink the place of the psychological in the study of childhood. In this section, I want to point the way to a number of possible directions that this work can take.

The first thing I want to stress is the necessity to move beyond a number of dualisms. The most obvious is the dualism of sociology and psychology. It is not helpful simply to attempt to replace interiority with exteriority, individual with social and so forth, because all that achieves is to leave the dualisms that created the problem intact. If it is clear that there is no essential state of childhood or adulthood, what we need to understand is how people of particular ages become subjects within specific, local practices and to understand how those subject positions and practices operate within complex circuits of exchange (Castenada 2002). The theoretical framework that underpins this move is derived from a post-foundational approach to the social sciences (Henriques *et al.* 1998). In this account, the subject is not made social, but rather the social is the site for the production of discursive practices which produce the possibility of being a subject. I would argue that it is absolutely essential for a different approach to the psychological study of childhood not to understand psychology as one part of a dualistic divide. Rather, it is important to understand how those classic aspects of psychology – learning, reasoning, emotions and so forth are produced as part of social practices. I want to gesture towards some of my own work in this area and also to mention other work which presents us with the possibility of approaching the study of children in a different way.

The production of children as subjects within educational practices

Some years ago, I attempted to rethink an approach to mathematics learning as cognitive development by approaching school mathematics as a set of discursive practices and asking how children became subjects within those practices in such a way that the learning of mathematics was accomplished (Walkerdine 1989). I wanted to understand how school mathematics discourse had specific properties and how it formed a particular relation between signifier and signified. I argued that we could explore in detail how children learned mathematics through an understanding of their production as subjects within school mathematics practices. In addition to this, however, I argued that as Rotman (1980) has also argued, mathematics was 'reason's dream', a dream of mastery over the physical universe. I suggested that this meant that it embodied particular fantasies of mastery over a calculable universe which were powerful fantasies linked to an omnipotent masculinity.

Childhood in this analysis contains two key elements: difference (not all childhoods are the same) and an emotional or libidinal economy. I want to think about these issues as they relate to one kind of difference, that of gender. British discourses of childhood have tended to implicitly define the child as male. If, for example, we examine educational writings about natural childhood, they often assume attributes that are understood as masculine: activity, breaking rules, naughtiness. Girls are often defined within education as displaying characteristics of passivity, rule-following and good behaviour, which makes their status as natural children quite problematic (Walkerdine 1989). I want to explore some of the ways in which girls and girlhood figure as an Other to adult men and the way in which this produces a set of practices for the production of the girl as a subject. Castenada (2002) argues that all children can be understood as figures in complex global circuits of exchange. With this in mind, we can think about how the relation between woman and girl, adulthood and childhood, is always a difficult one for women in the contemporary West. Are women only women when they are no longer considered sexually desirable to men? How does the idea of adult women as girls portray the girl as always and already a sexual object for a man? Women then must always strive to continue to be girls and the status of little girls with respect to sexuality is a complex one. Although there is a very clear discourse about girls as children, I have argued that there is a ubiquitous, but completely disavowed and eroticized gaze at the little girl within popular culture (Walkerdine 1997). Girls are used to sell anything from yoghurt to cars. Indeed, the adverts play on the innocence, vulnerability and hidden eroticism of the little girl. In this way the girl is never unproblematically a child. It is her production as the object of an erotic male gaze that renders her always potentially a woman. But the production of the girl as a problematic figure is made possible by the centrality of a male fantasy of conquering and deflowering innocence, projected onto the girl and the woman. The girl then is a complex figure in a circuit of exchange between men. In order to understand the practices in which girls are produced as subjects, we would need to understand just how those fantasies become embodied in the actual discourses and practices of girlhood. But more than this. We are also talking about emotions – about circuits of desire and power. The girl as object of male fantasy and desire struggles to be desirable. The relation of both the man and the girl's emotions and fantasies can be understood as both interior and exterior – that is, contained within the desires, pains and anxieties of the subjects themselves, but inseparable from the embodiment of those emotions within the discourses and practices of both girlhood and masculinity: in girls' dreams of becoming.

It is difficult to imagine becoming an adult without a place within the circuits of sexual exchange. In these practices, she is the object exchanged, while the masculine assumes the subject position of both proper child and proper adult. To illustrate this, I want to make brief mention of a debate that ensued in the press following a 1980s television series called *Minipops*, in which young children sang pop songs. What particularly caught the attention of the broadsheet press was the fact that many little girls wore quite heavy make-up, 'lashings of lipstick on mini-mouths', according to one critic. The discussion that ensued in the press was about whether the girls in particular were being stripped of their childhood by the intrusion of adult sexual fantasies. The producers of the show argued that the girls had wanted the make-up, a fact hardly difficult to imagine. On the other hand, the tabloid press compared the children to the 'kids from *Fame*' and talked about future talent, not mentioning sexuality at all. Thus it seems that childhood innocence and the intrusion of adult sexuality was a middle-class concern, fame and making it a working-class one and the desire to wear make-up another. It is not difficult to see that the actual little girls in the show were located at the intersection of all these competing discourses which not only claimed to know them but also to have their best interests at heart.

How then does any little girl herself come to understand her own desire to wear lipstick? Is she not always positioned as a human becoming? Is she not always, whatever she does, already positioned as a problem? The broadsheet critics wanted to remove her lipstick and give her a childhood, while the tabloids wanted her talent to be allowed to reach its potential. If she herself wants the lipstick, then she must be some kind of deviant. I am trying to say that any girl's desires are caught inside these complex circuits of exchange, which position her in complex and contradictory ways. Her task, it would seem, is to be able to manage those contradictory positions and to find a way through them. We could understand subjectivity as composed of just that relation between the discourses, practices and circuits of exchange and the practices of self-management through which those contradictory positions are held together and lived. This allows us to study childhood as simultaneously both exterior and interior, being and becoming, psychological and social.

Understanding the social production of children as subjects

I argue that the study of childhood must be able to understand the discourses and practices in which childhood is produced and the way that the positions within those practices are experienced and managed to produce particular configurations of subjectivity. The examples I have given above do point to some aspects of how this work might be done. However, we need to develop tools for the micro analysis of practices and their place in the positioning of subjects. I want to point finally and briefly to three approaches to this that already exist and which might be developed to assist in this work. The first is work on situated learning and apprenticeship (Cole and Scribner 1990; Haraway 1991; Lave and Wenger 1991); the second is actor network theory (Law and Moser 2002); and the third is the idea of assemblages (Deleuze and Guattari 1988; Lee 2002).

Work on the idea of learning being situated rather than general comes from two sources. The first is the work of feminist theorist Donna Haraway (1991), who questioned the idea of a 'god-trick' of large macro stories told by science as universalized accounts freed from context. The other trajectory comes from the work in the 1970s of Michael Cole and Sylvia Scribner (1990), who aimed to demonstrate that reasoning is not a generalized accomplishment but something produced in specific and local practices. This idea has been taken up by many psychologists and anthropologists in the last 30 years, perhaps the best-known of whom is Jean Lave. This body of work, known as situated cognition, has developed the study of apprenticeship (Lave and Wenger 1991) as a way of thinking about specific accomplishment of competencies without having to look to a generalized developmental model. Lave and Wenger report a number of studies of traditional and modern apprenticeship. What they demonstrate is the way in which apprentices participate peripherally in the practices of the craft or skill they are learning. They argue that learning involves an inculcation into the culture of the practices being learnt:

> From a broadly peripheral perspective, apprentices gradually assemble a general idea of what constitutes the practice of the community. This uneven sketch of the enterprise (available if there is legitimate access) might include who is involved; what they do; what everyday life is like; how masters talk, walk, work, and generally conduct their lives; how people who are not part of the community of practice interact with it, what other learners are doing; and what learners need to learn to become full practitioners. It includes an increasing understanding of how, when, and about what old-timers collaborate, collude and collide, and what they enjoy, dislike, respect, and admire. In particular it offers exemplars (which are grounds and motivation for learning activity), including masters, finished products, and more advanced apprentices in the process of becoming full practitioners.
>
> (Lave and Wenger 1991: 95)

This approach gives us a clear way of thinking about how children both are and become outside a developmental framework. The approach does not locate learning within the child but within the culture of practice. It is not at all incompatible with one which draws upon an idea of the production of children as subjects within particular practices as I discussed earlier. However, the approach which I proposed did also stress the importance of power in terms of understanding of the kind of subject needed by liberalism. In addition, I stressed the importance of the complex emotional economies which form part of the production of the child as subject within a practice.

Other approaches, which are also compatible are the reference by Lee (2001) to Deleuze and Guattari's (1988) idea of assemblages in which, for example, horse and rider as an assemblage manage to produce more than, or a supplement to, what either could accomplish alone. For Lee, the child learns by supplementation to take their place within the adult world. Finally, it is worth also considering the work of Bruno Latour and what is often described as actor network theory (Law and Moser 2002). Law and others have developed Latour's approach to science studies to take in the idea that organizations work to produce subjects in quite complex ways, so that what we might classically think of as power and agency are distributed. So, for example, when exploring how the subjectivity of a manager of a science laboratory is created, Law and Moser (2002: 3) demonstrate that all actions within the organization are joined in a complex network so that 'it is no longer easy to determine the locus of agency, to point to one place and say with certainty that action emerges from that point rather than from somewhere else'. The manager only knows where 'he' is because his subjectivity as manager is an effect of a performance that is distributed in a network of other materials and persons, jobs and activities. It is these which produce the manager as an effect of power, power distributed in the complexities of networks, the 'intersecting performance of multiple discourses and logics' (2002: 6). Like Lee, Law and Moser propose that the manager is an assemblage. In this approach, as in the others explored, the subject (in this case the manager) is not an essential psychological beingness. Rather it is created as a nodal point at an intersection of complex discourses and practices. Could it be that children as subjects are created as both beings and becomings through the production of them as subjects who are created in practices, through what Law *et al.* call intersecting performances of discourses and practices, yet also in a way which means that they are constantly apprenticed into new practices? Could we also say that the practices themselves involve complex circuits of exchange between children and between adults and children, which not only link locals to globals in Castenada's sense but also make connections within emotional economies in which, as with the case of the little girls I explored, girlhood does work for both adults and children and catches them up emotionally through the emotional investments in the contradictory positions which they enter? I am proposing that all of these approaches potentially offer us ways of approaching childhood which take us beyond development but which do not throw out the psychological, but then also attempt to go beyond a number of dualisms, thus displacing the binaries of interior and exterior, individual and social, psychology and sociology.

Childhood, within these approaches, is mobile and shifting. Yet, potentially, change and transformation can just as easily be studied as within the developmental approach. But we are no longer in the terrain of an essential childhood with a fixed and universalized psychology of development. Rather, the practices in which we are produced as subjects from birth to death, and the ways in which they produce our subjectivity as both being and becoming, always in relation, always at once interior and exterior, provide us with a different way of studying and understanding the many and varied childhoods in their local variants and global forms.

References

Ariès, P. ([1960] 1986) *Centuries of Childhood: A Social History of Family Life.* Harmondsworth: Penguin.

Buckingham, D. (2000) *After the Death of Childhood: Growing Up in the Age of Electronic Media.* Cambridge: Polity.

Castenada, C. (2002) *Figurations.* Durham, NC: Duke University Press.

Cole, M. and Scribner, S. (1990) *The Psychology of Literacy.* MA: Harvard University Press.

Darwin, C. (1887) A biographical sketch of an infant, *Mind, 7*.

Deleuze, G. and Guattari, F. (1988) *A Thousand Plateaus: Capitalism and Schizophrenia.* London: Athlone.

Foucault, M. (1979) *Discipline and Punish*, Harmondsworth: Penguin.

Hamilton, D. (1981) *On Simultaneous Instruction and the Early Evolution of Class Teaching.* Glasgow: University of Glasgow.

Haraway, D. (1991) Situated knowledges: the science question in feminism and the privilege of partial perspective, in D. Haraway *Simians, Cyborgs and Women: The Reinvention of Nature.* New York: Routledge.

Henriques J. *et al.* (1998) *Changing the Subject: Psychology, Social Regulation and Subjectivity*, 2nd edn. London: Routledge.

James, A. and Prout, A. (eds) (1997) *Constructing and Reconstructing Childhood: Contemporary Issues in the Sociological Study of Childhood*, 2nd edn. London: Falmer.

Jones, K. and Williamson, J. (1979) The birth of the schoolroom, *Ideology and Consciousness*, 6: 59–110.

Lave, J. and Wenger, E. (1991) *Situated Learning: Legitimate Peripheral Participation.* Cambridge: Cambridge University Press.

Law, J. and Moser, I. (2002) *Managing Subjectivities and Desires.* Lancaster: Centre for Science Studies, University of Lancaster.

Lee, N. (2001) *Childhood and Society.* Buckingham: Open University Press.

Postman, N. (1983) *The Disappearance of Childhood.* London: W. H. Allen.

Rose, N. (1985) *The Psychological Complex.* London: Routledge.

Rose, N. (1990) *Governing the Soul.* London: Routledge.

Rotman, B. (1980) *Mathematics: An Essay in Semiotics.* Bristol: University of Bristol.

Stewart, W. A. C. (1972) *Progressives and Radicals in English Education 1750–1970.* London: Macmillan.

Venn, C. (1984) The subject of psychology, in J. Henriques *et al. Changing the Subject: Psychology, Social Regulation and Subjectivity*, 2nd edn. London: Routledge.

Walkerdine, V. (1984) Developmental psychology and the child-centred pedagogy: the insertion of Piaget into early education, in J. Henriques *et al. Changing the Subject: Psychology, Social Regulation and Subjectivity*, 2nd edn. London: Routledge.

Walkerdine, V. (1989) *Counting Girls Out.* London: Virago.

Walkerdine, V. (1997) *Daddy's Girl: Young Girls and Popular Culture.* Basingstoke: Macmillan.

45

DISCOURSES OF THE CHILD

Erica Burman

Source: *Deconstructing Developmental Psychology*, London: Routledge, 1994, pp. 48–64.

Once upon a time we all lived in the land of childhood.
(*Adolescence*, Channel 4, 26 April 1992)

Childhood is the kingdom where nobody dies
Nobody that matters, that is.
(Edna St Vincent Millay, 1892–1950)

Discourses of childhood are central to the ways we structure our own and others' sense of place and position. They are part of the cultural narratives that define who we are, why we are the way we are and where we are going. This chapter addresses the range of ways childhood is depicted, the extent to which developmental psychological accounts reflect these representations, and the consequences of this for the adequacy of current forms and functions of developmental psychology.

The definition and demarcation of childhood are replete with social and political meanings. Whether cast in terms of nostalgia or repugnance, the category of childhood is a repository of social representations that functions only by virtue of the relationship with other age and status categories: the child exists in relation to the category 'adult'. While most developmental accounts treat movement within, and transition beyond, childhood as largely maturationally determined (as reflected in the chronological organisation of textbooks), a moment's reflection reveals that the membership prerequisites and privileges associated with the entry to adulthood are only tenuously linked with some criterial common point. As Jo Boyden and Andy Hudson (1985) note:

The distinction between children and adults is given as a basis on the one hand for granting additional rights (for instance, the first to receive relief in times of distress), and on the other, for restricting both the enjoyment of certain rights and the exercise of certain obligations.

(Boyden and Hudson, 1985: 4)

To take just a few contemporary and immediate examples, in Britain today there are a number of competing definitions of adult maturity simultaneously applied to different spheres of activity which vary in the age of maturity employed: political majority, legal responsibility and sex. In the last case it should be noted that different criteria for maturity are employed depending on whether your sexual partner is of the same or opposite sex. The entry limits on these three arenas of adult activity vary within Western Europe as well as across wider cultural spheres. There is variation within systems as well, with different criteria employed on the basis of gender. In Judaism, for example, boys are considered adult at age 13 while girls attain this status at 12. At a more general level, to take perhaps the most telling example, in many countries, the UK included, young men of 16 are treated as too young to vote or marry without permission, but old enough to kill or be killed for their country. But even before we look to 'other' cultures or to history, a diversity of definitions of maturity is apparent. To what extent is this diversity reflected in developmental psychological accounts? The question of whether 'we all lived in the land of childhood' (as the documentary claimed) turns out to be indissociable from that of who 'we' are, and whose land it is.

Developmental psychology and
the cultural categorisation of the life span

Do children grow or are they made? This variant of the nature–nurture question is what structures both the popular and the academic imagery of child development. The cover of one current textbook (Dworetzky, 1990) shows a budding flower emerging from the soil beneath the beneficent glow of a sun (with bud and sun of the same colour) – all this in a naive child-like style. Another (Kaplan, 1991), entitled *A Child's Odyssey*, conveys a picture of development as a journey, beset with difficulties and dangers, which are, moreover, negotiated sequentially and separately. Reproductions of Impressionist rural and garden scenes are interspersed throughout this text. The corresponding nuances of nostalgic romanticism this conveys perhaps underscore how as readers we learn about developmental psychology through the lens of our own recollected childhood as retrospectively reconstituted within dominant models of the child. Small wonder perhaps at the alternation between a rhetoric of mystery or wonder and businesslike calculation of how much further there is yet to go.

The important point here is that both varieties of account portray development as natural and inevitable. The trajectory of development is seen as basically uniform, with 'cross-cultural perspectives' appearing as optional extras within 'Applications' sections, in which it is largely child-rearing strategies or differences in moral codes that are presented for consideration. That is, cultural issues are treated as informing the 'content' of development rather than entering into its structure in any more fundamental way. Further, the distinctions most textbooks make between the main account and 'applications' or 'issues' maintains an implicit assumption that developmental psychological knowledge is not otherwise informed by 'applied' interests or values – an assumption that I questioned in Chapter 1.

One reason why culture can be portrayed as a kind of optional or exchangeable extra in this way lies in the structure of the texts. Firstly, most textbooks follow a chronological format from birth (or even conception) to adolescence or, with the recognition that development is 'life span', to death. Some accounts specify age limits on the periods they distinguish, as in Dworetzsky and Davis (1989) who distinguish 'Beginnings: 0–1 years; Early Childhood: 1–6 years; Middle Childhood: 6–12 years; Adolescence: 12–18 years; Early Adulthood: 18–40 years; Middle Adulthood: 40–65 years; Late Adulthood: 65+ years of age' (vii–x). It is impossible to read this without noting at the very least the remarkable lack of sensitivity to cultural and class variation in life expectancy. Most accounts distinguish between early and middle childhood, with 'toddlerhood' emerging as a new category between infancy and early childhood (in Kaplan, 1991). At a more detailed level, Fogel's (1991) account of infancy breaks this period down into seven sections, each of which is accorded not only age limits but also a specific subjective orientation (in some instances even assuming the 'voice' of the infant), with 'The psychology of the newborn (the first two months)'; 'Attention and anticipation (two to five months)'; 'The origins of initiative (six to nine months)'; 'Becoming a cause and becoming vulnerable (ten to twelve months)'; 'Expression, exploration and experimentation (twelve to eighteen months)'; 'Conflict, doubt and power (eighteen to twenty four months)' and 'I'm not a baby anymore (twenty four to thirty six months)' (Fogel, 1991: ix–xiv).

In one sense this kind of 'developmental tasks' approach simply represents the application within an age category of what is frequently portrayed as the preoccupations that separate and govern age categories. But how much do these actually have to do with age? Dworetzsky and Davis (1989) treat 'Loving and working' as the subtitle for 'Early adulthood' (p. xx) with the 'Applications' section devoted to 'Finding your one and only'. In 'Late adulthood' (subtitled 'Relationships and retirement'), the 'Applications' is about 'Stopping elder abuse'. Are these inevitable, or even prevalent, features of the human life span? Surely 'elder abuse' can occur only in societies where older people are infantilised and treated as dispensable, rather than integrated and revered. Important questions arise from these reflections. What we have here are features of white middle-class US society mapped onto models of development which are then treated as universal. What are the effects of condensing the intervals between stages from multiples of years to mere months, as in the infancy example? The earlier in the life span, the more crucial it seems the developmental achievements must be within an ever-contracting period of time. Are these achievements as culture-free as they are represented? What kinds of injunctions do they make to parents?

Secondly, the categorisation into age-graded intervals brings with it a further segmentation of developmental description. Many of these comprehensive texts subdivide each period into 'physical', 'cognitive' and 'psychosocial' (or 'social and personality'), in some cases with a chapter on each (e.g. Seifert and Hoffnung, 1987), but more often combining the treatment of 'physical and cognitive development' and 'social and personality development' (e.g. Dworetzky, 1990; Dworetzky and Davis, 1989; Kaplan, 1991; Santrock, 1989). There are two features to note here: firstly, the connection between the cognitive and the physical works to privilege the realm of the cognitive as the primary arena for psychological development (and incorporates the physical within this), and places it in linear succession to the emphasis on biology in development; and, secondly, it reinstates the now familiar division between the rational and the irrational, that is, the cognitive and the emotional (see Chapter 2) with the first seen as essential and the second as contingent.

Bringing up baby: variability in childcare advice

A rather different picture emerges from the history and sociology of childhood. Here, debates focus on the extent and variability of conceptions of childhood, conceived of as a modern, Western notion (Ariès, 1962). While it is not possible to make a simple translation from representations (whether pictorial or literary) of children to child-rearing practices, or from newspaper accounts to what parents actually did to, and felt for, their children (Pollock, 1983), nevertheless childcare advice does constitute an important resource from which to speculate about the cultural content of, and importance accorded to, childhood and parenting practices. It can therefore provide an alternative vantage point from which to look at contemporary developmental psychological accounts.

Various models have been put forward to categorise historical fluctuations in childcare advice discernible even within England and the US. Newson and Newson (1974) and Hardyment (1983) write in terms of prevailing moralities which have governed approaches to childcare. From the mid-eighteenth century to mid-nineteenth century they identify a 'religious' morality, with a focus on preparing children for death since, with the high infant mortality rates of the time, a parents' duties were seen as best fulfilled in striving to ensure their child's life in the hereafter. With the prospect of little time to prove a child's goodness in life, a battle ensued to save the child's soul. For some this means there was little scope for indulgent, permissive parenting. As Susanna Wesley wrote to her son John (founder of the Methodist movement) 'Break his will now and his soul will live' (in Newson and Newson, 1974: 56). Child activists Ennew and Milne relate the powerlessness of children to their status as legal minors in every society, pointing out that in eighteenth-century Europe,

> child theft was not theft unless the child was wearing clothes. Otherwise child theft was like the theft of a corpse. The body was not inhabited by a legal person in either case.
> (Ennew and Milne, 1989: 12)

After World War I medicine succeeded religion as the dominant moral authority governing childcare. This is sometimes attributed to a decline in infant and child mortality rates due to sanitation reforms in the mid- to late nineteenth century (combined with a general crisis of faith from the War), but it should be recalled that the highest recorded infant mortality rates in Britain were reported in the first part of the twentieth century (Rose, 1985). The narrative of modern progress that sometimes informs these accounts of childcare advice must therefore be problematised.

With the shift from medical to mental hygiene, the emerging psychology partook of medicine's authority to promise earthly survival in return for adherence to 'scientific mothercraft'. The earlier preoccupation with hereditary inclinations and predispositions was superseded by the application of behaviourist principles to childcare. The work of Watson and the New Zealand stockbreeder Truby King, who applied principles he developed rearing cattle to the upbringing of children, both advocated 'regularity of habits', and gave rise to what Daniel Beekman (1979) has called the 'mechanical' child.

> The establishment of perfect regularity of habits, initiated by feeding and cleaning by the clock is the ultimate foundation of all round obedience. Granted good organic foundations, truth and honour can be built into the edifice as it grows.
> (Truby King, 1937, cited in Newson and Newson, 1974: 61)

The authoritarian religious expert on child development was succeeded by the equally authoritarian medical expert. But the 1930s to the 1950s saw the rise of a different moral orientation towards children, emphasising children's 'needs' and 'natural development'. This was the period when psychoanalytic ideas were beginning to make their impact in early child education and with this came the importance accorded to play, to emotional as well as physical needs, and to continuity of care (Urwin and Sharland, 1992). As Newson and Newson put it 'At last the dirty, happy, noisy child could be accepted as a good child' (1974: 63). A less punitive approach was advised in dealings with children, particularly in relation to those enduring preoccupations of childcare advice: toilet training, thumb sucking and masturbation. But this was uttered in no less coercive pronouncements to parents.

The final period Newson and Newson (1974) distinguish is what they call 'Individualism and the fun morality' which they identify with the period after World War II. In part they attribute this change to the inward turn towards personal, domestic matters as an escape from recalling the atrocities of Hiroshima and Nazi death camps, and otherwise as part of a new confidence and assertiveness that marked this more affluent (for some) period. These developments (in 'choice' and consumption) were reflected in the childcare advice, firstly, in the less authoritarian tone of address and, secondly, by an emphasis on flexibility rather than prescription. The problem here is that enjoying parenting has become mandatory. In terms of the contemporary situation, this aspect still seems predominant, although there are rumblings of a backlash to permissive parenting in favour of more punitive parent-centred approaches within moral panics about childhood crime and failure at school. Contrariwise, in publicity about child abuse, moralities of 'natural needs and development' are still very much in evidence (Kitzinger, 1990; Stainton Rogers and Stainton Rogers, 1992).

It seems, then, that even within a relatively homogeneous cultural group, different historical periods have represented the process of rearing children very differently. While only one of these periods employs an explicit rhetoric of needs, it is important to recognise that all types of advice laid claim to the moral authority to define the requirements not only for good parenting, but also for what made an appropriate child, albeit often concerned with what the children would become rather than how they fared at the time. In this sense, the rhetoric of children's needs, while attractive, has been invoked over the years in quite diverse and often conflicting terms. There is a corresponding danger that children's 'needs' become some kind of inviolable category that is treated as self-evident rather than as informed by and reflecting the socio-political preoccupations of particular cultures and times (Woodhead, 1990).

Childhood as dependency

Changing images of the child can be related to broader social tensions within emerging modern industrialising states. There are three points to note here. Firstly, the contrasting models frequently coexist and compete, rather than succeed each other in a harmonious fashion. Secondly, and following from this, there are continuities between images at different times – many conceptions reverberate on in powerful ways today. Thirdly, debates about the nature of the child have been central to the ways the State has interacted with, and regulated, its citizens. The eighteenth-century French philosopher Rousseau is credited with inventing the modern notion of childhood as a distinct period of human life with particular needs for stimulation and education. In contrast to evangelical doctrines of 'original sin', this model upheld the innocence of the child, the proximity of children to nature, and their freedom from contamination with the ugly lessons of civilisation. But this was not all it achieved:

> The new child was a figure of the 'Cult of Sensibility' associated with Rousseau. . . . At the basic level, therefore, this construction related to the contest for a particular kind of society – for a particular kind of beliefs – which was to stand between eighteenth century rationalism and nineteenth century industrialisation.
>
> (Hendrick, 1990: 38–9)

Industrialisation in the late eighteenth century ushered in the formalisation of child labour in factories. Outrage over the conditions of child labourers had less to do with exploitation than with fears of unruly and potentially undesirable activities made possible by an independent income. Martin Hoyles (1989) relates the invention of childhood innocence to the cult of the 'infant Jesus' which worked to eclipse children's active political resistance. Harry Hendrick (1990) argues that a debased version of the eighteenth-century philosophy of child nature was invoked to justify making children dependent through schooling, imposing a middle-class ideal of childhood as a period of helplessness. This was then treated as a cultural universal to block the reproduction of working-class resistance through controlling the activities of young people.

> They [eighteenth-century notions of child nature] were thoughtful expressions of a developing social and political philosophy (extending well beyond a concern with children) which was finding an audience among a class anxious about what it deemed to be the rebellious and aggressive attitudes and behaviours of young people (and of their parents). Thus juvenile lawlessness was seen as one of the heralds of political insurrection.
>
> (Hendrick, 1990: 44–5)

This was achieved through the introduction of compulsory mass schooling, linked to a theory of child nature which presented the initial state of the child as ignorant (thereby disenfranchising their community and 'street' knowledge) and positioning the working-class child as in need of education and socialisation. A standard curriculum produced a segregated and surveyed population with an emphasis on Bible study, along with gender-appropriate training suited to working-class boys and girls' allotted station in life (Hunt, 1985). A national childhood was constructed through schooling, which, although it was officially classless, rendered the child (and therefore the family) always available for reformation of their working-class morals. The process of schooling demanded a state of ignorance in return for advancement of opportunities for limited few. In terms of the impact on children at the time, Hendrick (1990) suggests that the main effect of the introduction of compulsory schooling was to diminish children's sense of their own value and take them out of the sphere of 'socially significant activity':

> [T]here was nothing coincidental in mid-century penologists and social investigators seeking to return children to their 'true position' (to their nature), as it also involved making them more amenable to the classroom. . . . The reconstruction of the factory child through the prism of dependency and ignorance was a necessary precursor of mass education in that it helped prepare public opinion for shifts in the child's identity (from wage-labourer to school pupil), for a reduction in income of working class families (as a result of the loss of children's earnings), and for the introduction of the state into childrearing practices.
>
> (Hendrick, 1990: 46)

Childhood as universal

From this specific historical picture based in mid-nineteenth century Europe, we can see a move away from a diversity of class and cultural conceptualisations of childhood to the imposition of a standardised model that drew together a set of concerns with child education, management and control as well as philanthropy. This standard childhood, as administered in part through schooling, achieved uniformity and coherence among urban and rural populations; it reflected the Victorian domestic ideal of the family – based on order, respect and love – with corresponding organisation around age and gender asymmetries; and it made possible the twentieth-century construction of the compulsory relation between family, State and public welfare. Childhood, conceived of as a period of dependency, meant that education and socialisation were required to lead and train the child in the 'appropriate' direction. Hence representations of childhood were central to social policies.

It is worth reflecting on the links between notions of childhood, schooling and child labour when considering contemporary debates on the welfare of children in Third World countries. The mass media encourage us to think about 'all our children' (the BBC leaflet to the series of this name is subtitled 'A guide for those who care'), and charitable aid to Third World countries is focused on the welfare of children (as in sponsoring a child: 'Experience the joy of sponsorship says Michael Aspel', advertisement in the *Guardian*, 13 February 1992). We are exhorted by Plan International UK to 'change the world . . . one child at a time', to consider ourselves 'A World Family'.

Cosy and caring as this 'world family' sounds, it ignores cultural and economic differences and treats economic inequalities outside the history of colonialism and imperialism which produced the impoverishment of the Third World in the first place. It positions those countries as responsible for their own 'underdevelopment' instead of recognising the vested interests that maintain Third World countries as dependent markets and sources of cheap labour – primarily that of women and children. In evaluating the significance of the suppression of the impact of imperialism within these texts, we should recall that children are directly involved in the sex tourism industry which was made possible by imperialist (often specifically US) wars in South East Asia (Boyden and Hudson, 1985), as was international trafficking in children (Ramirez, 1992). Moreover, additional consequences follow from this focus on the child. Social change is rendered gradual, discretionary and individual through working at the level of 'one child at a time'.

In these ways the child *as child* functions as an index, a signifier of 'civilisation' and modernity. The 'right' to childhood is adopted as a transcultural universal that links First and Third Worlds in a relationship of patronage and cultural imperialism. The adoption of this notion (which is structured in the 1959 UN Declaration of the Rights of the Child and the 1989 Convention on the Rights of the Child) bears witness to interests which, while seeking to enable and protect children, are also in danger of rendering them passive, dependent and malleable. This is useful in evaluating current discussions of child labour in Third World countries, involving around 150 million children (Boyden with Holden, 1991). The issue here is to proscribe exploitative and dangerous work practices rather than pathologise Third World cultures and families for failing to uphold modern Western notions of dependent and playing children. What Boyden (1990) calls the 'globalization of childhood' functions as a medium for perpetuating ethnocentric and racist assumptions and prevents us from attending to the specific conditions and meanings of children's participation within local economies, without which little real aid and action is possible (see Chapter 13 for more on these issues).

From this historical perspective on legal and social policy, therefore, a certain ambivalence about the State's role in relation to children can be detected. While the model of the vulnerable, ignorant child positioned them as requiring protection, children were also portrayed as a source of disruption requiring control and discipline. In their analysis of policy and welfare practices relating to children that have given rise to legislation in Britain, Dingwall *et al.* (1984) argue that childhood has generally been treated as a 'social problem' whereby the dominant focus of social policy and practice has been on the perceived capacities of young people to threaten public order. Children's problems of abuse and neglect have tended to be collapsed together with the treatment of child *as* problem, as reflected even now within the types of care and provision available.

Returning to the developmental psychology textbooks, a similar elision is distinguishable. Dworetzky and Davis (1989) move from discussing children's needs in early life to taking as their 'Application' for their 'Adolescent social and personality development' chapter the question of 'Preventing teenage pregnancy'. It is worth pointing out here that the majority of the world's children are born to women under 20 (Phoenix, 1991), and that this is the time considered by most cultures as appropriate for childbearing. So whose development is being depicted here? 'Sexual precocity' is, however, a threat to the dominant, sanctified, passive model of childhood. New arrivals within US child development texts are coverage of 'teenage suicide' (Dworetzky, 1990; Seifert and Hoffnung, 1987) and 'childhood obesity' (Kaplan, 1991), both of which are problems within the US (but while most of the world is starving and struggling to survive). In Bukatko and Daehler (1992) the chapter on 'Social cognition' treats this as equivalent to 'self regulation'. Issues of social inequalities, disaffection and unemployment are alluded to in the last of the new (to the second edition) sections on 'The child and the year 2000' in Kaplan (1991). These, however, are presented as choices or almost life careers for young people, with the headings 'The non-college bound student'; 'Gender and achievement; minorities in high school; dropping out of school'; and 'Delinquency'. The focus on individual development leads to an acknowledgement of structural disadvantage only insofar as it is treated as a property of the individual: yet another reminder of the problems with opting for a model of change 'one child at a time'.

Significance of advice literature

The identification of these problems is often coupled with advice. Firstly, there is the significance of its presence (and volume). Newson and Newson (1974) comment on the paucity of this literature prior to the mid-twentieth century. They provide a useful reminder that the preconditions for a psychology of child development, with its concerns about psychological adjustment and abilities, are a low rate of infant mortality and an adequate standard of living. Consider then what they term the 'cult of child psychology', the explosion of popular as well as academic literature that assaults us in supermarket queues and newsagents, and that finds its way among the recipes and quizzes in general newspapers as well as in those magazines specifically directed to women. Developmental psychology participates within the everyday popular understanding of parental roles, family relations and indeed personal identities of mothers, fathers, children and all who are involved in teaching or caring for them in contemporary Western culture. In Britain, the Royal College of General Practitioners has recently approved a publication, *Emma's Diary* (Lifecycle Marketing, 1991), to be distributed free in doctors' surgeries and clinics. This contains adverts not specifically associated with childcare as well as a week-by-week description of the progress of pregnancy and childcare. The demand for information about childcare and development is presented in newspaper coverage as aiming 'to satisfy pregnant women's craving for facts about parenthood', with pregnant women described as 'information guzzling' (*Independent on Sunday*, 16 February 1992: 24). The popular notion of pregnancy as producing compulsive appetites is here extended to include women's desires to know. So essential is the role currently accorded to knowledge about child development that it can even be represented as part of a pregnant woman's bodily needs. Nested within these ideas is a form of biological reductionism which collapses the biological fact of pregnancy into a period of receptivity to information about children (shades here of Winnicott's 'primary maternal preoccupation', and of the attachment and 'bonding' research discussed in Chapter 6). And following from the biologistic analogy, the notion of critical periods, or deadlines by which this knowledge must be demonstrated, is maintained.

But, secondly, what functions does this advice play? Do we find it helpful, reassuring? How can we understand the development of this eager market? It has been suggested that one reason why mothers (and fathers) turn to books arises from the erosion of extended family ties within which cultural understandings of child rearing would otherwise be communicated. Indeed, distinct class differences have been noted between those mothers who rely on their mothers' advice and those who seek out professional sources of information (Jones, 1987; Vukelich and Kumar, 1985). Again this is a useful prompt to recall the social divisions that make spurious simple descriptions of 'society' as homogeneous even within one geographical area. While the readership of the early child manuals was primarily middle class, one clear reason for the increasing dependence on professional advice lies in the ways this explicitly devalues oral sources as uninformed and old-fashioned, cautioning women not to rely on their mothers' or older women's advice. In this sense the advice is self-maintaining.

It is clearly difficult to assess the impact or 'effects' of this literature. Harriette Marshall's (1991) analysis of the content of some influential contemporary British sources highlights their dominant themes. Motherhood is presented as a woman's 'ultimate fulfilment', with mother love as 'natural' (and, correspondingly, failure to love as requiring psychiatric treatment). There is an emphasis on 'modern' motherhood, with a dependence on professional experts for advice, and the desirable forum for the bringing up of a child is defined as a happy, heterosexual, nuclear family. This was presented as both inevitable and enduringly stable, wherein the expressed commitment to flexibility and 'sharing the caring' in the accounts gave way to positioning the mother as primarily and ultimately responsible for the 'normal development' of her child through actively stimulating, as well as caring for, her child. Rather as indicated by the slip in the Sorce *et al.* (1985) study discussed in Chapter 3, her identity as a woman is absorbed into that of mother, she is treated as responsible for her child's subsequent deeds and misdeeds through the emphasis on the importance of early experience and she is drawn into the discourse of developmental psychology through this positioning, as both originator and monitor of her child's development.

Marshall speculates how, given this load, it is possible for a woman to feel confident that she is fulfilling her maternal duty. While the women in Cathy Urwin's (1985a) survey report consulting manuals for reassurance, these are also the source of considerable anxiety. Developmental milestones structure mothers' observations of their offspring, such that they worry about the rate of progress, and induce competition between parents by inviting comparisons between children, reflecting the structuring of 'normal development' as measurable through the ranking of individuals. Development thus becomes an obstacle race, a set of hoops to jump through, with cultural kudos accorded to the most advanced, and the real or imagined penalties of professional intervention or stigmatisation if progress is delayed. Small wonder then at the marginalised position of 'learning disabled' children and their families. As well as the tendency to load responsibility for the next generation's moral performance on women, and to locate social problems within 'faulty mothering', this account also fails to accord any role to societal and structural influences.

The cultural organisation of development

The popular and 'academic' literature on how children develop reflects dominant cultural assumptions about children's natures and treatment. It also informs these to the extent that they become the resource for the circulation of everyday understandings about what children (and through them mothers, fathers and others) around them are like. The variability of advice gives rise to variability of practice. Newson and Newson (1974) take as their example the case of breast-feeding, which has been subject to fluctuation according to class and generation. While in the 1920s and 1930s bottle-feeding was a means for the British middle classes to display their status as able to afford the technology to feed and manage babies, by the 1980s breast-feeding had come to be associated with a middle-class commitment to the notion that 'Breast is best' (Stanway and Stanway, 1983), a principled desire to give your baby the best start to life, backed up by studies correlating breast-feeding with subsequent cognitive performance. The point here is not to advocate one form of feeding over another, but to indicate how the fluctuating demands on women made by medicine and psychology neglect the social factors that constrain women's choices, and thus often function simply to stigmatise further those who fail to measure up to this moral imperative.

A major consequence of this variability is that women are segmented and separated from each other's experiences and solidarity, both by generation and by class. Firstly, women who adhered to the expert advice of their day, by, for example, staying home with their child rather than engaging in paid work, are now portrayed as over-involved and clinging. Before them, their mothers who had not indulged their children and had fed them by the clock had gone on only to be later positioned as cruel and heartless. Meanwhile, within the current rhetoric of 'flexibility', women are presented with the 'choice' about feeding method. But the decks are heavily loaded in favour of breast-feeding: what mother can resist the injunction to foster the development of her child or, worse, impede it by failing to provide 'baby's birthright'? What of the mothers who do not have 'the choice' not to work, or who cannot for other reasons breast-feed their baby? This is not to condone the cynical peddling of baby milk substitutes to poor women in the Third World. Rather, in both contexts, the rhetoric of freedom of choice functions as a more subtle form of oppression by failing to recognise the inequality of access to the conditions it presupposes.

Consequences

This chapter has focused on the forms and variations of discourses of childhood, and the significance of these variations. Three main issues emerge. Firstly, definitions of childhood are relational, they exist in relation to definitions of adults, of mothers and fathers, of families, of the State. These relational terms of child, adult and State have come to function in mutually dependent, mutually constitutive ways. While this may be an easy point to accept at an intellectual level, its ramifications are far-reaching. Discussions of children's natures necessarily reflect, and invoke, models of political organisation. Just as the needy, dependent child requires the attentive, indulging mother, so the child on whom environment inscribes its learning schedules requires the regulating, training mother.

Secondly, as feminists have recognised (Thorne, 1987), changes in gender relations will bring about changes in our conceptualisation of children. Developmental psychology's commitment to a view of children and child development as fixed, unilinear and timeless is not only ethnocentric and culture-blind in its unwitting reflection of parochial preoccupations and consequent devaluation of differing patternings, but is also in danger of failing to recognise changes in the organisation of childhood subjectivity and agency. Ann Solberg (1990) documents the increased power gained by the greater participation in household labour of Norwegian children of dual earner parents, as indicated both by their own and their family's perceptions. This study involves analysis of the subjective meanings invested (by children as well as adults) in being older or younger, or more or less big or grown up. The participation of women in paid work outside the home in this example has created the conditions for new forms and variations of childhood to emerge. If childhood is seen as static, universal and timeless then this can only be viewed as an aberration to be deplored. But to do this would be to proscribe any change from existing social arrangements and to refuse to recognise opportunities for the development of new subjectivities. Further, the fact that this study seems so novel in testifying to a relation between children's productive labour and enhanced social position itself speaks volumes about the ignorance or repression of the fact that most of the world's children work. That is, we fail to recognise the cultural specificity of our developmental models, which are not only partial and unaware of this, but also oppressive in prescribing what are Western norms for Third World countries.

Thirdly, and finally, there is the question of the positioning of children and knowledge. Children are defined as lacking knowledge, hence requiring protection and education. To challenge this conception may seem to render children responsible for the difficulties that befall them, as is evident in discussions of child abuse (Kitzinger, 1990). In their textbook, Seifert and Hoffnung (1987), alongside a section on 'The concept of childhood in history', present an account of the modern construction and institutionalisation of children as benign, noting that:

> In the twentieth century, society became increasingly concerned about protecting children from the harsh world outside the family. Children were thought to need the special protection of parents and institutions dedicated to serving children, such as schools.
> (Seifert and Hoffnung, 1987: text to figures pp. 12–13)

Attribution of knowledge to children is bound up with images of the child and what we imagine them and ourselves to be. Discourses of childhood function as regulatory both overtly and internally. They produce a sense of adulthood and childhood not only for us but also for children. Accounts such as that quoted above fail to distinguish between a variety of social relations, both within and between cultures, that constitute a 'society'. They portray as unproblematic both the position of the family as haven in a heartless world, and the State as involved in protecting and educating children. These are the issues to which we turn next.

References

Ariès, P. (1962) *Centuries of Childhood*, Cape: London.

Beekman, D. (1979) *The Mechanical Baby: a popular history of the theory and practice of childraising*, London: Dobson.

Boyden, J. (1990) 'Childhood and the policy makers: a comparative perspective on the globalization of childhood', in A. James and A. Prout (eds) *Constructing and Reconstructing Childhood: contemporary issues in the sociological study of childhood*, Basingstoke, Hants: Falmer.

Boyden, J. with Holden, P. (1991) *Children of the Cities*, London: Zed Books.

Boyden, J. and Hudson, A. (1985) *Children: rights and responsibilities*, London: Minority Rights Group.

Bukatko, D. and Daehler, M. (1992) *Child Development: a topical approach*, Boston, Mass.: Houghton Mifflin.

Dingwall, R., Eekelaar, J. M. and Murray, T. (1984) 'Childhood as a social problem: a survey of the history of legal regulation', *Journal of Law and Society, 11, 2:* 207–32.

Dworetzky, J. (1990) *Introduction to Child Development*, St Paul, MN: West.

Dworetzky, J. and Davis, N. (1989) *Human Development: a lifespan approach*, St Paul, MN: West.

Ennew, J. and Milne, B. (1989) *The Next Generation: lives of Third World children*, London: Zed Books.

Fogel, A. (1991) *Infancy: infant, family and society*, St Paul, MN: West.

Hardyment, C. (1983) *Dream Babies*, Oxford: Oxford University Press.

Hendrick, H. (1990) 'Constructions and reconstructions of British childhood: an interpretive survey, 1800 to the present', in A. James and A. Prout (eds) *Constructing and Reconstructing Childhood: contemporary issues in the sociological study of childhood*, Basingstoke, Hants: Falmer.

Hoyles, M. (1989) *The Politics of Childhood*, London: Journeyman.

Hunt, F. (ed.) (1985) *Lessons for Life*, Oxford: Blackwell.

Jones, D. (1987) 'The choice to breast feed or bottle feed and influences upon that choice: a survey of 1525 mothers', *Child Care, Health and Development, 13, 1:* 75–85.

Kaplan, P. (1991) *A Child's Odyssey: child and adolescent development*, St Paul, MN: West.

Kitzinger, J. (1990) 'Who are you, kidding? Children, power and the struggle against sexual abuse', in A. James and A. Prout (eds) *Constructing and Reconstructing Childhood: contemporary issues in the sociological study of childhood*, Basingstoke, Hants: Falmer.

Marshall, H. (1991) 'The social construction of motherhood: an analysis of childcare and parenting manuals', in A. Phoenix, A. Woollett and E. Lloyd (eds) *Motherhood: meanings, practices and ideologies*, London: Sage.

Newson, J. and Newson, E. (1974) 'Cultural aspects of childrearing in the English-speaking world', in M. Richards (ed.) *The Integration of the Child into a Social World*, London: Cambridge University Press.

Phoenix, A. (1991) *Young Mothers?*, Oxford: Polity.

Pollock, L. (1983) *Forgotten Children*, Cambridge: Cambridge University Press.

Ramirez, A. (1992) 'Honduras: the traffic in children', *Central America Report, 55:* 5.

Rose, N. (1985) *The Psychological Complex: psychology, politics and society in England 1869–1939*, London: Routledge & Kegan Paul.

Santrock, J. W. (1989) *Life-span Development*, Dubuque, Iowa: Wm. C. Brown.

Seifert, K. L. and Hoffnung, R. J. (1987) *Child and Adolescent Development*, Boston, Mass.: Houghton Mifflin.

Solberg, A. (1990) 'Negotiating childhood: changing constructions of age for Norwegian children', in A. James and A. Prout (eds) *Constructing and Reconstructing Childhood: contemporary issues in the sociological study of childhood*, Basingstoke, Hants: Falmer.

Sorce, J. F., Emde, R. N., Campos, J. and Klinnert, M. (1985) 'Maternal emotional signalling: its effect on the visual cliff behaviour of one year olds', *Developmental Psychology, 21, 1*: 195–200.

Stainton Rogers, R. and Stainton Rogers, W. (1992) *Stories of Childhood: shifting agendas of child concern*, Hemel Hempstead: Harvester Wheatsheaf.

Stanway, P. and Stanway, A. (1983) *Breast is Best: a commonsense approach to breast-feeding*, London: Pan.

Thorne, B. (1987) 'Revisioning women and social change: where are the children?', *Gender and Society, 1, 1*: 85–109.

Urwin, C. (1985a) 'Constructing motherhood: the persuasion of normal development', in C. Steedman, C. Urwin and V. Walkerdine (eds) *Language, Gender and Childhood*, London: Routledge & Kegan Paul.

Urwin, C. (1985b) 'Review of *War in the Nursery* (D. Riley, Virago, 1983)', *Feminist Review, 19*: 95–100.

Urwin, C. (1986) 'Developmental psychology and psychoanalysis: splitting the difference', in M. Richards and P. Light (eds) *Children of Social Worlds*, Oxford: Polity/Blackwell.

Urwin, C. and Sharland, E. (1992) 'From bodies to minds in children literature: advice to parents in inter-war Britain', in R. Cooter (ed.) *In the Name of the Child: health and welfare 1880–1940*, London: Routledge.

Vukelich, C. and Kumar, D. S. (1985) 'Mature and teenage mothers' infant growth expectation and use of child development sources', *Family Relations: Journal of Applied Family and Child Studies, 34*: 189–96.

Woodhead, M. (1990) 'Psychology and the cultural construction of children's needs', in A. James and A. Prout (eds) *Constructing and Reconstructing Childhood: contemporary issues in the sociological study of childhood*, Basingstoke, Hants: Falmer.

46

MORALITY AND THE GOALS OF DEVELOPMENT

Erica Burman

Source: *Deconstructing Developmental Psychology*, London: Routledge, 1994, pp. 177–189.

Developmentalism is a beguiling creed, to be a developer of backward lands an attractive vocation. We all want to see ourselves as bearers of aid, rectifiers of past injustice. To be sent among a distant nation as a conveyer of progress can only make one feel good. . . . It boosts self esteem. It is to regain certainty and purpose, to cast away the ennui and despair of decaying industrial society and to restore bracing faith in the goodness and charity of one's fellow men and women.

(Morris, 1992: 1)

It has been clear that an underlying project of developmental psychology has been to produce moral citizens appropriate to the maintenance of bourgeois democracy, but it has been less clear what notion of morality it subscribes to. This chapter addresses the treatment of morality in developmental psychology. The debates and criticisms generated in this area can be regarded as encapsulating in a microcosm the limitations of current developmental models. While the moral assumptions permeating models of moral development have attracted some critical attention, their exhibition within this arena should be understood as only one particular instance of what is a general problem. In this chapter the moral status of models of moral development is located within the broader cultural and political landscape within which developmental psychology functions. The remaining questions about whether developmental psychology can outgrow rather than simply process, mature and recycle the conservative and culture-bound presentations of early twentieth-century privileged men are complex. But a prerequisite for this is to understand what these theories are and do.

Piaget's rules on children's games

In *The Moral Judgement of the Child* (1932) Piaget describes his investigations of children's developing appreciation of morality. He conceived of morality as systems of rules, and his aim was to understand how we acquire these rules. In line with his paradoxical model of the child both as asocial and as party to insights that civilisation has knocked out of us, Piaget held that most of the moral rules we learn are imposed and enforced on us ready-made by adults. However, he saw in the 'social games' played by children the opportunity to see how these rules are constructed and interpreted by children. By asking children to teach him how to play the game of marbles and asking questions about who had won the game and why, Piaget built up a picture of characteristic ways in which children of different ages both practised and accounted for the rules.

Piaget traced a development in children's play from regularities or rituals that an individual child devises to amuse herself which are full of idiosyncratic habits and symbols, to an imitation of some aspects of what others are doing in terms of rules she has devised but assumes hold generally. At this point, he argued, children may believe themselves to be playing together, but may in fact be playing entirely different games in parallel, without seeing the need for a shared set of rules. This clearly ties in with Piaget's ideas about childhood egocentrism. By about 7–8 years, he claimed, children began to see the game of marbles as a competitive game structured by rules. The success of the game depends on mutual co-operation between players according to collectively upheld rules. By 11–12 years (in what he later termed formal operational thinking) Piaget argued that children are interested not only in rules governing the particular game or version of the game they are playing, but in reflecting upon the total set of possible variations that might be called upon in a given case – in other words a hypothetico-deductive approach characteristic of formal reasoning. At this point we should note that, for Piaget, it is the appreciation and engagement with *competition* that is taken as the indicator of sociality.

This work formed the basis for a wide-ranging exploration of children's moral understanding. He explored children's awareness of rules by asking children such questions as 'Can rules be changed?', 'Have rules always been the same as they are today?' and 'How did rules begin?'. At the second stage (which would be called 'preoperational' in his later work), children's imitation of rules was based on a perception of rules as sacred and unalterable, despite violating these rules in their own play. Once again childhood egocentrism is used to account for this paradox. Piaget identified a developmental progression from *heteronomy*, where the self is undifferentiated from the (social, moral, physical) context, to *autonomy*, where the individual chooses to engage in particular social contracts. He traced a change in approach towards rules from an initial *unilateral respect* (where rules are obeyed due

43

LIVERPOOL JOHN MOORES UNIVERSITY
LEARNING SERVICES

to adult constraint) to *mutual respect* (where rules are social conventions operating to maintain fairness). He went on to pose stories involving minor misdeeds to children, investigating their ideas about responsibility in terms of moral questions he considered relevant to children, such as stealing and lying. The outcome of his clinical interviews with children was that he claimed, in contrast to older children and adults, young children judged the naughtiness of an action by its results rather than by the agent's intentions, that is, the magnitude of the damage is treated as the index of the scale of the misdeed.

Kohlberg on Piaget

Laurence Kohlberg (1969a, 1969b, 1976), a US developmental psychologist, elaborated on and developed Piaget's work on moral reasoning to put forward a series of six stages and three levels in the development and articulation of moral judgement from childhood to adulthood. He based his work on the classification of the kinds of moral reasoning displayed by individuals of different ages when they were confronted with hypothetical dilemmas. The most celebrated 'dilemma' used to elicit the underlying structure of people's moral reasoning was about a penniless man, Heinz, who urgently needs an expensive medicine to save his wife's life, and which the pharmacist refuses to give or supply on credit. Should he steal the drug? Here there is a conflict between the values of property and life. We should pause to note that, in the transition from Geneva to the US and from the 1930s to the 1960s, a process of methodological and taxonomical rigidity has taken place. The ascription of moral level has become a question of classification according to age or stage; from premoralism, to conformism, to individual principled morality.

A number of claims underlie the framework. Firstly, the stages are said to be universal and fixed. Secondly, the sequence is invariant, with variation only in rate of progression or fixation at a particular stage. And, thirdly, each stage is a structured whole, with characteristics of reasoning associated with a stage related together into a total world-view. All this is reminiscent of Piaget's model of the relations that hold between the organisation of cognitive operations. In terms of evidence used to support this model, there is apparently fairly widespread support for the claim that the stages occur in a fixed order (Colby *et al.*, 1983). There is also cross-sectional support, in that higher stages are reported among older subjects. In addition, some longitudinal studies suggest that over a period of years individuals tend to advance to higher stages (Walker, 1989). Even some cross-cultural work lent support, with Kohlberg (1969b) identifying the same sequence of stages (with the stories slightly adapted), in the US, Britain, Taiwan, Mexico and Turkey, and the stages and sequences confirmed in other societies by Edwards (1981). So it seemed as though the arena of moral development had been pretty well sorted out. Or had it?

Kohlberg's dilemmas

From the 1970s some critical voices emerged which suggested that the sorting process was on a less than equitable basis. It seemed that the ascription of the moral highground was of uncertain validity, of contested value and unfair distribution.

In terms of methodological criticisms, a first problem arises from basing a classification of moral level on verbal reports. Unlike Piaget's early work, Kohlberg's model relies exclusively on what people say about what (other) people should do, based on hypothetical situations. But being more thoughtful, circumspect, taking more factors into consideration does not necessarily mean that people behave more morally. Further, the practice of investigating moral reasoning via hypothetical situations makes the moral problems posed even more detached and distanced. In this context Carol Gilligan's (1982) work on women's reasoning about the real-life dilemma of whether or not to terminate a pregnancy provides a particularly striking contrast.

Secondly, corresponding to the work challenging what is seen as Piaget's rather pessimistic view of children's abilities, there has been some work which seeks to analyse and minimise the linguistic and narrative demands of the task. Stein *et al.* (1979) reformulated Heinz's dilemma into a story about a lady who had a sick husband and had to steal some cat's whiskers in order to make the only medicine that would save his life. Despite the fairy tale genre and simplicity of the story, they report young children as having difficulties understanding it. They suggest that the children do not draw the obvious inference that the medicine will save the man's life since they cannot maintain the major goal in mind while trying to pursue the subgoals of securing the whiskers and making the medicine. In order to engage with the dilemma, the task presupposes the ability to understand a complex narrative and to think through alternative courses of action, both of which may be more complicated than the process of making moral judgements alone.

Criticisms addressed to the theory rather than the procedures by which it was arrived at also take a number of forms. In the first place, it is claimed that it addresses only a very restricted notion of morality. While this is not the place to go into alternative (such as behavioural or psychoanalytic) models of morality, the Kohlbergian model of morality as moral reasoning cannot engage with issues of moral commitment, and individual priorities or differences of moral salience of particular issues. Nor does it address the subjective experience of feelings of guilt and shame which, as Kagan (1984) notes, children exhibit from an early age. Once again we see that a cognitive developmental model which prioritises rationality cannot theorise its relation with emotions except insofar as emotions are regarded as subordinate to, or at best by-products of, cognition.

The rigidity of representation of morality also fails to deal with domain specificity, familiarity and, further, the reality of the conflicting moral codes and priorities we are subject to (Turiel, 1983; Song *et al.*, 1987). Moreover, not only is this a model which treats talk about moral behaviour as equivalent to moral activity, it also fails to address how accounting for the morality of one's behaviour tends to follow rather than precede the actions. Hence these accounts measure moral rationalisation rather than reasoning (Hogen, 1975).

Double standards: Gender-differentiating rights and responsibilities

One of the most influential criticisms of the model is that the stages do not fit female development. Carol Gilligan (1982) points out that both Piaget and Kohlberg derived their stage norms from studying boys and men. She challenges the capacity of the model to express women's psychological development. She reinterprets boys' and girls' accounts of Heinz's dilemma, where in terms of Kohlbergian criteria the girls would be scored as reasoning at a lower moral stage of development. She points out that the girls' and women's reservations about stealing the drug were based on additional considerations arising from an engagement with the context, such as the effect on the wife if the man was imprisoned for the crime and the worry about who would care for her if she fell ill again.

Although it is unclear whether she is advocating improving or abandoning it, Gilligan therefore throws the model of moral development that Kohlberg proposes into question. In tracing a linear progression from undifferentiation or attachment to autonomy, she argues that it subscribes to a model of morality based on individual rights and freedoms of the kind enshrined in Western legal systems, whereas, she holds, women's moral development is characterised by a much more contextualised morality concerned with conflicting responsibilities and care – that is, concerned with responsibilities and relationships rather than rights and rules. She argues that Kohlberg's model emphasises separation rather than connection by taking the individual rather than the relationship as the primary unit of analysis.

Gilligan ties these different conceptions of morality to the different roles traditionally accorded to men and women. Since women define their identity through relationships of intimacy and care, the moral issues women face are to do with learning to assert their own needs without seeing this as 'selfish'. For both sexes, she argues, the issues that we face are to do with the conflict between integrity (separateness) and care (attachment), but that men and women approach these issues with different moral orientations. For men the emphasis is on 'equality', based on an understanding of fairness, equal respect, balancing the claims of other and self. In contrast, women's morality, she claims, is more oriented to issues of responsibility, with recognition of differences in need that an equal rights approach cannot address – an ethic of compassion and care and not wanting to hurt. Gilligan calls for the necessity for these contrasting moral orientations to be seen as complementary rather than one being systematically downgraded, and ultimately for them to be integrated into a more adequate vision of moral maturity. While there are problems with the idealisation of women's qualities within this account (see Sayers, 1986), the value of this work lies in demonstrating the limited application and far-reaching devaluation of women structured within the cognitive developmental model.

Culture and the goals of development

A further serious difficulty with Kohlberg's model lies in the status of the sixth stage, which represents individual moral conviction as the most advanced morality beyond the respect for democratically arrived at and contractually maintained rules (Stage Five). Firstly, few people are designated as attaining the higher points on the developmental ladder (with Jesus Christ, Mahatma Gandhi, and Martin Luther King named by Kohlberg as among the lucky few – among whom he also includes himself!). This raises questions about the theoretical status of the highest point of development. Secondly, some cultures are recorded as not reaching even beyond the second stage. There are clearly methodological difficulties involved in the study of people from one culture by those of another. These are issues that anthropologists routinely address, although some have been known to rely on psychology with disastrous results (see, e.g., Hallpike, 1979). The suggestion that Kohlberg's stages can be related to the 'complexity' of societies (Edwards, 1981) sets up a hierarchy from 'primitive' to 'complex' which simply reflects a Western cultural bias. It may, however, be more accurate to make a distinction between rural and urban societies, with Stage Five reported much less frequently in the former (Snarey, 1985). But this calls for an analysis that connects cognitive/moral development with culture and context.

However, a further issue comes into play when researchers measure indigenous people's abilities and interests by means of a test devised outside their own culture. Here developmental psychology reproduces and bolsters the dynamic of imperialism by offering tools that produce a picture of inferiority and moral underdevelopment through the ethnocentric and culturally chauvinist assumptions that inform both theory and tool (Joseph *et al.*, 1990). Kohlberg later reformulated some of his claims about Stage Six so that it is now seen as an ideal, rather than a necessary, endpoint of development (Levine *et al.*, 1985). This, however, seems to offer a rather cosmetic change which leaves the methodological, and moral-political, problems intact.

In this we can see played out problems common to all developmental psychological theories that claim to hold generally. The postulation of a starting state and an endstate involves the prescription of the endpoint, the goal, of development. We talk in terms of 'progressing', 'advancing' from one stage to the next. But the norms by which we evaluate that development may be far from universal. In particular, as we have seen, the individual autonomy of conscience of Stage Six fits well with the modern, Western ideology of individualism. But this is not the highest point of moral development for all cultures, many of which value obedience and respect for elders and tradition over personal conviction. Kagan (1984) notes that in Japan the guiding principle of social interaction is to avoid conflict and maintain harmonious relationships. With such a different value system and contrasting view of the relationship between individuals, we could expect that a Kohlbergian Stage Six person would be considered aberrant and amoral in according personal principles more importance than societal expectations.

Further, the model of 'man' prescribed in Kohlberg's (and by implication Piaget's) model derives from particular social interests, based on a liberal model of society seen as functioning by means of social contractual arrangements between people (Simpson, 1974; Sampson, 1989). The rationality which is so highly valued in the cognitive developmental model ties in with a bourgeois conception of the individual which either accepts class divisions or denies their existence (Sullivan, 1977; Buck-Morss, 1975). In its celebration of autonomy, Kohlbergian theory therefore partakes of a liberal view that sees society as composed of independent units who co-operate only when the terms of co-operation are such as to further the ends of each of the parties. This also clearly recalls Piaget's definition of social interaction in game playing through competition. Not only does this lead to an asocial view of the individual, in terms of the ascription of pre-social interests, it also sets up a form of conceptual imperialism in its application to cultures which do not share this underlying model. Sullivan treats this model as a case example of the political and conceptual problems wrought by an inadequate theory of the social: thought is severed from action, form from content, the abstract from the concrete and, ultimately, emotion from intellect.

Developmental psychology and the developing world

Some of the methodological and moral difficulties described above have been reflected in the failure of the project of cross-cultural psychology. On practical grounds researchers were forced to recognise that the cultural assumptions held by research 'subjects' about the nature of the task demanded of them did not always correspond with that intended by the researchers. Cole *et al.* (1971) found that the African Kpelle consistently failed Piagetian classification tasks when asked 'how a wise man' would organise piles of foods and household items together. It was only when in despair the researcher asked how 'a fool would do it' that they exhibited the typical Western classification based on type (sorting similar items together) that had been defined as task success, rather than functional relations that reflected the ways the items were used.

Such examples highlight that the problems are more than mere practical or technical difficulties, and cast doubt on the entire project of developmental psychology. The presentation of a general model which depicts development as unitary irrespective of culture, class, gender and history means that difference can be recognised only in terms of aberrations, deviations – that is, in terms of relative progress on a linear scale. The developmental psychology we know is tied to the culture which produced it. And, while such insights have had some impact within academic psychology, they are maintained in policy and in popular representations of childhood and child development.

The image of the active, natural, innocent child functions within the economy of cultural representations of children in so-called developing countries in ways which castigate poor people for their poverty, lapse into racist assumptions about child neglect and penalise the children of the poor rather than promote their welfare. Claire Cassidy (1989) discusses how, when poverty and ignorance lead to malnutrition in Third World countries, this is sometimes treated by welfare workers as an example of parental neglect. There is a failure to distinguish between culturally normative and deviant forms in evaluating child development in 'other' cultures. In purveying what is advertised as a general, universal model of development, developmental psychology is a vital ingredient in what Jo Boyden (1990) has termed the 'globalization of childhood'. While Western sentimentalised representations of children are rooted in the attempt to deny children's agency (notwithstanding the claims of child-centredness) and prevent social unrest, the key dimensions that have come to structure Western organisation of childhood are being inappropriately imposed in 'developing' countries. The division between public and private has been central to Western industrialisation, but it should be recalled that poor people have less privacy, and that street children may have none at all (although see Glauser (1990) for an analysis of the distinction between children *of* the street and children living *on* the streets). But Western conceptions of children as unknowing, helpless and in need of protection from the public sphere may actually disable and criminalise children who are coping as best they can. All too often, policies and practices developed in the West function more in punitive than protective ways for Third World children – even in literal ways by being dispensed by the police, who in some Third World countries have been responsible for the murder of children in their custody.

Similarly, while the regulation of child labour is clearly important, attempts to abolish this in line with Western practice frequently ignore the extent to which families (and children) are dependent on the incomes children generate, and would therefore need to be compensated in order to let their children attend school. Further, the schooling which is on offer is often of varying quality, and may often take the form of enforced assimilation to a colonial language. The schooling experience may therefore be one which fails rather than enables children. The Western priority accorded to education may therefore be misplaced in the sense that this is unlikely to be organised around principles of personal development or enlightenment.

The undifferentiated, globalised model of childhood not only fails to address the varying cultural value and position of children (Zelizer, 1985), but also ignores gender as a structural issue in development (in both the senses of individual and economic development). Aid agencies are now being forced to recognise that specific priorities need to be set up for girls and women (e.g. Wallace and March, 1991), while the role of gendered meanings in structuring not only entirely different subjectivities and livelihoods, but actual nutrition and survival is gradually emerging through the efforts of women's organisations (Scheper-Hughes, 1989b; Batou, 1991).

In general, the concept of childhood on offer is a Western construction that is now being incorporated, as though it were universal, into aid and development policies (Burman, in press b). Associations between the development of the child and the development of the nation or State are familiar. Indeed many aid policy documents present their rationale for promoting child survival and development in terms of the future benefit to the State (e.g. Myers, 1992). But there are other resonances I want to mobilise here. Tim Morris opens his account of his experiences as an aid worker in the Middle East (in the extract I have positioned at the beginning of this chapter) with a critique of the cultural chauvinism, complacency and personal investments set up within aid work. Just as he is exposing the problems inherent in defining goals for societal development, so too do the same problems arise within the determination of the direction and endpoint of individual development. The notion of 'progress', whether of societies or through 'the life span', implies linear movement across history and between cultures. Comparison within these terms is now being recognised as increasingly untenable. In particular, the implication that there is a detached, disinterested set of devices or techniques for this purpose, such as developmental psychology purports to provide, illustrates the extent to which we have come to believe in the abstract disembodied psychological subject, and dismiss all it fails to address as merely either supplementary or inappropriate. In this regard, it should be noted that the focus within this book on literature and interpretations produced by researchers in Britain and especially the US, is not, or not merely, a reflection of my own parochialism. Anglo-US psychology extends its influence much further than its own linguistic and cultural domains through the dynamic of imperialism. Developmental psychology therefore functions as a tool of cultural imperialism through the reproduction of Western values and models within post-colonial societies.

Developmental psychology and the production of childhood

Closer to home, these issues arise in analogous ways within discussions of child abuse, in particular the recognition of child sexual abuse. Part of the reason why this issue commands such media attention lies in the challenge to the image of the safe, happy and protected child. Not only do the family, or trusted parental figures, no longer necessarily provide a safe, caring environment for children, but the model of the child as innocent can render the 'knowing' child as somehow culpable within her own abuse (Kitzinger, 1990). Issues of power that constitute the abuse are eclipsed within the effort to ward off children's agency and sexuality and maintain a romantic sentimental image of the passive, innocent child (Stainton Rogers and Stainton Rogers, 1992).

While developmental psychology plays a key role in the legitimation and perpetuation of these dangerously limited and sometimes plainly false conceptions of childhood, they mesh with dominant cultural imagery which glorifies and markets childhood as a commodity. In the green and caring 1990s, children signify as icons of simplicity and naturalness, the necessary accessory for any soap, shampoo and caring (especially male) figure. But according intrinsic, natural qualities to children gives rise to representations of gender and sexual orientation as somehow essential and inherent, as where child models are portrayed engaging in heterosexual dating postures as a means of selling clothes that are simply scaled-down versions of their parents' (Burman, 1991).

Discussions of the impact of developmental psychological knowledge often flounder on the issue of whether it reflects or produces the practices it describes. While it would be naive to accord too much significance to a minor arena of academic and popular culture, nevertheless the act of reproduction of both common-sense and technical-political understandings within the seemingly objective arena of scientific research functions to re-cycle existing historically and culturally specific ideas as legitimised, eternal knowledge. Models about children and child rearing, achieve a reality in part because they comprise the fabric of both professional and everyday knowledge about ourselves and our relationships. We cannot easily get outside them since they have constituted our very subjectivities, and in that sense notions of 'reflection' and even 'production' fail to convey their reality within our lives.

Baker and Freebody (1987) discuss how a particular cultural form, in this case, children's first reading books, acts to 'constitute the child' by presenting a particular, school-endorsed set of representations of child, family, school and social relations within the materials. While purporting to reflect the children's development, these function to organise it. They map out their school and personal careers and ambitions as pupils, boys and girls, with class positions (see also Rose, 1985), and relay sets of ideas about the positions and rights of adults and children. The consequences of this may even enter into the children's abilities to engage with educational processes. As they put it:

Young readers, whose identities as children differ from the images embedded in the texts, may have particular difficulties in relating to these books. For all children there may exist the practical problems of knowing how to treat these images while taking part in a reading instruction based on them, in such a way as to appear to be concurring with school-endorsed portraits in the texts.

(Baker and Freebody, 1987: 57)

Morality and change

We have moved very fast in this chapter from a discussion of Piaget's work on morality to the role developmental psychology plays in the new world, and now the new world order. What developmental psychology all too often neglects, even when it studies morality, is its own moral status as a moral science, and its moral positions in the world. We have seen how developmental psychology has functioned as an instrument of classification and evaluation, as a tool for 'mental hygiene', a euphemism for the control and surveillance of populations deemed likely to be troublesome or burdensome – working-class children, single parents, minority groups and poor people the world over. Clothed in the rhetoric of scientific rigour and detachment, it has worked in very partial ways. The denial of moral-political assumptions underlying developmental psychology has merely worked to maintain reactionary practices. Now it is time to recognise that the 'science' of development is not separate from concerns of 'truth', and therefore of morality, politics and government.

This book started with an account of how developmental psychology arose, and the moral-political agendas it served and expressed. From the constitution of the isolated, individual 'child' as its unit of study, to an equivalent focus on families, mothers, and now fathers, developmental psychology functions as a key resource for legislating upon and distributing welfare interventions. Parts I and II of this book demonstrated how development is portrayed as either divorced from social and material circumstances, or within so over-simplified and sanitised a conception of the 'social' that it diverts and proscribes critical evaluation and colludes in the pathologisation of individuals and groups on the basis of their failure to reflect the Western, middle-class norms that have structured developmental psychological research. In Parts II and III we saw how these assumptions structure not only the explicit accounts of how to care for, and who should care for, children, but also enter in less direct but equally evaluative ways into accounts of language and learning. 'Sensitive' mothers are not only better mothers in the ways that they respond to and look after their charges, they also maximalise (Rose, 1990) their children's learning. We may claim, as the theories of cognitive development and education discussed in Part IV do, to deal with the 'whole child', but this child is endowed with a false unity conferred by its abstraction from social relations. These last chapters have argued that the rationality and individualism that 'he' is accorded construct an image of mental life that privileges cultural masculinity and mirrors market demands for skills and efficient functioning. The costs of accounting for 'mastery' and development in these ways are that, beneath the facade of the whole, adjusted and integrated self, the subject of developmental psychology is fragmented, alienated and split.

In over seven years of teaching a wide range of undergraduate and professional groups, within each group I have encountered two sorts of reactions to developmental psychology. One is that it is mystificatory and jargon-ridden, which creates some hostility on the grounds of its exclusivity and inaccessibility; the other is to dismiss it as simply common sense. And both reactions are correct. What should be clear from this book is that dressed up in its claims to present some particular expertise (of which it devotes considerable energy to maintaining sole control), developmental psychology (like the rest of psychology) imports ideological understandings into its theories that are incorporated into 'science'. As I have shown, the methodologies as well as the theories reflect these assumptions, but coded at a deeper level through the relation between science and modern States.

Constructing and deconstructing

This book has attempted to identify and evaluate the central themes that structure contemporary developmental psychology. In part the journey has been a historical one, in aiming to understand the specific conditions that prompted the emergence of, and agenda for, what has come to be a central agency for the regulation and control of individual and family life. In other ways we have had to look beyond the theories to understand the cultural and political role that the academic practice of developmental psychology fulfils. Both home and school are informed by developmental psychology, and it enters into the ways we talk and reflect upon our feelings and intellect, and, more than this, produces 'us' in its image.

The process of delineating and commenting on these discourses is part of the process of deconstructing, of dismantling the power of this apparatus for the construction of subjects by which we are disciplined and constituted. We have seen how inequality and differential treatment on the basis of class, culture, gender, age and sexuality permeate the deep structure of developmental psychological practice. Developmental psychology therefore contributes to the maintenance of the social formation which gave rise to it.

I have been using the term deconstruction as a mode of analysis which invites scrutiny of the limits and presuppositions that have guided research. While deconstruction threatens to disallow absolute justification of any position (Burman, 1990) – including mine here – there nevertheless can be no fully practising deconstructor. Instead, the issue is to bring to light, acknowledge, the investment and hidden subjectivity that lie beneath the claims to disinterested, true knowledge. The impetus behind this book reflects Gayatri Chakravorty Spivak's (1990) characterisation of the 'corrective and critical' role of deconstruction:

> in one way or another academics are in the business of ideological production. . . . Our institutional responsibility is of course to offer a responsible critique of the structure of production of the knowledge we teach even as we teach it, but, in addition, we must go public as often as we can.
>
> (Spivak 1990: 103)

What is achieved by such a process of deconstruction? I would like to hope that at the very least some caution about the indiscriminate application of general models should follow. Ideas are tools for change, and they are certainly used to prevent change. The purpose of this deconstruction is to lay bare, to make public, the parameters by which our own change and development has been structured. The domain of developmental psychology is a modern, Western construction, which is itself contested and under revision, though currently often continually reinvented. Taking apart, challenging its scientific certainty and grip on common sense may help us to recognise other ways of talking about those issues that currently are dealt with within the terms of developmental psychology. Exploitation and oppression suffuse the structure of developmental psychology. Our task is to deconstruct it.

References

Baker, C. D. and Freebody, P. (1987) '"Constituting the child" in beginning school reading books', *British Journal of Sociology of Education, 8, 1*: 55–76.

Batou, J. (1991) '100 million women are missing', *International Viewpoint, 206*: 26–8.

Boyden, J. (1990) 'Childhood and the policy makers: a comparative perspective on the globalization of childhood', in A. James and A. Prout (eds) *Constructing and Reconstructing Childhood: contemporary issues in the sociological study of childhood*, Basingstoke, Hants: Falmer.

Buck-Morss, S. (1975) 'Socio-economic bias in Piaget's theory and its implications for cross-cultural studies', *Human Development, 18*: 35–45.

Burman, E. (1990) 'Differing with deconstruction: a feminist critique', in I. Parker and J. Shotter (eds) *Deconstructing Social Psychology*, London: Routledge.

Burman, E. (1991) 'Power, gender and developmental psychology', *Feminism and Psychology, 1, 1*: 141–54.

Burman, E. (in press b) 'Poor children: charity appeals and ideologies of childhood', *Changes: International Journal of Psychology and Psychotherapy*.

Cassidy, C. (1989) 'Worldview conflict and toddler malnutrition: changeagent dilemmas', in N. Scheper-Hughes (ed.) *Child Survival and Neglect*, Dordrecht: Reidel.

Colby, A., Kohlberg, L., Gibbs, J. and Lieberman, M. (1983) 'A longitudinal study of moral judgement', *Monographs of the Society for Research in Child Development, 48, (1–2)*: (no 200).

Cole, M., Gay, J., Glick, J. and Sharp, D. W. (1971) *The Cultural Context of Learning and Thinking*, New York: Basic Books.

Edwards, C. P. (1981) 'The comparative study of the development of moral judgement and reasoning', in R. H. Munroe, R. L. Munroe and B. B. Whiting (eds) *Handbook of Cross Cultural Human Development*, New York: Garland.

Gilligan, C. (1982) *In a Different Voice: psychological theory and women's development*, Cambridge, Mass.: Harvard University Press.

Glauser, B. (1990) 'Street children: deconstructing a construct', in A. James and A. Prout (eds) *Constructing and Reconstructing Childhood*, London: Falmer.

Hallpike, C. (1979) *The Foundations of Primitive Thought*, Cambridge: Cambirdge University Press.

Hogen, R. (1975) 'Moral development and the structure of personality', in D. DePalma and J. Foley (eds) *Moral Development: current theory and research*, New York: LEA.

Joseph, G., Reddy, V. and Searle-Chatterjee, M. (1990) 'Eurocentrism in the social sciences', *Race and Class, 31, 4*: 1–26.

Kagan, J. (1984) *The Nature of the Child*, New York: Basic Books.

Kitzinger, J. (1990) 'Who are you, kidding? Children, power and the struggle against sexual abuse', in A. James and A. Prout (eds) *Constructing and Reconstructing Childhood: contemporary issues in the sociological study of childhood*, Basingstoke, Hants: Falmer.

Kohlberg, L. (1969a) 'The child as moral philosopher', in J. Sants (ed.) *Developmental Psychology*, Harmondsworth: Penguin.

Kohlberg, L. (1969b) 'Stage and sequence: the cognitive developmental approach', in D. A. Goslin (ed.) *The Handbook of Socialization Theory and Research*, Chicago: Rand McNally.

Kohlberg, L. (1976) 'Moral stages and moralisation', in T. Lickona (ed.) *Moral Development and Moral Behaviour: theory, research and social issues*, New York: Holt, Rinehart & Winston.

Levine, C., Kohlberg, L. and Hewer, A. (1985) 'The current formulation of Kohlberg's theory and a response to critics', *Human Development, 28*: 94–100.

Morris, T. (1992) *The Despairing Developer: diary of an aid worker in the Middle East*, London: IB Taurus.

Myers, R. (1992) *The Twelve Who Survive: strengthening programmes of early childhood development in the Third World*, London: Routledge/UNESCO.

Piaget, J. (1932) *The Moral Judgement of the Child*, London: Routledge & Kegan Paul.

Rose, N. (1985) *The Psychological Complex: psychology, politics and society in England 1869–1939*, London: Routledge & Kegan Paul.

Rose, N. (1990) *Governing the Soul: the shaping of the private self*, London: Routledge.

Sampson, E. (1989) 'The deconstruction of self', in J. Shotter and K. Gergen (eds) *Texts of Identity*, London: Sage.

Sayers, J. (1986) *Sexual Contradictions: feminism, psychology and psychoanalysis*, London: Tavistock.

Scheper-Hughes, N. (1989b) 'Culture, scarcity and maternal thinking: motherlove and child death in Northeast Brazil', in N. Scheper-Hughes (ed.) *Child Survival: anthropological perspectives on the treatment and maltreatment of children*, Dordrecht: Reidel.

Simpson, E. (1974) 'Moral development research: a case of scientific cultural bias', *Human Development, 17:* 81–106.

Snarey, J. R. (1985) 'Cross cultural universality of social-moral development: a critical review of Kohlbergian research', *Psychological Bulletin, 97*: 202–32.

Song, M. J., Smetana, J. G. and Kim, S. Y. (1987) 'Korean children's conceptions of moral and conventional transgressions', *Developmental Psychology, 23, 4*: 577–82.

Spivak, G. C. (1990) 'Practical politics of the open end', in S. Harasym (ed.) *The Postcolonial Critic: interviews, strategies, dialogues*, London: Routledge.

Stainton Rogers, R. and Stainton Rogers, W. (1992) *Stories of Childhood: shifting agendas of child concern*, Hemel Hempstead: Harvester Wheatsheaf.

Stein, N., Trabasso, T. and Garfin, D. (1979) 'Comprehending and remembering moral dilemmas', in S. Goldman (ed.) *Understanding Discourse: interactions between knowledge and process*, symposium presented to American Psychological Association, September.

Sullivan, E. (1977) 'A study of Kohlberg's structural theory of moral development: a critique of liberal social science ideology', *Human Development, 20*: 352–75.

Turiel, E. (1983) *The Development of Social Knowledge: morality and convention*, Cambridge: Cambridge University Press.

Walker, L. J. (1989) 'A longitudinal study of moral reasoning', *Child Development, 60*: 157–66.

Wallace, T. and March, C. (1991) *Changing Perceptions: writings on gender and development*, Oxford: Oxfam.

Zelizer, V. A. (1985) *Pricing the Priceless Child: the changing social value of children*, New York: Basic Books.

47

THE YOUNG CITIZEN

Nikolas Rose

Source: *Governing the Soul*, New York: Routledge, 1990, pp. 87–97.

Childhood is the most intensively governed sector of personal existence. In different ways, at different times, and by many different routes varying from one section of society to another, the health, welfare, and rearing of children have been linked in thought and practice to the destiny of the nation and the responsibilities of the state. The modern child has become the focus of innumerable projects that purport to safeguard it from physical, sexual, or moral danger, to ensure its 'normal' development, to actively promote certain capacities of attributes such as intelligence, educability, and emotional stability. Throughout the nineteenth century and our own, anxieties concerning children have occasioned a panoply of programmes that have tried to conserve and shape children by moulding the petty details of the domestic, conjugal, and sexual lives of their parents.

Along this maze of pathways, the child – as an idea and a target – has become inextricably connected to the aspirations of authorities. The environment of the growing child is regulated financially, through benefits and allowances to the family, and pedagogically through programmes of education directed at the parent-to-be. Legislative obligations are imposed upon parents, requiring them to carry out social duties from the registration their children at birth to ensuring that they receive adequate education up into their teens. Health visitors exercise a surveillance, in principle comprehensive and universal, over the care of young children in their homes. Child protection legislation has imposed powers and duties upon local authorities, requiring them to evaluate the standards of care being provided to children by their parents through the agencies of social work, and to intervene into the family to rectify shortcomings, utilizing legal mechanisms where necessary. To adjudicate upon a child accused of a crime now requires scrutiny and evaluation of family life as a condition of the possibility and legitimacy of judgement. Doctors in general practice and in hospital have professional, if not legal obligations to scrutinize the children they see for whatever reason for signs that they may be 'at risk' and notify statutory authorities of their suspicions. And universal and compulsory schooling catches up the lives of all young citizens into a pedagogic machine that operates not only to impart knowledge but to instruct in conduct and to supervise, evaluate, and rectify childhood pathologies.

Thus, over the present century, a new visibility has been accorded to the child in its life within the household and outside it, and the 'private' family has been opened up to social powers and allocated social duties. Reflecting upon these events, among others, in his 1949 Alfred Marshall Lectures at Cambridge, T. H. Marshall argued that what had occurred amounted to the extension of citizenship to the child. Citizenship denoted 'a kind of basic human equality associated with the concept of full membership of a community'; the developments in techniques and conceptions of government since the eighteenth century showed its gradual progress or evolution over the last two and a half centuries.[1] As far as children were concerned, while they were not citizens in the sense of having political rights to participate in the exercise of political power, and perhaps were only beginning to gain civil rights necessary for individual freedom such as liberty of the person and the right to justice, they had gained social rights. The educational system and the social services extended to each child the right to a modicum of economic welfare and security, to share in the social heritage and live the life of a civilized being according to the standards prevailing in the society at large. Universal education, for Marshall, was a decisive step in the re-establishment of social rights of citizenship in the twentieth century, for it was an attempt to stimulate the growth of citizens in the making. Education was a personal right for the child irrespective of his or her parents' wishes, but it also recognized and imposed a social and collective right – the duty of each individual to improve and civilize themselves for the benefit of the social health of the community. Other sociologists have developed this argument, suggesting that special protective legislation and other forms of social provision for children in the nineteenth century were also developments of citizenship, recognizing the claims of the child, as citizen *in potentia*, upon the social collectivity.[2]

Now Marshall and his followers acknowledged that citizenship imposed obligations as well as rights, obligations both on the community and on the individuals who made it up. But, nonetheless, endowing children with the status of citizenship, making them full and equivalent members of a community, was a profoundly progressive recognition of a principle of equality, and one ultimately in conflict with the principles of inequality that lay at the heart of a capitalist economic system. Since the 1960s, however, most sociological analysts of the welfare state have interpreted these developments differently.[3] Even the most sanguine of these commentators see the apparatus of welfare as ambiguous and contradictory, and regard welfare as having more to do with the disablement of conflict than with the recognition of rights. For more than a century and a half, it is argued, the poor and oppressed, supported by progressive elements of the bourgeoisie, have campaigned and struggled to get the state and the powerful to recognize their social obligations – in the form of education, health care, social support in times of sickness and hardship, and so forth. However, the policies and practices vouchsafed were the minimum necessary to buy off the discontented; far from being inspired by a recognition of collective social obligations, their goal has been to preserve the efficiency of those who provide necessary labour power and military might, to provide antidotes to social unrest, and to ward off demands for truly progressive measures of equalization of wealth and status. The policies and practices of welfare, far from extending citizenship in any benign sense, have in fact functioned to maintain inequality, to legitimate existing relations of power, and to extend social control over potentially troublesome sectors of society.

Further, it appeared that the extension of social regulation to the lives of children actually had little to do with recognition of their rights.[4] Children came to the attention of social authorities as delinquents threatening property and security, as future workers requiring moralization and skills, as future soldiers requiring a level of physical fitness – in other words on account of the threat which they posed now or in the future to the welfare of the state. The apparent humanity, benevolence, and enlightenment of the extension of protection to children in their homes disguised the extension of surveillance and control over the family. Reformers arguing for such legislative changes were moral entrepreneurs, seeking to symbolize their values in the law and, in doing so, to extend their powers and authority over others. The upsurges of concern over the young – from juvenile delinquency in the nineteenth century to sexual abuse today – were actually moral panics: repetitive and predictable social occurrences in which certain persons or phenomena come to symbolize a range of social anxieties concerning threats to the established order and traditional values, the decline of morality and social discipline, and the need to take firm steps in order to prevent a downward spiral into disorder. Professional groups – doctors, psychologists, and social workers – used, manipulated, and exacerbated such panics in order to establish and increase their empires. The apparently inexorable growth of welfare surveillance over the families of the working class had arisen from an alignment between the aspirations of the professionals, the political concerns of the authorities, and the social anxieties of the powerful.

Feminists argued that the regulation of children had to be located within a wider history, in which 'the family' had become a key mechanism of social control and ideological support for a patriarchal capitalism that maintained both women and children in a state of dependency.[5] 'The family' was an ideological mechanism for reproducing a docile labour force, for exploiting the domestic labour of women under the guise of love and duty, for maintaining the patriarchal authority of men over the household. The notion of the family as a voluntary arrangement – entered into out of love, suffused by positive emotions, naturally wishing to have and to cherish its children, the site of self-realization for mothers and of mutual regard and protection of family members – was an ideology that disguised the oppressive relations within this intimate sphere, and the social and economic coercion upon women to enter into family life and motherhood. The function of this familial ideology was to mask the realities of family life, and to preserve a social institution that provided vital economic functions for capitalism: reproduction of the labour force, socialization of children, exploitation of the unpaid domestic labour of women, compensation to men for the alienating nature of their work, and so forth.

Radical criticism of the techniques of family regulation came to focus on the notion of the family as a 'private' domain, seeing this as the central element in the ideology masking the social and economic role of the family.[6] The language of privacy disguised and legitimated the authority of men in the household over both women and children, and obscured the extent to which the state actually shaped and controlled relations in the intimate sphere for public, political ends. The division of public and private is, of course, central to liberal political thought, demarcating the boundaries between the domain over which the powers of the state and law can properly be exercised and that where they have no place. Within these terms the family represents the private sphere *par excellence* – indeed it is doubly private, not only being outside the proper authority of the state but also outside the scope of market relations. The division between public and private is traced back in political and social philosophy at least as far as Aristotle's distinction between *polis* and *oikos* and up to the natural rights theories of John Locke. However, in the eighteenth and nineteenth centuries the distinction was posited in terms of the division between home and market. It was given a philosophical foundation in the liberal political philosophy of J. S. Mill and his followers, with the opposition between the realm of legitimate public regulation and the realm of freedom from intrusion, personal autonomy, and private choice. Writers point to the particular associations in these texts between the public sphere (the world of work, the market, individualism, competition, politics, and the state) and men, and the corollary association of women with the private, domestic, intimate, altruistic, and humanitarian world of the home.

Critics argued that this public/private divide, and the conception of the private that it uses, has always functioned to sustain a particular and oppressive set of relations between men and women. However, developments within capitalism in the nineteenth century reworked this public/private divide to suit the interests of a ruling, property owning male elite. This accounted for the emergence of the cult of domesticity with its idealization of motherhood. While allowing that this allotted certain powers to women, it did so only in their status as mothers confined to the private sphere, and hence failed fundamentally to challenge either the patriarchal separation of realms, or the economic power that men wielded over the family unit.

Analyses of the legal regulation of marriage, divorce, sexual behaviour, and domestic violence were deployed to show that the ideology of individual choice and personal freedom in the private domain of home and family legitimated a refusal by public authorities to intervene into certain places, activities, relationships and feelings. Designating them personal, private, and subjective made them appear to be outside the scope of the law as a fact of nature, whereas in fact non-intervention was a socially constructed, historically variable, and inevitably political decision. The state defined as 'private' those aspects of life into which it would not intervene, and then, paradoxically, used this privacy as the justification for its non-intervention.

Like *laissez faire* in relation to the market, the idea that the family could be private in the sense of outside public regulation was, according to these critics, a myth. The state cannot avoid intervening in the shaping of familial relations through decisions as to which types of relation to sanction and codify and which types of dispute to regulate or not to regulate. The state establishes the legal framework for conducting legitimate sexual relations and for procreation, and privileges certain types of relation through rules of inheritance. Further, the state, through public law, set up complex welfare mechanisms especially those surrounding the proper development of children. And however potent is the legal ideology of family privacy, in decisions as to the best interests and welfare of children in cases concerning care and custody, and in the division of family property and other aspects of family disputes, legal functionaries operate according to ideological and patriarchal beliefs as to morality, responsibility and family life and what is best for children. On the one hand, the state, representing dominant male interests, chooses the nature and objectives of public regulation; on the other, a domain is constituted outside legal regulation and designated 'private', where welfare agencies enforce the ideology of motherhood, and where male power is not even subject to limited protections of the rule of law.

These analyses have much to commend them. But in designating the public/private division as an ideology that disguises the hand of the state and has primarily a social control function in relation to women, they fail to register or come to grips with two key issues. The first concerns the way in which the privacy of the family was a vital element in the technologies of government that made liberal democratic rule possible, allowing a fundamental transformation in the scope and responsibilities of 'the state' and the organization of power. The second concerns the ways in which these new rationales and technologies of government did not simply control individuals through the family but played a constitutive role in the formation of citizens of such democracies, acting at the level of subjectivity itself.

'Familialization' was crucial to the means whereby personal capacities and conducts could be socialized, shaped, and maximized in a manner that accorded with the moral and political principles of liberal society. The languages of the regulatory strategies, the terms within which they thought themselves, the ways in which they formulated their problems and solutions, were not merely ideological; they made it possible and legitimate to govern the lives of citizens in new ways. In doing so, they actually brought new sectors of reality into existence, new problems and possibilities for personal investment as well as for public regulation. If the familialization of society worked, it was because it both established its political legitimacy and commanded a level of subjective commitment from citizens, inciting them to regulate their own lives according to its terms.

The emergence of an institutionally distinct political domain, the sovereign state, entailed the gradual concentration of formal political, juridical, and administrative powers that had hitherto been dispersed among a range of authorities – guilds, justices, landowners, and religious authorities.[7] This concentration, and the concomitant legitimation and delimitation of political authority by the doctrines of 'rule of law', entailed the conceptualization of certain domains that were freed from the threat of punitive sanction and detailed internal regulation. These developments coincided with the major transformations in the lives of the working population associated with the growth of urban capitalism, and hence with the decomposition of the extensive mechanisms by which the church, the local powers, and the community had specified, monitored, and sanctioned the detailed aspects of personal, conjugal, sexual, and domestic conduct. The private family was to emerge as a solution to the problems of regulating individuals and populations and of producing social solidarities that were posed by these ruptures in socio-political relations.[8]

The private family did not reactivate the independence of patriarchal authority and political allegiance of the pre-liberal household, but nor did it require the extension of the scope and prerogatives of the state into the details of everyday existence. The domesticated private family was both to be distinguished from political life and to be defined and privileged by law; it was to be both freed from detailed prescriptions of conduct and to be permeable to moralization and normalization from outside. It was to become the matrix for the government of the social economy.

The reconstruction of the working-class family in the nineteenth century took place not through the activities of the state, but through an initiative that maintained a certain distance from the organs of political power – philanthropy. Philanthropic activity was certainly mobilized by the perceived threats posed to the wealthy by the dangerous classes, the amalgam of crime, indigence, pauperism, and vice that appeared to be multiplying in the cities. But it was a response unlike either repression or charity, for it sought a prophylactic mode of action, endeavouring to promote certain kinds of moral conduct by coupling the provision of financial aid with conditions as to the future conduct of recipients. In England and France philanthropists sought not to 'preserve' the families of the urban masses – for family life was widely believed to be virtually unknown in the rookeries and at the heart of the great towns – but to organize the conjugal, domestic, and parental relations of the poor in the form of the domesticated family. Assistance was thus conditional upon marriage, good housekeeping, sobriety, moral supervision of children, and the search for wage labour.[9]

Throughout the nineteenth century a multitude of little and large projects were undertaken, each using the human technology of the family for social ends. It appeared that the family could play a vital role in eliminating illegality, curbing inebriety, and restricting promiscuity, imposing restrictions upon the unbridled sensualities of adults and inculcating morality into children. Bourgeois women sought to recruit their working class sisters as allies, arguing that marriage, domestic hygiene, and so forth were not only moral in their own right, but would further women's interests by increasing their powers *vis-à-vis* their menfolk. The legal relation of marriage was to promote emotional and economic investment by both men and women into the home, cathecting domesticity at the expense of street life, public bawdiness, and vice. Such campaigns served a vital function, operating as relays through which the imperatives of social regulation could become linked with the wishes and aspirations of individuals for security and advancement.

In such campaigns, public authorities were seldom centrally involved, although they did provide a legal framework for philanthropic action and often supported private campaigns with funds and information. A more significant ally of philanthropy, which operated not so much by *moralization* as by *normalization*, was medicine. Medico-hygienic expertise began to elaborate a set of doctrines concerning the conditions for rearing healthy children and to pose many issues of moral conduct – (drunkenness, debauchery, viciousness, masturbation, insanity) – in medical terms. They not only were detrimental to individual health but arose from weaknesses incurred through faulty government in childhood and could themselves be passed down from parents to children in the form of a susceptible constitution. Such advice was disseminated through literature and personal contact, principally into the homes of the well-to-do; its message was that the preservation of the lineage depended upon the active concentration of mothers upon the rearing of their offspring. In their turn, hygienists and philanthropists took this message into the homes of the poor, to reinforce the demands of morality with the norms of medicine. Thus a set of standards for family life began to be established and generalized that were grounded neither in political authority nor religious duty; the norms of medicine appeared to arise directly from life itself.

Philanthropists and hygienists campaigned to have their strategies enshrined in law and their expertise linked to the activities of social institutions such as courts, hospitals, prisons, and schools. By the start of the twentieth century the family was administered and policed by practices and agencies that were not 'private' (many of their powers were constructed legally, they were often recipients of public funds, and their agents were frequently publicly accredited by some form of licencing), but nor were they organs of central political power. Their operations and objectives were not specified by the decrees and programmes of political forces but operated under the aegis of moral principles and, increasingly, by professional expertise underpinned by the power of a claim to truth. In France and England, however, the turn of the twentieth century saw the linking of these moralizing and normalizing projects more centrally into the calculations and policies of the political authorities. What was involved here was not so much an expansionary project on behalf of the ruling classes, as an attempt to resolve some rather specific social troubles. The remit of the public power was to extend to the government of the physical, moral, and mental capacities of citizens. The autonomy of the poor family was not to be destroyed but re-modelled through enhancing and modifying the family machine.

A web of legal powers, social agencies and practices of judgement and normalization began to spread around troubled and troublesome children.[10] These were linked to the formal government machine at three principal points. The medical apparatus of public health extended its scrutiny to all children from birth, in their homes and in the schools, through registration of births, infant welfare centres, health visitors, school medical officers, education in domestic sciences, and schools for mothers, using legal powers and statutory institutions to provide a platform for the deployment of medico–hygienic norms and expertise, seeking to turn the school into a medical station and the home into a site of prophylaxis. Around the juvenile court, new powers of judgement and scrutiny were brought to bear upon the families of troubled and troublesome children, utilizing the legal process as a kind of case conference or diagnostic forum and deploying social workers and probation officers to scrutinize and report upon the homes of their cases, and to undertake at least a part of the normative assessment and reformation of children and their families. And the child guidance clinic acted as the hub of a programmatic movement for mental hygiene, drawing together the powers of the courts over children who had done wrong and parents who had wronged them, the universal and obligatory scrutiny of conduct in the school, and the private anxieties of family members about the behaviour of their children, into a powerful network linked by the activities and judgements of doctors, psychologists, probation officers, and social workers. These technologies of government, which Donzelot terms the 'tutelary complex', enabled the difficulties posed by working-class families and children to be acted upon with a degree of force, universality, and certainty but without disabling the family mechanism. Families would neither be lured into dependency by especially favourable treatment, nor forced into resistance by measures that were frankly repressive. Through the ministrations of expertise in the service of health, hygiene, and normality, the family would be returned to its social obligations without compromising its autonomy and responsibility for its own members and destiny.

Expertise also resolved a further problem at the junction of the family mechanism and the goals of government. This was that of achieving a harmony between the private authority, self-concern, and aspirations of the autonomous family and the best procedures for the socialization of its members. Donzelot refers to the techniques along this dimension as 'the regulation of images'. The representations of motherhood, fatherhood, family life, and parental conduct generated by expertise were to infuse and shape the personal investments of individuals, the ways in which they formed, regulated and evaluated their lives, their actions, and their goals. Of course, the construction of subjective values and investments was the aim of many of the familializing projects of the nineteenth and twentieth centuries. It was an explicit rationale of the moralizing philanthropy of the nineteenth century, and of the arguments for universal education. The concern for the health and welfare of children in the early twentieth century certainly sought to utilize 'the family' and the relations within it as a kind of social or socializing machine in order to fulfil various objectives – military, industrial and moral – but this was to be done not through the coercive enforcement of control under threat of sanction, but through the production of mothers who would want hygienic homes and healthy children. The promotion of hygiene and welfare could only be successful to the extent that it managed to solicit the active engagement of individuals in the promotion of their own bodily efficiency.

The family could come to serve these new social objectives only to the extent that it would operate as a voluntary and responsible machine for the rearing and moralizing of children, in which adults would commit themselves to the task of promoting the physical and mental welfare of their offspring. Once such an ethic came to govern our existence, the images of normality generated by expertise could come to serve as a means by which individuals could themselves normalize and evaluate their lives, their conduct, and those of their children. The means of correct socialization could be implanted in families concerned with the self-promotion of their members without the threat of coercion and without direct intervention by political authorities into the household. Such families have come to govern their intimate relations and socialize their children according to social norms but through the activation of their own hopes and fears. Parental conduct, motherhood, and child rearing can thus be regulated through family autonomy, through wishes and aspirations, and through the activation of individual guilt, personal anxiety, and private disappointment. And the almost inevitable misalignment between expectation and realization, fantasy and actuality, fuels the search for help and guidance in the difficult task of producing normality, and powers the constant familial demand for the assistance of expertise.

To be sure, the contemporary disquiet about the powers of welfare professionals in relation to the family have an old fashioned *laissez faire* ring. But the extent that they can be reactivated in the late twentieth century is testament to the success of the socializing project of the last hundred years, to the incorporation of the expert doctrines for the government of children into our own free will. Socialization, in the sense in which we see it here, is not the anthropological universal beloved by functionalist sociologists; it is the historically specific outcome of technologies for the government of the subjectivity of citizens.

The notion of the normal child and family has an ambiguous status in these technologies of subjectivity. Normality appears in three guises: as that which is natural and hence healthy; as that against which the actual is judged and found unhealthy; and as that which is to be produced by rationalized social programmes. Criteria of normality are simultaneously used to construct an image of the natural child, mother and family, to provide a more or less explicit set of instructions to all involved as to how they should identify normality and conduct themselves in a normal fashion, and to provide the means of identifying abnormality and the rationale for intervention when reality and normality fail to coincide.

Yet our conceptions of normality are not simply generalizations from our accumulated experience of normal children. On the contrary, criteria of normality are elaborated by experts on the basis of their claims to a scientific knowledge of childhood and its vicissitudes. And this knowledge of normality has not, in the main, resulted from studying normal children. On the contrary, in tracing the genealogy of normality we are returned to the projects of the government of children that provided the platform for the take-off of expertise. It is around pathological children – the troublesome, the recalcitrant, the delinquent – that conceptions of normality have taken shape. It is not that a knowledge of the normal course of development of the child has enabled experts to become more skilled at identifying those unfortunate children who are in some way abnormal. Rather, expert notions of normality are extrapolated from our attention to those children who worry the courts, teachers, doctors, and parents. Normality is not an observation but a valuation. It contains not only a judgement about what is desirable, but an injunction as to a goal to be achieved. In so doing, the very notion of 'the normal' today awards power to scientific truth and expert authority.

Since World War II psychologists have increasingly provided the vocabularies with which the troubles of children have been described, the expertise for diagnosing and categorizing such children, the languages within which the tasks of mothers and fathers have been adumbrated, and the professionals to operate the technology of childhood regulation. Psychology has played a key role in establishing the norms of childhood, in providing means for visualizing childhood pathology and normality, in providing vocabularies for speaking about childhood subjectivity and its problems, in inventing technologies for cure and normalization. Through the connections established between the norms of childhood and images of family life, parenting, and motherhood, the psyche of the child and the subjectivity of the mother have been opened up for regulation in a new way. It has become the will of the mother to govern her own children according to psychological norms and in partnership with psychological experts. The soul of the young citizen has become the object of government through expertise.

Notes

1 T. H. Marshall, 'Citizenship and social class', in *Sociology at the Cross-roads*, London: Heinemann, 1963. The phrase quoted is from p. 72.
2 B. S. Turner, *Citizenship and Capitalism*, London: Allen & Unwin, 1986, esp. pp. 92–96. Cf G. M. Thomas and J. W. Meyer, 'The expansion of the state', *Annual Review of Sociology* 10 (1984): 461–82.
3 See, for example, I. Gough, *Political Economy of the Welfare State*, London: Macmillan, 1979.
4 For two examples of this literature, see A. Platt, *The Child Savers*, Chicago, Il: University of Chicago Press, 1969; N. Parton, *The Politics of Child Abuse*, London: Macmillan, 1984. See also the overviews given in M. Freeman, *The Rights and Wrongs of Children*, London: Pinter, 1983, and R. Dingwall, J. M. Eekelaar, and T. Murray, 'Childhood as a social problem: a survey of legal regulation', *Journal of Law and Society* 11 (1984): 207–32.
5 This picture, of course, obliterates many conceptual and political distinctions. For examples of this literature see: A. Oakley, *Sex, Gender and Society*, London: Temple Smith, 1972; L. Comer, *Wedlocked Women*, Leeds: Feminist Books, 1974; E. Zaretsky, *Capitalism, The Family and Personal Life*, London: Pluto Press, 1976; E. Wilson, *Women and the Welfare State*, London: Tavistock, 1977; J. Lewis, *The Politics of Motherhood: Child and Maternal Welfare in England 1900–1939*, London: Croom Helm, 1980; J. Lewis, 'Anxieties about the family and the relationships between parents, children and the state in twentieth-century England', in M. Richards and P. Light, *Children of Social Worlds*, Cambridge: Polity Press, 1986.
6 These paragraphs draw on my article 'Beyond the public/private division: law, power and the family', *Journal of Law and Society* 14 (1987): 61–76. For some of this literature see M. Stacey, 'The division of labour revisited', in P. Abrams *et al.*, (eds), *Development and Diversity: British Sociology 1950–1980*, London: British Sociological Association, 1981; M. Stacey and M. Price, *Women, Power and Politics*, London: Tavistock, 1981; E. Gamarnikow *et al.*, (eds), *The Public and the Private*, London: Heinemann, 1983. Much of the recent debate refers back to M. Rosaldo, 'Women, Culture and Society', in M. Rosaldo and L. Lamphere, (eds.), *Women, culture and society*, Stanford: Stanford University Press, 1974. See also S. Ardener (ed.), *Women and Space*, London: Croom Helm, 1981, and J. B. Elshtain, *Public Man and Private Woman*, Brighton: Harvester, 1981. The argument has been particularly influential in disputes over the legal regulation of families: see F. Olsen, 'The family and the market: and study of ideology and legal reform', *Harvard Law Review* 96 (1983): 1497;

K. O'Donovan, *Sexual Divisions in Law*, 1985; M. Freeman, 'Towards a critical theory of family law', *Current Legal Problems* 38 (1985): 153; A. Bottomley, 'Resolving family disputes: a critical view', in M. Freeman (ed.), *State, Law and the Family*, London: Tavistock, 1984.

7 For a useful discussion see J. Minson, *Genealogies of Morals*, London: Macmillan, 1985, Ch. 5.

8 J. Donzelot, *The Policing of Families*, London: Hutchinson, 1979.

9 I discuss philanthropy further in N. Rose *The Psychological Complex*, London: Routledge & Kegan Paul, 1985.

10 These are discussed in detail for England in my *Psychological Complex* and for France in Donzelot, op. cit.

48

WHOSE 'CHILDHOOD'?
WHAT 'CRISIS'?

Phil Scraton

Source: *Childhood in Crisis*, London: University College London Press, 1997, pp. 163–186.

Childhood is mapped by rituals imposed from above. From the moment of birth, through family and community induction, religious and cultural initiation and on to the seemingly unquestioned gradation of formal schooling, the baby–toddler–child is celebrated and processed through the ritualizing of his or her progress. The progression of the person-in-the-making or adult-in-waiting is predominantly temporal. Children are 'big/small for their age' or 'ahead of/behind their class/grade'. They are 'backward', 'forward', 'slow', 'quick', 'gifted' and classified. Until recently, and still present in popular discourse, such classifications included 'handicapped', retarded or educationally subnormal. Common-sense and popular assumptions dovetail with institutional practices and policies in conferring appropriateness as 'childhood' behaviour and its progression is subjected to routine assessment. The scrutiny and classification to which they are subjected is not restricted to physical growth and academic attainment. Dress, manners, speech, hair, jewellery, beliefs, style, music . . . the list is endless. Each is measured against standards imposed by those adults significant in children's lives and they are regularly reminded of the consequences of a 'bad attitude' or mixing with the 'wrong people'. Their gullibility and corruptibility is taken-for-granted and emphasized. Within this context children's experiences are reconstructed by adults who easily portray power as responsibility, control as care and regulation as protection. Typically, adults direct and children obey, with age and status (parent, guardian, professional) ensuring legitimacy.

The ritualization of childhood, steeped in the symbolism of celebration, maps the 'progression' of the child through his or her stages of development. At the level of appearances the moments of celebration, from birthdays to prize-givings to religious ceremonies, are child-centred. Yet they function also as adult-defined practices of conformity. Beginning with initiation into familial, community, religious, cultural and institutional practices they become profound processes through which children are socialized and conditioned. Deviation from the charted path inevitably leads to condemnation, punishment and even expulsion (from school, from church, from home). Within this context of discipline, regulation and correctionalism, passive or active resistance by children and young people is always defined as negative, as a challenge to legitimate authority. Perhaps the most disturbing feature of the control imposed on children, both in formal institutions and in informal interaction, is the overarching and shared assumption that left to their own devices children lack collective responsibility, run wild and destroy each other. Writing only days after the death of James Bulger, for example, Melanie Phillips and Martin Kettle commented '. . . it begins to seem that William Golding's fictional universe of juvenile savagery in *Lord of the Files* lies all around us in our housing estates and shopping malls' (*Guardian*, 16 February 1993). As noted in Chapter 2, Golding's fiction is taken as a pseudo-scientific cautionary tale that children abandoned or bereft of the discipline and guidance of adults will sink to unknown depths of cruelty and individualism normally avoided by the civilizing process of adult society. What an incredible irony this represents given the apparently insatiable appetite that much of the adult, patriarchal world has for violence, brutality, war and destruction.

Deliverance from 'evil'

As a process of normalization, the ritualization of childhood is about power relations. The socialization of the child and the definitions of appropriate development are not open to negotiation, except between 'knowledgeable' adults. This text provides a mass of contemporary evidence, derived in a wide range of children's experiences, which consistently demonstrates the silence of their voices, the absence of their feelings, the neglect of their needs and the denial of their ideas from political debates, institutional decision-making and policy initiatives which shape their lives. The regulation and control of children's behaviour, that which amounts to the imposition from above of disciplinary power, is effective precisely because of its invisibility, its taken-for-granted legitimacy. As Foucault (1977) maintains, the most effective exercise of power is that which operates through 'subtle coercion'. It is not simply that adults conspire to exclude or marginalize children and young people from the processes of consultation, decision-making or institutional administration but that there is no conceptualization or recognition that such processes might be appropriate. What this amounts to, however, is a coincidence of adult interests across all institutions in both the private and public spheres.

Children and young people have always posed problems for the adults in their lives yet there remains the much-promoted and oft-quoted myth, usually based on childhood reminiscences of the defining adults, that there was once a 'golden age' of compliance and discipline in which authority prevailed and every child knew its place. The idea that childhood deviance, youth lawlessness and anti-authority attitudes have escalated and are indicative of a broader moral decline within a previously stable and conforming social order is enduring. Each generation progressing through parenthood and into middle-age cannot remember a time when children were so ill-disciplined and so dismissive of their elders. Pearson (1993/94:190) quotes a range of sources which indicate that harking back to an earlier period of 'civility and order when the traditions of family and community were still intact' has become a regular British pastime. He quotes a Christian youth worker, James Butterworth, writing in 1932, as bemoaning the 'passing of parental authority, defiance of pre-war conventions, the absence of restraint, the wildness of extremes, the confusion of unrelated liberties, the wholescale drift away from churches . . .' (1993/94:190). In 1930 F. R. Leavis talked of the 'vast and terrifying disintegration of social life' with catastrophic change destroying the family; 'the generations find it hard to adjust themselves to each other . . . parents . . . helpless to deal with their children' (1993/94:190). 'We have arrived', wrote T. S. Eliot, 'at a stage of civilization at which the family is irresponsible . . . the moral restraints so weak . . . the institution of the family is no longer respected' (1993/94:190). Roy and Theodora Calvert identified a national 'crisis in morals'. Pearson closes his discussion of the inter-war years with a quote from A. E. Morgan in 1939:

> Relaxation of parental control, decay of religious influence, and the transplantation of masses of young persons to new housing estates where there is little scope for recreation and plenty of mischief . . . a growing contempt for the procedure of juvenile courts . . . The problem . . . is intensified by the extension of freedom which . . . has been given to youth in the last generation.
>
> (1993/94:191)

Pearson is insistent, and the evidence is convincing, that the 'same rhetoric' which is 'utterly misleading in its emphasis on the novelty and unprecedented dimensions of juvenile crime', has been employed for over a century. He concludes:

> The fact that we seem to be able to persuade ourselves in the 1990s that we are passing through an unprecedented crisis of public morals, while expressing our fears in a language which is indistinguishable from that of generations which are long dead, is an extraordinary historical paradox which reflects an equally extraordinary historical amnesia about even the more recent past.
>
> (1993/94:191)

What Pearson's work shows is that the grand delusion of an 'unprecedented crisis of public morals' has remained a persistent feature within popular discourse throughout the twentieth century. The issue is not simply that the past is forgotten, but that it is idealized. Undoubtedly, there has been an increase in community tensions, anti-social behaviour and the fear, if not the reality, of crime. The disruption of community identities and their social cohesiveness has contributed to a range of predatory and threatening behaviours as loosely-defined and poorly-serviced communities turn in on themselves. But there is a tendency to interpret the back-to-back nineteenth century neighbourhoods, the impoverished tenements and the twentieth century under-resourced redevelopments as honourable environments virtually free of disruption, disorder or mischievous children.

Just as Pearson's work illustrates the extent and depth of adult indignation as each ageing generation wrings its hands at the declining moral fibre of its children, so the process is renewed, often in more measured published or broadcast commentaries. In July 1994, for example, *The Sunday Times* published an article by Gerald Warner on the 'ills' of contemporary childhood which encompassed the full range of reactionary opinion towards all things progressive. He centred his analysis on childhood in Scotland and warned 'Civilisation menaced by adolescents from hell' (*The Sunday Times*, 3 July 1994). His starting point was the James Bulger case which established his key themes:

> What I did on my holidays the 1994 version. Put concrete block on railway line, am; abducted toddler from supermarket and beat him to death, pm. Who said that today's youngsters do not know how to make their own entertainment?

Quite apart from representing one of the most untypical crimes of the decade as typical, almost casual, these opening lines trivialized a tragic case and, on its back, condemned a generation of children. Warner warmed to his task: 'releasing the school population into general circulation [school holidays] is a life-endangering exercise.' Why? Because it is a population of 'sullen, introverted, ignorant and loutish young people' who threaten the 'future of our country' and 'civilisation itself'. A 'nation of vipers' has been bred whose 'prevailing ethos is anti-social' (*The Sunday Times*, 3 July 1994).

Warner's world is one of absolutes, a world in which 'political correctness' portrays children as the 'victims' of unemployment and poverty. Schools are 'appalling', denied the essential tool of discipline: corporal punishment. Teachers 'live under a regime of terror, fearing physical assault or false accusations of "abuse".' This, he argues, is evidence that the 'balance of power' in schools has been inverted. While teachers run scared, parents 'spawn' the 'monsters'. The political context of Warner's 'breeding-ground of anarchy' is 'two decades of political correctness' dominated and sustained by the 'Leftist thought police' who banned the works of authors such as Enid Blyton. But,

> Blyton children had two parents and fought crime; politically correct children should have one parent (or live with two homosexuals) and commit crime . . . 'The youth of a nation are the trustees of posterity,' claimed Disraeli. He was right; in this generation that is a terrifying thought.
>
> (*The Sunday Times*, 3 July 1994)

Warner's article could be dismissed as being no more than a reactionary rant against progressive trends, the kind of contribution so much the stock-in-trade of Conservative Party Conference fringe meetings, occasionally spilling onto the main conference agenda. It cannot be so lightly passed over. For it represents the sharp end of a continuum of child rejection. It is a sharp end most accurately described as child-hate, in the same vein as race-hate, misogyny or homophobia. This form of argument takes an event which is atypical, in this case the killing of James Bulger, and represents it as typifying a generation lost to the basics of morality, discipline and responsibility. The hatred, apparently reserved for cases marked by exceptional and unusual cruelty and brutality, is extended to include a range of behaviours construed as offensive or anti-social. Thus the atypical transforms into the stereotypical.

What this rhetoric appeals to, and it has been successful in maintaining its constituency, is the notion of inherent evil. There is no shortage of reference points for this construction of the evil spirit lying dormant, waiting to be triggered, within the apparently innocent body. Christianity, for example, despite its diverse religions, holds steadfastly to the conceptualization of original sin and the intrinsically imperfect or flawed soul of the individual. It represents an ever-present feature of belief systems which implore that their 'faithful' be 'delivered from evil' and led 'not into temptation'. Further, the biological determinism of the early medical models of deviant behaviour, although challenged by rationalism, promoted the construct of inherent, if not inherited, evil. Rationalism, which argued that individuals knowingly and voluntarily took decisions to commit crime, become deviant or behave offensively, did little to challenge the proposition that evil originated within the individual. The conceptualization of 'evil' within the aberrant child has a long tradition with religious, academic and child-care institutions. It resides permanently beneath the surface which presents a veneer of tolerance and understanding in direct contrast to the forces released once children and young people step out of line.

The killing of James Bulger unleashed a level of adult vindictiveness unprecedented in recent times. Children suspected of the murder and taken into custody for questioning, despite their innocence, were unable to return with their families to their homes. Following their arrest, the two boys charged with the murder of James Bulger made court appearances marked by scenes of mass, adult hysteria. Hostile crowds attempted to break through police cordons to attack the vehicles in which it was assumed they were being transported. Once convicted, and following the trial judge's statement that their act was of 'unparalleled evil' (*Daily Express*, 25 November 1993), the press lost no time in presenting full-page photographs of the 'Freaks of Nature' (*Daily Mirror*, 25 November 1993). Another headline, 'How Do You Feel Now, You Little Bastards' (*Daily Star*, 25 November 1993) encapsulated and reflected on an adult nation's demand for revenge. As Chapter 2 shows, there was hatred evident in much of the public's response and the demand for the boys' execution. It was endorsed with enthusiasm by media coverage, a sense of moral outrage closely aligned to the demand for retribution. This process not only influenced the trial, the sentence and an intervention by the Home Secretary setting a minimum period for the boys' imprisonment (declared unlawful in July 1996), but it promoted a severe backlash directed against progressive and successful youth justice – and other institutional – policies. The case became a metaphor for children's 'lost innocence' and the triumph of 'evil' over 'good'. Within five months Home Office Minister, David McLean, had the line 'our job is to drive the vermin off the streets' removed from a speech by his advisors.

The political reaction which followed the death of James Bulger, although rarely as vitriolic as Warner's later article or McLean's censored statement, reflected a broad consensus and some specific similarities. Within days of the murder the Prime Minister, John Major, called for a 'crusade against crime' and a 'change from being forgiving of crime to being considerate to the victim' (*Mail on Sunday*, 21 February 1993). While there was no evidence in the public domain of people being forgiving, particularly of the much-proclaimed misbehaviour and ill-discipline of children and young people, the Prime Minister was eager to regain the initiative in the law and order debate. Over the previous 12 months there had been continual media coverage of the supposed post-1960s liberalism and permissiveness which allegedly had dominated the youth justice and youth morality debates. The former had focused on alternatives to custody programmes, particularly those involving groupwork and rehabilitation at outdoor centres. Without any reference to the relative costs (diversionary programmes were significantly cheaper than custodial regimes), benefits or objectives of such programmes, they had been roundly dismissed as holidays or rewards for offenders. At the same time, as Chapter 6 shows, the Association of Chief Police Officers and other police organizations announced a crisis in youth crime, specifically centred on 'persistent young offenders' and joyriders. The message, endorsed by John Major, was that in order to redeem the harm done to victims of crime, there was required a return to harsher, punitive regimes geared to the disciplining of children and young people.

Kenneth Clarke, then Home Secretary, was unequivocal in his attack on 'persistent, nasty, little juvenile offenders' and their apologists. For him, they were indicative of 'a loss of values and a loss of a sense of purpose . . . partly due to a weakening of some of our institutions . . .'. He railed against social workers as 'not succeeding with children' concluding that 'it is no good mouthing political rhetoric, as some of them do, about why children in their care are so delinquent' (*The World this Weekend*, BBC Radio 4, 21 February 1993). This suggested 'loss of values', together with what was alluded to consistently as weak or permissive professional intervention, addressed the issue as one of moral philosophy rather than one of structural and material conditions. As the chapters on schooling and sexuality demonstrate, the political and media rhetoric suggested the moral degeneration of childhood, aided and abetted by irresponsible parents and liberal professionals. It was an issue taken beyond the confines of crime and offending behaviour to represent a multi-dimensional crisis in children's social identity and moral responsibility. Rather than the Labour Party opposition addressing concerns about the experiences, opportunities and frustrations of children and young people as a disenfranchised group facing the erosion of welfare provision, under-resourced schooling and diminishing work opportunities, its leaders appeared to mouth the same rhetoric as Government ministers. In his submission to Labour's Commission on Social Justice the then Shadow Health Minister, David Blunkett, echoed his Conservative counterparts:

> Those committed to a new twenty-first century welfare state have to cease what has been seen as paternalistic and well-meaning indulgence of the sub-culture of thuggery, noise, nuisance, and anti-social behaviour often linked to drug abuse. Understanding the causes of decline is not the same thing as tolerating the consequences.

For Tony Blair, then Shadow Home Secretary and aspirant Prime Minister, recent events were 'like hammer blows against the sleeping conscience of the country'. Learning and teaching the 'value of what is right and what is wrong' offered the only safeguard against 'moral chaos' (*Guardian*, 20 February 1993). Labour policies, Blair argued, would challenge the 'moral vacuum' and be 'tough on crime and tough on the causes of crime'. Noting its 'grave disquiet at the growth of vicious and unprovoked attacks on the most vulnerable in society . . .' an all-party group of MPs tabled a House of Commons motion locating the crisis in 'a decline in standards of personal responsibility and respect for others' (*Hansard*, 19 February 1993). Conveniently ignoring the statistical evidence which showed that Britain locked away more young people, earlier in their lives and for longer periods of time, than any other European Union member state, the demands for punishment, retribution and deterrence became overwhelming. Sir Ivan Lawrence QC, Chairman of the Home Affairs Select Committee on Juvenile Crime, captured the reactionary spirit of the moment:

> There is a hard-core of persistent young offenders, and too many of them are simply laughing at authority and thumbing their noses to the court. The biggest punishment is simply to take away their freedom. But they should also learn discipline and a respect for authority there.
>
> (*Guardian*, 22 February 1993)

In October 1993 Michael Howard, the new Home Secretary, delivered his uncompromising message to the Conservative Party's Annual Conference – unveiling his 27 steps to 'crack crime'. In an atmosphere which drew sustained and enthusiastic applause for a delegate's demand for execution, castration and beating, headlined in *Today*, (7 October 1993) as 'Hang 'Em High, Hang 'Em Often', Howard reiterated almost word-for-word the earlier censored statement of his under-minister, David McLean: 'we are sick and tired of these young hooligans . . . we must take the thugs off the streets' (*The Sun*, 7 October 1993). His commitment, previously announced by Kenneth Clarke, was to integrate into youth justice provision secure accommodation for 12–14-year-old children. Added to this would be USA-style boot camps based on the principles and practices of military correction. Within months, James Bulger's death had become a catalyst for the consolidation of an authoritarian shift in youth justice. It was a shift which, in legal reform and policy initiatives, was replicated throughout all institutional responses to children and young people. It carried media approval and popular (adult) consent, reflecting the well-established Thatcher agenda of the 1980s.

The social construction and political management of the 'crisis'

As previously discussed, the portrayal of 'dangerous children' or 'lawless youth' has remained a prominent feature of British social life over the last two centuries. Constructions of childhood rebels and delinquent gangs have remained high in the public consciousness, fuelled by associated moral panics and media amplification. Broader social trends or specific events at any moment, or in any given location, can only be fully interpreted through recognizing the social construction of reality in which popularly-held assumptions and media portrayals converge. As Chapter 2 illustrates so clearly, the media plays both a formative and a reflective role in this process of social construction. It mobilizes and reproduces images that have a resonance within its audience, reflecting and mirroring the prejudices, beliefs and anxieties that hold sway. Chomsky argues that in the 'manufacture of news', there is conformity to ideological pressures which reflect internalized values derived in structural power relations. He states:

> The system protects itself with indignation against a challenge to the right of deceit in the service of power, and the very idea of subjecting the ideological system to rational enquiry elicits incomprehension or outrage, though it is often masked in other terms.
>
> (1989:9)

While Chomsky's analysis is concerned with the creation of those 'illusions' necessary to maintain the US state's credibility with regard to foreign policy and military interventions, the significant point is that the media not only reflects back to its audience that which is expected – patriotism, for example – but also that it endorses and underwrites the interests of the powerful within any given social order. It generates a subtle mix, appealing to constituencies of prejudice, manipulating – even inventing – 'the truth' and servicing, not always without mild criticism, established-order priorities. The communications' revolution has provided the media with unprecedented capacities to reach vast audiences in an instant. As photographs, reports, comment and televisual data flash around the world, courtesy of media conglomerates' satellites, new technologies secure the images in seconds and broadsheets are published in hours. With political futures won and lost on television presentations, with wars broadcast live into sitting-rooms and computer-enhanced images of slow-motion, action-replays routinely used to identify the 'deviants', the power of the media to manufacture news has entered a new, global era dictated by its attendant global market-place.

There exists a considerable body of primary research illustrating the capacity, and apparent willingness, of the media to manipulate coverage to satisfy political–ideological agendas or to win readership or ratings battles. Within this broader context the media, particularly the press, has been culpable in the purposeful fabrication of stories relating to quite different events or incidents. Examples such as coverage of the 1984–85 coal dispute (Wade, 1985), prison protests in Scotland (Scraton, Sim and Skidmore, 1991) or in 1991 at Strangeways, Manchester (Jameson and Allison, 1995) and the Hillsborough Disaster (Coleman *et al.*, 1990; Scraton *et al.*, 1995) parallel the coverage of St Saviours School, Toxteth, discussed in Chapter 2. The images of 'militant' trade-unionists, 'psychopathic' prisoners, football 'hooligans' and 'lawless' children were created without supporting evidence and sustained over time, guaranteeing their acceptance without question. They appealed to an already established constituency within the public domain where the 'language of law and order . . . sustained by moralisms' (Hall, 1979:19) has succeeded in delivering the syntax of 'good' against 'evil', the standards of 'civilized' against 'uncivilized' and the choice of 'anarchy' against 'order'.

It was the appeal to values and morality which cemented the Thatcherite agenda bringing popular consent to the worst excesses of economic libertarianism and social authoritarianism. The media has played a significant part in this process. As Herman and Chomsky state:

> the 'societal purpose' of the media is to inculcate and defend the economic, social, and political agenda of privileged groups that dominate the domestic society and the state. The media serve this purpose in many ways: through selection of topics, distribution of concerns, framing of issues, filtering of information, emphasis and tone, and by keeping debate within the bounds of acceptable premises.
>
> (1988:298)

The 'privilege' enjoyed by adults when set against the experiences of children and young people is their function as active participants, namely citizens, within society. The media's participation in the social construction of reality is framed inevitably around the marginalization and exclusion of children, reflecting a broad adult consensus around 'childhood', its social identity and political management. The stories about children's behaviour which have dominated the press throughout the 1990s represent a conscious blend of imagery and ideology. Journalists and editors have taken the sensationalist, dramatic images of troublesome children and lawless youth, regardless of their accuracy, and touched the raw nerve of established ideologies. So strong are the ideologies which prevail over crime, disorder and deviance, saturated with dominant notions of 'evil', 'viciousness' and 'savagery' that the constituency thirsts for the grotesque and the horrific. On the one hand is the moral indignation of condemnation, harsh punishment and retribution, on the other is the amoral infatuation with the violent and brutal details of tragic cases.

Crime, disorder and deviance are part of a broader context of social construction in which images reflect shared and persistent ideologies. Popular assumptions about racial superiority and 'lesser breeds', deeply embedded in the English national psyche, and given credence by a century of eugenics, are regularly reinforced in media coverage of 'alien cultures' and immigration policy. Similar assumptions about 'problem estates' and 'sink schools', reflecting established class ideologies, are reinforced by media stereotypes of an underclass which inhabits 'no-go' areas. There are many examples which connect commonly-held assumptions based on internalized prejudices and bigotry to news coverage and political commentary within the media. Whatever the publishing and broadcasting guidelines require, the media is not in the business of education but in the business of news production, literally selling news. It is a cut-throat and competitive world in which the supply must be responsive to the demand. And truth, accuracy or enlightenment are often the first casualties.

The social construction of reality, manifested in and maintained by popular discourse, however, creates expectations and requires responses. If it constitutes a shared 'way of seeing', the political management of 'social problems' forms the basis for 'ways of responding'. The popular discourses outlined above have gained credibility from mainstream academic discourses and their 'domain assumptions'. 'Wayward children', 'dysfunctional families' and 'degenerate communities', whatever the tensions between competing theories, have been closely associated with an implicit, and often explicit, acceptance of pathological models. While early physiological theories of the 'deviant' or the 'delinquent' were overtaken by more refined theoretical constructs, focusing on genetic predisposition, and by the more socially contextualizing arguments of 'under socialization', the focus remained the same: individual pathology. Although quite different and distinct premises underpinned such models, ranging from biological/social determinisms to rationality and voluntarism, the emphasis remained consistent: the abnormal individual.

Similarly, the early sociological studies of the inner-city by late nineteenth century reformers, emphasized the corrupting influence of moral degeneration. Through the application of medical frameworks and analogies the social environment, or laboratory, was pathologized. In this construction people might not be born with criminality in their genes but they could be infected. As Mort (1987) so clearly shows, the medico-legal discourses of the late nineteenth century pulled together a range of quite unconnected social issues: poverty, sin, vice, crime and political sedition. From these early discourses emerged a growing academic analysis of environment and culture. Just as the body could be infected, creating a 'sick' person, so communities could be infected, creating a 'sick' society. Whatever the broader, structural relations of class, unemployment, poverty and appalling housing, the issue was reduced to morality. The political rhetoric and academic accounts fused together in their common assault on the 'idlers' and the 'unemployables' whose parlous state was represented as being of their own choosing. It was a fusion of like prejudices which remained almost untouched, and certainly intact, to be mobilized with a vengeance as the New Right of the 1970s invoked the 'Old Right' of the 1870s: the 'return to Victorian Values'.

The significance of medico-legal discourses which centre on some combination of individual and social pathology models – the bad, mad, sad individual or the bad, sick, infected and infectious community – is not only that they dignify and legitimate the bigotry of popular discourses but also that they actively promote policies of correction. For, if individuals or communities can be identified as being inherently pathological, they can be classified, targeted and disciplined accordingly. As Foucault (1977) demonstrates, in the pursuit of the 'disciplined subject' the regulatory functions of the 'professionals' become institutionalized. In this process Foucault's 'regimes of truth' are not dissimilar to Berger's 'ways of seeing' as prioritized 'social problems' become politically managed through state agencies. Knowledge might be diverse and differentiated but if it carries the weight of state agencies and their regulatory intervention it is knowledge interwoven with authoritative power. While power takes many diverse and relative forms, manifestly pluralized through complex social relations, in its political–economic forms it is persuasive. For those pushed to the political and/or economic margins, the relative surplus population and/or political activists, it is their personal or social worlds which become the focus of attention. Their actions are targeted, policed and regulated and their knowledge is contested, ignored and disqualified.

This is not to suggest that seriously disruptive, antisocial and criminal behaviours do not exist, are to be denied or can be reduced simply to political–economic determinants. Although, as Bea Campbell (1993) notes, it is no coincidence that young working-class men terrorize communities within a broader socio-economic context which presents the rhetoric of stake-holding while purposefully and institutionally denying their participation. It is also no coincidence that they are men behaving badly within patriarchies which make virtues of male aggression, bonding, camaraderie, homophobia and misogyny (Stoltenberg, 1991). While deeply offensive and threatening behaviours require appropriate policing, there is a lack of political will to examine and reform the structural, determining contexts which sustain the threats, the violence and the fear. It is not just a case of historical amnesia, as Pearson (1993/94) notes, but a remarkable reluctance to learn from history.

Consequently, authoritarianism, so much the hall-mark of Thatcherism, is not simply a populist dogma carefully orchestrated to win the hearts and minds of 'middle England'. It is the ever-present flip-side of the liberal, benign state. The social authoritarianism of the New Right has been unwavering in its commitment to the politics of correctionalism through punishment. In responding to individuals who transgress the law, the driving force has been a combination of punishment, retribution and deterrence. The popular appeal is that offenders 'get what's coming to them' and are compelled to conform through experiencing thoroughly unpleasant regimes of harsh punishment. At the community level the process of pathologizing identifiable families and groups has meant the growth of surveillance, targeting and regulation. What the pathology models suggest is a policy orientation towards normalization through correctionalism. This suits policies whose popular appeal is derived in demands for retribution and 'just desserts'. The political management of 'dangerous children' and 'lawless youth', then, reflects the social construction of 'dangerousness' and 'lawlessness' more broadly rooted in popular discourse.

Taking the moral high ground

Charles Murray, writing on the emergence of a British underclass during the 1980s, identifies three primary 'phenomena' which together form its structural foundation. These are illegitimacy, violent crime and drop-out from the labour force. 'Illegitimacy', however, constitutes the 'best predictor of an underclass in the making' (Murray, 1990:4). Murray's thesis is that children become 'responsible parents and neighbours and workers' because they copy the role models in their communities. Given that the 'responsible' community is one of 'appropriately' formed nuclear families with functioning parental roles, Murray's identification of dysfunction is as predictable as it is simplistic and crudely reductionist. It begins with an easily recognized stereotype, the 'lone mother', and quickly shifts to the pathologization of entire communities.

> A child [by which he means boy-child] with a mother and no father, living in a neighbourhood of mothers and no fathers, judges by what he sees . . . in communities without fathers, the kids [by which he means boy-kids] tend to run wild. The fewer the fathers, the greater the tendency . . . no set bedtime . . . left in the house at night while mummy goes out . . . an 18-month-old toddler allowed to play in the street . . . children who are inordinately physical and aggressive in their relationship with other children.
>
> (Murray, 1990:11–12)

For Murray young men 'are essentially barbarians' and it is marriage, 'the act of taking responsibility for a wife and children' that is 'an indispensable civilising force' within society (1990:23).

Murray's thesis not only appealed to the New Right, it gained indirect support from self-styled realists on the liberal left, particularly ethical socialists. Prominent among the regular contributors to this debate is *Guardian/Observer* columnist, Melanie Phillips. Central to her argument is the preeminence of 'adult gratification' over the 'best interests' of children. Discussing the 'catastrophic failure of the parental relationship' Phillips argues:

> . . . the assumption that long-distance fatherhood is just another dish to be chosen from the menu of alternative family structures, the peripatetic plight of children torn between two households, are . . . familiar features now of everyday life. And their consequences are becoming all too familiar: the rising levels of childhood and adult distress in Britain, Europe and America, from depression and eating disorders, through educational underachievement, truancy and

the flight from what is sometimes laughingly called home, into lives of homelessness, crime, drug abuse, failed relationships, suicide and despair.

(*Observer*, 13 June 1993)

Phillips shares with Murray the belief that settled marriage constitutes the 'civilising force' essential to societal stability and the primary socialization of children. For Phillips the 'crisis of the family' is a 'crisis in authority' and the 'attempt to rebuild a decent society will founder unless the two-parent family takes its place again as the template for a society based on co-operative, responsible and altruistic relationships' (*Observer*, 13 June 1993). Concluding that a father is 'a vital necessity for a child's emotional health', Phillips drives home her argument:

Two parent families . . . are the model of a healthy society . . . the cohesiveness of our society is at risk, too many of our children are in trouble and *all* parents urgently need help and support. We need to move from self-indulgence to social responsibility.

(*Observer*, 13 June 1993)

Phillips persistently returns to this social tension between 'self-indulgence' and 'social responsibility'. Writing on 'no-fault divorce', for example, she refers to criticism of 'pro-family campaigners' as embodying the 'increasing shrillness of the libertarian hedonistic tendency' (*Observer*, 29 October 1995). In discussing the case of Sarah Cook, a 13-year-old girl who married an 18-year-old Turkish national, she condemned it as a 'fitting take for the nihilistic nineties' (*Observer*, 28 January 1996). She railed against the 'astonishing' attitude of Sarah Cook's 'ordinary parents':

Their behaviour demonstrated a complete breakdown of any moral code whatsoever . . . an utter failure to understand what parenting is . . . It showed they had no concept of any values beyond immediate gratification. . . .

(*Observer*, 28 January 1996)

'Self-indulgence', 'hedonism', 'nihilism' and 'immediate gratification' form the judgmental currency employed by Phillips in specifying a 'decline in family values'. As illustrated above, the repeated attacks on 'lone parents' or 'dismembered families' by the ethical socialists, together with those made by the New Right on 'illegitimacy', are instrumental in laying blame on specific individuals and communities. The tone of the writing assumes that those who endure misfortune, poverty and under-resourced environments make conscious choices to exacerbate their suffering. It is the perception of voluntarism so evident in this work that makes it so detached from reality. There is also what Ros Coward refers to as 'horrendous middle-class bigotry' as 'the problem then becomes the sub-human culture of the poor threatening to overwhelm fundamental human decency' (*Guardian*, 2 December 1994). As Suzanne Moore puts it:

> Flaunting one's idyllic marriage and achieving children does little to help those who have tried and failed, not because we are immoral, irresponsible people but because we are full of human failings and may have made wrong choices or felt that there was no choice to make ... Pronouncements about the social good of the marital institution do little apart from propagating the idea that, when it comes to families, some are more equal than others ... Children are suffering through material, not maternal or paternal, deprivation. This, for me is the real moral issue.
>
> (*Guardian*, 9 March 1995)

Phillips' journalism, however, cannot be dismissed lightly as the writings of an individual, torch-carrying media commentator. It is well-respected and reflects a growing and influential constituency. She identifies closely with the writings of 'ethical socialists' such as Norman Dennis, George Erdos and A. H. Halsey and her work is consistent with the public statements of 'left realist' politicians such as Labour leader Tony Blair, and his shadow cabinet minister for education, David Blunkett. Dennis and Erdos (1992) take the debate away from the confines of Murray's inner-city underclass to propose a more universal, far-reaching social breakdown connecting 'illegitimacy' and family 'breakdown' to a reduction in the work ethic and spiralling crime. Halsey (Foreword: Dennis and Erdos, 1992:xi) argues that the traditional family provided a 'coherent strategy for the ordering of social relations in such a way as to equip children for their own eventual adult responsibilities'. Accepting that family life has been eroded he identifies (1992:xiii) an 'overlooked consequence' of 'family breakdown':

> the emergence of a new type of young male, namely one who is both weakly socialised and weakly socially controlled so far as the responsibilities of spousehood and fatherhood are concerned ... he no longer feels the pressure his father and grandfather and previous generations of males felt to be a responsible adult in a functioning community.
>
> (1992:xiii)

For Dennis and Erdos the lack of 'responsible fathers' is the persistent theme as 'young males ... no longer take it for granted that they will become responsible fathers' (1992:27). Dennis, 'by the summer of 1993, under the pressure of the cumulative evidence from common experience and statistical evidence' had established 'beyond doubt the superiority, for the children and for the rest of society, of the family with two publicly and successfully committed natural parents' (1993:69). In attempting to sustain this position he quotes an article published in *The Atlantic Monthly*, a 'leading journal of the liberal-left' in which Barbara Dafoe Whitehead wrote:

> The social science evidence is in: though it might benefit the adults involved, the dissolution of intact two-parent families is harmful to large numbers of children. Moreover . . . family diversity in the form of increasing numbers of single-parent and step-parent families does not strengthen the social fabric but, rather, dramatically weakens and undermines society.
>
> (1993:70)

Again, the emphasis is that adults, steeped in selfishness, nihilism and self-indulgence put their interests before the established 'needs of children' and the identified 'good of society'. For the ethical socialists it is a state of affairs encouraged by, and indicative of, a deepening social and moral shift supported by a post-1960s 'received wisdom'. Dennis and Erdos (1992:25) argue that such 'received wisdom' suggests that 'institutions which normatively held these areas [sexuality, procreation, child-care, child-rearing and adult mutual-aid] together in a tight inter-locking package [lifelong heterosexual socially-certified marriage] were "not deteriorating, only changing"'. As with Melanie Phillips, Dennis and Erdos propose that such a position constitutes a serious and sustained ideological attack on the family which collectively represents an 'anti-family consensus'. Underpinning this attack, and providing academic credibility to this subversive consensus are the 'betrayals' of the 'intellectuals': 'ad hoc combinations of destabilizing Marxism whose long march through the institutions began and ended in the family, altruistic anarchism, hedonistic nihilism . . . which excited the undergraduates of 1968 and which until recently were the stock-in-trade of serious journalism' (1992:107). It is this 'spirit of 68' which has prevailed in the 'weakening of the link between sex, procreation, child-care, child-rearing and loyalty in the life-long provision on a non-commercial basis of mutual care within a common place of residence'. It extends to include, without qualification, the 'new generation of feminists, in revolt against "capitalist patriarchy" or "patriarchal capitalism", whether as "feminist Marxists", "material feminists", or "radical feminists"' (1992:61–2) whose 'attack on the family is the last fling of Marxism' (1992:65).

The ease with which these authors dismiss the research and scholarship of critical analysis, including the full range and diversity of feminist critiques, provides a damning indictment of their academic approach, demonstrating a poverty of theory and lack of rigour. Yet their work not only enjoys a significant constituency, appealing to a politically broad church, it is also influential in establishing unexpected alliances. David Green, Director of the right-wing Institute of Economic Affairs, acknowledges the close association of the work of journalists Norman Macrae (*The Sunday Times*) and Melanie Phillips (*Guardian/Observer*) and the research and writings of Murray, Halsey, Dennis and Erdos, concluding (1992:viii, emphases added):

> The freedom of the press and the courage of a few academics . . . has saved us from monolithic political correctness. The next task is to discover what can be done to restore the ideal of the two-parent family, supported by the grandparents and aunts and uncles of the extended family, and in doing so avoid the extremes, always a possibility when *it becomes necessary to correct fundamentals.*
>
> (1992:viii)

To resolve the problem of Murray's pathologized communities, the objective is the correction of 'fundamentals'. The focus is those individuals whose actions collectively have destroyed Halsey's 'traditional family system'. According to Green this system is the ideal, and idealized, nuclear family as the kernel of the extended family. Both Murray and the ethical socialists are united in the belief that this system is the primary 'civilising force' within society and all consider that 'dismembered' or 'dysfunctional' families have prevailed because of voluntaristic and avoidable choices made by post-1960s nihilists and hedonists. While judgmentalism is implicit throughout this range of early 1990s work, the affirmation of moral absolutes is its most prevalent feature.

Towards a rights agenda for children and young people

The abuse, degradation and exclusion of children by adults is a global issue. While guarding against false universalism, the suffering of children at the hands and words of adults is not bounded by class, culture, gender, state or religion. Their enslavement as marginal, easily expendable and unprotected workers in sweatshops, mines, factories and, more recently, highly sophisticated light industry in the world's economic free zones is well-documented. Less thoroughly researched has been the essential contribution made by children and young people in the domestic sphere, as surrogate mothers, cleaners, carers, fetchers and carriers. The street children of Latin American, African and Asian shanty towns are represented in the media as condemnatory evidence of the decivilizing of whole cultures. Stories of child executions at the hands of death squads on the streets of Sao Paulo are matched by disturbing revelations of the sex trade in children in Thailand. The full horror of Rwanda's civil war, like so many others, is transmitted through the experiences of traumatized children who survived as the bereaved witnesses of the terrible slaughter of their loved ones. Undoubtedly, these are matters of profound concern. Their portrayal, however, unacceptably distances media consumers in the West from the depth and complexity of such experiences. Also, it enables those consumers to stand apart from any direct or indirect responsibility for such suffering.

By defining or portraying the experiences of children solely within cultural or societal boundaries, their pain and their exploitation is identified as a domestic issue, yet another expression of ethnic pathology. Yet it is the West, the self-appointed First World, which remorselessly exploits the labour in the sweatshops, the rice fields, the deregulated industrial plants and the mines. It is their affluent men who do business in the vicious and degrading child sex industry. It is the financial dealing of their political leaders and captains of multinational industry which create, without any reciprocal responsibility, the undermining dependency of national debts. At a distance, however, these are worlds apart. Closely associated to economic dominance through dependency is a form of cultural imperialism which implicitly assumes that the children of the First World are protected, cared for and provided for, nurtured, loved and educated, free from poverty, abuse, exploitation, illness and premature death. It is a cruel lie. For, whatever the relative material benefits, quality of life and opportunities self-evident within advanced capitalist societies, structural inequalities, ritualized abuse and the systematic denial of citizen's rights to all under the age of 18 are deeply etched into Britain's social and political landscape.

The Children's Rights Office notes that the United Kingdom is one of the richest nation-states in the world – with its children protected from the fundamental 'difficulties experienced by those in many developing countries of, for example, absolute poverty, malnutrition, death from preventable diseases, bonded child labour and illiteracy' (CRO, 1995a:8). Yet, there are serious problems for children in the UK:

> growing inequality, increased poverty, drug abuse, teenage pregnancy, high levels of violence to children including sexual abuse, growing levels of child prostitution, homelessness, rapidly rising divorce rates, growing problems of suicide and mental illness, a deteriorating environment and alienation from the political process.
>
> (CRO, 1995a:8)

Work has focused on these issues and on the lack of appropriate forums in which children and young people can voice their concerns or participate in their resolution. While politicians, media commentators and academics continue to lay the problems of childhood at the door of the 'disintegrating community' or the 'dismembered family' – arguing, as illustrated in the last section, that the issue is primarily one of moral values – the material realities derived in the determining contexts and structural relations of production (class), reproduction (patriarchy) and neocolonialism ('race') are ignored.

The Association of Metropolitan Authorities, in noting that 'children are the most vulnerable group in society', concludes:

> They have no voting rights and therefore no formal avenues to exercise power. They can only experience change through the actions of adults. Adults in positions of responsibility therefore have a duty to ensure that the rights of children and young people are respected.
>
> (1995:11)

What this process of adult mediation in all matters means is that ranging from the use of physical punishment in the home, in childcare or in schools, across the board to accessing contraception and abortion advice it is left to adults to decide on the 'best interests' of children in any given situation. As Liberty argues, 'there is a danger that children's rights in areas such as privacy and freedom of information, to name but two, can be randomly violated on the grounds that it is in their best interests' (in NCCL, 1991:69).

Again, the issue tends to be determined primarily on the grounds of moral values and judgments. In this line of moral argument there has been a commitment by adults to 'protecting' children and young people from knowledge and information relevant to their developing sexualities until such a time as adults/professionals/judges consider that they have matured sufficiently to cope with such matters. This returns the discussion to the notion of childhood innocence, effectively a state of ignorance or assumption based on rumour and imagination. It leads to a false prolonging of childhood in which physical and emotional development are allowed to run ahead of appropriate knowledge and understanding. Yet, at the same time in other spheres, children are expected to be rational and all-knowing in identifying the potential consequences of their actions. Nowhere has this been more evident than in the debate over criminal responsibility. Following the decision to prosecute two 10-year-old boys for murder in the case of James Bulger, the aftermath revealed the underlying contradictions implicit in the discourses which contextualize the political management and legal regulation of children. The decision to prosecute flew in the face of the principle, accepted by Parliament in 1969, that there should be no punishment of children without proven moral responsibility and, further, that children should benefit from care and regulation rather than incarceration and punishment. Allan Levy QC, a leading authority on children and the law remains unequivocal in his response to the 'sad message' of the trial of the two boys:

> The full adversarial process of a major criminal prosecution enveloped the two boys ... The Bulger case has revealed the

unacceptable face of our criminal justice system concerning children. It provides an unpalatable insight into outmoded thought, reform denied and the appearance of political calculation.

(*Guardian*, 29 November 1994)

The final reference, concerning political calculation, was directed against the Home Secretary's intervention to set a minimum-served sentence of 15 years. Gitta Sereny, an authority on the case of Mary Bell (who in 1968 at the age of 10 killed two toddlers) also strongly rejected the 15 year sentence:

It is outrageous, utterly outrageous. What hope do you give them? . . . 15 years for an 11-year-old is the other side of the moon. It is very important for them to be punished for something so wrong but it is not right for all hope to be taken away and for them to be put in a situation in which they cannot but be corrupted.

(*Guardian*, 8 February 1995)

Apart from the long-term consequences of a sentence eventually leading to young offenders' institutions and adult prisons the issue of equating moral responsibility with age remains critical. In May 1996 an 11-year-old boy was found guilty of manslaughter after he had pushed a concrete block from the top of a nine-storey tower block, killing a 74-year-old woman below. The subsequent trial turned on the issue of whether, in the circumstances, he could distinguish between right and wrong. He was found guilty of manslaughter, which suggests that despite his age the jury considered he could be held fully responsible for his actions. The judge, however, revealed that this conclusion left him with a 'real sentencing problem' (*Guardian*, 14 June 1996) as incarceration would put the boy 'at risk' and seriously inhibit his rehabilitation. Consequently he was given a 3 year supervision order and returned to his family.

Drawing the line of moral responsibility in relation to age and personal development is not straightforward. In May 1996 in Richmond, California, a 6-year-old boy was charged with attempting to unlawfully kill a one-month-old baby. The prosecutor argued that the boy acted with malice aforethought and that it was 'patently obvious' that he 'knew the difference between right and wrong' (*Independent*, 10 May 1996). Jeffrey Butts, of the National Centre for Juvenile Justice, considers that the issue is not restricted simply to the point at which as adults 'we are willing to acknowledge that children don't have the capacity to make good judgments'. More fundamentally, he argues, it extends to preventing 'the rush to take away the status of childhood from children'. This is precisely the point made by Allan Levy in condemning the 'increasingly reactionary approach' in the British criminal justice process which is actually contributing to the 'victimisation of children' (*Guardian*, 29 November 1994). He continues:

The relevance of childhood and children's special need for protection are well recognised in civil law. It is ironic that in circumstances where the fact of childhood needs more, not less, recognition, the agenda often politically motivated, is geared towards equating the child with the fully responsible adult.

Inevitably, what this leads to is the proposition that the 'fact' of childhood, in itself, becomes a mitigating circumstance in the commission of a serious offence. If drawing the line is to be more than an arbitrary endeavour, who draws it and the criteria used to achieve sound and fair judgments are significant issues.

On the one hand, then, there is the denial of children as rational, responsible persons able to receive information, participate in frank and open discussions and come to well-reasoned and appropriately-informed decisions about their interpersonal relationships (family, friends, sexual), about school and about developing sexuality. On the other, there is the imposition, using the full force of the law, of the highest level of rationality and responsibility on children and young people who seriously offend. The paradox is that the same sources appear to propose that childhood represents a period of diminished adult responsibility governing certain actions while being a period of equal responsibility governing others. What is clear from the work of children's advocacy agencies, and from consultation with children and young people, is the lack of any systematic attempt to resolve these contradictions and evolve institutional arrangements which recognize and actively promote the rights of children and young people in accord with the responsibilities placed on them.

The framework for such arrangements is contained in the UN Convention on the Rights of the Child (United Nations, 1989). The Convention was adopted by the UN General Assembly in 1989 and ratified by the UK Government in December 1991. By 1996 it had received almost universal ratification by the 190 UN member states. The convention comprises over 50 Articles, the main aims of which are to establish the rights of children and young people to adequate and effective care and protection, provide services and facilities appropriate to their fundamental needs and encourage institutional arrangements which enable them to be active participants in their society. The UN Committee expects ratifying states to initiate legal and policy reform and to develop professional agency practices in accordance with the Articles. As an international agreement the Convention is binding in international law. The Articles cover rights and duties across the entire social and community spectrum, providing direction for all state institutionally-based interventionist policies and practices. It recognizes the role and function of the state in supporting parents and carers in the growth, development and socialization of children.

Certain articles frame precise and unambiguous objectives. Article 19, for example, proclaims the right of the child to protection from all forms of physical and mental violence, abuse and neglect. Others, however, are more circumspect but no less significant. Crucial here is Article 3 which states the duty, in all actions, to consider the 'best interests of the child'. Again, the issue of who determines, defines and administers 'best interests' is not so easily identified. If this Article is placed alongside Article 5, which imposes a duty on governments to respect the rights and responsibilities of parents to provide guidance for children 'in line with their evolving capacities', the issue becomes compounded. In England and Wales the 1989 Children Act addressed parental responsibilities in terms of the sum total of 'rights', 'duties', 'power', 'responsibilities' and 'authority' which legally a parent has in relation to its child/children and their property. Most state institutions, childcare professionals and parents/carers would accept that parenthood involves responsibility, if not active decision-making, for the social development and personal guidance of the child. Article 5 underwrites this responsibility, directing states to do the same in providing support, but it is a responsibility left to the discretion of parents or carers as they quantify the 'evolving capacities' of the children in their care. While Article 3 establishes 'best interests' and declares a duty of care and protection there is no formula for establishing 'best interests' in any given circumstance.

The spirit of Articles 5 and 3 does reverse the traditional relationship of parents and carers to children by focusing on some broader conceptualization of 'evolving capacities' and 'best interests'. As the Children's Rights Office states, parents' rights are limited: 'to override the actions of a child only where the child is not competent to understand fully the consequences of their actions, or where failure to intervene would place the child at risk . . .' (CRO, 1995b:12). Much of this, however, carries little weight or relevance while children and young people are excluded and marginalized from the processes, including their status in the family, which govern and determine their lives. How are they to know any different? The Convention proclaims the right to express an opinion and have it taken seriously (Article 12), the right to freedom of expression (Article 13) and the right of access to appropriate information (Article 17). As has been stated elsewhere, 'a balance has to be struck between . . . the child's right to receive information and . . . their right to be protected from material that is likely to be harmful to them' (CRO, 1995b:35). Parents and carers are expected to mediate on these conflicting processes, again reflecting the dichotomy of liberty versus freedom. They become, as they already are, the definers of appropriateness as it relates to their perception of a child's competence. While Article 12 states the right to freedom of expression, legislation does not provide for this within the family, as it is conceived, if not reinforced, as a 'private domain'.

The reservations implicit in the above discussion are not meant to undermine the potential of the UN Convention as a significant forward move for the lives, experiences and decisions of children and young people. Progress can be made, however, only if the ratifying states actively promote, through legislation and policy, the Convention's Articles. Within the UK there is significant complacency linked to a 'little Englander' mentality concerning political sovereignty which has mitigated against the realization of the Convention's objectives. As stated previously, the complacency is derived in the mistaken assumption that the UK already meets most of the key demands made by the Convention and that the Articles are directed elsewhere, towards less 'civilized' societies. The sovereignty issue reflects a deep-seated and mistaken ideology which conflates nationalism, patriotism and xenophobia. It leads to a reluctance to move forward on any initiatives which are seen to be derived outside the narrow confines of the 'British' Parliament and to an explicit rejection of external, progressive, social and political initiatives for change.

Accordingly, in implementing the UN Convention, the UK Government failed 'to undertake a critical self-appraisal of the extent to which UK legislation, policies and practice comply with its principles and standards' (CRO, 1995a:8). Following ratification the UK Government put forward a series of reservations to the UN Secretary General. These focused primarily on immigration, employment and youth justice. In January 1995, following consideration of the UK's initial report, the UN Committee on the Rights of the Child responded by raising 15 substantive issues of concern (CRC, 1995). These included: immigration policy and legislation; coordination of the Convention's implementation; Northern Ireland; healthcare; sex education; physical and sexual abuse; children in care; youth justice, particularly the extension of imprisonment through secure training orders; poverty. One of the most serious issues was that the 'principle of the best interest of the child appears not to be reflected in legislation in such areas as health, education and social security . . .' (1995:3). Further, with regard to schooling, 'the right of the child to express his or her opinion is not solicited' (1995:3). The Committee was 'deeply worried' over 'judicial interpretations of the present law permitting the reasonable chastisement in cases of physical abuse of children within the family context' (1995:4). This led to concern that 'the physical integrity of children' as defined within the Convention was not protected by UK legislative or policy measures. It directed that in terms of 'best interests' and consultation the UK Government should incorporate appropriate and effective measures into rights' policies and legislation. It recommended 'further mechanisms to facilitate the participation of children in decisions affecting them . . .' (1995:5). The force and extent of the UN Committee's response left no doubts as to its dismay at the lack of progress made by the UK Government.

Inevitably, the UK Government 'expressed considerable anger at the explicit criticism of the poor record of the UK in implementing the Convention . . . given the poor record of respecting children which pertains in so many other countries in the world' (CRO, 1995a:8). This brought an immediate rebuke from Thomas Hammerberg, Vice Chair of the UN Committee, who stated that 'of more than 30 governments that have now appeared before the Committee, none has reacted with such hostility as the UK Government to its [the Committee's] observations and recommendations' (CRO, 1995a:8). The UK Government's response typifies a much wider denial of directives, agreements, treaties and conventions initiated and instituted beyond its borders yet demanding monitored, transparent progress within. Again, the politics of sovereignty were easily mobilized and invoked to popularize and represent international agreements as 'destabilizing' or 'interfering' with established, internal state policies and practices. Yet, as argued by the Children's Rights Office (CRO, 1995a:9), the objective of international, binding agreements and their monitoring 'is not to produce a league table of comparative progress' but to consider progress towards agreed aims and given 'resources, political situation, history, stability and culture'. A commitment to such progress, however, cannot be realized through rhetoric. It has to be carried through political will, informed debate and legislative and policy change.

The apparent reluctance of the UK Government to take appropriate action, through legal and policy reform, in implementing the UN Convention does not inspire confidence for the future of a rights agenda in Britain. As this book shows, legal reform and policy initiatives regarding children and young people have been regressive rather than progressive, imbued with characteristic authoritarian principles. The enduring popular imagery continues to promote caricatures of poorly-disciplined children, lawless youth, inadequate parents and failing teachers and social workers. With material realities submerged under wave after wave of adult moral indignation there is little popular constituency for a rights agenda. What has been evident throughout the 1990s is a sustained backlash directed against critical analysis and child-centred policies and practices. While the backlash has been sustained it has failed to eradicate the gradual progress towards a positive rights agenda which aims to secure rights for children and young people independent of but equal in standing to those of adults.

A positive rights agenda has the potential to create conditions necessary for the full and active participation of children and young people. At local, regional and national levels voluntary agencies continue to resist the blend of indifference and hostility directed towards their efforts as advocates and providers. These agencies have been effective, as have some health providers and youth/community services, in promoting the interests and meeting the needs of children. This interventionist and proactive work, along with the resistance of young people themselves, reveals a clear commitment to responding to children as persons rather than as dependants. This includes their active participation in decisions, both in the private and public spheres, which affect their lives. Of particular significance is the quality of life experienced in both family and community contexts.

As children develop, their right to knowledge and information necessarily extends beyond that which is provided within families or through school curricula. While these are the primary sites of their social experiences and socialization they are also institutional settings which limit and confine children's knowledge and understanding. The recent emergence and success of community drop-in centres as providers of informed advice, support and advocacy, governing a range of social, health and economic issues, demonstrates the significance of independent consultation opportunities for children and young people. These processes identify and target children as receivers of information and knowledge through which they can make responsible decisions underpinned by appropriate support. A positive rights agenda also perceives and promotes children as providers of information concerning their social and familial relationships and the administration of their schools, their communities and their physical environment. It challenges the reductionism which has characterized children as no more than passive consumers of community services. In contrast, it promotes full and active participation including effective consultation and monitoring. Until central and local government accept the need to establish children's rights departments which recognize and endorse the unique and developing needs of children and young people, the formal agenda will remain, at best, tokenistic.

The primary obstacles in the path of sound, progressive reform remain the structural relations and social arrangements through which adult power is endured by children. Adult power dominates their personal and social lives and is institutionalized in 'caring' and 'disciplining' agencies alike. As has been evident in the plethora of contemporary scandals, it is a power readily and systematically abused. It is a dangerous and debilitating power, capable of stunting the personal development and potential of even the most resilient children. It is physically and mentally painful, damaging good health and often wreaking havoc in those interpersonal relationships which require love, care and trust. What is so difficult for adults, as the power-brokers, to accept is that the 'crisis' is not one of 'childhood' but one of adultism. In the struggle against the full spectrum of the oppression of children, adults have to address the oppressor within and alongside them. It is imperative that the dominant lie, that adult power and its manifestations are conceived and administered for the benefit of children, is exposed. Equally important is an awareness of the damage done under the guise of protection and through the idealization of 'childhood' and the 'family'. The removal of these obstacles will enable children and young people to experience a more effective, participatory context supported by a positive rights agenda.

References

ASSOCIATION OF METROPOLITAN AUTHORITIES (1995) *Checklist for Children: Local Authorities and the UN Convention on the Rights of the Child*, London, AMA/CRO.

CAMPBELL, B. (1993) *Goliath: Britain's Dangerous Places*, London, Methuen.

CHOMSKY, N. (1989) *Necessary Illusions: Thought Control in Democratic Societies*, London, Pluto.

COLEMAN, S., JEMPHREY, A., SCRATON, P. and SKIDMORE, P. (1990) *Hillsborough and After: The Liverpool Experience: First Report of the Hillsborough Project*, Liverpool, Liverpool City Council.

CRC (1995) Consideration of Reports Submitted by States Parties under Article 44 of the Convention: Concluding observations of the CRC: UK and Northern Ireland Committee on the Rights of the Child 8th Session, 27 January 1995.

CRO (1995a) *Making the Convention Work for Children*, London, Children's Rights Office.

CRO (1995b) *Building Small Democracies*, London, Children's Rights Office.

DENNIS, N. (1993) *Rising Crime and the Dismembered Family: How Conformist Intellectuals Have Campaigned Against Common Sense*, London, Institute of Economic Affairs.

DENNIS, N. and ERDOS, G. (1992) *Families Without Fatherhood*, London, Institute of Economic Affairs.

FOUCAULT, M. (1977) *Discipline and Punish: The Birth of the Prison*, London, Allen & Unwin.

HALL, S. (1979) 'The great moving right show', *Marxism Today*, January, pp. 14–19.

HERMAN, E. S. and CHOMSKY, N. (1988) *Manufacturing Consent: The Political Economy of the Mass Media*, New York, Pantheon Books.

JAMESON, N. and ALLISON, E. (1995) *Strangeways 1990: A Serious Disturbance*, London, Larkin Publications.

MORT, F. (1987) *Dangerous Sexualities*, London, Routledge.

MURRAY, C. (1990) *The Emerging British Underclass*, London, Institute of Economic Affairs.

NCCL (1991) *A People's Charter: Liberty's Bill of Rights*, London, Liberty.

PEARSON, G. (1993/1994) 'Youth crime and moral decline: Permissiveness and tradition', *The Magistrate*, December/January.

SCRATON, P., JEMPHREY, A. and COLEMAN, S. (1995) *No Last Rights: The Denial of Justice and the Promotion of Myth in the Aftermath of the Hillsborough Disaster*, Liverpool, Alden Press/LCC.

STOLTENBERG, J. (1991) *Refusing to Be a Man*, London, Fontana.

UNITED NATIONS (1989) *The United Nations Convention on the Rights of the Child*, New York, United Nations.

WADE, E. (1985) 'The miners and the media: Themes of newspaper reporting', in SCRATON, P. and THOMAS, P. (Eds) *The State v. The People: Lessons from the Coal Dispute*, Oxford, JLS/Basil Blackwell.

49

THE EVERYDAY WORLD
OF THE CHILD

Matthew Speier

Source: J. Douglas, ed., *Understanding Everyday Life*, London: RKP, 1970, pp. 74–82.

I. A new look at the empirical content
of childhood socialization

Sociology considers the social life of the child as a basic area of study in so-called institutional analyses of family and school, for example. What is classically problematic about studying children is the fact of cultural induction, as I might refer to it. That is, sociologists (and this probably goes for anthropologists and psychologists) commonly treat childhood as a stage of life that builds preparatory mechanisms into the child's behavior so that he is gradually equipped with the competence to participate in the everyday activities of his cultural partners, and eventually as a bona fide adult member himself. This classical sociological problem has been subsumed under the major heading of socialization. In studying the organization of culture and society it seems quite natural to inquire into the process by which a new entrant acquires the status of a member in the eyes of others in his surrounding cultural milieu (unlike those entrants who arrive as adults, as 'strangers' or immigrants, tourists and the like, the child enters upon the scene with a clean slate, because the process takes place without the underlay of previous cultural experience).

The classical formulation of the problem of socialization has centered on treatments of the child's entry and incorporation into culture as a *developmental process*. Its working paradigm has been to ask questions about child development, such as the general one: How does the child internalize the norms, values, attitudes, etc., of others in his society? Traditional anthropological ethnography has asked in addition: How does the child develop particular skills in social and economic ways of life? Psychologists have focused on maturational growth and on personality development. Lately, researchers from all these disciplines have become interested in the development of language skills.

I would like to propose an approach that differs sharply from the developmental one found in the classical formulations of socialization research. This approach sets aside questions of development yet retains the substantive interests of adult-child interaction central to the study of socialization.

I propose a simple definition of socialization that if acceptable to developmentally oriented research would imply the investigation of a hidden frame of analysis altogether: *socialization is the acquisition of interactional competences.* We can readily admit to the fact that children acquire 'a sense of social structure,' to use Cicourel's phrase. That is, for the child to develop from a newborn entrant to a participating member in social arrangements around him, he must undergo a learning process over the course of growing up through successive stages of life. However, to study this implicitly recognized acquisition process, presupposes a good knowledge of the features of interactional competences that are acquired. That is, what in fact are children developmentally acquiring? An investigation of the concrete features of competent interaction is nothing more or less than a study of what children normally and routinely do in their everyday activities, and as such it is not a study at all in the development of competence but a study in descriptive interactional analysis. It is my firm belief that no investigation of acquisition processes can effectively get underway until the concrete features of interactional competences are analyzed as topics in their own right. Without this preliminary step, which deliberately refrains from treating the topic of development, discussions of social competence must necessarily remain too vague and abstract to be of any direct use in empirical socialization research.

The target phenomena I propose to examine, interactions and concerted activities, are not customarily the subject of childhood socialization research. I refer to those sorts of interactions and activities that are *naturally situated* in the stream of everyday life. Naturalistic interactions and activities regularly take place by means of one very dominant mode of human communication, namely, talk. The centrality of talk in the everyday organization of human activity . . . is perhaps the major contribution by so-called ethnomethodologists to the history of modern sociology, a discipline that has remained oddly sluggish in recognizing the central role of speech in the organization of group life.

Talk and its conversational properties (including, where necessary, accompanying nonspoken aspects of interaction such as gestures, facial organization, and ecological spacing) therefore comprise an altogether new set of empirical dimensions in the study of childhood social organization. It can easily be shown how investigators of childhood socialization have regularly relied on the speech communications of cultural participants in making inferences about 'childrearing practices,' though the speech practices themselves are never treated explicitly as analytic topics in their own right, directly relevant to the abstractions that are constructed about organized native knowledge presumably underlying children's and parents' situated courses of action.

This new direction in childhood socialization encourages the generation of topical analyses dealing with problems in how children talk to other children and how they talk with parents and other adults. These constitute, in part, problems in conversational analysis. . . . Unlike past researchers who have only noted in passing the most general significance of language (as in symbolic interactionism), this new direction in studying speech as the living performance of language has emphasized the *methods* participants use when building talk and practical activity around each other. By methods is meant what others have alluded to as the *procedural basis* for everyday interactions, or, as Turner puts it, our enterprise consists of 'the uncovering of members' *procedures* for doing activities,' talking or 'doing things with words' being a major component of those procedures.

Our task in research, then is to gather 'samples' (and at this point no sampling rules can be evinced) of concrete instances of natural interactions involving children. What can we explicate about the formal properties of those conversational procedures, for example, that we find participants using in the concrete instance coming before our analytic scrutiny?

The reader accustomed to the conventional paradigm in childhood socialization will not find hypothetical inquiries about 'socialization influences and aims,' nor problems in the social-structural basis for the child's 'internalization of norms,' etc. He will find, instead, that that interactional orientation to childhood organization will supply a frame of reference that precludes the posing of such abstract problems, and that in fact such problems as are found in the classical formulations will be dissolved and replaced by a whole new set of analytic considerations. In searching out the procedural properties of children's conversational interactions, a vast variety of studies in childhood social organization could be attempted, encompassing parent-child interactions in everyday household activity, adult-child interactions in other families' homes, in public places, in schools, or interactions exclusively among children themselves. Children's exclusive contacts constitute problems of study in what might be called the organization of 'children's culture,' and as such open up a wholly new sociological domain.

In this reformulated context for studying children's everyday activity the notion of development takes on a new shape. The temporal scale is vastly reduced to interactional units of *occasioned and situated activity*. The focus now is upon developing sequences of interaction from one moment to the next, rather than upon stages of development in the child's life; on the way interactants build a social scene and build a conversation together, episodically, beginning with procedures for opening and entering into copresent interactions, next for sustaining them around practical purposes using conversational resources for so doing, and finally for terminating the interaction or shifting into new activities or situations along natural junctures. The notion of development, then, enters into the analysis of interactional sequences moving naturally through time as participants do and say things methodically together. Children presumably have sufficient competence to cooperate in interactional development over a great variety of social circumstances. As interactants they must be able to employ conversational procedures with those they routinely encounter in everyday life. What conversational resources are available to children and to their interlocutors when routine interactions arise and take shape? That is, how are such procedures for interacting employed resourcefully by participants as they go about their talking and acting and their everyday practical achievements?

In the discussion that follows I will attempt to demonstrate how a concrete instance of data in the child's everyday life can be analyzed so as to yield some key issues in the organization of childhood activity.

II. Treating an instance as an opening gambit

I will open with an analysis of a piece of data from the study of children's everyday activities. From it I hope to generate a few important issues that I will take up in more detail in the sections following this one. These issues will center on the analysis of interactional development as a sequence of conversation, and on the nature of some of the conversational resources used by participants in that sequence. I take it that the instance is typical of a mundane routine that children confront in daily life, namely, calling on their friends. Children's contacts often involve and sometimes require the intervention of adults. This is a point about the organization of childhood to keep in mind when examining the instance I am about to present.

The following complete event took place in an encounter between a neighborhood child and a household mother. I was a guest in this home and at the time of the interaction was alone in a bedroom whose window was situated in a favorable position to overhear and record the entire sequence. It lasted for about one minute. The ecological arrangement is very important for an interpretation of the data. This house, on a street of private attached homes in San Francisco, has a front gate off the street that is always locked and that leads onto a tunnel or passage that has a staircase at the far end going up to the front door of the house. The staircase turns and a caller at the front gate at street level cannot see the front door one flight above. To gain entry a caller must always ring the bell at the gate first. This is a standard architectural arrangement for many homes in this city. It structures an interaction between caller and door-answer in such a way that neither party can see the other unless the answerer descends the staircase and turns the corner to look down the passageway at the caller. The entire passage and staircase are actually outdoors. The following transpired:

1. Caller: (Boy rings bell and waits for an answer to his ring.)
2. Mother: Who's there?
3. Caller: Can your son come out?
4. Mother: What?
5. Caller: Can your son come out?
6. Mother: What do you want?
7. Caller: Can your son come out?
8. Mother: (pause) Who is it?
9. Caller: Jerry. Can your son come out?
10. Mother: Oh – No he can't come right now. (Closes the front door.)
11. Caller: When do you think he could come out?
12. Mother: (Silence, since mother has not heard, having closed the door before the boy spoke utterance 11.)
13. Caller: (leaves)

I want to make the following points about this piece:

1 One of the features of family arrangements consists of an ecological containment of members inside the confines of a physical setting, commonly thought of as a residence. Family members therefore carry on their household activities in a home territory. In this instance we find that home territories have entrance points, such as doors and front gates. Those who are bona fide residents of the territory have the right of free passage into their own homes and in fact need not knock or ring to ask permission to be granted entry. In the case at hand, adults have keys, and others wishing entry, such as household children, ring, wait for voice identification, and without further question get passage by means of an electric button pressed by the door answerer. This does *not* constitute asking for and receiving permission where household members are concerned but merely requests clearance, a form of mechanical security to control the entry of *out-siders*. In other words it is an inconvenience to children of the house who may not own a key to the gate, the price paid for such security measures in big cities. But where nonhousehold members are concerned, entry does indeed involve the granting of permission to come in through the front door (guests are treated as temporary household members and therefore the simple clearance pattern of ring-voice identification-entry applies).

2 A child wishing to call on another child must attend to this problem of entering another home territory (whether gates, locks, closed front doors, or some other physical arrangements exist). Now as far as conversational interaction or a state of talk goes, *the child must be prepared to identify himself as a caller and likewise the person on whom he is calling.* He must therefore have at his disposal the conversational resources to make such

relevant identifications as necessary conditions, perhaps, for paying a visit to another child or getting him to come out to play.

3 As the data shows, the opening of the interaction is founded upon the principle of getting an adequate identification from the caller *as a second step in the sequence*, the first being the summoning of a household member by the bell-ring. The structural parallel is to that of the opening sequences of telephone calls, as analyzed by Schegloff. Where in telephoning activity the answerer speaks first after hearing the ring summon him, so too in the household entry situation in our data. But unlike the telephoning interaction, here the answerer provides a question that calls for explicit identification from the caller: 'Who's there?' Unlike the telephone answerer, who cannot know where the caller is located, the door-bell answerer knows precisely his location and thereby presumably his most general intention: to speak to some member of the house and possibly to gain entry.

4 Now the boy caller in the data hears the mother's call for an identification, but rather than supplying it with an *identification term* he relies on voice recognition to do this identificational work. But it does not. His question, moreover, is his reason for being there. Instead of identifying himself in the terms of reference carried within his utterance, he offers an identification of the one he is calling on, the thirteen-year-old boy of the house: 'Can your son come out?'

5 What can be gathered from this question? The caller could have made an identification by using the boy's first name (*FN*), but instead he has selected a term from an altogether different set of possible calling terms. He uses what I might call a *relational term*, that is one of a number of such terms applying to members of a unit of social membership called 'family.' The selection of 'your son' is interactionally viable because the caller has performed an analysis of his interlocutor, the mother of the house. Hearing (not seeing) her as the mother, because either he is familiar with her voice or he assumes any woman's voice will typically be that of the mother of the house, he transforms his own identification term for his friend, a *FN*, used to address him, into relational terms for the benefit of the answerer. In other words, when a child talks to another child's mother he can refer to his friend in terms of his relationship to her as her son. Now another consideration about this selection procedure suggests itself, namely, that when a neighborhood child doesn't in fact know the name of a boy on the block he has played with in the past, he can formulate an identification using familial relationships in households. This is a conversational resource to accomplish the purpose of his call. Perhaps he just wants *someone* to play with.

6 The mother's failure to make voice identification leads her to ask the boy to repeat his first utterance. After he does, she still cannot identify him, so she then goes on to inquire about the purpose of his call: 'What do you want?' The caller repeats himself for the third time, still waiting at the front gate and out of sight, and the mother calls once more for an identification of the caller. This is preceded by a brief pause in which she appears to be scrutinizing the voice for familiarity. It brings the boy's identification: 'Jerry. Can your son come out?' He selects *FN*, but he doesn't employ a parallel term for the rest of his utterance, and continues to identify the boy of the house in family-relationship terms. I cannot prove it, but I would speculate that he does not know the *FN* of the boy of the house.

7 The mother then grasps fully the purpose of the call and what its interactional consequences might be, that her son is being asked to go outside and play. However, at that moment she knows that her son is playing with another child in the house, and also that he has not discerned the occasion of the caller's visit. This raises the next interesting point for our discussion. Instead of relaying the matter to her son, she instead tells the caller herself that he can't come out. Two aspects of this suggest themselves for consideration of the nature of adult interventions in children's contacts and on the nature of children's rights. On the one hand, this mother has the entitlement, as does presumably any mother, to make decisions about contacts between her child and other children. On the other hand, she does not feel obligated to inform her son of the event *before closing it off* on her own. Finally, she does not show obligation to the caller to provide for future contacts by saying 'Come back later,' for example. So, in no sense has she assigned herself the responsibility of being a go-between in a fully developed way. Her intervention then might be characterized in terms of the parental rights she typically exercises to *answer for or talk for* her child. In this way we see that a child has restricted rights as a speaker, given that we do indeed find in many different situations that parents enforce their entitlements to speak for their own children. Needless to say, the restriction of rights to speak is intimately connected to the restrictions on responsibilities, such as the child's presumed responsibility to take appropriate courses of action or to make suitable interactional decisions where other children are concerned. By talking for her son, a mother can practice interactional control over household activity.

8 Finally, the sequence terminates when the caller places a question designed to provide for future contact, and, recognizing that the answerer has retreated inside the house, leaving only silence, he takes leave of the front gate, never having gained entry.

LIVERPOOL
JOHN MOORES UNIVERSITY
AVRIL ROBARTS LRC
TEL. 0151 231 4022

50

THE CHILD'S RELATIONS
WITH OTHERS

Maurice Merleau-Ponty

Source: *The Primacy of Perception*, Evanston, Illinois: Northwestern University Press, 1964, pp. 107–119.

I pass to the fact that appeared to me to be worthy of mention by way of introduction to this course: the relation that can be established between the development of intelligence (in particular, the acquisition of language) and the configuration of the individual's affective environment.

I call your attention to a short article by Francois Rostand entitled 'Grammaire et affectivité.'[1] Rostand begins by remarking that from the start there is a correlation between the age at which the child is most dependent on his parents (i.e., about two years) and the age at which he begins to learn language. There is a period when the child is 'sensitive' with regard to language, when he is capable of learning to speak. It has been shown that if the child up to two years of age does not have a linguistic model to imitate, if he does not find himself in an environment in which people are speaking, he will never speak as do those who have learned language during the period in question. This is the case with those children who are called 'savages,' who have been raised by animals or far from contact with speaking subjects. In no case have these subjects ever learned to speak with the linguistic perfection that is found among ordinary subjects. Deaf children whose retraining has been delayed and who consequently have not learned to speak during the 'sensitive' period never speak their language in exactly the same way as do those who can hear. One can show, in fact, that in their syntax or their morphology there exist, after retraining, some very odd peculiarities: for example, the absence or rarity of the passive voice in verbs. This allows us to presume that there will be a profound link between the acquisition of language (which would seem to be a strictly intellectual operation) and the child's place in the family environment. It is this relation that Rostand seeks to define exactly.

It is a commonplace that the child's acquisition of language is also correlated with his relation to his mother. Children who have been suddenly and forcibly separated from their mothers always show signs of a linguistic regression. At bottom, it is not only the word 'mama' that is the child's first; it is the entire language which is, so to speak, maternal.

The acquisition of language might be a phenomenon of the same kind as the relation to the mother. Just as the maternal relation is (as the psychoanalysts say) a relation of *identification*, in which the subject projects on his mother what he himself experiences and assimilates the attitudes of his mother, so one could say that the acquisition of language is itself a phenomenon of identification. To learn to speak is to learn to play a series of *roles*, to assume a series of conducts or linguistic gestures.

Rostand mentions an observation made by Dr. Dolto-Marette in a case of jealousy in a child. The younger of two children shows jealousy when his new brother is born. During the first days of the newborn child's life, he identifies with it, carrying himself as though he himself were the newborn baby. There is a striking regression in language as well as in character. In the following days one notices in him a change of attitude. The subject identifies himself with his older brother and overcomes his jealousy; he adopts all the characteristics of the eldest, including an attitude toward the new baby that is identical to what, until now, had been his older brother's attitude toward him. Thanks to a fortunate circumstance his jealousy is overcome. By chance, just as the baby is born, a fourth child comes to stay in the family. This fourth child is bigger than all three brothers in the family. The presence of a child who is older than the eldest brother robs the latter of his status as the 'absolute eldest.' The eldest is now no longer 'absolutely big,' since there are others who are bigger than he is. The fourth child aids in the middle brother's transition and assimilation of the role of the eldest.

It is in this way that a case of neurotic stuttering is cured and a marked linguistic progress realized from day to day. The subject acquires the use of the simple past tense, the imperfect, the simple future, and the future with the verb *to go* ('I am *going* to leave'). Coming back to this observation, Rostand interprets it in the following fashion: The jealousy that invades the subject when he confirms the arrival of a new brother is essentially a refusal to change his situation. The newcomer is an intruder and is going to confiscate to his own advantage the place in the family that was held until now by our jealous subject. It is in the phase of the 'surpassing' of jealousy that one notices the appearance of a link between the affective phenomenon and the linguistic phenomenon: jealousy is overcome thanks to the constitution of a scheme of past-present-future. In effect, jealousy in this subject consists in a rigid attachment to his present – that is, to the situation of the 'latest born' which was hitherto his own. He considered the present to be absolute. Now, on the contrary, one can say that from the moment when he consents to be no longer the latest born, to become in relation to the new baby what his elder brother had until then been in relation to him, he replaces his attitude of 'my place has been taken' with another, whose schema might be somewhat like this: 'I *have been* the youngest, but I *am* the youngest no longer, and I *will become* the biggest.' One sees that there is a solidarity between the acquisition of this temporal structure, which gives a meaning to the corresponding linguistic instruments, and the situation of a jealousy that is overcome. For the subject the situation of jealousy is the occasion both for restructuring his relations with the others he lives with and at the same time for acquiring new dimensions of existence (past, present, and future) with a supple play among them.

Speaking Piaget's language, one might say that the whole problem of overcoming jealousy is a problem of 'de-centering.' Until now the subject has been centered on himself, centered on the situation of the latest born that he has occupied. In order to accept the birth of a new child, he must de-center himself. But the de-centering involved here is not, as it was for Piaget, a primarily intellectual operation, a phenomenon of pure knowledge. It is a matter of a lived de-centering, aroused by the situation of the child inside the family constellation.

One might even say that what the child learns, in solving the problem of jealousy, is to relativize his notions. He must relativize the notions of the youngest and the eldest: he is no longer *the* youngest; it is the new child who assumes this role. He thus must come to distinguish the absolute 'youngest' from the relative 'youngest' which he now becomes. And in the same way he must learn to become the eldest in relation to the newborn child, whereas until now the notion of 'eldest' had only an absolute meaning.

In Piaget's language, the child must learn to think in terms of reciprocity. Rostand himself cites Piaget's terms. But these terms take on a new meaning from the fact that training in reciprocity, relativity, and de-centering occurs here not by intellectual acts of 'grouping' but by operations within the vital order, by the manner in which the child restores [*réétablit*] his relations with others.

To this preliminary observation Rostand adds the following personal one: He noticed in a little girl of thirty-five months an interesting linguistic phenomenon that followed a frightening emotional experience (an encounter, while walking alone, with a big dog). Two months later this experience seemed to bear fruit. There was an abrupt acquisition of certain modes of expression (in particular, the imperfect tense of verbs) which until then the child had not used.

This step occurred at the birth of a younger brother. What we have to understand is the exact relation between this linguistic phenomenon, the birth of the younger brother, and the emotional experience of two months earlier.

The child had come across a dog who was nursing its young. At the time she encountered the dog, she knew already from her parents that she was going to have a little brother or sister in about two months. Meeting the dog which was nursing its litter was not an indifferent experience for the child; it was a visible symbol of something analogous that was about to happen in her own world. The pattern about to be realized two months later in the child's environment (parents, little girl, little brother) was already prefigured by the pattern (big dog; me, the little girl; the little dogs). The sight of the dogs was of paramount significance by virtue of its relation to the situation in which the child was about to find herself.

In order for her to accept the birth of a younger brother, what was basically necessary was a change of attitude. Whereas the little girl had been, until then, the object of all attention and of all caresses, she now had to accept the fact that some of this attention and these caresses would be transferred to another, and to associate herself with this attitude. She had to pass from an ingratiating [*captative*] attitude (i.e., one in which the child receives without giving) to a selfless [*oblative*], quasi-maternal attitude toward the child about to be born. It was necessary for her to accept a relative abandonment, to turn and confront a life that would henceforth be *her* life, that would no longer be supported, as it had been until then, by the exclusive attention of her parents. In short, the girl had to adopt an active attitude, whereas until then, her attitude had been passive.

The linguistic phenomenon that emerges at this same time can be understood in this perspective. I said earlier that the imperfect tense appeared in the child's language after the birth of her brother. More important, however, was the emergence of four verbs in the future tense; there was also a great increase in the use of 'me' and 'I.' If the future is a time of aggressiveness, a time when projects are envisioned, when one takes a stand in the face of what is to come and, instead of allowing it to come, moves actively toward it – then how was it made possible by the new situation of the little girl? The answer is that this was precisely the attitude demanded of the child by the birth of her brother. The acquisition of 'me' and 'I' presented no problems; it indicated that the subject adopted a more personal attitude and lived to a relatively greater degree by herself. Finally, the acquisition of the imperfect tense at the birth of her little brother indicated that the child was becoming capable of understanding that the present changes into the past. The imperfect is a former present which, moreover, is still referred to as present, unlike the past definite. The imperfect is 'still there.' The acquisition of the imperfect thus presupposes a concrete grasp of the movement from present to past which the child, on her part, was just in the process of achieving in her relations with her family. The fact is, all the verbs she used in the imperfect after the birth of her brother had to do with the baby. The baby *is* what the elder sister *used to be* in the world of the family.

To be sure, emotion plays a role only to the extent that it gives the subject the occasion to re-structure her relations with her human environment, and not at all simply as emotion. If the problem had not been resolved, if the subject had shown herself incapable of overcoming her jealousy or her uneasiness, nothing good would have come from the experience. Inversely, there can be cases in which the subject progresses in language without apparent emotion. In such cases, however, linguistic progress always has an interrupted character; the acquisition of the modes of expression always represents a sort of crisis, in which a whole realm of expression is annexed in a single stroke.

In sum, the intellectual elaboration of our experience of the world is constantly supported by the affective elaboration of our inter-human relations. The use of certain linguistic tools is mastered in the play of forces that constitute the subject's relations to his human surroundings. The linguistic usage achieved by the child depends strictly on the 'position' (in psychoanalytic terms) that is taken by the child at every moment in the play of forces in his family and his human environment.

Here again it is not a question of a causal analysis. There is no question of saying that the linguistic progress is *explained* by the affective progress, in the sense in which expansion is explained by heat. One might reply that the affective progress itself is also a function of the intellectual progress and that the entire intellectual development makes possible a certain affective progress. And this would also be true.

What we are seeking here is not a causal explanation, any more than before. My effort is to show the solidarity and unity of the two phenomena, not to reduce the one to the other, as is traditionally done by both empiricist and intellectualist psychologists. The child's experience of the constellation of his own family does more than impress on him certain relations between one human being and another. At the same time that the child is assuming and forming his family relations, an entire form of thinking arises in him. It is a whole usage of language as well as a way of perceiving the world.

The problem of the child's perception of others:
the theoretical problem

Before studying the different relations established between the child and his parents, his peers, other children, brothers, sisters, or strangers, before undertaking a description and analysis of these different relations, a question of principle arises: How and under what conditions does the child come into contact with others? What is the nature of the child's relations with others? How are such relations possible from the day of birth on?

Classical psychology approached this problem only with great difficulty. One might say that it was among the stumbling blocks of classical psychology because it is admittedly incapable of being solved if one confines oneself to the theoretical ideas that were elaborated by academic psychology.

How does such a problem arise for classical psychology? Given the presuppositions with which that psychology works, given the prejudices it adopted from the start without any kind of criticism, the relation with others becomes incomprehensible for it. What, in fact, is the psyche [*psychisme*] – mine or the other's – for classical psychology? All psychologists of the classical period are in tacit agreement on this point: the psyche, or the psychic, is *what is given to only one person*. It seems, in effect, that one might admit without further examination or discussion that what constitutes the psyche in me or in others is something incommunicable. I alone am able to grasp my psyche – for example, my sensations of green or of red. You will never know them as I know them; you will never experience them in my place. A consequence of this idea is that the psyche of another appears to me as radically inaccessible, at least in its own existence. I cannot reach other lives, other thought processes, since by hypothesis they are open only to inspection by a single individual: the one who owns them.

Since I cannot have direct access to the psyche of another, for the reasons just given, I must grant that I seize the other's psyche only indirectly, mediated by its bodily appearances. I see you in flesh and bone; you are there. I cannot know what you are thinking, but I can suppose it, guess at it from your facial expressions, your gestures, and your words – in short from a series of bodily appearances of which I am only the witness.

The question thus becomes this: How does it happen that, in the presence of this mannequin that resembles a man, in the presence of this body that gesticulates in a characteristic way, I come to believe that it is inhabited by a psyche? How am I led to consider that this body before me encloses a psyche? How can I perceive across this body, so to speak, another's psyche? Classical psychology's conception of the body and the consciousness we have of it is here a second obstacle in the way of a solution of the problem, Here one wants to speak of the notion of *cenesthesia*, meaning a mass of sensations that would express to the subject the state of his different organs and different bodily functions. Thus my body for me, and your body for you, could be reached, and be knowable, by means of a cenesthesic sense.

A mass of sensations, by hypothesis, is as *individual* as the psyche itself. That is to say, if in fact my body is knowable by me only through the mass of sensations it gives me (a mass of sensations to which you obviously have no access and of which we have no concrete experience), then the consciousness I have of my body is impenetrable by you. You cannot represent yourself in the same way in which I feel my own body; it is likewise impossible for me to represent to myself the way in which you feel your body. How, then, can I suppose that, in back of this appearance before me, there is someone who experiences his body as I experience mine?

Only one recourse is left for classical psychology – that of supposing that, as a spectator of the gestures and utterances of the other's body before me, I consider the totality of signs thus given, the totality of facial expressions this body presents to me, as the occasion for a kind of decoding. Behind the body whose gestures and characteristic utterances I witness, I project, so to speak, what I myself feel of my own body. No matter whether it is a question of an actual association of ideas or, instead, a judgment whereby I interpret the appearances, I transfer to the other the intimate experience I have of my own body.

The problem of the experience of others poses itself, as it were, in a system of four terms: (1) myself, my 'psyche'; (2) the image I have of my body by means of the sense of touch or of cenesthesia, which, to be brief, we shall call the 'introceptive image' of my own body; (3) the body of the other as seen by me, which we shall call the 'visual body'; and (4) a fourth (hypothetical) term which I must reconstitute and guess at – the 'psyche' of the other, the other's feeling of his own existence – to the extent that I can imagine or suppose it across the appearances of the other through his visual body.

Posed thus, the problem raises all kinds of difficulties. First, there is the difficulty of relating my knowledge or experience of the other to an association, to a judgment by which I would project into him the data of my intimate experience. The perception of others comes relatively early in life. Naturally we do not at an early age come to know the exact *meaning* of each of the emotional expressions presented to us by others. This exact knowledge is, if you like, late in coming; what is much earlier is the very fact that I perceive an expression, even if I may be wrong about what it means exactly. At a very early age children are sensitive to facial expressions, e.g., the smile. How could that be possible if, in order to arrive at an understanding of the global meaning of the smile and to learn that the smile is a fair indication of a benevolent feeling, the child had to perform the complicated task I have just mentioned? How could it be possible if, beginning with the visual perception of another's smile, he had to compare that visual perception of the smile with the movement that he himself makes when he is happy or when he feels benevolent – projecting to the other a benevolence of which he would have had intimate experience but which could not be grasped directly in the other? This complicated process would seem to be incompatible with the relative precociousness of the perception of others.

Again, in order for projection to be possible and to take place, it would be necessary for me to begin from the analogy between the facial expressions offered me by others and the different facial gestures I execute myself. In the case of the smile, for me to interpret the visible smile of the other requires that there be a way of comparing the visible smile of the other with what we may call the 'motor smile' – the smile as felt, in the case of the child, by the child himself. But in fact do we have the means of making this comparison between the body of the other, as it appears in visual perception, and our own body, as we feel it by means of introception and of cenesthesia? Have we the means of systematically comparing the body of the other as seen by me with my body as sensed by me? In order for this to be possible there would have to be a fairly regular correspondence between the two experiences. The child's visual experience of his own body is altogether insignificant in relation to the kinesthetic, cenesthesic, or tactile feeling he can have of it. There are numerous regions of his body that he does not see and some that he will never see or know except by means of the mirror (of which we will speak shortly). There is no point-for-point correspondence between the two images of the body. To understand how the child arrives at assimilating the one to the other, we must, rather, suppose that he has other reasons for doing it than reasons of simple detail. If he comes to identify as bodies, and as animated ones, the bodies of himself and the other, this can only be because he globally identifies them and not because he constructs a point-for-point correspondence between the visual image of the other and the introceptive image of his own body.

These two difficulties are particularly apparent when it comes to accounting for the phenomenon of imitation. To imitate is to perform a gesture in the image of another's gesture – like the child, for example, who smiles because someone smiles at him. According to the principles we have been entertaining, it would be necessary for me to translate my visual image of the other's smile into a motor language. The child would have to set his facial muscles in motion in such a way as to reproduce the visible expression that is called 'the smile' in another. But how could he do it? Naturally he does not have the other's internal motor feeling of his face; as far as he is concerned, he does not even have an image of himself smiling. The result is that if we want to solve the problem of the transfer of the other's conduct to me, we can in no way rest on the supposed analogy between the other's face and that of the child.

On the contrary, the problem comes close to being solved only on condition that certain classical prejudices are renounced. We must abandon the fundamental prejudice according to which the psyche is that which is accessible only to myself and cannot be seen from outside. My 'psyche' is not a series of 'states of consciousness' that are rigorously closed in on themselves and inaccessible to anyone but me. My consciousness is turned primarily toward the world, turned toward things; it is above all a relation to the world. The other's consciousness as well is chiefly a certain way of comporting himself toward the world. Thus it is in his conduct, in the manner in which the other deals with the world, that I will be able to discover his consciousness.

If I am a consciousness turned toward things, I can meet in things the actions of another and find in them a meaning, because they are themes of possible activity for my own body. Guillaume, in his book *l'Imitation chez l'enfant* (1925), says that we do not at first imitate others but rather the actions of others, and that we find others at the point of origin of these actions. At first the child imitates not persons but conducts. And the problem of knowing how conduct can be transferred from another to me is infinitely less difficult to solve than the problem of knowing how I can

109

represent to myself a psyche that is radically foreign to me. If, for example, I see another draw a figure, I can understand the drawing as an action because it speaks directly to my own unique motility. Of course, the other *qua* author of a drawing is not yet a whole person, and there are more revealing actions than drawing – for example, using language. What is essential, however, is to see that a perspective on the other is opened to me from the moment I define him and myself as 'conducts' at work in the world, as ways of 'grasping' the natural and cultural world surrounding us.

But this presupposes a reform not only of the notion of the 'psyche' (which we will replace henceforth by that of 'conduct') but also of the idea we have of our own body. If my body is to appropriate the conducts given to me visually and make them its own, it must itself be given to me not as a mass of utterly private sensations but instead by what has been called a 'postural,' or 'corporeal, schema.' This notion, introduced long ago by Henry Head, has been taken over and enriched by Wallon, by certain German psychologists, and has finally been the subject of a study in its own right by Professor Lhermitte in *l'Image de notre corps* (1939).

For these authors, my body is no agglomeration of sensations (visual, tactile, 'tenesthesic,' or 'cenesthesic'). It is first and foremost a *system* whose different introceptive and extroceptive aspects express each other reciprocally, including even the roughest of relations with surrounding space and its principal directions. The consciousness I have of my body is not the consciousness of an isolated mass; it is a *postural schema.* It is the perception of my body's position in relation to the vertical, the horizontal, and certain other axes of important co-ordinates of its environment.

In addition, the different sensory domains (sight, touch, and the sense of movement in the joints) which are involved in the perception of my body do not present themselves to me as so many absolutely distinct regions. Even if, in the child's first and second years, the translation of one into the language of others is imprecise and incomplete, they all have in common a *certain style* of action, a certain *gestural* meaning that makes of the collection an already organized totality. Understood in this way, the experience I have of my own body could be transferred to another much more easily than the cenesthesia of classical psychology, giving rise to what Wallon calls a 'postural impregnation' of my own body by the conducts I witness.

I can perceive, across the visual image of the other, that the other is an organism, that that organism is inhabited by a 'psyche,' because the visual image of the other is interpreted by the notion I myself have of my own body and thus appears as the visible envelopment of another 'corporeal schema.' My perception of my body would, so to speak, be swallowed up in a cenesthesia if that cenesthesia were strictly individual. On the contrary, however, if we are dealing with a schema, or a system, such a system would be relatively transferrable from one sensory domain to the other in the case of my own body, just as it could be transferred to the domain of the other.

Thus in today's psychology we have one system with two terms (my behavior and the other's behavior) which functions as a whole. To the extent that I can elaborate and extend my corporeal schema, to the extent that I acquire a better organized experience of my own body, to that very extent will my consciousness of my own body cease being a chaos in which I am submerged and lend itself to a transfer to others. And since at the same time the other who is to be perceived is himself not a 'psyche' closed in on himself but rather a conduct, a system of behavior that aims at the world, he offers himself to my motor intentions and to that 'intentional transgression' (Husserl) by which I animate and pervade him. Husserl said that the perception of others is like a 'phenomenon of coupling' [*accouplement*]. The term is anything but a metaphor. In perceiving the other, my body and his are coupled, resulting in a sort of action which pairs them [*action à deux*]. This conduct which I am able only to see, I live somehow from a distance. I make it mine; I recover [*reprendre*] it or comprehend it. Reciprocally I know that the gestures I make myself can be the objects of another's intention. It is this transfer of my intentions to the other's body and of his intentions to my own, my alienation of the other and his alienation of me, that makes possible the perception of others.

All these analyses presuppose that the perception of others cannot be accounted for if one begins by supposing an ego and another that are *absolutely* conscious of themselves, each of which lays claim, as a result, to an absolute originality in relation to the other that confronts it. On the contrary, the perception of others is made comprehensible if one supposes that psychogenesis begins in a state where the child is unaware of himself and the other as different beings. We cannot say that in such a state the child has a genuine communication with others. In order that there be communication, there must be a sharp distinction between the one who communicates and the one with whom he communicates. But there is initially a state of pre-communication (Max Scheler), wherein the other's intentions somehow play *across* my body while my intentions play across his.

How is this distinction made? I gradually become aware of my body, of what radically distinguishes it from the other's body, at the same time that I begin to live my intentions in the facial expressions of the other and likewise begin to live the other's volitions in my own gestures. The progress of the child's experience results in his seeing that his body is, after all, closed in on itself. In particular, the visual image he acquires of his own body (especially from the mirror) reveals to him a hitherto unsuspected isolation of two subjects who are facing each other. The objectification of his own body discloses to the child his difference, his 'insularity,' and, correlatively, that of others.

Thus the development has somewhat the following character: There is a first phase, which we call pre-communication, in which there is not one individual over against another but rather an anonymous collectivity, an undifferentiated group life [*vie à plusieurs*]. Next, on the basis of this initial community, both by the objectification of one's own body and the constitution of the other in his difference, there occurs a segregation, a distinction of individuals – a process which, moreover, as we shall see, is never completely finished.

This kind of conception is common to many trends in contemporary psychology. One finds it in Guillaume and Wallon; it occurs in Gestalt theorists, phenomenologists, and psychoanalysts alike.

Guillaume shows that we must neither treat the origin of consciousness as though it were conscious, in an explicit way, of itself nor treat it as though it were completely closed in on itself. The first *me* is, as he says, virtual or latent, i.e., unaware of itself in its absolute difference. Consciousness of oneself as a unique individual, whose place can be taken by no one else, comes later and is not primitive. Since the primordial *me* is virtual or latent, egocentrism is not at all the attitude of a *me* that expressly grasps itself (as the term 'egocentrism' might lead us to believe). Rather, it is the attitude of a *me* which is unaware of itself and lives as easily in others as it does in itself – but which, being unaware of others in their own separateness as well, in truth is no more conscious of them than of itself.

Wallon introduces an analogous notion with what he calls 'syncretic sociability.' Syncretism here is the indistinction between me and the other, a confusion at the core of a situation that is common to us both. After that the objectification of the body intervenes to establish a sort of wall between me and the other: a partition. Henceforth it will prevent me from confusing myself with what the other thinks, and especially with what he thinks of me; just as I will no longer confuse him with my thoughts, and especially my thoughts about him. There is thus a correlative constitution of me and the other as two human beings among all others.

Thus at first the *me* is both entirely unaware of itself and at the same time all the more demanding for being unaware of its own limits. The adult *me*, on the contrary, is a *me* that knows its own limits yet possesses the power to cross them by a genuine sympathy that is at least *relatively* distinct from the initial form of sympathy. The initial sympathy rests on the ignorance of oneself rather than on the perception of others, while adult sympathy occurs between 'other' and 'other'; it does not abolish the differences between myself and the other.

Note

1 In *Revue Française de Psychoanalyse*, vol. 14 (April–June, 1950), pp. 299–310.

51

EMBODIMENT AND CHILD DEVELOPMENT

A phenomenological approach

John O'Neill

Source: H. P. Dreitzel, ed., *Recent Sociology No. 5*, New York: Collier Books, 1973, pp. 87–99.

Any theory of child socialization is implicitly a theory of the construction of social reality, if not of a particular historical social order. In this essay I propose to give an account of the phenomenological approach to the basic pre-suppositions of child socialization. I shall restrict my account to the writings of Maurice Merleau-Ponty, who, although widely known as a philosopher and political theorist, remains to be known for the lectures on child psychology which he gave for many years at the Sorbonne.[1] For reasons of economy it is not possible to follow the whole of Merleau-Ponty's interpretation and critical evaluation of the literature with which he familiarized himself concerning the physiological, intellectual, moral, and cultural development of the child, not to mention his close reading of psycho-analytical and American anthropological research. Much of the literature is in any case now all too familiar to workers in child psychology, although Merleau-Ponty's close reading and phenomenological critique of Piaget's work might be given special mention because of its continuing interest.

Merleau-Ponty's analysis of the child's relation to others, his family, and the world around him may serve as introduction to the whole of Merleau-Ponty's phenomenology of perception, expression, and the sociohistorical world of human institutions. At all events, the topic and its phenomenological horizons are inseparable and can only be managed in a short space by focusing upon the very fundamental presuppositions of the phenomenon of the child's orientation to the world and others around him through the mediations of the body, language, perception, and reflection. The phenomenological concern with these basic structures of child development involves an implicit concern with the way in which they may be prejudged by the assumptions of unreflexive research.

The starting point in any study of child psychology and socialization must be the child's relation to the adult world, its social relations, linguistic, perceptual, and logical categories. By insisting on this point, Merleau-Ponty dismisses any notion of a psychology of the child, the sick person, man, woman, or the primitive as an enclosed nature. Indeed, there is a *complementary feature* of the child-adult relationship, namely, the reverse adult-child relationship. This obliges us in the methodology of child studies to design research procedures which are sensitive to the two-way and even asymmetric relation between the child's orientation to the adult world and the adult world's interests in fostering, enforcing and moralizing upon its own interests and hopes in the child world. We cannot here look down the path toward the 'politics of experience' which this first methodological observation opens up. It must suffice to remark that it points to a cultural dilemma that is generic to human relations and thus makes it impossible to conceive of child psychology and psychoanalysis outside of specific cultural frameworks.

Another general conclusion which we may elicit from the interactional nature of the object of child studies refers to a phenomenon that is common to the object of all social studies. The natural scientist for most purposes is concerned only with the observer's experience, however mediated by his instruments, of the object under study. Even if we take into account the problems of interference referred to by the Heisenberg uncertainty principle, the problem here is merely that the scientist must allow for changes in the behaviour of experiemental objects due to the interference effects of his own methods of study. But although this problem produces a greater similarity between the natural and social sciences than was imagined earlier, it leaves unchanged an essential difference between them. Namely, where the object of science is a human relationship or set of human relationships, a custom or institution, the 'ordering' of the relationship it is not merely a scientific construct. It is first of all a pre-theoretical construct which is the unarticulated 'commonsense' knowledge of others as 'relatives' who experience dependable needs and wants expressed through the 'relevances' of the human body, time, and place.

The burden of Merleau-Ponty's methodological critique of research methods in studies of child perception, language, and morals is that they proceed without the benefit of any reflection upon the way their methods already prejudge the nature of the phenomena they are intended to elicit. In the first place we must rid ourselves of a 'dogmatic rationalism' which consists in studying the child's world from above and thereby construing the child's efforts as pre-logical or magical behaviour which must be sloughed off as a condition of entry into the objective, realist world of adults. Such a prejudice overlooks the way in which child and adult behaviour are solidary, with anticipations from the side of the child and regressions on the side of the adult which makes their conduct no more separable than health and sickness. Indeed, the real task of a genuine psychology must be to discover the basis of *communication* between children and adults, between the unconscious and consciousness, between the sick and the sane.

'We must conceive the child neither as an absolute "other" nor just "the same" as ourselves, but as polymorphous.' This remark may serve as a guiding principle in following Merleau-Ponty's subtle interweaving of the processes of structure and development in the child's relation to others. The notion of *development* is, of course, central to the psychology of the child; it is, however, a complex notion since it implies neither an absolute continuity between childhood and adulthood nor any complete discontinuity without phases or transitions. It is here that we need to avoid the twin reductions of the phenomena of development which Merleau-Ponty labels 'mechanist' and 'idealist' exemplified respectively by the learning theory approach originated by Pavlov and the cognitive approach of Piaget. Here we are on explicitly philosophical ground because the continuity between childhood and adult life raises the question of how it is in principle that individual and inter-subjective life are possible.

Mechanist, reflex or learning theory accounts of child development involve us in the difficulty that their causal explanations fail to cover the phenomena of adult initiative, creativity and responsibility. Reflex theory reduces conduct to a structure of conditioned reflexes built into increasingly complex patterns whose principle of organization is always conceived as an environmental stimulus to which the responses of adaptation occur without internal elaboration. Reflex theory attempts to explain conduct in terms of physiological process without norms or intentionality. But even at its own level reflex theory is not sure of its foundations. Once one attempts to make the notions of stimulus, receptor and reflex more precise, reflex theory becomes riddled with question-begging hypotheses about mechanisms of inhibition and control, acquired drives and the like. The case of 'experimental neurosis' in one of Pavlov's dogs involved in repeated experiments reveals that the consequences of the restriction of a biologically meaningful environment in order to induce conditioned reflexes results in pathological behaviour. By the same token, the acquisition of human habits is not a strictly determined reflex but the acquisition of a capability for inventing solutions to situations which are only *abstractly* similar and never identical with the original 'learning situation.' What is involved in the formation of human habits is the aquisition of a 'categorical attitude' or a power of 'symbolic expression,' and it is only in pathological conduct that atomistic and associationist explanations appear plausible.

While rejecting naturalistic reductions of child development, Merleau-Ponty is equally critical of idealist or cognitive accounts of the phenomena of perception, intelligence and sensory-motor behaviour. The basic fault in cognitive approaches to the child's relation to the world and others is that they sacrifice the immediate, *visceral knowledge* of self, others and the world which we possess without ever having apprenticed ourselves to the 'rules' of perception language, and movement. This preconceptual knowledge is neither subjective nor objective and requires a conception of *symbolic form* which rests neither upon a realist nor an idealist epistemology but instead seeks what is complementary in them. Because the philosophical presuppositions of psychology are implicitly dualistic, consciousness is usually described as the transparent possession of an object of thought in distinction from perceptual and motor acts which are described as a series of events external to each other. Thought and behaviour are juxtaposed or else set in a speculative hierarchy. Against these alternatives, Merleau-Ponty proposes to classify behaviour according to a continuum whose upper and lower limits are defined by the submergence of the structure of behaviour in content, at the lowest level, i.e. 'synenetic forms,' and, at the highest level, the emergence of structure as the proper theme of activity, i.e., 'symbolic forms.'

The conceptualization of behaviour requires the category of Form in order to differentiate the structures of quantity, order and value or signification as the dominant characteristics respectively of matter, life and mind and at the same time to relativize the participation of these structures in a hierarchy of forms of behaviour. Form is itself not an element in the world but a limit toward which biophysical and psychobiological structures tend. In a given environment each organism exhibits a preferred mode of behaviour which is not the simple aim or function of its milieu and its internal organization but is structured by its general attitude to the world. In other words, the analysis of form is not a matter of the composition of real structures but the perception of wholes. Human behaviour, which is essentially symbolic behaviour, unfolds through structures or gestures which are not in objective space and time, like physical objects, nor in a purely internal dimension of consciousness unsituated with respect to historical time and place.

Merleau-Ponty calls the objects of perception 'phenomena' in order to characterize their openness to perceptual consciousness to which they are not given *a priori* but as 'open, inexhaustible systems which we recognize through a certain style of development.' The matrix of all human activity is the *phenomenal body* which is the schema of our world, or the source of a vertical or human space in which we project our feelings, moods and values. Because the human body is a 'community of senses' and not a bundle of contingently related impression, it functions as the universal setting or schema for all possible styles or typical structures of the world. These, however, are not given to us with the invariable formula of a *facius totius universi* but through the temporal synthesis of horizons implicit in intentionality. 'For us the perceptual synthesis is a temporal synthesis, and subjectivity, at the level of perception, is nothing but temporality, and that is what enables us to leave to the subject of perception his opacity and historicity.' The cognitive approaches to child development overlook the *tacit* subjectivity which does not constitute its world *a priori* nor entirely *a posteriori* but develops through a 'living cohesion' in which the embodied self experiences itself while belonging to this world and others, clinging to them for its content.

Thus in his analysis of the child's perception of causal relations Merleau-Ponty argues that it is not a matter of a simple ordering of external data but of an 'informing' [*Gestaltung*] of the child's experience of external events through an operation that is properly neither a logical nor a predicative activity. Similarly, in the case of the child's imagination, it proves impossible to give any objective sense of the notion of *image* even as photograph, mimicry, or picture, apart from an 'affective projection.' Imagination is therefore not a purely intellectual operation but is better understood as an operation beneath the cognitive relation of subject and object. The 'imaginary' and the 'real' are two *forms of conduct* which are not antithetical but rest upon a common ambiguity which occasionally allows the imaginary to substitute for the real. The child lives in the hybrid world of the real and the imaginary which the adult keeps apart for most purposes or is otherwise careful of any transgression wherein he catches his own conscience. Again, in the analysis of the child's drawing, it is also improper to treat the child's efforts as abortive attempts to develop 'adult,' or rather perspectual, drawing, which is itself an historical development in art dominated by the laws of classical geometric perspective. The child's drawing is not a simple imitation of what he sees any more than of what he does not see through lack of detailed 'attention.' The child's drawings are expressive of his relations to the things and people in this world. They develop and change along with his experience with the objects, animals, puppets, and persons around him, including his own experience of his body, its inside and outside. 'The child's drawing is *contact* with the visible world and with others. This tactile relation with the world and with man appears long before the looking attitude, the posture of indifferent contemplation between the spectator and the spectacle which is realized in adult drawing.'

It is above all in the child's acquisition of language that we observe the complex interrelation of cognition and affectivity which can only be made thematic in later phases of development by presupposing the massive inarticulatable background of the world into which we import our categories, distinctions and relations. Language and intelligence presuppose one another without priority and their development rests rather upon the ability of the child to assimilate his linguistic environment as an open system of expression and conduct, comparable to his acquisition of all his other habits. Again, for reasons of economy we cannot deal with the broad range of the phenomenology of language. Instead, we must focus attention upon

Merleau-Ponty's interpretation of the social contexts of the acquisition of language.

> It is a commonplace that the child's acquisition of language is also correlated with his relation to his mother. Children who have been suddenly and forcibly separated from their mothers always show signs of a linguistic regression. At bottom, it is not only the word 'mama' that is the child's first; it is the entire language which is, so to speak, maternal.
>
> The acquisition of language might be a phenomenon of the same kind as the relation to the mother. Just as the maternal relation is (as the psychoanalysts say) a relation of *identification*, in which the subject projects on his mother what he himself experiences and assimilates the attitudes of his mother, so one could say that the acquisition of language is itself a phenomenon of identification. To learn to speak is to learn to play a series of *roles*, to assume a series of conducts or linguistic gestures. ('The Child's Relations with Others')

This hypothesis on the development of language in relation to the child's familial roles is illustrated in terms of analysis of the expression of child jealousy. Upon the birth of a new baby the younger of two children displays jealousy, behavioural regression (carrying himself as though he were the baby), and language regression. There, phenomena represent an initial response to the threatened structure of the child's temporal and social world of the 'latest born' child. The emotional response of jealousy expresses the child's attachment to a hitherto eternal present. A little later the child begins to identify with his older brother, adopting the latter's earlier attitudes towards himself as the 'youngest.' The chance circumstance of the visit of another child bigger than his older brother relativizes once and for all the 'absolute eldest' and the child's jealousy recedes. At the same time as these 'sociometric' experiences are acquired the child's linguistic experience of temporal structure also expands. 'He considered the present to be absolute. Now, on the contrary, one can say that from the moment when he consents to be no longer the latest born, to become in relation to the new baby what his elder brother had until then been in relation to him, he replaces the attitude of "my place has been taken" with another whose schema might be somewhat like this: "*I have been* the youngest, but I *am* the youngest no longer, and I *will become* the biggest." One sees that there is a solidarity between the acquisition of this temporal structure, which gives a meaning to the corresponding linguistic instruments, and the situation of jealousy that is overcome.'

The child's resolution of his jealousy permits us to make some general remarks upon the relation of the cognitive and affective elements in the child's conception of the world and others around him which will then permit us to deal finally with the fundamental problem of the possibility of social relations of any kind. In overcoming his jealousy we might, as Piaget would say, speak of the child having solved the egocentric problem by learning to decenter himself and to relativize his notions by thinking in terms of reciprocity. But these are clearly not purely intellectual operation; rather, what is called *intelligence* here really designates the mode of intersubjectivity achieved by the child. The intellectual and linguistic elaboration of our experience of the world always rests upon the 'deep structures' of our affective experience of the interpersonal world against which we elaborate only later our modes of inductive and deductive thinking.

The perception of other people and the intersubjective world are problematical only for adults. The child lives in a world which he unhesitatingly believes accessible to all around him. He has no awareness of himself or of others as private subjectivities, nor does he suspect that all of us, himself included, are limited to one certain point of view of the world. That is why he subjects neither his thoughts, in which he believes as they present themselves, without attempting to link them to each other, nor our words, to any sort of criticism. He has no knowledge of points of view. For him men are empty heads turned towards one single, self-evident world where everything takes place, even dreams, which are, he thinks, in his room, and even thinking, since it is not distinct from words. Others are for him so many gazes which inspect things, and have an almost material existence, so much so that the child wonders how these gazes avoid being broken as they meet. At about twelve years old, says Piaget, the child achieves the *cogito* and reaches the truths of rationalism. At this stage, it is held, he discovers himself both as a point of view on the world and also as called upon to transcend that point of view, and to construct an objectivity at the level of judgement. Piaget brings the child to a mature outlook as if the thoughts of the adult were self-sufficient and disposed of all contradicitons. But, in reality, it must be the case that the child's outlook is in some way vindicated against the adult's and against Piaget, and that the unsophisticated thinking of our earliest years remains as an indispensible acquisition underlying that of maturity, if there is to be for the adult one single intersubjective world. My awareness of constructing an objective truth would never provide me with anything more than an objective truth for me, and my greatest attempt at impartiality would never enable me to prevail over my subjectivity (as Descartes so well expresses it by the hypothesis of the malignant demon), if I had not, underlying my judgments, the primordial certainty of being in contact with being itself, if, before any voluntary *adoption of a position* I were not already *situated* in an intersubjective world, and if science too were not upheld by this basic δοξα. With the *cogito* begins that struggle between consciousnesses, each of which, as Hegel says, seeks the death of the other. For the struggle ever to begin, and for each consciousness to be capable of suspecting the alien presences which it negates, all must necessarily have some common ground and be mindful of their peaceful co-existence in the world of childhood. (*Phenomenology of Perception*)

Classical psychology, however, renders the intersubjective world which is the presupposition of all socialization entirely problematic. This arises from the assumption that the psyche is *what is given to only one person*, intrinsically mine and radically inaccessible to others who are similarly possessed of their own experiences. The same assumption is also made with regard to the body, namely, that it is as *individual* as the psyche and know-able by me only through the mass of sensations it gives me. So conceived, the problem of the experience of others presents itself as a system with four terms: (1) myself, my 'psyche'; (2) the image I have of my body by means of the sense of touch or cenesthesia, i.e., the 'introceptive image' of my own body; (3) the body of the other as seen by me, i.e., that 'visual body'; (4) the hypothetical 'psyche' of the other, his feeling of his own existence which I must reconstitute by means of (3) the 'visual body.'

The difficulties intrinsic to the operation of this schema are apparent from what it assumes in the analysis of the child's response to the other's smile. The child responds very early to facial expressions and, of course, verbal expressions of 'do's' and 'don'ts' without being able either to compare his 'motor smile' with the 'visible smile' of the other or to correlate just what it is that he is doing that meets with approval or disapproval. Rather than engage in point for point comparisons the child can only respond to global situations and attitudes, in other words to his surround-ings as motivation or conduct. This means that we must reject the individualist and solipsistic conceptions intrinsic to the dual worlds of the mind and body as conceived in classical psychology and its philosophical tradition. We can no longer conceive of the psyche as a series of enclosed 'states of consciousness' inaccessible to anyone but myself. Consciousness is turned towards the world; it is a mode of conduct toward things and persons which in turn reveal themselves to me through their style and manner of dealing with the world. By the same token we must revise our conception of the body as an agglomeration of senses that are mine and which are only to be guessed at in the case of others. My awareness of body is the activity of a postural or corporeal schema which is the lived experience of a cenestesia or play between my various senses and the senses of others visible in their comportment.

Thus in today's psychology we have one system with two terms (my behaviour and the other's behaviour) which functions as a whole. To the extent that I can elaborate and extend my *corporeal schema*, to the extent that I acquire a better organized experience of my own body, to that very extent will my consciousness of my own body cease being a chaos in which I am submerged and lend itself to a transfer to others. And since at the same time the other who is to be perceived is himself not a 'psyche' closed in on himself but rather a *conduct*, a system of behaviour that aims at the world, he offers himself to my motor intentions and to that 'intentional transgression' (Husserl) by which I animate and pervade him. Husserl said that the perception of others is like a 'phenomenon of coupling' [*accouplement*]. The term is anything but a metaphor. In perceiving the other, my body and his are coupled, resulting in a sort of action which pairs them [*action à deux*]. This conduct which I am able only to see, I live somehow from a distance. I make it mine; I recover [*reprendre*] it or comprehend it. Reciprocally I know that the gestures I make myself can be the objects of another's intention. It is this transfer of intentions to my own, my alienation of the other and his alienation of me, that makes possible the perception of others. ('The Child's Relations with Others')

Here we can only point to the complementarity between the role of the corporeal schema and the work of social actors in elaborating the field of impressions and visual data inadvertently and deliberately presented to him as the motives and expectations of social interaction or the typification of personal and institutional conduct. Likewise, without any further comment upon the relation between transcendental phenomenology and mundane intersubjectivity, we must now conclude with an analysis of the formation of the child's corporeal schema in the early stages of socialization.

The problem is to account for how it is that we become aware of the distinction between our own body and the other's body while simultaneously acquiring the ability to transfer our intentions to the facial and linguistic expressions of the other as the *prima facie* basis of their further elaboration and making our own gestures similarly available to the other's intentions and expectations. We may distinguish three principal stages in this process, at each point commenting upon the conceptual revisions which are implicit in their structure and development during the first three years of the child's life.

The first phase is that of *pre-communication* in which the child does not experience himself as a single individual set over against all others. The first *me* is still a latent or vertical possibilty within our experience of an anonymous or collective existence. What is sometimes called egocentrism at this stage refers not to an experience of self-other contrast but precisely to the experience of a *me* which dwells as easily in others as in itself and is in fact no more aware of itself than it is of others. For this reason, however, the child's *me* can be extremely demanding and volatile. But the phenomena of the child appearing to be wilfully different from situation to situation, playing several roles with himself and even attributing his experiences to others ('transitivism') mislead us into attributing them to the child's egocentrism. But these phenomena are actually symptomatic of the as yet unacquired structure of his own perspective as an *I* and that of others in which every *you* is also an *I* and neither he nor they an undifferentiated *me* without limits of time and space. The full development of this structure of experience has as its 'correlate' the development of lingistic competence with the system of pronouns which in turn elaborates an interpersonal order through this very perspective.

The second phase which we distinguish intervenes, in the development of the first phase from pre-communication to the acquisition of personal perspective and its implicit competence with orderly social life gained by the child's second year or so. This is the stage of the child's awareness of his *own body (corps propre)* and the *specular image (l'image speculaire)*. At this stage the development of consciousness towards what is called intelligence proceeds by means of an expanded awareness of the child's own body through the acquisition of its specular image which in turn involves a general mode of conduct beyond the episodic event of seeing his body image in a mirror. Moreover, the mastery of this specular image is more difficult for the child to achieve than the distinction between his father, say, and his father's image in the mirror – even though he still allows the image a quasi-reality similar to that we feel in the presence, of portraits, however much we 'know better.' But in the case of his own specular image the child can make no visual comparison to establish the difference between the experience of his body seen in the mirror and his body of which he can only see the hands, feet or other parts but is otherwise a totality of which he has only a lived experience. Yet the child has now to understand that although he is his own body and not its image in the mirror, his own body is nevertheless visible to others like its mirror image.

Since Merleau-Ponty is not concerned to make an absolute distinction between the three phases of early child development, we may mention the overlap between the second and third phase here, i.e., the 'crisis at three years.' This phase is marked by the child's refusal of his body and thoughts falling under any perspective or interpretation than his own. He wants his own way and this he works out by stubbornly requiring the resistance of others to his own negativity. Through everything the child refuses, his parents, their words, and their food, there arises the structure of oedipal relations in which again the child's world and his conception of social reality are reducible neither to cognitive nor solely affective factors.

The interpretation of the development of the specular image again involves taking a position on the reduction of cognitive and affective behaviour. Merleau-Ponty rejects the view that the specular image involves a cognitive process in which the relation between reality and image, the body here and its image or shadow over there, is established once and for all. The specular image involves a new form of conduct, a shift from the lived body to the visible body, the object of social attention, projection and mimesis. The body is now a form of conduct, of an identification with others which is never quite stabilized but is the basis of the child's joys and sorrows, his jealousies and tender loyalties which are the experiences of growing up among others – the possibility of a super ego.

> Thus one sees that the phenomenon of the specular image is given by psychoanalysts the importance it really has in the life of the child. It is the acquisition not only of a new content but of a new function as well: the narcissistic function. Narcissus was the mythical being who after looking at his image in the mirror of water, was drawn as if by vertigo to rejoin his own image in the mirror of water. At the same time that the image of oneself makes possible the knowledge of oneself, it makes possible a sort of alienation. I am no longer what I felt myself, immediately, to be; I am that image of myself that is offered by the mirror. To use Dr. Lacan's terms, I am 'captured, caught up' by my spatial image. Thereupon I leave the reality of my lived *me* in order to refer myself constantly to the ideal, fictitious, or imaginary *me*, of which the specular image is the first outline. In this sense I am torn from myself, and the image in the mirror prepares me for another still more serious alienation, which will be alienation by others. For others have only an exterior image of me, which is analogous to the one seen in the mirror. Consequently others will tear me away from my immediate inwardness much more surely than will the mirror. 'The specular image is the "symbolic matrix,"' says Lacan, 'where the I springs up in primordial form before objectifying itself in the dialectic of identification with the other.' ('The Child's Relations with Others')

The acquisition of the specular image introduces the child into the drama of social life, the struggle with the other, ruled by desire and recognition, even to death. It lies outside of the scope of this essay to pursue these themes in terms of the conjuncture between Hegelian phenomenology and Lacanian psychoanalysis. But this is certainly a direction in which we might pursue the dialectic between personal and public life which we repeat in the spectacle of the *body-politic* and the struggle between the 'organization' of authority and the delinquencies of love's body.

123

Note

1 These lectures are contained in the form of student notes published with Merleau-Ponty's approval in *Bulletin de Psychologie*, No. 236, tome XVIII 3–6, November 1964. Of these lectures 'The Child's Relations with Others' has been translated by William Cobb in Maurice Merleau-Ponty, *The Primacy of Perception*, and other essays, edited by James M. Edie, Evanston, Northwestern University Press 1964, pp. 96–155.

Part 8

CHILDHOOD,
VIOLENCE AND RISK

52

PUBLIC PERCEPTIONS OF CHILDHOOD CRIMINALITY

Allison James and Chris Jenks

Source: *British Journal of Sociology* (June 1996): 314–331.

Introduction

The innocence of childhood has finally come of age. Initiated by Rousseau, the lyrical image of childhood as the 'sleep of reason' was amplified by Goya into the more sinister version that 'the sleep of reason produces monsters!' In Britain in 1993, this was a prophecy which, at last, seemed to have come true through the violent murder of one child by two others. Not yet quietened by the passage of time nor by the imposition of guilty verdicts on two young boys and the Home Secretary's subsequent retributive recommendation of a fifteen year minimum period of containment for them both, more than two years after this 'shocking' event a feeling of terrible uncertainty and public unease remains. Our concern here is to tease out the nature and import of that unease.

We begin with the suggestion that the murder was not just disturbing, but was, quite literally, unthinkable. Unthinkable, that is, because it occurred within the conceptual space of childhood which, prior to this breach, was conceived of – for the most part and for most children – as innocence enshrined. In essence, what the British public seemed to have to come to terms with in 1993 was that childhood could no longer be envisioned unproblematically as a once-upon-a-time story with a happy and predictable ending.

And yet, in vaunting the apparent originality of this transgression of our childhood categories, we are not forgetful of the spectacular precedent provided by the double child-murder committed by the child Mary Bell in 1968, nor the largely unwritten history of child-by-child murder that undoubtedly preceded it. What was remarkable in 1993, however, was an apparent dense public amnesia about these earlier events. Little evidence in the highly voluble and condemnatory public concern about children and violence which took place in the press, this forgetting sheds some light, albeit refracted, on the divergent understandings of childhood which were expressed at that time.

For example, as anguish vied with outrage, calls for retribution and revenge at least matched those for compassion and understanding and a demand for the increasing secular policing of children was championed in the context of a tardy response by the church to condemn. Indicative of an ambivalence abroad in the wider population, the rapid yet unconsidered reaction of some sections of the laity simply served to underline the apparent general unwillingness of the clergy to engage in such a high profile moral issue, seemingly providing further evidence, besides the murder, of a nation in moral decline.

None the less these varied responses shared common themes, themes which questioned the idea of 'the child' and the institution of childhood in the late twentieth century. They centred on two interlinked issues: first, what is 'the child's' nature and second, what are the limits of 'the child's' capacity for action? That these are neither new nor uncommon questions about childhood is pertinent to our concerns for they underline the socially constructed nature of childhood, a childhood with which children themselves must daily engage (James 1995).

Thus, our paper begins with an examination of the conceptual framework that has provided for the continued dominance of the image of childhood innocence in British culture. We then seek to understand one particular range of public responses to the Bulger murder – the opinions expressed through the pages of the quality press – and to highlight, from the perspective of sociology, the issues it raised about the place of children in contemporary British society through its seeming negation of that dominant image of a complete absence of evil.

It is important to emphasize at this point that it is not our intention to write a paper about criminology or the media *per se*. Furthermore, and in relation to methodology, even though our original data collection involved an exhaustive accumulation of newspaper articles about the Jamie Bulger case, we have purposefully chosen to restrict our consideration of media representation to a limited range of articles and commentaries available from the quality press during the short period of the trial when public interest was at its highest. Our intention had never been to achieve a representative sample but rather the reverse, that is, to demonstrate the spectrum of responses that were available, thus providing further evidence, we would suggest, of the radical disruption which children who commit violent crime bring to our concepts of 'the child'. We have not aimed at a distillation of the overall 'public perception' of the event, even if such a consensus had been available, but we have sought instead to record and analyse 'preferred' or 'dominant readings' (Philo 1990) of the case that emerged directly from the voices of eminence, but was also reported and undiluted by the skilled and informed journalism of the broadsheet editorial desk.

Our final task is to indicate what this debate portends for actual children through exploring the questions it prompted about the ideological construction, and therefore purpose, of 'childhood' itself.

At the outset, however, we note some dramatic and powerful consequences of this rupturing of our culturally and historically specific vision of childhood: not only has the murder given rise to a broad public debate about the nature of childhood, albeit often ill-informed, it may have also depotentiated the ideological role which 'childhood' has traditionally played in public perceptions of children and social relations more generally. Beyond this lies the potential consequences of such a changed perception of 'childhood' for children themselves which, as yet, remain to be fully spelled out.

Traditional conceptions of childhood?

That there is a particular vision of western childhood which is both historically and culturally specific is now well established. The French historian Ariès (1962) was one of the first to demonstrate that while children are present in all cultures their presence has been and still is differently regarded (see also DeMause 1976; Stone 1977; Pollock 1983; Demos 1986; Houlbrooke 1984 and Boswell 1988). The biological facts of infancy are but the raw material upon which cultures work to fashion a particular version of 'being a child'. Thus, to have been a child in seventeenth-century England was, so the argument goes, a very different social experience from being a twentieth-century child, not only in terms of the material conditions of their existence but, more importantly, in relation to the duties, obligations, restraints and expectations placed upon children. In brief, what a child is reflects the particularities of particular socio-cultural contexts.

More recently, however, attention has been paid within sociology and anthropology to the dissonance which exists between children's own experiences of being a child and the institutional form which childhood takes (James and Prout 1990; James 1993). This has sharpened a theoretical focus on the plurality of childhoods, a plurality evidenced not only cross-culturally but also within cultures. At the very least, it is suggested, the experience of childhood is fragmented and stratified, by class, age, gender and ethnicity, by urban or rural locations and by particularized identities cast for children through disability or ill health.

But, despite these different social experiences, children themselves remain enmeshed in the forced commonality of an ideological discourse of childhood. Routinely, children find their daily lives shaped by statutes regulating the pacing and placing of their experience. Compulsory schooling, for example, restricts their access to social space and gerontocratic prohibitions limit their political involvement, sexual activity, entertainment and

129

consumption. Children are further constrained not only by implicit socializing rules which work to set controls on behaviour and limits on the
expression of unique intent, but also by customary practices which, through
the institution of childhood, articulate the rights and duties associated
with 'being a child'.

For western children these are, as we detail below, still largely the rights
and duties of the innocent abroad. Constrained by dominant paediatric and
psychological theories of child development (Jenks 1982), contemporary
childhood remains an essentially protectionist experience. Obliged by the
adult world to be happy, children, Ennew (1986) argues, are seen 'as lacking
responsibility, having rights to protection and training but not to autonomy'
(1986: 21). Although derived from a particular spatio-temporal location,
these ideal behavioural traits have been identified, none the less, as pertinent for all children. And, in doing so, simultaneous images of otherness are
produced: those parents who fail to promulgate or accommodate this vision
of childhood within the family are effectively seen to fail as parents and
those children who fail to conform to the image of 'the child' are seen as
some of childhood's failures (Armstrong 1983).

Testimony of the insidious and assiduous power of this particular discourse
on childhood is found in the extensive globalization of western ideas of
childhood. As a post-colonial legacy, variation in the form which childhood
might take is denied (Boyden 1990) as, through the Declaration of the Rights
of the Child and the work of charitable agencies and international bodies in
the Third World, one particular vision of childhood has been and continues
to be exported as 'correct childhood' (Ennew 1986: 21). Not only does this
cast doubt, and comparative judgment, upon different family forms and
parenting practices in the Third World through the misguided assumption
of a uniformity of childhood in western Europe, it also disguises the socially
constructed character of 'the child' upon which it rests (Last 1994).

But what, then, are the supposed intrinsic characteristics of 'the child'
from which such a dominant idea of childhood springs? In their historical
account of the emergence of contemporary ideas of 'the child' Hockey and
James (1993) note four contributory themes which, during the last three
centuries, have shaped a particular vision of what childhood is: (1) that
the child is set apart temporally as different, through the calculation of
age; (2) that the child is deemed to have a special nature, determined by
Nature; (3) that the child is innocent; and (4) therefore is vulnerably dependent. In sum, these are themes which centre first, on questions of the child's
morality (2 and 3), and, second, on its capability (1 and 4). And, as we have
already suggested, it is precisely these themes which surfaced in the recent
public debates about children and violent crime. Thus, to what extent the
events of 1993 marked a significant shift in our understanding of childhood
or whether it was simply an old debate in a new guise is a central question
for this paper.

The moral ground?

From a sociological perspective the issues raised by children who commit violent crime are, first, conceptual and, are second, empirical. But the two are intimately linked, for it is clear that the way in which we think about children and conceive of childhood has very practical consequences for children themselves. If, as we argue, childhood is a social construction which provides both form and content to children's experiences, then the ways in which children relate and are related to in everyday life is, inevitably, in terms of the conceptual structures through which they are previously envisaged. In brief, children are locked, for their intelligibility, within the contingency of social conventions. The negotiable character of these conventions is a question of power, which children exercise only in a partial form. They can demand attention but not redefinition. How then is 'the child' defined and what might be the child's response?

An archaeology of the ideas which give rise to the modern 'child' reveals a strong and continuous commitment to conceptions of childhood purity. First, emanating from Rousseau, children are deemed initially free from corruption by virtue of their special nature. Emerging from the Enlightenment, they are the Ideal immanence, and the messengers of Reason. It is the experience of society which corrupts them. Left to Nature the child would be a stranger to guilt. A second engagement with childhood's supposed absence of evil stems from Locke: children are thought to be innocent, not innately, but, like halfwits, as a consequence of their lack of social experience. Through time the unknowing child may become corrupted by society.

Although formulated in the eighteenth-century these perceptions of the child's moral nature and development have retained a powerful and persuasive hold upon the public imagination, reappearing in different guises and with different consequences for children themselves. For example, Freud's discussion of childhood sexuality (Freud 1905) led to a contemporary furore and two decades of abuse for reinvoking 'original sin' in a libidinal form. Similarly, the contesting voices of nineteenth-century social reformers, discussed by Hendrick (1990), reveal, by turns, a concern to rescue the vulnerable child forced into factories and productive work and a desire to restore the Romantic vision of childhood for all children, perceived to be under threat from working-class juvenile delinquency. Similarly, Kitzinger (1990) shows how the purity of childhood has more recently been mobilized in a variety of forms in discussions about child sexual abuse, arguing that, for children themselves, such imagery is double-edged.

Notwithstanding differences in accounts of childhood's pure state, nor yet of the purpose and intent of its usage, over time, the theme of innocence has remained closely tied to 'the child'. It would be hard to envisage any other group in modern society content to be suspended within such essentially anachronistic visions.

Nevertheless they persist. Charity adverts for overseas development and aid, for example, manipulate images of children's utter dependency as playing a part in their own deprivation (Burman 1994), emphasizing that children are the least complicit in causality yet the most effected. Similarly, it is as a passive victim of abuse, neglect and poverty that 'the child' is often displayed for the British public through mass media and government rhetoric. In sum, a dominant modern discourse of childhood continues to mark out 'the child' as innately innocent, confirming its cultural identity as a passive and unknowing dependent, and as therefore a member of a social group disempowered, but for good, altruistic reasons.

Regarding children as being in possession of a special and distinctive nature, which is both untainted and vulnerably dependent, is what makes any link between children and violent crime particularly problematic, for the imagery of childhood and that of violent criminality are iconologically irreconcilable. It is still difficult, for example, to regard the video films of Jamie Bulger's abduction from the shopping mall as anything other than pictures of children holding hands. For the same reasons, it is impossible to ascribe blame to the inaction of the many adults who witnessed the subsequent dismal procession to the fateful railway embankment.

That these images were not of post-Enlightenment children but of children perpetrating a violent crime has, we suggest, had two important and highly disruptive consequences. First, the traditional image of 'the child' has been shattered through the dramatic denial of childish purity. Second, the unitary idea of 'the child', which such an ideology so long encouraged, has been revealed as illusory. No longer confined to the academy, the idea that childhood is contestable and culturally variable has entered a more public arena. No longer can 'different' children be othered from the category of 'child'.

However, as stated in the introduction, it does not follow from our argument here that we regard the recent conflation of the categories of 'child' and 'murderer' as instancing a unique state of affairs. Just as it has been established (Jenks 1994) that although child-abuse has only been rendered visible as a phenomenon during the last thirty years, despite its rate of historical occurrence being virtually constant, so, we might suppose that children did not kill children for the first time either in the case of Mary Bell or in Merseyside in 1993. We must assume and acknowledge that some children have always killed other children. What concerns us more here, as sociologists, is the social context, the climate of collective sentiment which made this particular event utterly 'shocking' and disruptive in its consequences. Child-by-child murder may not constitute a social trend, nor is it an original event, but the magnitude of the public reaction to the Bulger case certainly does comprise a social phenomenon. Our concern here, then, is not to account for the death of a child, but to attempt to explain the imminent, and historically located, death of 'childhood' which, in 1993, became a pressing public concern.

Two main but contradictory themes dominated the developing debate about childhood begun in the autumn of 1993. First, that children can and do commit acts of violence voiced the possibility that, after all, the Puritans were correct; that children are born sinful and have a natural propensity for evil unless properly and rigorously restrained. This doctrine of Adamic 'original sin' is a model of childhood, elsewhere formulated as the 'Dionysian' by Jenks (1995a) as an image of the wilful and unconstrained potential, which has always provided the dark side or inarticulate backdrop of our contemporary and dominant images of the child. As noted earlier, for instance, it was awakened this century in the powerful form of Freud's 'Id' and, more contemporarily, in debates about child sexual abuse.

A second, more liberal, interpretative frame suggested that children who kill are simply anomalous. Such children, it was said, are literally out of step with the staged intellectual, social and moral development of 'normal' children. They were not, however, to be subsequently regarded as the falsifying 'black swans' of Popper's philosophy of science, but rather as the abhorrent cases in a search for the security, and dubious consensus, of the confirmation of childhood innocence.

To foreshadow some conclusions: the consequences of either the 'origin sin' or the 'anomalous case' responses is a re-construction, rather than radical re-think, of our attitudes to children through shifting and strengthening the existing conceptual boundaries of childhood so as to exclude, as pathological or peculiar, those children who exceed the limits of what it is to be a child. For children themselves this raises the possibility of an increased governing (Rose 1989; Donzelot 1986) of their activities through calls for visible forms of containment or, perhaps more implicit and possibly more repressive, calls for the reaffirmation of a concept of 'the normal child'. Such a response addresses not the moral grounds of the problem but rather defers this question through the modern recourse to further surveillance in the place of understanding. The dark spectre of Foucault's watchtower is brought to mind along with the mechanical reduction of human conduct wrought through the one-sided emphasis on the 'voir' in 'savoir' (Foucault 1973).

In November 1993 the rough framework of these debates began to be sketched in as, seemingly, society struggled to comprehend a growing disillusionment with what children are or might become in the modern world. It was not, we suggest, just two children who were on trial for the murder of a third but childhood itself. The death of Jamie Bulger became, in the broadest sense, a metaphor for the supposed moral decline of a society which experiences the exponential acceleration of social change (Virilio 1991) in late-modernity as the constant confrontation with 'risk' (Beck 1992).

What is 'the child'?

That children are capable of violence, of rape, muggings and even murder is an idea that clearly falls outside traditional formulations of childhood. As people privately struggled to make sense of the events of 1993, newspaper headlines echoed their confusion, a confusion engendered by children revealed in a new role as suspects in a hitherto adult crime

> ... it is supposed to be the age of innocence so how could these 10 year olds turn into killers?
>
> (*The Sunday Times* 28 November 1993)

Sentiments parallel with those of the Archbishop of York, Dr John Hapgood, who stated that

> ... the importance of the crime lies in what it says about the potential for evil in children at an age at which innocence was once taken for granted.
>
> (quoted in *The Times* 25 November 1993)

The problem voiced here is one of classification: children who commit such violent acts pose a conundrum for they disassemble the traditional binary opposition between the categories of 'child' and 'adult', an opposition previously legitimized by the peculiar gloss of the moral ground, outlined above, whereby innocence is a hallmark of 'the child' and corrupting knowledge, that of 'adult'. These categories became badly blurred as the literally unthinkable was transformed by a grim reality. The conceptual boundaries once containing the child, through 'is' or 'ought', became utterly indefensible. Public attempts at propitiation in the face of this potentially dangerous confusion were conducted in different ways.

One approach was through conceptual eviction: children who commit acts of violence should be removed from the category of 'child' altogether. Such expulsion facilitates the restoration of the old moral order and re-establishes the discourse of childhood in its traditional ideological form. The lead for this practice was offered by Mr Justice Morland, the trial judge, in his summing up

> The killing of James Bulger was an act of unparalleled evil and barbarity ... This child of two was taken from his mother on a journey of over two miles, and then on a railway line battered to death without mercy. Then the body was placed across the railway line so that it would be run over by a train, in an attempt to conceal the murder. In my judgment your conduct was both cunning and very wicked.
>
> (Reported in *The Times* 24 November 1993)

These strategies were subsequently apparent in press commentaries and readers' letters during November 1993 where images of radical alterity were routinely employed

> ...evil freaks (local police, reported in *The Sunday Times* 28 November 1993)

with

> ...the Satan Bug inside (Ellis quoted in *The Sunday Times* 28 November 1993)

and having

> ...adult brains (Hymas quoted in *The Sunday Times* 5 December 1993)

as

> ...the spawn of Satan ...who committed ...acts of unparalleled evil and barbarity.
>> (quoted in *The Guardian* 27 November 1993)

These

> ...little devils.
>> (*The Sundary Times* 28 November 1993)

were no longer to be classified as children. And *The Times* leader of 25 November 1993 was titled

> The Three Evils (being 'metaphysical', 'physical' and 'moral').

and the substance of the piece deplored not just the awfulness of the killing but our contemporary failure to acknowledge and respond to 'a darker side' of childhood.

Within these quotations two kinds of 'Otherness' can be identified: (a) the child possessed of an inherently evil nature; and (b) the composite creature, the 'adult-child'. Both are highly transgressive images, at once wilful, bizarre and demonic. In that these images instance acute fractures from the commonplace idea of 'the child' as it is understood within western society, they both constitute a powerful, and volatile, ambiguity in public accounts of childhood. Anthropological work on social classification enables us to understand such a response as one emitting from a people whose cosmologies are under threat. As Mary Douglas (1970) has shown, the identification of anomalies, whether in the form of people, plants or animals, is integral to the establishment of social order. Anomalies are, in essence, the by-products of systems of ordering. Through their remarked differences, ironically, they work to firm up the boundaries which give form and substance to the conceptual categories from which they are excluded. In this sense, by refusing children who commit acts of violence acceptance within the category of child, the public was reaffirming to itself the essence of what children are. That is, it was a way to restore the primary image of the innate goodness of children through relegating some would-be children (those who commit acts of violence) to another category essentialized through images of evil or pathology. Thus, the stigma of anomaly works to explain how certain children are capable of actions which other, 'normal', children are not: the system of classification stays intact by resisting the 'defilement' of the abhorrent case. This analytic issue was well stated as a legal dilemma by Edward Pilkington in *The Guardian* when he wrote that

> At the centre of this anxiety is a simple question. Do children exist in a special state, qualitatively different from adulthood, in which they merit unique status and treatment? Or are they small adults, as capable of evil as any grown-up and who deserve to be treated with equal severity?
>
> (*The Guardian* 30 May 1994)

That the kinds of responses, previously reported, were to be found in the pages of the quality press (and were not just tabloid rhetoric) indicates the powerful magnetism which the idea of 'the child' exercises in our thinking about the quality of our culture, its past achievements and the future collective moral 'good'. The child has become emblematic.

Other extracts from contemporaneous press reports suggest that eroding the idea of 'the child' in late-modernity portends an even greater social loss: the loss of society itself. Thus, alongside the positing of innate evil and depravity as ways of accounting for why children commit violent crimes, other accounts struggled to explore the particularity of the social contexts, like dysfunctional families, which might foster, in the child, the ability to perform adult-like actions. As such they were attempting to salvage the idea of the child, by regarding it as an epiphenomenon.

Although seeming to represent an oppositional voice, this latter perspective shares a common ground: it too individualizes acts of violence in an attempt to cling onto traditional accounts of what children are. As an explanatory narrative it has as its source the fact that, as Jenks (1995b) has argued, 'the child' has become a way of speaking about sociality itself. Any assault on what the child is, or rather, what the child has evolved into, threatens to rock the social base. The child through the passage of modernity came to symbolize futurity and was thus guarded and invested. In the late-modern context, where belief in progress and futures has diminished, has the child come now to symbolize the solidity and adhesion of the past? And is it therefore defended through nostalgia and seen as a hedge against 'existential anxiety' (Giddens 1991).

The divergent spectrum of public attitudes towards childhood criminality featured in the press sublimated these contradictions. For those who would adhere to the view that evil is a genuine motivational force within the social world, the fact that children can commit acts of violence was simply an indication of how far we, as a society, had fallen from grace. Perhaps it even provided the spur for a 'return to basics' campaign. However, for those others adopting a more liberal stance, childhood criminality was regarded as a harbinger of how our nemesis would appear if we did not act to arrest the postmodern malaise. One notable pronouncement from the Secretary of State with responsibility for the family summarized this divergence as a paradox

> That two young boys at an age, when most of their peers are riding bikes and playing computer games, could commit such an appalling act of violence leaves one numb with disbelief. Some people wrote the murders off as peculiarly, even uniquely, evil. Others saw the killing as a reflection of the times in which we live ... Yet those who were quick to pronounce sentence on society overlooked an important paradox. For nothing was clearer, after the terrible facts had become known, than the united sense of mourning from which a whole community drew strength.
>
> (Virginia Bottomley quoted in *The Guardian* 28 December 1993)

A reader's letter published in *The Guardian* exemplifies one end of the spectrum of attitudes, that of the child-as-society

> I was not surprised by the murder of James Bulger, it seemed to me just the sort of thing that could happen in nineties Britain, just one symptom of the insidious brutalism that has permeated every aspect of life. Why should we expect children to have any sense of mutuality when they grow up in a society where human life is accorded no value.
>
> (*The Guardian* 27 November 1993)

The opposite end appears in an adjacent letter

> ... As children are treated, so they treat others. Each time a child is struck, it dies a little inside. Each time a society refuses to deal with causes of violence, it dies a little too.
>
> (*The Guardian* 27 November 1993)

And the two accounts are brought together under a shared headline which underscores the conceptual links, and the public conflation, between the idea of the child and the idea of society

TRAGIC PROOF THAT SOCIETY HAS LOST ITS SOUL.
(*The Guardian* 27 November 1993)

Writing in the same edition of the newspaper, Walter Schwarz concludes that if public consciousness has been stirred

> ... it is because children in a moral vacuum seem the most spectacular victims of a society in which people have ceased officially to count.
> (*The Guardian* 27 November 1993)

The events of November 1993 thus yielded a three-fold restatement and confirmation of what, in the public mind, children are as the loss of childhood itself seemed immanent. First, 'the child' is not evil; second, 'the child' is not adult and third, 'the child' is a symbol of society's optimism, a search for a hopeful future or a recollection of good times past. And in doing so children who commit acts of violence were by definition firmly excluded from the conceptual category of 'child'. Through their actions, such children contravene its boundaries and in so doing threaten, most fundamentally, each of our senses of attachment to the social bond.

What does the child need?

The differing accounts as to why and how it is possible for children to commit crimes of violence were, as we have shown, partially synthesized in public perceptions through the redrawing of the traditional boundaries of childhood. While this momentarily dissolved the conundrum, it offered little comfort for the future. Thus it was in pursuit of a solution to, rather than simply an explanation of, the conceptual problem posed by children not behaving as children that the broad band of public opinion widened to ask more searching questions about childhood. Views about what children need ranged from a harshly repressive response to a more liberal one.

For those who would pinpoint evil nature as the locus of violence in some children, repression and retribution were simple solutions

> ... we must recognise, and act to ensure that, society is protected from evil individuals of whatever age. If criminals act against society then they must be removed from society.
> (*The Guardian* 27 November 1993)

Predictably, similar calls have been made before. In 1989 after the assault of a paralysed woman by three boys, aged nine, seven and six, a superintendent of police remarked that

> ... we would like to see the age of criminality lowered and we would like to see the boys facing criminal action.
>
> (*The Guardian* 13 April 1989)

For those others who would espouse a more liberal viewpoint, preferring to blame society as the legitimating source of some children's violence, the solution was less individualized and certainly less clear cut.

> Parents cannot cope and schools are left without adequate resources or training to pick up the pieces. Year after year the same patterns of behaviour recur. There is all too frequently nowhere for disturbed children to go, so they do not get the care and treatment they need. As a society we are failing all our children if we do not have the will and the commitment to enable them to grow up with the support and guidance they need.
>
> (*The Guardian* 27 November 1993)

Thus, between, on the one hand, the clamour for punishment, revenge and retribution and, on the other hand, demands for understanding and loving care, it would seem that public perceptions of what children need are indeed in disarray. Even a rational gloss on the preceding divergence of views could only suggest a public demand for better material provision for child support. The problem is not peculiarly British. In France, despite the collective assertion that children who commit violent crimes are still children and cannot be held responsible, unlike the British case, a similar dilemma remains about what measures might be taken to prevent children committing acts of violence (this is reported by Lowry in *The Daily Telegraph* 2 December 1993).

If, as Woodhead (1990) has argued, concepts of children's needs are integral to the social construction of childhood itself, then the collective indecision and social paralysis, previously discussed, becomes comprehensible. As a society, and presumably as individuals, we do not know what actions to take because we do not know what children are. They are steadily slipping from our conceptual grasp, and because we no longer know what children are then we can neither understand nor articulate their needs.

What can be done?

What can be done is complex and, as yet, uncertain. But what is being done, in the name of prevention, is both simple and deceptively straightforward.

As ever with contemporary crisis management, we witness a convenient 'scapegoating', the searching out of something or somebody to blame. The targets have been as banal as the unspecified causality of video games and their suspicious 'hyperreality', lack of discipline in homes and schools, declining standards of morality, and truancy. All these are seen as key antagonistic elements in the battle to recover the lost innocence of children, explanatory devices dedicated to recreating yesterday's children not to forging tomorrow's adults.

Taking the lead from the Bulger trial judge's remarks, the government's response to the growing moral panic about the nation's children has been to establish a set of controls upon children's activities. 'Truancy Watch', launched in Autumn 1993, was designed to encourage the public policing of children and takes its cue from a scheme already running 'successfully' in Stoke-on-Trent

> Shops display 'truant-free zone' stickers and staff are trained to challenge suspects and fill in confidential forms for education welfare officers. Buses carry posters asking: 'Are you sure your child is in school.'
>
> (*The Guardian* 27 November 1993)

The resonances with Foucault's 'Panopticon' are clear. Described by the teacher's unions as being akin to

> ... unleashing 'an army of spies and informants into the streets.'
>
> (*The Guardian* 27 November 1993)

such public accountability for children represents a revival of concepts of 'the child' as public property taking us back to the pragmatic origins of mass education, the economic policy of 'human capital' and the educational ideology of vocationalism. A diffuse and spurious sense of the collective is invoked in political discourse and charged with the role of 'guardian of the nation's future'. All these are paradoxical claims in the face of earlier government pronouncements concerning the rolling back of the state and the celebration of individualism. This confused response was, however, put forward by John Pattern, Secretary of State for Education, in the autumn of 1993

> ... until such time as we can rely on all parents to fulfil their side of the bargain there is going to be an important role for the community.
>
> (quoted in *The Guardian* 27 November 1993)

Such a brand of community care may have a continuity with the, now disbanded, policy of mobilizing a 'Mum's Army' for infant education, but it is very much at odds with the spirit of the newly instituted Children's Act whose enlightened philosophy strains towards the child's liberty rather than its further containment. Similarly, the call for the restriction of children's access to video games and films as being the 'likely' source of illicit knowledge which prematurely ages children's minds may run counter to more liberal or, indeed, more informed claims. For example, the call for children's increased need for earlier sex education, a demand being made currently in response to growing numbers of schoolgirl pregnancies and the threats to health posed by HIV and AIDS. A similar polarity centres around the value of school uniform as a deterrent to truancy and a method of social control as against the child's freedom to self expression through the opening up of choice. But such stabs at reform or social engineering offer few solutions. They are mostly about containment. They universally fail to resolve a more central problematic: if we don't know what children are then we don't know what they need and, if we don't know what they need then. . . . ? What?

There is, however, one way out of this dilemma which has still to be fully explored. Yet, unless the socially constructed nature of childhood becomes more widely registered, it is an opportunity which may not even be taken. One way of discovering why children commit acts of violence, what motivates them or what stays their hands, would be to know more from children themselves about crime and violence. Just as in the 1980s when child sexual abuse was high up the agenda we found that we did not know much about the extent of children's knowledge about sex, so too now the adult world finds itself in a state of ignorance about what ordinary children do ordinarily to one another. For example, an emerging body of work from the USA indicates that most child abuse, sexual, physical and psychological is, in fact, peer abuse (Ambert 1995). We need to know what bullying is and how and why it occurs; when does teasing become bullying and when does taunting turn to violence? But to ask children such questions is, unsurprisingly, a course of action fraught with conceptual and perhaps even ethical problems.

Given the dominance of particular models of child development in public perceptions of children, models which are both unilinear and on the whole uniform, children are rarely seen as competent articulators of their own experiences (Jenks 1982). Children as social actors may gradually become visible and acceptable within sociology but in the public world children themselves may still have little opportunity to have their voices listened to. Children's words may continue to be viewed with suspicion, or indifference, by an adult audience as in cases of child sexual abuse where age, rather than experience, may still often be deemed the more important indicator of a child's ability to tell, or even know, the truth. Thus, in trying to ask children about violent crime would what they have to say be judged as insightful or would it be tempered, even nullified, by adult listeners? And should what children have to say prove unacceptable to the adult world, with what value would it be credited? Would it be simply dismissed as evidence of children's inability to be articulate observers, further justification for not including them in decisions made about their welfare? These problems are real, but not insurmountable, as ethnographic work with children by sociologists and anthropologists is beginning to demonstrate.

To our knowledge there has been just one public attempt to ask children about violent crime and the tone of its reporting hints at the unacceptability of the responses which were obtained. Under the headline 'Bulger: chill verdict of the children', Charles Hymas recounts what he terms as the 'cynical' opinions of the young people with whom he talked. He expresses surprise at their 'moralistic, even reactionary' attitudes

> Everybody is responsible for their own thoughts and the way they deal with these thoughts. The kids were wrong and they got what they deserved. They have nobody else to blame apart from themselves.
>
> (quoted in *The Sunday Times* 5 December 1993)

That children should express the attitude that 'basically society is better off without them', that the punishment given to the child murderers 'was not severe enough', poses Hymas with a conceptual problem. But his problem is also ours. Is the punitive line taken by these children merely a callow replication of received views, a sign of their immaturity and lack of experience; is it, as it were, a sign of their innocent immaturity? Or, more troubling perhaps, might their desire for revenge and harsh justice be an indication of a cruel propensity in all children, the image entertained by adults only through fiction from *The Midwich Cuckoos* to *The Lord of the Flies*? If so, then our traditional idea of 'the child' must be abandoned. If not, then surely we have to reject any monolithic category of 'the child' and work instead with the more pluralistic concepts of 'childhoods', 'children' and 'childlikeness'? But to abandon a shared category of the child is to confront a daunting paradox. If as adults we do just that, what happens to the concept of 'childhood' through which we, as adults, see ourselves and our society's past and future? If, as we have argued here, the concept of 'childhood' serves to articulate not just the experience and status of the young within modern society but also the projections, aspirations, longings and altruism contained within the adult experience then to abandon such a conception is to erase our final point of stability and attachment to the social bond. In an historical era during which issues of identity and integration (Giddens 1991) are, perhaps, both more unstable and more fragile than at any previous time, such a loss would impact upon the everyday experience of societal members with disorienting consequences. Only by interrogating the possessive adhesion of adults to the concept of childhood in the context of postmodernity can we begin to understand the fear behind those distorted masks of hatred and retribution that disfigured the faces of the crowd outside of the courthouse in Liverpool during 1993 where two sad little boys were being charged with the murder of a third.

Bibliography

Ambert, A.-M. 1995 'The Problem of Peer Abuse', *Sociological Studies of Children*, 7: 177–206,

Ariès, P. 1962 *Centuries of Childhood*, Harmondsworth: Penguin.

Armstrong, D. 1983 *Political Anatomy of the Body: Medical Knowledge in Britain in the Twentieth Century*, Cambridge: Cambridge University Press.

Beck, U. 1992 *Risk Society: Towards a New Modernity*, London: Sage.

Boswell, J. 1988 *The Kindness of Strangers: the Abandonment of Children in Western Europe From Late Antiquity to the Renaissance*, Harmondsworth: Penguin.

Boyden, J. 1990 'Childhood and the policy makers: A comparative perspective on the globalization of childhood' in A. James and A. Prout (eds) *Constructing and Reconstructing Childhood*, Basingstoke: Falmer.

Burman, E. 1994 'Innocents abroad: Western fantasies of children and the iconography of emergencies', *Disasters*, 18(3): 238–53.

Demos, J. 1986 *Past, Present and Personal*, Oxford: Oxford University Press.

DeMause, L. (ed.) 1976 *The History of Childhood*, London: Souvenir Press.

Donzelot, J. 1986 *The Policing of Families,* London: Hutchinson.

Douglas, M. 1970 *Purity and Danger*, Harmondsworth: Penguin.

Ennew, E. 1986 *The Sexual Exploitation of Children*, Cambridge: Polity Press.

Foucault, M. 1973 *Discipline and Punish*, London: Allen Lane.

Freud, S. 1905 *Three Essays on the Theory of Sexuality*, see edition trans. J. Strachey 1949 London: Imago Press.

Giddens, A. 1991 *Modernity and Self-Identity*, Cambridge: Polity Press.

Hendrick, H. 1990 'Constructions and reconstructions of British childhood: an interpretive study 1800 to the present' in A. James and A. Prout (eds) *Constructing and Reconstructing Childhood*, Basingstoke: Falmer.

Hockey, J. and James, A. 1993 *Growing Up and Growing Old: Ageing and Dependency in the Life Course*, London: Sage.

Houlbrooke, R. 1984 *The English Family 1450–1700*, London: Longmans.

James, A. 1993 *Childhood Identifies: Self and Social Relations in the Experience of the Child*, Edinburgh: Edinburgh University Press.

—— 1995 'On being a child: the self, the group and the category' in A. P. Cohen and N. J. Rapport (eds) *Questions of Consciousness*, London: Routledge.

James, A. and Prout, A. (eds) 1990 *Constructing and Reconstructing Childhood*, Basingstoke: Falmer.

Jenks, C. (ed.) 1982 *The Sociology of Childhood*, London: Batsford.

—— 1994 'Child Abuse in the Postmodern context: An Issue of Social Identity', *Childhood* 2: 111–121.

—— 1995a 'Decoding Childhood' in P. Atkinson, S. Delamont and B. Davies (eds) *Discourse and Reproduction: Essays in Honour of Basil Bernstein*, New York: Hampton Press.

—— 1995b 'Constituting Child Abuse: A Problem of Late Modernity', *Sociological Studies of Children* 7: 155–76.

Kitzinger, J. 1990 'Who are you kidding? Children, power and the struggle against sexual abuse' in A. James and A. Prout (eds) *Constructing and Reconstructing Childhood*, Basingstoke: Falmer.

Last, M. 1994 'Putting children first', *Disasters* 18(3):.

Philo, G. 1990 *Seeing and Believing: The Influence of Television*, London: Routledge.

Pollock, L. 1983 *Forgotten Children: Parent–Child Relations from 1500 to 1900*, Cambridge: Cambridge University Press.

Rose, N. 1989 *Governing the Soul*, London: Routledge.

Stone, L. 1977 *The Family, Sex and Marriage in England 1500–1800*, London: Weidenfeld and Nicolsen.

Virilio, P. 1991 *Speed and Politics*, New York: Semiotext(e).

Woodhead, M. 1990 'Psychology and the cultural construction of children's needs', in A. James and A. Prout (eds) *Constructing and Reconstructing Childhood*, Basingstoke: Falmer.

53

SAFETY AND DANGER

Childhood, sexuality, and space at the end of the millennium

Valerie Walkerdine

Source: *Research in Childhood: Sociology, Culture and History*, Denmark: University of Southern Denmark, 2000, pp. 197–212.

Introduction

In recent years a number of major concerns have been raised regarding the safety of children in public and private spaces, both in relation to their vulnerability to dangerous adults but also the problem of dangerous children who prey on others. British examples of incidents leading to these concerns include the James Bulger case, where two ten-year-old boys murdered a two-year-old boy, and the Dunblane massacre, in which children in a primary school were shot by a gunman. American examples include the spate of recent school killings by boys and the murder of the child beauty queen JonBenet Ramsey. We might also include the recent furor in Belgium over the discovery of pedophile rings. In all of these examples there is one of two features: the dangerous adult (almost exclusively male) who is violent and/or sexually predatory on young children, or the protoviolent boy or protosexual girl, as in the cases of James Bulger and JonBenet Ramsey, respectively. As one British judge put it in a case of child sexual abuse, the girl involved was understood to be "no angel."

Anxieties about the safety of children in public and private space and the specter of dangerous children, in particular boys who commit murder, feed anxieties about a world out of control and in which it is no longer possible to protect children. I want to look at this in two ways. The first involves the need to rethink concepts of what childhood means in postmodernity and childhood's relation to a concept of space that can no longer be contained within traditional developmental discourses. The second is to think about how adult anxiety about child protection in public and private space relates to complex issues about adult sexuality, what Jacqueline Rose (1985) called "the desire of adults for children."

This anxiety manifests itself not only in the well-known examples given but also in fears that there is no longer any place or space in which children are safe—certainly not school with its crazy lone killers or teenage gunmen; not home with the threat of child abuse; and not the street, park, or playground with its lurking strangers. I make this contrast because, as we will see, thirty years ago, within educational practices, the home and school were often envisaged as safe havens in which children could develop normally and naturally. What then has happened to our idea of childhood and development within this context in which sex and violence feature so prominently?

I want to explore the way in which this huge anxiety about children and the status of childhood has erupted at the end of the twentieth century. It is understood in terms, on the one hand, of pathological adults who sully the otherwise sound barrel so that it is not necessary to ask questions about masculine sexuality. On the other hand, I want to argue that indeed such issues raise profound questions about the status of adult sexuality and its object. In particular I want to raise some issues about the easy separation of normality and pathology. In addition to this, I want to think about the way in which models of childhood from within developmental theory also privilege a particular model of normality, to the extent that it is certain children, children who are Othered, who become the object of pathologization discourses. Normal, and hence natural, boys are naughty and playful, not violent. Normal girls are well behaved, hardworking, and asexual (Walkerdine, 1989, for example).

What is the relation between the changes in the understanding of public and private space and the constitution of the subjectivities of children within those spaces? Traditionally, within the discourses of modernity, it has been developmental theory that has been marshaled to tell the truth about a naturally developing child within a natural environment. That environment was meant to protect children from the dangers understood as inherent in an industrialized urban landscape. Now in a context of a postindustrial and postmodern landscape there is no longer taken to be any safe haven, no environment safe for natural development.

Anxieties about children in public space

So much has changed since the individualist developmentalism of earlier decades in which children's exploration of physical space was seen as basic to development. Now there are increasing fears about the safety of children in any kind of public space. For example, we have moved from the idea of the primary school as a safe environment in which the right kind of development might be accomplished through the easy exploration of concrete physical space—as in the applications of Piaget, with the school being understood as a safe and nurturing environment in which development can occur naturally in contrast to sometimes difficult environments outside (see in particular the government report "Children and their Primary Schools," 1967, discussed in Walkerdine, 1984)—to the primary school as a site of danger. The concern about safety is less a worry about environmental danger (though that certainly plays a part) and more about the threat posed by the violence and sexuality of adults. In this sense then, a great deal has changed, from even the 1960s and 1970s, as the idea of development as unhindered play in a natural environment is less and less on the agenda. This is very significant in terms of our approach to the assumptions about space made within developmental theory.

Most work on space from within traditional developmental theory depends upon distinctions made by Piaget in 1967 between topological and euclidean space, arguing that children acquired spatial concepts through their active manipulation of objects within the physical world, recognizing first that there were two dimensions and later three. However, this model of solid space fits neither subatomic physics nor cyberspace. Piaget argued that children cannot master three dimensions before two, suggesting also that young children had difficulty with the abstract, needing first to experience the concrete. Cyberspace requires a conception of space as flow and energy, not as fixed, solid, and geographical. Quite young children playing computer games handle with ease the complex relation of two to three dimensions, the n dimensional space of levels in platformers (accomplishments that concretely they should not be able to do), for example, with its intricate relation of movement in virtual space and reaction time, suggesting the necessity of a different conception not only of the space that children inhabit but of the processes of acquisition of modes of understanding of that space itself. If the spaces in which children grow up have changed fundamentally from those of previous generations, in terms of the anxieties and possibilities that surround them, and if a space of flows and energies replaces that of solids, then the time has come for us to rethink the concepts of childhood and of space as well as the relationship between them.

In addition to this, adults are presented as not only part of the problem (especially of course adult men) but also as unable to put a stop to what is happening to children and indeed to the destruction of the environment: children are left to their own devices, as is graphically illustrated in television series like *Teenage Mutant Ninja Turtles* (Urwin, 1995) and *Rugrats*. In this context, a new space is often put forward as being outside these concerns, one in which rational play may be offered, without the fears attached to public space and indeed without undue interference from adults: cyberspace is adult-free, unknown, and unsupervised. To the technophile, it is a new frontier, an untamed and anarchic space in which transformation might still be possible (Fuller & Jenkins, 1998). However, this is crosscut by technophobia, in terms of discourses about media effects, which play upon the dangers of new technologies to the vulnerable minds of the children of the masses as the producer of addiction on the one hand and violence on the other. In particular, in Britain at least, two forms have been singled out for concern: videos (movies) and computer and video games. The murder of James Bulger in Liverpool by two young boys brought to the surface not only the danger to children in public space but the danger wrought by children themselves. The children in danger have to be saved from dangerous children, but those dangerous children have minds made vulnerable and oversuggestible by their environment (these are, of course, the children of the poor) and the effects of the media are most marked upon them, thus both videos and games are blamed for addiction and for violence. Actually, then, in effect, we have at the end of the twentieth century the twin poles that were there at its birth: the vulnerable-minded protoviolent masses and the superrational explorers of the unknown (in this case, the information superhighway). In relation to this, femininity is still constituted as Other and girls rarely figure as either murderers or superrational explorers, though those categories are constantly challenged.

Children and new technologies

I will summarize the major conditions of possibility (Henriques, Hollway, Urwin, Venn, & Walkerdine, 1998) for the discursive constitution of the present concern with children and new technologies. The emergence of social psychology at the end of the nineteenth century, with its emphasis on the group as a crowd (Le Bon, 1895; Tarde, 1890), built on earlier concerns about the irrationality, vulnerability, suggestibility, and absence of morality of the "dangerous classes." These characteristics paved the way for the understanding of poor peoples as psychologically lacking and pathological and can be related directly to the kind of assumptions that became taken for granted in work on children of the poor in general and children and the media in particular. That is, that certain children had minds that were vulnerable to outside influences, hence concerns about violence and addiction. These become very clear in the debates surrounding the James Bulger case and video nasties, for example. This generated strategies of population management in relation to psychopathology on the one hand and popular entertainment and crowd control on the other.

The ready use of existing concepts in the emergent pre- and postwar traditions of mass media and communication studies, principally in the United States, and the use of, for example, theories of vulnerable masses and social psychology, in the work of the Frankfurt school, helped to cement this discursive apparatus. American social psychology made moves in the 1950s to make psychoanalytic insights amenable to scientific inquiry. One of the kinds of work on children to emerge from this was Bandura's work on social learning theory, producing a number of key studies, highlighting the role of imitation in the production of antisocial behavior and signaling the way in which children could be understood as aggressively and violently imitating what they saw on television. In Britain, the 1956 study by Himmelweit, Openheim, and Vince argued that children could be addicted to television, with the worst addicts being working-class children whose viewing habits were less likely to be supervised by their parents.

Moral concern about violence and addiction was generated at this time, building upon the moral technologies from the nineteenth century (and indeed before this). Concern about violence and addiction were two of the major concerns addressed by research on video games, as was previously also the case with the arrival of video technology. In the United States in particular, such research appears to have developed in tandem with the anxiety about the loss and disappearance of childhood itself, with figures such as Neil Postman (1994) arguing that television signaled the erosion of childhood, to arguments about addiction and abuse (for example, Best, 1990; Ivy, 1995; Jenkins, 1992), which suggested that 95 percent of American adults are addicted and/or had abused childhoods, presenting this as one of the major American anxieties of the late twentieth century. This can be put together with the fact that almost all research on violence and the media comes from the United States. In Britain too, however, there has been a sharp increase in anxiety about children as victims of abuse and per-petrators of crime, with a number of psychologists lining up behind Elizabeth Newson (1994) to argue, controversially, that the only thing to have accounted for the change in children's behavior (pace the Bulger case) is violent videos. British media and cultural studies have tended to use notions of media literacy to counter notions of passively imitating children (Buckingham, 1991). However, this tends to build upon preexisting strateg-ies and technologies that stress rationality as a counter to the irrationality of the dangerous classes.

Discourses of modernity

Grand metanarratives of modernity elide the specificities of childhoods. In order to understand these metanarratives it is necessary to work not with a general theory but with an approach that understands the discourses and practices through which particular subjectivities are produced. This means that childhood is understood not as a natural state best described through developmental accounts but that these very accounts can be understood as historically specific "regimes of truth" that constitute what it means to be a child at a particular time and place (Walkerdine, 1998).

The theoretical framework underlying this approach has been articulated in a number of publications (for example, Foucault, 1977; Henriques et al.,

1998). In brief, what is particularly important is the concept of subjectivity, that is, that the human subject is produced in the discursive practices that make up the social world (as opposed to a pregiven psychological subject who is made social or socialized). This means that we need an understanding of how what Foucault (1977) called the microphysics of power actually works to form the discourses that produce and regulate what it means to be a subject within different social practices. In this analysis, the subject is produced through the discursive relations of the practices themselves and is not coterminous with the actual embodied and lived experience of being a subject. To understand the relation between subjectification (the condition of being a subject) and subjectivity (the lived experience of being a subject), it is necessary to examine what subject-positions are created within specific practices and how actual subjects are both created in and live those diverse positions. The reason that I am laboring this point is that to understand subjectivity is not the same as understanding "learning" or "cognition"; rather, the issue becomes how to examine both how social and cultural practices work and how they create what it means to be a subject inside those practices. Thus, the understanding of how practices operate and how subjects are formed inside them becomes one and the same activity. For Foucault, power/knowledge is a central component of the current social order. To examine what counts as childhood, therefore—as well as the relation of children to popular culture—we need to examine how that relation is formed inside the discourses that constitute the technologies of the social (Foucault, 1977).

Understanding the historical dimension

In Foucault's approach to the "history of the present," it is necessary to examine how the present is constituted through the historical production of power/knowledge relations. In relation to children and popular culture, we need to look at least to the post-Enlightenment concern about the over-suggestible, irrational poor (Blackman, 1996). Work on the suggestibility of crowds (for example, Le Bon, 1895; Tarde, 1890) paves the way for the later emergence of social psychology and of mass communications research. The important twin issues of the mass medium and the vulnerable and suggestible mind cohere to produce a social psychology and a psychopathology of groups in which mass irrationality and suggestibility have a central place (Walkerdine, 1997). I want to argue that the concern about the regulation of the masses through their mass suggestibility and irrationality became one of the central aspects of the technologies through which they were regulated.

In brief, concern about rationality and irrationality and the vulnerability of the minds of certain children to the media finds its antecedence within the emergence of these discourses and technologies. We can trace the surveillance of children's viewing, for example, in and through the technologies of the regulation both of what counts as childhood and what was shown to children (films, television, video games). This intersected with concerns about children and rationality that also tied in with the production of the rational government of the masses and the bourgeois order, in which to be civilized was to be understood as ultimately rational, with women, the masses, and colonial peoples being defined as dangerously outside rationality. To produce the individual in the image of reason, therefore, was to produce a subject who would accept the moral and political order of a liberal democracy apparently according to their own free will and not rebel (Walkerdine, 1984). It is out of these intersecting discourses and claims to truth that we can find the current concerns about children and the new media and technologies. Indeed, if we are to examine current concerns we can find that they cohere largely around concerns about the vulnerability and suggestibility of young minds, with those being understood as most at risk being the children of the masses, the poor. Alongside that, however, we can also find a utopian discourse of the new information superhighway as a new frontier, a new space for the production of a new, and perhaps super, rationality. In this way, the concerns about children and space split into an opposition between cyberspace as a new space for the production of a new rationality (which replaces a traditional developmentalism) and the pathologized others—the children of the poor, who may be subject to the breakdown of these other spaces.

The eroticization of little girls

While we can identify boys as a target for discourses about the relation of dangers to children to dangerous children, we also need to examine the issue of what is often taken to be the intrusion of adult sexuality into the lives of young girls. How can little girls be safe if adult men take them as sexual objects, as in concerns about pedophilia and child sexual abuse? Nevertheless, young girls themselves, especially working-class girls, are often understood as being part of the problem, which raises the difficult issue of the relation of childhood to adult sexuality. The topic of popular portrayals of little girls as eroticized, little girls and sexuality, is an issue that touches on a number of very difficult and often taboo areas. Feminism has had little to say about little girls, except through studies of socialization and sex-role stereotyping. With regard to sexuality, almost all attention has been focused on adult women. Little girls enter debates about women's memories of their own girlhood in the main: discussions of little girls' fantasies of sex with their fathers or adult men, as in Freud's Dora case, the debate surrounding Masson's claim that Freud had suppressed the evidence that many of his female patients had been sexually abused as children, and, of course, the discourse of abuse itself. The topic of little girls and sexuality has come to be seen as being about the problem of the sexual abuse of innocent and vulnerable girls by bad adult men, or conversely, less politically correct but no less present, the idea of little girls as little seductresses. I want to open up a set of issues that I believe are occluded by such debates—the ubiquitous eroticization of little girls in the popular media and the just as ubiquitous ignorance and denial of this phenomenon. In the rest of the chapter, I want to concentrate on this issue in particular.

Childhood innocence and little Lolitas

Janie is six. In the classroom she sits almost silently well behaved, the epitome of the hardworking girl, so often scorned as uninteresting in the educational literature on girls' attainment (Walkerdine, 1989). She says very little and appears to be constantly aware of being watched. She herself watches the model that she presents to her teacher, classmates, and me, seated in a corner of the classroom making an audio recording. She always presents immaculate work and is used to getting very high marks. She asks to go to the toilet and leaves the classroom. Since she is wearing a radio microphone I hear her cross the hall in which a class is doing music and movement to a radio program. The teacher tells them to pretend to be bunnies. She leaves the hall and enters the silence of the toilets, and in there alone she sings loudly to herself. I imagine her swaying in front of the mirror. The song that she sings is one on the lips of many of the girls at the time I was making the recordings: Toni Basil's "Mickey" (see Walkerdine, 1997).

"Mickey" is a song sung by a woman dressed as a teenager. In the promotional video for the song she wears a cheerleader's outfit complete with a very short skirt and is surrounded by large, butch-looking women cheerleaders who conspire to make her look both smaller and more feminine. "Oh Mickey, you're so fine, you're so fine, you blow my mind," she sings. "Give it to me, give it to me, any way you can, give it to me, give it to me, I'll take it like a man." What does it mean for a six-year-old girl to sing these highly erotic lyrics? It could be argued that what we have here is the intrusion of adult sexuality into the innocent world of childhood. Or indeed, that because she is only six, such lyrics do not count because she is incapable of understanding them. I shall explore the issue of childhood innocence in more detail, and rather than attempting to dismiss the issue of the meaning of the lyrics as irrelevant, I shall try to place these meanings in the overall study of little girls and sexuality. In moving out of the public and highly surveilled space of the classroom, where she is a good, well-behaved girl, to the private space of the toilets she enters a quite different discursive space, the space of the little Lolita, the sexual little girl, who cannot be revealed to the cozy sanitized classroom. She shifts in this move from innocent to sexual, from virgin to whore, from child to little woman, from good to bad. The public surveilled space of the classroom is still understood as a space in which sexuality is left out or kept at bay. It is in the unsurveilled private space that the child-woman can be manifest and which therefore presents problems within educational discourse. Of course, what is also pointed up by the research on Janie is that by the use of new technology (she wears a radio microphone) the public/private space dichotomy becomes blurred because the very act of recording her brings that space to the public attention. Such a shift is also central to many practices of "real people" television (see Pini & Walkerdine, forthcoming) and popularized in such Hollywood films as *EdTV*.

Children and the popular

I want to explore some of the "gazes" at the little girl, the ways that she is inscribed in a number of competing discourses. I will concentrate on the figure of the little girl as an object of psychopedagogic discourse and as the eroticized child-woman of popular culture. I have argued in previous work that the nature of the child is not discovered but produced in regimes of truth created in those very practices that proclaim the child in all his naturalness. I write "his" advisedly, because a central plank of my argument has been that although this child is taken to be gender-neutral, actually he is always figured as a boy, a boy who is playful, creative, naughty, rule breaking, rational. The figure of the girl, by contrast, suggests an unnatural pathology: she works to the child's play; she follows rules to his breaking of them; she is good, well behaved, and irrational. Femininity becomes the Other of rational childhood. If she is everything that the child is not supposed to be, it follows that her presence, where it displays the above attributes, may be considered to demonstrate a pathological development, an improper childhood, a danger or threat to what is normal and natural. However, attempts (and they are legion) to transform her into the model playful child often come up against a set of discursive barriers: a playful and assertive girl may be understood as forward, uppity, overmature, too precocious (in one study a primary school teacher called such a ten-year-old girl a "madam"; see Walkerdine, 1989). Empirically then, "girls," like "children," are not discovered in a natural state. What is found to be the case by teachers, parents, and others is the result of complex processes of subjectification (Henriques *et al.*, 1984). Yet, while this model of girlhood is at once pathologized, it is also needed: the good and hardworking girl who follows the rules prefigures the nurturant mother figure, who uses her irrationality to safeguard rationality, to allow it to develop (Walkerdine & Lucey, 1989). Consider then the threat to the natural child posed by the eroticized child, the little Lolita, the girl who presents as a little woman, not of the nurturant kind, but rather the seductress, the unsanitized whore to the good girl's virgin. It is my contention that popular culture lets this figure into the sanitized space of natural childhood, a space from which it must be guarded and kept at all costs. What is being kept out and what is safe inside this fictional space?

153

The discourse of natural childhood builds upon a model of naturally occurring rationality, itself echoing the idea of childhood as an unsullied and innocent state, free from the interference of adults. The very cognitivism of most models of childhood as they have been incorporated into educational practices leaves both emotionality and sexuality to one side. Although Freud posited a notion of childhood sexuality that has been very pervasive, it was concepts like repression and the problems of adult interference in development that became incorporated into educational practices rather than any notion of sexuality in children as a given or natural phenomena. Indeed, it is precisely the idea that sexuality is an adult notion that sullies the safe innocence of a childhood free to emerge inside the primary school classroom that is most important. Adult sexuality interferes with the uniqueness of childhood, its stages of development. Popular culture then, insofar as it presents the intrusion of adult sexuality into the sanitized space of childhood, is understood as very harmful.

Visually these positions can be distinguished by a number of gazes at the little girl. Psychopedagogic images are presented in two ways: the fly on the wall documentary photograph in which the young girl is seen always engaged in some educational activity and is never shown looking at the camera, and the cartoon-type book illustration in which she appears as a smiley face, rounded (but certainly not curvy) unisex figure. If we begin to explore popular images of little girls they present a stark contrast. I do not have room in this piece to explore this issue in detail, but simply let me make reference to newspaper and magazine fashion shots and recent television advertisements—for example, ads for Volkswagen cars, Yoplait yogurt, and Kodak Gold film. All present the highly eroticized alluring little girl, often (at least in all three TV ads) with fair hair and ringlets, usually made up and with a look that seductively returns the gaze of the camera. Indeed, such shots bear far more similarity to images taken from child pornography than they do to psychoeducational images. However, the popular advertisement and fashion images are ubiquitous: they are an everyday part of our culture and have certainly not been equated with child pornography.

It would not be difficult to make a case that such images are the soft porn of child pornography and that they exploit childhood by introducing adult sexuality into childhood innocence. In that sense they could be understood as the precursor to child sexual abuse in the way that pornography has been understood by some feminists as the precursor to rape. However, I feel that such an interpretation is oversimplistic. The eroticization of little girls is a complex phenomenon, one in which a certain aspect of feminine sexuality and childhood sexuality is understood as corrupting of an innocent state. The blame is laid both on abuse—and therefore pathological and bad men who enter and sully the terrain of childhood innocence—and on the little Lolitas who lead men on. But popular images of little girls as alluring and seductive, at once innocent and highly erotic, are contained in the most

154

respectable and mundane of locations: broadsheet newspapers, women's magazines, television advertisements. The phenomenon that we are talking about therefore has to be far more pervasive than the approach that some men are rotten apples, pathological and abusive. This is not about a few perverts but about the complex construction of the highly contradictory gaze at little girls, one that places them as at once threatening and sustaining rationality, little virgins that might be whores, to be protected yet to be constantly alluring. The complexity of this phenomenon, in terms of both the cultural production of little girls as these ambivalent objects and the way in which little girls themselves as well as adults live this complexity, how it produces their subjectivity, has not begun to be explored.

Eroticized femininity and the working-class girl

Let us return to Janie and her clandestine singing. I have been at some pains to point out that Janie presents to the public world of the classroom the face of hardworking diligent femininity, which, while pathologized, is still desired. She reserves the less-acceptable face of feminity for more private spaces. I imagine her dancing as she sings in front of the mirror, which can be understood as an acting out, a fantasizing of the possibility of being someone and something else. I want to draw attention to the contradictions in the way in which the eroticized child-woman is a position presented publicly for the little girl to enter but simultaneously treated as a position that removes childhood innocence, allows entry of the whore, and makes the girl vulnerable to abuse. The entry of popular culture into the educational and family life of the little girl is therefore to be viewed with suspicion, as a threat posed by the lowering of standards, of the intrusion of the low against the superior high culture. It is the consumption of popular culture that is taken as making the little working-class girl understood as potentially more at risk of being victim and perpetrator. Janie's fantasy dirties the sanitary space of the classroom. But what is Janie's fantasy and at the intersection of which complex fantasies is she inscribed? I want to explore some of the popular fictions about the little working-class girl and to present the way in which the eroticization presents for her the possibility of a different and better life, of which she is often presented as the carrier. The keeping at bay of sexuality as intruding upon innocent childhood is in sharp contrast to this.

There have been a number of cinematic depictions of young girls as capable of producing a transformation in their own and others' lives, from Judy Garland in *The Wizard of Oz*, through Shirley Temple, *Gigi*, and *My Fair Lady*, to (orphan) *Annie*. In the majority of these films the transformation effected relates to class and to money through the intervention of a lovable little girl. Charles Eckert (1991) argued that Shirley Temple was often portrayed as an orphan in the depression whose role was to soften the hearts of the wealthy such that they would identify her as one of the poor, not dirty and radical, but lovable, to become the object of charity through their donations. In a similar way, Annie is presented as an orphan for whom being working class is the isolation of a poor little girl, with no home, no parents, no community. She too has to soften the heart of the armaments millionaire, Daddy Warbucks, making him soften at the edges, as well as find her own happiness through dint of her lovable personality. It is by this means that she secures for herself a future in a wealthy family, which she creates by bringing Daddy Warbucks and his secretary, Grace, together. By concentrating on these two characters alone it is possible to envisage that the little working-class girl is the object of massive projections. She is a figure of immense transformative power who can make the rich love, thereby solving huge social and political problems, and she can immeasurably improve her own life in the process. At the same time she presents the face of a class turned underclass, ragged, disorganized, orphaned, for whom there is only one way out: embourgeoisement. Thus she becomes the epitome of the feminized and therefore emasculated, less threatening, proletariat. In addition to this, Graham Greene pointed to something unmentioned in the tales of innocent allure: the sexual coquettishness of Shirley Temple. His pointing to her pedophilic eroticization led to the closure of *Night and Day*, the magazine he edited, after it was sued for libel.

What does the current figure of the eroticized little girl hold? What fantasies are projected onto her and how do these fantasies interact with the fantasy scenarios little working-class girls create for themselves and their lives? If she is simultaneously holding so much that is understood as both good and bad, no wonder actual little girls might find their situation overwhelming. It would be easy to classify Janie and other girls' private eroticization as resistance to the position accorded to her at school and in high culture, but I hope that I have demonstrated that this would be hopelessly simplistic.

Fantasies of seduction

Let us see then what psychoanalysis has had to say about seduction and the eroticization of little girls. It is easy to pinpoint Freud's seduction theory and his account of an autoerotic childhood sexuality. We might also point to the place of the critiques of the seduction theory in the accusation that psychoanalysis has ignored child abuse, the raising of the specter of abuse, as a widespread phenomenon and the recent attacks on therapists for producing false memories of abuses that never happened in their clients. In this sense then, the issue of little girls and sexuality can be seen as a minefield of claim and counterclaim focusing on the issue of fantasy, memory, and reality. If one wants therefore to examine sexuality and little girls as a cultural phenomenon, one is confronted by a denial of cultural processes: either little girls have a sexuality that is derived from their fantasies of seduction by their fathers or they are innocent of sexuality, which is imposed upon them from the outside by pathological or evil men who seduce, abuse, and rape them. Culturally, we are left with a stark choice: sexuality in little girls is natural, universal, and inevitable; or, a kind of male gaze is at work in which the little girl is produced as object of an adult male gaze. She has no fantasies of her own, and to paraphrase Lacan we could say that "the little girl does not exist except as symptom and myth of the masculine imaginary." Or, in the mold of the Women Against Violence Against Women approach of "porn is the theory, rape is the practice," we might conclude that popular representations of eroticized little girls is the theory and child sexual abuse is the practice. Girls' fantasies prove a problem in all these accounts because only Freud credited them with any of their own, although he made it clear that, like others working on psychopathology at the time, feminine sexuality was the central enigma. Indeed his main question was, What does the woman, the little girl, want? A question to which Jacqueline Rose in her introduction to Lacanian writing on feminine sexuality (1985) asserts that "all answers, including the mother are false: she simply wants." So little girls have a desire without an object, a desire that must float in space, unable to find an object, indeed to be colonized by masculine fantasies, which create female desire in their own image. Of course, Laura Mulvey's original 1974 work on the male cinematic gaze has been much revised and criticized (e.g., Screen, 1992), but critics have tended to ignore the complex production of subjectivity.

Let us return to the psychoanalytic arguments about sexuality. Laplanche and Pontalis (1985) discuss seduction in terms of "seduction into the fantasies of the parents." Those fantasies can be understood in terms of the complex intertwining of parental histories and the regimes of truth, the cultural fantasies that circulate in the social. This may sound like a theory of socialization, but socialization implies the learning of roles and the taking on of stereotypes. What we have here is a complex interweaving of the many kinds of fantasy, both "social" in the terms of Geraghty (1991) and others and psychic, as phantasy in the classic psychoanalytic sense (in psychoanalysis it is spelled with a "ph"). Lacan, of course, argued that the symbolic system carried social fantasies that were psychic in origin, an argument he made by recourse to structuralist principles from de Saussure and Lévi-Strauss. However, it is possible to understand the complexity in terms that conceive of the psychic/social relation as produced not in ahistorical and universal categories but in historically specific regimes of meaning and truth (Henriques et al., 1998).

However, what Freud did argue for was what he called a "childhood sexuality." What he meant was that the bodily sensations experienced by the baby could be very pleasurable but this pleasure was, of course, always crosscut by pain, a presence marked by the absence of the caregiver, usually the mother. In this context little children could learn in an omnipotent way that they too could give these pleasurable sensations to themselves, just as they learned, according to Freud's famous example of the cotton reel game, that in fantasy they could control the presence and absence of the mother. So for Freud there is no tabula rasa, no innocent child. The child's first senses of pleasure are already marked by the phantasies inherent in the presence and absence of the Other. However, as Laplanche and Pontalis (1985) point out, the infantile sexuality, marked by an "infantile language of tenderness," is crosscut by the introduction of an adult "language," the language of passion. "This is the language of desire, necessarily marked by prohibition, a language of guilt and hatred, including the sense of orgastic pleasure" (p. 226). How far does this view take us down the road of sorting out the problems associated with models of childhood innocence?

The model suggests that there are two kinds of sexuality: an infant one about bodily pleasures and an adult one that imposes a series of other meanings upon those pleasures. We should note here that Laplanche and Pontalis do go as far as implying that not all of the fantasy is on the side of the child but that the parents impose some of their own. The sexuality would then develop in terms of the admixture of the two, in all its psychic complexity. Let me illustrate that briefly by making reference to a previous study of mine (Walkerdine, 1985) in which I discussed my own father's nickname for me: Tinky, short for Tinkerbell. I was reminded of my nickname by a father, Mr. Cole, whose nickname for his six-year-old daughter, Joanne, was Dodo. I argued that Tinky and Dodo were fathers' fantasies about their daughters: a fairy with diminutive size but incredible powers on the one hand and a preserved baby name (Dodo, as a childish mispronunciation of JoJo) on the other. But a dodo is also an extinct bird, or for Mr. Cole, that aspect of extinction that is preserved in his fantasy relationship with his daughter as a baby. Joanne is no longer a baby; babyhood—like the dodo—has gone, but it is preserved in the fantasy of Mr. Cole's special nickname for his daughter, and in so designating her, he structures the relationship between them: she remains his baby.

In the case of my own father's fantasy, Tinky signified for me the most potent aspect of my specialness for him. I associated it with a photograph of myself aged three winning a local fancy dress competition, dressed as a bluebell fairy. This is where I won and "won him over": my fairy charms reciprocated his fantasy of me, designating me "his girl" and fueling my oedipal fantasies. But I am trying to demonstrate that those fantasies are not one-sided on either the parent's or the little girl's side but, as the Tinky example illustrates, that the "language of adult desire" is entirely cultural. Tinkerbell and bluebell fairies are cultural phenomena that can be examined in terms of their semiotics and their historical emergence as well as their production and consumption. My father did not invent Tinkerbell or the bluebell fairy; rather he used what were available cultural fantasies to name something about his deep and complex feelings for his daughter. In return, I, his daughter, took those fantasies to my heart and my unconscious, making them my own. Of course it could be argued that this sails very close to Laura Mulvey's original position, following Lacan, that woman (the little girl) does not exist (or have fantasies that originate with her) except as symptom and myth of male fantasy. But I am attempting to demonstrate that a position that suggests that fantasies come only from the adult male is far too simplistic. My father might have imposed Tinkerbell on me but my own feelings for my father had their own role to play.

I want to argue that the culture carries these adult fantasies, creates vehicles for them. It carries the transformation of this into a projection onto children of the adult language of desire. In this view the little seductress is a complex phenomenon that carries adult sexual desire but also hooks into the equally complex fantasies carried by the little girl herself. The idea of a sanitized natural childhood in which such things are kept at bay, having no place in childhood, becomes not the guarantor of the safety of children from the perversity of adult desires for them but a huge defense against the acknowledgement of dangerous desires on the part of adults. In this analysis, "child protection" begins to look more like adult protection.

It is here then that I want to make a distinction between seduction and abuse. Fantasies of Tinky and Dodo were enticing, seductive, but they were not abuse. To argue that they were is to make something very simplistic out of something immensely complex.

As long as seduction is subsumed under a discourse of abuse, issues of "seduction into the fantasies of the parents" are hidden under a view that suggests that adult sexual fantasies about children are held only by perverts who can be kept at bay by keeping children safe and childhood innocent. But if childhood innocence is really an adult defense, adult fantasies about children and the eroticization of little girls is not a problem about a minority of perverts from whom the normal general public should be protected. It is about massive fantasies carried in the culture, fantasies that are equally massively defended against by other cultural practices, in the form of the psychopedagogic and social welfare practices incorporating discourses of childhood innocence. This is not to suggest that children are not to be protected. Far from it. Rather, my argument is that a central issue of adult sexual projections onto children is not being addressed.

So the issue of fantasy and the eroticization of little girls within popular culture becomes a complex phenomenon in which cultural fantasies, fantasies of the parents, and little girls' oedipal fantasies mix and are given a cultural form that shapes them. Laplanche and Pontalis (1985) argue that fantasy is the setting for desire, "but as for knowing who is responsible for the setting, it is not enough for the psychoanalyst to rely on the resources of his (sic) science, nor on the support of myth. He (sic) must become a philosopher!" (p. 17). In poststructuralist terms this would take us into the domain of the production of knowledges about children and the production of the ethical subject. I want to explore lastly this latter connection by suggesting several courses of action and to examine briefly the issue through a specific example of a "moral panic" about popular culture and the eroticization of children.

Minipops

I want to end by examining briefly the case of *Minipops*, a series transmitted on Channel Four television in 1983. The series presented young children, boys and girls, white and black, singing current pop songs, dressed up and heavily made up. This series became the object of what was described as a moral panic. The stated intention of the director was to present a showcase of new talent, the idea having come from his daughter, who liked to dress up and sing pop songs at home. The furor caused by the programs was entirely voiced by the middle classes. The broadsheet papers demanded the axing of the series on the grounds that it presented a sexuality that spoiled and intruded into an innocent childhood. One critic wrote of "lashings of lipstick on mini mouths" (*Sunday Times*, 1983). By contrast, the tabloids loved the series. For them, the programs represented a chance for young children to be talent spotted, to find fame. There was no mention of the erosion of innocence. Why this difference? It would be easy to imagine that the tabloids were more exploitative, less concerned with issues of sexual exploitation so rampant in their own pages, with the broadsheets as upholders of everything that is morally good. However, I think that this conclusion would be erroneous. While I deal with this argument in more detail elsewhere (Walkerdine, 1997), let me point out here that I have argued that the eroticized little girl presents a fantasy of Otherness to the little working-class girl. She is inscribed as one who can make a transformation, which is also a self-transformation, which is also a seductive allure. It is not surprising therefore that the tabloid discourse is about talent, discovery, fame: all the elements of the necessary transformation from rags to riches, from flower girl to princess, so to speak. Such a transformation is necessarily no part of middle-class discourse, fantasy, and aspiration. Rather, childhood for the middle class is a state to be preserved, free from economic intrusion and producing the possibility of the rational and playful child who will become a rational, educated professional, a member of the "new middle class."

Seduction and the eroticization of little girls are complex cultural phenomena. I have tried to demonstrate that the place of the little working-class girl is important because her seductiveness has an important role to play in terms of both a social and personal transformation, a transformation that is glimpsed in the fantasies of fame embodied in series like *Minipops*. The figure of the little working-class girl then simultaneously holds transformation of an emasculated working class into lovable citizens and the fear against which the fantasy defends. This is the little Lolita: the whore, the contagion of the masses that will endanger the safety of the bourgeois order. On the other hand, child protection as the outlawing of perversion and preservation of a safe space for innocent childhood can also be viewed as class specific and is indeed the fantasy of the safe space that has not been invaded by the evil masses.

I have tried to place an understanding of unconscious processes inside of all of this because, as I hope that I have demonstrated, psychic processes form a central component of how social and cultural fantasies work. Some may argue that my recourse to psychoanalysis presents such psychic processes as universal and inevitable but I have tried to show the social and the psychic merge together to form any particular fantasies at a specific moment. This is only a very small beginning that may help to sort out how we might approach a hugely important topic that has been badly neglected.

Conclusion

Let us return then to the notion of public and private space. How are the current imaginaries about the child and the adult related to a regeneration of childhood and the positions of children in postmodernity? With the example of the eroticization of young girls, I have tried to show just what might be at stake inside the concerns about child safety in public and private spaces, that is, questions about adult male sexuality and the place of that desire. It is clear that we need to rethink our approach to the study of childhood to encompass an understanding of the specificity through which children become subjected in the practices of postmodernity, in which we can understand a post-Enlightenment discourse of nature and natural rationality as one of the current fictions that functions in truth. The threat posed by the breaking apart of this fiction becomes a different problem than the one envisaged as simply about moving to a new space—in this case, cyberspace—in which development may still be properly accomplished by the isolated protorational boy. Might we therefore begin to examine what kinds of subjects and subjectivities are created in relation to popular media? What are the ways in which such discourses and practices prepare children for the world beyond the screen? The male figures of the rational middle-class explorer and the protoviolent and addicted working-class boy, the well-behaved protomother and the little working-class seductress certainly exist not only as subject positions but are constantly created as modes of subjectivity within the practices of game playing. These are neither ahistorical nor transcultural figures but quite specific to the time and place that produces them. They are also replete with the fears, phobias, and fetishes of late twentieth-century Western cities. How might we begin to explore the situated production of all subjectivities of the world's children as they face the huge differences confronting the new millennium? It is not only our approach to the understanding of space, of popular culture that must change but our approach to the issue of childhood itself.

Rationality and its Others—irrationality, madness, criminality, sexual perversion—are popularly understood as the effects of success or failure of sexual perversion or similarly the result of simplistic ideas about the effects of the media upon that socialization. If we are to begin to construct both alternative kinds of accounts and to intervene differently in work with children, we must take seriously the simple pathologization that is rooted in the long-established practices of regulation of the poor and the masses. In these modes of regulation, adult pathology is expressed mostly by those who were poorly socialized as children. This prohibits our gaze toward something else, that is, the way in which the practices of pathologization sit so neatly alongside those very discourses and practices in which the eroticization of little girls is commonplace and the Internet explorer one of today's anarcho-heroes. If we begin to interrogate both what is spoken and the way it sits so neatly alongside that which receives no comment, we may be able to approach the complexities of explanation and intervention in childhood in a different kind of way.

References

Best, J. (1990). Threatened children: Rhetoric and concern about child victims. Chicago: University of Chicago Press.

Bhabha, H. (1984). The other question: The stereotype in colonial discourse. *Screen, 24*, pp. 18–36.

Blackman, L. (1996). The masses: Retelling the psychiatric story, *Feminism and Psychology, 6*, (3), pp. 361–79. Special Issue on Class.

Buckingham, D. (1991). *Intruder in the house.* Fourth International Television Studies Conference, London.

Cole, M. *et al.* (1971). *The cultural context of learning and thinking.* New York: Basic Books.

Deleuze, G., & Guattari, F. (1987). *A thousand plateaux.* Minneapolis: University of Minnesota Press.

Eckert, C. (1991). Shirley Temple and the house of Rockefeller. In C. Gledhill (Ed.), *Stardom* (pp. 39–50). London: Routledge.

Foucault, M. (1977). *Discipline and punish.* Harmondsworth: Penguin.

Fuller, M., & Jenkins, H. (1998). Nintendo and new world travel writing. In S. Jones (Ed.), *Cybersociety* (pp. 55–70). Thousand Oaks, CA: Sage.

Geraghty, C. (1991). *Women and soap opera.* Oxford, UK: Polity.

Greene, G. (1980). *The pleasure dome: The collected film criticism, 1935–40, (of) Graham Greene.* J. R. Taylor (Ed.), Oxford: Oxford University Press.

Henriques, J., Hollway W., Urwin, C., Venn, C., & Walkerdine, V. (1998). *Changing the subject: Psychology, social regulation and subjectivity.* London: Routledge.

Himmelweit, H., Oppenheim, A., and Vince, P. (1958). *Television and the Child.* London: Oxford University Press.

Jenkins, R. (1992). *Intimate enemies: Moral panics in contemporary Great Britain.* New York: Aldine de Gruyter.

Laplanche, J., & Pontalis, J. B. (1985). Fantasy and the origins of sexuality. In V. Burgin, J. Donald, & C. Kaplan, *Formations of fantasy* (pp. 76–95). London: Routledge.

Le Bon, G. (1895/1968). *The crowd.* Dunwoody, GA: N. S. Berg.

McRobbie, A. (1979). Settling accounts with subcultures. *Screen Education, 34,* pp. 17–28.

Mulvey, L. (1974). Visual pleasure and narrative cinema. *Screen, 16,* (3), pp. 55–68.

Newson, E. (1994). Video violence and the protection of children. University of Nottingham Child Development Research Unit.

Piaget, J. (1967). *The child's conception of space.* New York: W. W. Norton.

Pini, N., & Walkerdine, V. (forthcoming). *Girls on film: New visible fictions of femininity.*

Postman, N. (1994). *The disappearance of childhood.* New York: Vintage Books.

Rose, J. (1985). *Peter Pan or the impossibility of children's fiction.* London: Macmillan.

Rose, J. (1985). Introduction. In J. Mitchell & J. Rose (Eds.), *Jacques Lacan and the Ecole Freudienne Feminine Sexuality* (pp. 1–58). London: Macmillan.

Screen (1992). *The sexual subject.* London: Routledge.

Sunday Times (1983, March 13). P. 36.

Tarde, G. (1890). *La Criminalité.* Paris: F. Alcan.

Urwin, C. (1995). Teenage mutant ninja turtles. In C. Bazalgette & D. Buckingham (Eds.), *Not in front of the children* (pp. 35–51). London: BFI.

Walkerdine, V. (1984/1998). Developmental psychology and the child centred pedagogy. In J. Henriques, W. Hollway, C. Urwin, C. Venn, & V. Walkerdine, *Changing the subject: Psychology, social regulation and subjectivity* (pp. 153–202). London: Routledge.

Walkerdine, V. (1985). Video replay. In V. Burgin, J. Donald, & C. Kaplan, *Formations of fantasy* (pp. 105–47). London: Routledge.

Walkerdine, V. (1988/1990). *The mastery of reason.* London: Routledge.

Walkerdine, V. (1989). *Counting girls out.* London: Virago.

Walkerdine, V. (1992). *Reasoning in a post-modern age.* Fifth International Conference on Thinking, Townsville, Australia.

Walkerdine, V. (1993). Beyond developmentalism. *Theory and Psychology, 3,* 4, 451–69.

Walkerdine, V. (1997). *Young girls and popular culture.* London: Macmillan; Cambridge, MA: Harvard University Press.

Walkerdine, V., & Lucey, H. (1989). *Democracy in the kitchen: Regulating mothers and socialising daughters.* London: Virago.

54

WHEN CHILDREN
KILL CHILDREN

The search for justice

Stewart Asquith

Source: *Childhood* 3(1) (1996): 99–116.

Children who kill children

The reported murders of young children by other children in a number of countries in recent years have prompted extensive discussion and debate. The main purpose of this article is to examine critically some of the key issues raised by such cases, and in particular the Bulger case in the United Kingdom, in the light of general comments about some of the current European developments in juvenile justice. The merit of adopting a European perspective is that it allows for some of the key ethical and legal concerns to be addressed in the pursuit of justice for the children involved and to articulate their relevance for our understanding of childhood, and the relationship between children, families and the state.

Though the issues surrounding the murders of children are complex, some of the questions posed by it are in fact very simple and must include consideration of the following: At what age should children be held criminally responsible? What explanations of criminal behaviour by young children are acceptable and what implications do they have for the pursuit of justice? Just how are we to deal with children who commit serious offences? How might offence behaviour by young children be prevented? What theories or constructions of childhood are implicit in the currently available models of justice for children?[1]

The Bulger case

In 1993 in England,[2] the death of the toddler James Bulger at the hands of two other young children provoked considerable public reaction when the details of what proved to be a particularly horrific murder were made known. Scenes outside the court where the two accused boys were being tried reflected clearly the level of feelings aroused by the case and many of us who are parents experienced a conflict of emotions — disbelief and horror at what happened to a toddler who had been with his mother in a public shopping environment familiar throughout Britain and a lack of comprehension at just what motivation and factors could induce two 10-year-old children to abduct, murder and mutilate a young child.

James Bulger had been taken away by the two boys from a shopping centre where he had been with his mother and despite the cries and protest he had displayed in front of many bystanders, no one had intervened to prevent the abduction from taking place — a fact many of the adult witnesses in the subsequent trial were to state as a cause of great regret. The fact also that the three boys were recorded in the shopping centre on a security video camera, later to be relayed round Britain on television, served at the same time to validate for some the use of surveillance cameras in public places. For others, it did little more than amplify the disbelief that such a public abduction could take place with no adults intervening to assist a young child in what, for many of them with hindsight, was apparent distress.

Taken to a railway line some distance from the shopping centre, James was repeatedly beaten and his body lain across the railway track to be found on 14 February 1993. The case provoked immense public and political reaction, with members of the police force involved expressing disbelief at the horrific nature of what had been done by two children (*The Independent*, 13 February 1994); extensive media coverage and the 'evil' portrayal of the two young boys; and, especially outside the courtroom where the boys were to appear, a public display of anger, demands for vengeance and near riot behaviour.

In terms of how to deal with the two boys who were, at the time of the offence, 10 years old, the parents of James Bulger initiated a campaign committed to life imprisonment for the murderers of their son. The Prime Minister, John Major, was also himself to say that more condemnation and less understanding was to be shown to such criminal acts, a position which very neatly fitted the stance taken by the Home Secretary, Michael Howard, more generally in promoting severe punishment for young offenders. Even as late as November 1994, Michael Howard was being challenged in the European Court on Human Rights about his decision to keep the murderers of James Bulger in custody indefinitely. The challenge had been made in terms of the right of every individual up to the age of 18 to have his or her case reviewed annually. In this way the Bulger case was also seen to raise broader questions of sovereignty in as much as concern was expressed once again at the way in which nation-states were subject to European law.

All in all, the Bulger case is one which has had dramatic reverberations in the United Kingdom, in a variety of policy and political areas. The case has forced discussion and debate on the nature of childhood; the role of parents; the role of the state in dealing with children who offend; the age of criminal responsibility; and most sharply, the nature of the justice afforded to children who do wrong.

In many respects, the Bulger case, and others like it, provide a barometer for the way in which a society views its children, the competencies we ascribe to children and the status we give to childhood. It is the more serious and horrific cases which present a site at which intersect very different modes of thinking about and conceiving of childhood, whether professional or lay. Indeed it could be argued that such cases blur the distinction between public and professional notions of childhood and justice for children, precisely because they challenge cherished assumptions about children at a time when there is an absence of clearly defined alternatives to put in their place — such is the postmodernist legacy.

But the Bulger case, dramatic as it was, is not the only such case involving children murdering children, as over the past 2 years a number of such cases have been reported in a number of countries. Shortly after the Bulger case in England, a 10-year-old girl in Scotland was charged with trying to smother a baby with a pillow. In the USA reports have appeared of what has been referred to as a 'revenge killing by a three year old' in which a 12-year-old confessed to murder when she was herself 3 years old, by drowning, of her 1-year-old cousin (Cleland, 1994). In Budapest, Hungary, two boys aged 13 and 14 were held on suspicion of killing a 9-year-old boy from an orphanage by binding him and then beating him to death (Reuters. 1994). More recently in England, a case has been reported of a 14-year-old girl who stabbed her classmate in the school playground (*Sunday Mail*, 13 November 1994)[3] and also a case of the murder of a 6-year-old boy involving an 11- or 12-year-old suspect (Harris, 1994).

Culture and explanation

But the case which has most similarities with the Bulger case is that of the death of 5-year-old Silje Marie Redergard in Trondheim, Norway, who froze to death in a school playground after a game with three boys (one aged 6 and the other two aged 5) (*Glasgow Herald*, 1994).[4] The case of little Silje has brought the discussions and debates about the Bulger case to centre stage once again. Some of the similarities were striking between the English and Norwegian cases, in particular, the way in which attention was focused on the extent to which TV programmes or videos with violent content had influenced the behaviour of the children. In the case of James Bulger, the video *Child Play III* was seen to be a contributing factor and the whole affair led to an inquiry into the effects of violence in the media on children's behaviour. In the case of Silje Redergard in Norway, TV programmes such as *Power Rangers, Ninja Turtles* or other imported American programmes were the focus of attention, at the highest political level. The Norwegian Prime Minister, Gro Harlem Brundtland, had also stated that 'Norwegians might have to think twice before allowing such "free market" violence to be broadcast by commercial networks' and that 'violence on the screen [could] possibly become violence on the retinas of even small children' (*Glasgow Herald*, 1994). Not long after, broadcasts of *Power Rangers* to Norway, Sweden and Denmark were suspended. The ultimate irony is that a few weeks after Silje's death in Norway, the *Power Rangers* characters almost had a number one hit record in the British musical charts with a song based on the show. What this surely illustrates is the way in which social, cultural and even historical differences in the explanations of childhood behaviour have to be taken into consideration in any analysis of such 'hard' cases as the Bulger and Redergard deaths.

This is particularly so when the striking difference in public and political responses to the children responsible for the deaths in the two countries is included in the analysis. In England, the general reaction was one in which the two 10-year-olds were characterized as evil, meriting severe punishment including being locked up in prison for life. As noted above, the parents of James Bulger themselves have also actively campaigned for their son's murderers to never be released. This contrasts sharply with what appears to be a very different Norwegian reaction where 'no one, not even Silje's mother, seems to blame the boys' (*Glasgow Herald*, 1994). In fact Beathe Redergard (Silje's mother), in publicly stating that 'I forgive the ones who killed my daughter. It is not possible to hate small children. They can't understand the consequences of what they have done' at one and the same time neatly crystallized one of the key issues — that of criminal responsibility. The issue of criminal responsibility is one which differentiates the United Kingdom from the rest of Europe as we discuss later, and which surely underpins the great differences in the pursuit of justice for children throughout Europe.

What further investigation of public attitudes to the Bulger case reveal is sharp contrast in views about how to deal with the two 10-year-olds, ranging from hanging and life imprisonment to more liberal measures designed to offer them care, support, guidance and counselling. Similarly, discussion quickly focused on the role played by parents, and the whole issue of the contribution of poor or inadequate parenting to crime and delinquency entered the public domain. Further, a number of commentators alluded to the 'the end of childhood' (Levy, 1994); 'the killing of innocence' (Pilkington, 1994); and, reflecting a common reaction to the assumed dangers of extending rights to children the 'growing uncertainty about the parameters of childhood and a mounting terror of the anarchy and uncontrollability of unfettered youth' (Pilkington, 1994). Pilkington also asserts that if the public demand for vengeance and even the hanging of the two boys who had murdered James Bulger were to be satisfied, 'we may be in danger of murdering childhood itself'. There are echoes of the work of Postman (1982) and others.

The social construction of childhood

It is clearly not the case that the end of childhood is nigh. Rather, how a society constructs childhood, its children and the nature of adult–child relations is clearly in transition. As Shamgar-Handelman puts it, rather more succinctly, childhood

> . . . is a social invention, no matter what form it may take, so that claims of 'the erosion of childhood' (Suransky, 1982) or of the liquidation of childhood (Hengst, 1987) or the need to 'escape from childhood' (Holt, 1974) mean only that the pattern of childhood, its boundaries or determinants, have aroused the disapproval of one or another observer.
>
> (Shamgar-Handelman, 1994: 252)

What the Bulger, Redergard and other cases, tragic as they are, alert us to is the malleability of childhood as a social construct, both from a historical and comparative cultural perspective, in which theories of childhood, the process of socialization and the relationship between the generations cannot be divorced from the structural makeup of society in general. Similarly, the relationship between how we speak of childhood has to be related to societal structures. Both sides of the relationship have to be taken into consideration for, as Boswell argues in his work on the abandonment of children throughout the ages, the analyst has to recognize that

> . . . two sets of problems overlap: the semantic variability of terms for children and childhood, and historical changes in social structures and expectations regarding both. Each deserves a separate study although they cannot be treated adequately in isolation.
>
> (Boswell, 1988: 27)

Precisely the same concerns prompt a more formal appraisal of the implications of the James Bulger case for the philosophy, policy and practice underpinning systems of justice for children and young people who commit offences, not only in the United Kingdom but also further afield in the international community. What followed were public debates about the need for more severe measures for dealing with children who commit serious offences, including what can be referred to as the 'constancies' of delinquency control rhetoric such as the need to bring back the birch, the short, sharp, shock, detention centres and a generally more punitive and severe response to the criminal acts of young child offenders. Similarly, and part of the backlash against the perceived inadequacies and failings of a more liberal approach to dealing with child offenders, the role of parents in failing to inhibit delinquent behaviour in their children through poor parenting was targeted.

The Norwegian reaction to the Redergard case does appear to have been very different from the English in being more liberal and supportive of the children involved. Nevertheless, both cases raise important issues about the very conceptual foundations on which major social institutions rest.

> Childhood is the life-space which our culture limits it to be i.e. its definitions through the courts, the school, the family, the economy and also through psychology and philosophy. But this is only part of the dialectics.
>
> (Qvortrup, 1994: 3)

In a sense, the notion of childhood is not simply defined or constituted by the courts, the school and our other social institutions. The relationship is indeed more dialectical than that, as the courts, the school and so on are themselves constituted by the very notion of childhood itself. Thus, if we are going through a period of reformulation of childhood, the process necessitates a fundamental, not an incremental, reappraisal of the very basis of the institutions which impact on the lives of children. The questioning of just what childhood is, prompted by the cases in question, merges neatly with current attempts in the international community to address the need for radical change in juvenile justice systems. In fact taking this one step further, such cases have forced adults to reassess the very notion of justice in its application to children who offend and in particular those who commit serious offences resulting in the death of other children.

The implication of the Bulger case in terms of seeking justice for children is that a balance has to be struck somehow in achieving justice for the death of a young child with the justice of the treatment meted out to the children who committed the murder. In terms of systems of criminal justice a number of alternative conceptions of justice in relation to young offenders are being deployed including 'restorative justice' (Walgrave, 1994) and 'la justice reparatrice' (Gazeau and Peyre, 1994). But cases such as the Bulger case have also led to consideration being given to the significance of 'distributive' or 'social justice' in terms of the distribution of life opportunities for children and their families, especially where structural social inequality and injustice are seen to contribute to society's ills including crime and delinquency (Report of the Commission on Social Justice, 1994).

LIVERPOOL
JOHN MOORES UNIVERSITY
AVRIL ROBARTS LRC
TEL. 0151 231 4022

Children who commit offences

Any system of justice for children has to be seen in the context of the social, political and economic climate in which it is located. Over the past two decades there have been important shifts in political ideology (some of which do not fit easily with a system of justice for children based on welfare principles); there have been significant changes in social work thinking about how to deal with children; the economic situation has changed considerably; there have been a number of dramatic occurrences involving the deaths of children, some of whom have actually been in care; child and sexual abuse have been 'discovered' (see Qvortrup, 1994); and, with the ratification of the United Nations Convention on the Rights of the Child by a number of countries, the very citizenship status of children and their rights are now firmly located on the political agenda. The Bulger case is remarkable in the way in which it touches on almost all of these areas, prompting a consideration not just of criminal policy as it relates to the young but also of other areas more traditionally associated with broader social policy concerns — parenting, childcare, poverty, social injustice and so on.

In referring to the alleged failure of welfare approaches to dealing with offenders, and suggesting that we should 'condemn more and understand less' (see earlier), the British Prime Minister, John Major, was implying that too much attention had been paid to identifying the factors which are used to account for criminal behaviour, whether by children or adults, and that more effort should be devoted to sanctioning offenders for what they have done. In this respect, what he had to say reflects a clear divergence between two basic ideologies of delinquency and crime control.

One might simply be called the 'justice' model in which offenders are seen to be responsible for what they have done, should be dealt with in a court of criminal law and can rightly be considered worthy of punishment. The other, again put rather simply, is the 'welfare' model in which offenders are necessarily viewed as responsible for what they have done (their behaviour explicable by individual or social factors), need not be dealt with in a court of criminal law, and should be dealt with by measures designed to promote their welfare or interests.

The James Bulger case had a considerable impact on discussions about future developments in delinquency control throughout Europe, including eastern Europe.[5] In particular, it gets to the very heart of the issue of just how to deal with those very young offenders who commit serious offences and tends to polarize 'welfare' and 'justice' philosophies and the conception of children as vulnerable and in need of care or as responsible and appropriate subjects of punishment. Nor was the English reaction unique, as Bourquin (1994) points out in commenting on the dilemma posed by the Bulger case for French commentators.

170

That this is not just a matter of purely academic concern is clear as illustrated by a reading of developments in the United Kingdom and throughout Europe, where most countries are currently reviewing their systems of justice for children along the dimension of the 'justice' and 'welfare' models (Dunkel, 1991). In relation to the United Kingdom, it has to be remembered that there are great institutional differences between Scotland and England, where juvenile justice, education and law are based on very different principles. With specific reference to crime and delinquency, most children in Scotland are dealt with by what is known as the Children's Hearings system (see Asquith, forthcoming) based on a philosophy of welfare where the decision as to how to deal with children who commit offences is made in reference not to the offence but, rather, to the child's need for compulsory measures of care. The comments made by the Prime Minister challenged the basic philosophy of the Scottish Children's Hearings system, and reinforced the obligation on analysts to locate any understanding of how children are conceived of and, in the case of children who offend, dealt with in a social, cultural and historical context.

But even in Scotland, children who commit serious offences may be dealt with in the criminal courts. And, throughout Europe, the general trend in relation to children who commit offences is best characterized as the 'twin track approach'. By this is meant that for the majority of children, punishment and judicial proceedings are seen to be inappropriate. For the minority of serious or persistent offenders, judicial intervention and punitive measures may be imposed.

Crime and delinquency in Europe

The danger of cases such as the Bulger case is that they are presented as an example of a general trend. Nothing could be further from the truth in relation to trends in crime and delinquency throughout Europe over the past 30 years or so (Junger-Tas, 1991). Since the end of the Second World War and until virtually the end of the 1980s, there had been a steady increase in the numbers of crimes and offences committed. But in relation to children and young offenders, the increase had been at a faster rate of growth. What even a cursory examination of the statistics available reveal is that:

- boys are largely responsible for delinquent and offending behaviour;
- girls are relatively invisible in the crime statistics (though there is recent evidence to suggest that they are increasingly becoming involved in fraud and drug-related offences);
- the increase in crime statistics relating to children and young people is accounted for largely by offences against property, mainly theft and damage (theft of cars has become a major preoccupation of young offenders throughout Europe);

- there is a small but increasing proportion of offences by children and young people involving violence against the person; and
- the age of peak offending has increased and now stands at around 16 or 17 in most European countries.

The main point to make here is that in comparison to the vast majority of cases, the Bulger, Redergard and other cases, serious and significant though they may be, are nevertheless atypical. Developments throughout Europe have to be seen against a backcloth of a small but increasing proportion of serious offences committed by young offenders, of a general involvement of young people in relatively less serious offences involving theft and a small but increasing proportion of female offenders. This is, of course, a gross oversimplification but it does highlight the general concerns expressed in most European countries and illustrates clearly the 'twin track approach'.

But as is clear in this and other policy areas involving children, the danger is that it is the atypical case which drives the movement for radical change in policy and practice. This is not to suggest that the Bulger case is not important and that it does not raise important issues. It does suggest however that the measures adopted for the majority of cases involving child offenders (who are involved in less serious offences) may well have to be different from those which are employed against the more serious offenders. It does not, however, resolve the difficulty of deciding upon how best, or justly, to deal with young children who commit serious offences.

Nevertheless, the Bulger case does put into focus the difficulties in seeking to devise a just system of treatment, or punishment for that matter, for child offenders and a number of issues have to be considered which relate not simply to systems of justice for children but more importantly to the very status we ascribe to childhood and the competencies we expect of our children.

Criminal responsibility

Throughout Europe there is wide variation in both philosophy and practice in relation to the distinctions between child, young adult and adult offenders. What most states share, though, is a current preoccupation with reviewing just how best to deal with child and young adult offenders. As Dunkel (1991: 2) points out, this may well indicate the search for a common philosophy on which to base systems of juvenile justice throughout Europe in the drive to harmonize policies and practices. Such harmonization of policies and practices, to be realized, would, however, have to accommodate very different cultural expectations of childhood and children in the countries involved. Legal, judicial and justitial transplants are notoriously ineffective where they ignore cultural differences.

Where differences are most obvious in relation to juvenile justice is in the age limits set both for criminal responsibility and for the application of penal measures. For example, Scotland is not the only country to have a low age of criminal responsibility. In Switzerland and the Republic of Ireland, the age of criminal responsibility is set at 7, and it is of course in England and Wales set at 10. This has to be compared with France, where it is 13, the Scandinavian countries, where the age is uniformly set at 15, and other European countries such as Belgium, Romania, Lithuania and others, where it is 18.

The two boys who murdered James Bulger were 10 and therefore, in terms of the English legal system, just above the age of criminal responsibility. The issue that has to be considered is the extent to which we are willing to maintain that children as young as 10, or even younger as in Scotland, Ireland and Switzerland, can be said to be capable of the appropriate mental capacity for criminal responsibility to be ascribed. The wider issue at stake is of course the whole issue of the competence and responsibility adults are prepared to ascribe to children generally and whether adulthood and childhood can be clearly differentiated on such dimensions. There is evidence, for example, to suggest that very young children may be just as capable as adults at making rational and responsible decisions in a number of areas of their lives (Weithorn and Scherer, 1994).

Even if that is the case, children who are technically criminally responsible may nevertheless not be subjected to the rigours of the penal system. For example, in many European countries where there is a low age of criminal responsibility, children and young people may not be subjected to custodial sanctions until they are near the age of penal majority. And, more generally, in Switzerland, though the age of criminal responsibility may have been set at 7, up to the age of 14 only educational measures can be employed. In Scotland, where the age of criminal responsibility remains technically at 8, the majority of children who commit offences are dealt with through the welfare and care measures supported by the Children's Hearings system. But again illustrating the tension experienced in all systems of juvenile justice across the world, even in Scotland the child who commits a serious offence will be dealt with in court. Again, recognition is made of the developmental aspect of childhood in the formulation of policies on the incarceration of children.

Nor does the raising of the age of criminal responsibility appear to be associated with particularly negative effects. As Dunkel (1991) again points out, where countries have recently raised their age of criminal responsibility (as in Norway from 14 to 15 in 1987) or have decriminalized petty offences (for 14- or 15-year-olds, as in Austria in 1989) there have been no negative consequences as a result of what he calls such 'reductionist policies'.

Again, this reflects the 'twin track approach' to the development of criminal policy in relation to children and young offenders currently adopted in a number of European countries. It has to be said that in other European countries, the drive to a more punitive reaction to dealing with young offenders, in the wake of the Bulger case, is taken to merely reflect the image of the English juvenile justice system as being located somewhere on the right of the criminal and penal policy spectrum.

But even in Scotland, known worldwide for a more explicit commitment to a welfare philosophy, the need to devise measures appropriate to the small group of serious and/or petty offenders was clearly reflected in the recent announcement (*Scotsman*, 23 September 1994) that £1,000,000 had been made available for the development of appropriate measures. Similarly, the establishment of a military style camp in Scotland, privately run and employing ex-members of the parachute regiment in the development of a strict regime for young offenders reflects clearly the fact that a more rigorous approach is thought necessary and appropriate, by central government, for this small but troublesome group of child and young offenders.

But in the continual search for both effective and just systems of justice for children who commit offences, there have recently been some dramatic developments which reflect the drive towards dealing with children in terms of justice models. I suggested above that there was a twin track approach throughout Europe and in general this would appear to be the case. Nevertheless, Sweden, renowned for the welfare approach of the Scandinavian countries, has recently returned to a juvenile justice system based on a justice model, involving court appearances for children who commit offences.

The Swedish developments are based on a criticism of the treatment ideology and

> . . . holds that a penal system concerning juvenile delinquents ought to be based on principles which meet the demands of legal security and reliability. By openly presenting the connection between the criminal offence and the punishment it ought to be possible to have the system play an important part in the struggle against juvenile crime.
>
> (Report of the Swedish Committee
> on Juvenile Delinquency, 1994: 27)

In reference to one of the key issues — the decision as to which authorities shall be responsible for deciding on sanctions and how decisions will be made, the Swedish Committee adopts the principle that all criminal offences whether committed by a juvenile or an adult shall be dealt with in the judicial system; there will be no juvenile court but a modified court of criminal law as applicable to adults; and young offenders should be punished for what they have done, particularly if this involves a serious offence.

What has to be remembered is that in the 'justice' model, as illustrated by the Swedish developments, children are governed by the same rules and procedures governing criminal cases involving adults. In that respect, there are two fundamental questions which have to be addressed. One is the extent to which the rules governing the presentation *and* hearing of evidence by children should be modified to take account of their age. Though no direct access was available to the court at the time of the actual case, press and other reports present a picture of two young children traumatically affected by the whole affair. In commenting on the trial of the Bulger murderers, Levy (1994) states

> . . . it seems extraordinary that while many other countries advance both their thinking and the age of criminal responsibility, we spend a generation failing to do either. The realities only confirm the sad message.

But the whole issue of criminal responsibility of children, their competence and the question of what decision-making forum is appropriate to their abilities and understanding is a matter not just for offenders. It also has significant reverberations for other children caught up in the criminal justice process. In particular, children who are witnesses to offences or who, in the case of child abuse and sexual abuse, are victim witnesses, will also find themselves in a legal or judicial context which displays evidence of the prevalent tendency to suppress the relevance of childhood and ignores the great differences between children and adults. Levy (1994) again comments:

> An increasingly reactionary approach in the criminal justice system is leading to the victimisation of children. The relevance of childhood and children's special need for protection are well recognised in civil law. It is ironic that in circumstances where the fact of childhood needs more, not less recognition, the agenda, often politically motivated, is geared towards equating the child with the fully responsible adult.

This is not to be taken to suggest that the offence committed by the Bulger murderers was not serious and demanded a formal response. That is not being questioned. What *is* being questioned, however, is whether judicial proceedings can be applied in the same way to children as they are to adults. It was in rejection of just such a position that the court was decided to be an inappropriate forum for dealing with the majority of children in Scotland (Kilbrandon Report, 1964). Similarly, the introduction of close circuit television in Scotland to allow children to present their evidence outwith the actual court is premised on similar arguments about the competencies of children (Murray, 1995).

Policing public places

What became clear after the arrest of the two young children charged with the murder of James Bulger is that instrumental in their detection was material made available from a close circuit security video camera used in surveillance of the shopping centre from where James was abducted. This has been used in a number of ways to support what had already been an increasing practice in a number of public spaces — the use of video cameras to police many of our public spaces with a view to reducing criminal and delinquent behaviour. A number of police authorities have adopted such a policy: Airdrie in Scotland, Liverpool, Northampton and Kings Lynn, for example, have all had a video surveillance system installed in the city centre in an attempt to reduce the opportunities for criminal behaviour and to increase the chance of early detection and identification of offenders. Such 'target-hardening' strategies have also received formal central government backing in Scotland with finance being made available for a Citywatch scheme in a number of major cities based largely on video and camera surveillance. The introduction of video surveillance in such public spaces has been justified on the basis that it will do for safety what gas street lighting did in the early 19th century (McCalpine, 1994).

But there is a cost with such an approach and one which was again highlighted by the Bulger case. On the one hand, there is no doubt that video surveillance is a useful and effective means of identifying actual offenders and thereby deterring would be offenders — it was certainly crucial in relation to the Bulger case. The problem though is that video surveillance, in the case of James Bulger at least, revealed its potential for detection, but not for prevention. On the other hand, however, there must be serious concern at the way in which civil liberties may be eroded through the increasing encroachment of surveillance techniques in public spaces. The makers of the surveillance equipment involved in the detection of the Bulger murderers have publicly stated that orders for their product soared after the trial (McCalpine, 1994).

Policing private places

One of the key questions prompted by the Bulger case must surely be the extent to which some form of control can be exerted over the kinds of experiences children encounter in the family and just how far the state can intervene in the family home and parenting role. The murder of James Bulger did not only raise fundamental questions about how we are to deal with children who commit offences but also directed attention to, at the very least, two other issues. One is of course the influence of the portrayal of violence through video and other forms of media on the behaviour of children. The other is the role of parents and the way in which parenting can contribute to, or fail to inhibit, criminal and delinquent behaviour. Debates about the increase of one-parent families have generally concentrated on the implications of the absence of one parent for the healthy growth and development of the child. What became the focus of attention in the wake of the Bulger and other cases was more the quality of the parenting afforded many of our children and the nature of child–parent relationships and contact at a time when increasing numbers of children and their families are in poverty; when the gap between rich and poor families is widening; when labour market opportunities for a large section of the population are low; when both parents in families work to meet the level of expense incurred for current life expectations; and when the social and political status of children, and the consequent implications for parenthood, is being reappraised.

In relation to the effects of the portrayal of violence on the behaviour of children, there is of course still considerable disagreement in the research community and it is not my task to consider that here. But the Bulger case has to be seen in the context of a European-wide concern at the potentially harmful effects of violent and other forms of behaviour relayed to children through videos, film, computer discs, CD-Roms and on-line computer facilities. In effect, the terms of what might be referred to as the Hart–Devlin debate (Hart, 1968; Devlin, 1968) in the 1960s about the legislation of private morality is currently being replayed in reference to children. Precisely the same policy issues are being addressed — the 'harmful' effects of certain behaviours, the prohibition of the public distribution and sale of offending material to children and the right of the state to intervene in the private lives of its citizens. The notion of harm in this respect is very relevant to our discussion and of course the debate derives from the John Stuart Mill dictum that intervention in the life of an individual is only justified if there is threat of harm to another: threat of harm to oneself does justify the intervention of others. For Mill, as for later commentators, children are to be exempted from this general principle on the grounds that they are not competent to judge what is in their best interests.

As for the issue of parenting, once again the Bulger case crystallized issues which were being addressed in other contexts. In particular, the break-down of family life both in terms of social and demographic trends and also the inadequacy of the parenting afforded to some children. The single-parent family has of course continued to receive considerable attention and has been the focus of much debate about the effects of lone parenthood on the behaviour of children and has indeed been identified as a potential variable in the explanation of the rise in the crime rates referred to above. Again, this is a European-wide phenomenon and it is no surprise that in the wake of discussions about such as the Bulger cases, concern about the levels and quality of state provision of childcare is increasingly on the political agenda.

The policing of private and the policing of public spaces does of course present important policy and practical considerations. But on a more theoretical level, it could also be argued that the boundaries between what constitutes private and public places are themselves being renegotiated and that the Bulger and other cases are an important element in the process of renegotiation.[6] In the renegotiation of the relationship between the private and the public, the 'ownership' and control of childhood and children's very behaviour becomes an issue. Shamgar-Handelman (1994) points out that as childhood as a social construction changes, so also does the nature and patterns of control over it — to repeat a point made above, in some respects the very concept of childhood serves to constitute the forms and structures of the institutions charged with a responsibility for children. What she also argues is that it is most likely that those with the least control over their lives and childhood are children themselves. The increasing erosion of the distinction between public and private spaces may well contribute to childhood more and more being the subject of surveillance, dependency and control.

Social crime prevention

But the Bulger case also directed attention more to the inadequacies of the parenting which might be being offered to some children, particularly to children who live in and come from lower socioeconomic backgrounds. This presents something of a problem. If it is the case that delinquent and criminal behaviour by young children can be explained in terms of their upbringing or the social and economic circumstances in which they live, then the notion of a low age of criminal responsibility becomes something of an anachronism, particularly if the necessity to treat a child as criminally responsible and to deal with him or her in a court based system of justice is governed more by the seriousness of the offence than by any consideration of the general competence of children. It also suggests that the focus for intervention is not necessarily, or at least not only, the child but may be more appropriately the circumstances in which he or she lives. The adoption of a harsh and severe punitive response to children who commit offences may then have all the hallmarks of what Bill Ryan referred to a long time ago as 'blaming the victim' (Ryan, 1971). That is, in relation to crime, the criminal justice system punishes those who themselves are the victims of social and economic circumstance. The inadequacy of parenting; the questionable childcare arrangements for many of our children; the general level of poverty experienced by many children in Britain and the rest of Europe; the general lack of life opportunities for many families cannot be ignored in the wake of the knee-jerk response so often adopted in the policy response to such horrific events as the death or murder of a child.

Nor is this purely an academic matter, since the adoption of what has been referred to as a social crime prevention policy (King, 1988; NACRO, 1992) in Europe, particularly in France, is committed to alleviating some of the more negative effects of many of the life experiences of children and their families. Based on the premise that the criminal justice system in itself can never solve crime, this involves the development of an integrated and multidisciplinary approach to improving the social and economic conditions in which many children and families find themselves; a close working relationship between criminal and social policy; and early intervention in the lives of children as an investment in their long term future. The aim is not simply the reduction of criminal or delinquent behaviour but a general improvement in the life opportunities of such children and families.

In relation to criminal justice intervention, no argument is being made in this article that judicial intervention in the lives of some children is necessarily unwarranted. Rather, the application of severe and punitive measures developed in response to cases such as the Bulger death, for the majority of children who offend, may not be only inappropriate but also ineffective and counter-productive in the attempt to reduce offending by the majority of children and young people involved. It was on the basis of such an argument that the Bonnemaison Report in France had questioned the value of criminal justice intervention in attempts to reduce crime and delinquency (King, 1988).

Cases such as that of James Bulger may well demand, for a number of reasons, criminal justice intervention, but they cannot be used as the basis for the development of policy for the majority of children who offend. The pursuit of justice for children must surely be based as much on a concern with the effects of social and economic inequalities and injustice as on the rules and standards set by the criminal law. That is, not only do they provoke questioning of the justice of the process by which children in such cases are dealt with, they also demand fundamental examination of the contribution of social inequalities and social injustice to the growth and development of children. And this is certainly the trend throughout Europe, where there is generally increasing recognition of the need, in relation to young offenders, to integrate a social policy perspective with more traditional criminal policy approaches. But even in relation to the two young boys who murdered James Bulger (and to other children who commit particularly serious offences) it is clear that dealing with them in the criminal justice system itself allows justice at least in part to be seen to be done and may assuage public reaction to what they did. The real problem, though, is in identifying how best to deal with such children and to prepare them for eventual release. On that there is less certainty.

On a more theoretical level, current debates and discussions about what philosophers call 'hard cases' have important implications for our understanding of childhood, children and the philosophies on which our social institutions are based. As notions of childhood alter so too the patterns of control imposed on the behaviour of children change. In many respects, changing notions of childhood may also be a measure of the extent to which society is itself undergoing change. It is for such reasons that the United Nations Convention on the Rights of the Child has to be viewed, if it is ever implemented fully and meaningfully, as a document with the potential for radical social change. The change in the social, political and economic status of children on which it is premised is inextricably linked to the need for change in the social and political structure of the situations children find themselves in around the world. The ready acceptance of an ideology of the child as a rational, responsible being and evil, wicked being and of childhood as essentially different from adulthood, in the light of some of the reactions to the murderers of James Bulger, is easily understood since it demands no radical change in our conception of children. More importantly for adults, it also thereby demands no change either in the structure of their social and political world or in the power relations between children and adults. Changing conceptions of childhood and associated expectations challenge cherished notions of adulthood and the rights of adults to control the behaviour of children. As Boswell (1988) illustrates clearly, this is considerably more than a semantic matter.

Notes

1 Sharon Stephens commented on a very early version of this article and I am grateful to her for insights and suggestions.
2 A distinction is often drawn in this article between England and Scotland. This is not due simply to nationalist tendencies. Rather, the major social institutions in Scotland relating to children — the law, education and juvenile justice — are very different from those south of the border and gross generalizations cannot be made about reactions in both countries to such cases as the murder of James Bulger. In fact, as I argue later, any understanding of the nature of the reactions to such cases must of necessity take into account the cultural, social and political assumptions regarding children and childhood in different countries.
3 Both the regional and national press are cited in this article; regional newspapers are the *Glasgow Herald*, the *Scotsman* and the *Sunday Mail*; nationals include *The Independent* and *The Guardian*.
4 Silje Redergard had been playing with the three boys who persuaded her to take off her outer clothes during their game and then had decided they were going to be 'bad' to her. Reports show that Silje was kicked, shoved and stoned and left unconscious in the snow in the playground not far from where she lived. Silje appears to have died not from the injuries but by freezing to death.
5 For example, on a recent trip by the author to Bulgaria on behalf of the Council of Europe, the Bulger case was discussed in a colloquium on juvenile justice.
6 I am grateful to Sharon Stephens for her views on this issue.

References

Asquith, S. (forthcoming) 'Juvenile Justice in Scotland', in L. Walgrave (ed.) *Juvenile Justice in Europe*. Leuven: ACCO.

Boswell, J. (1988) *The Abandonment of Children*. Harmondsworth: Penguin.

Bourquin, J. (1994) 'The James Bulger Case through the Eyes of the French Press', *Social Work in Europe* 1(1).

Cleland, A. (1994) *Report on Visit to American Bar Association*. Glasgow: Scottish Child Law Centre.

Devlin, P. (1968) *The Enforcement of Morals*. Oxford: Oxford University Press.

Dunkel, F. (1991) 'Legal Differences in Juvenile Criminology in Europe', in T. Booth (ed.) *Juvenile Justice in the New Europe*, Social Services Monograph: Research in Practice. Sheffield: University of Sheffield.

Gazeau, J.-F. and V. Peyre (eds) (1994) *La justice reparatrice et les jeunes*, Etudes et Seminaires series. Vaucresson: Centre de Recherche Interdisciplinaire de Vaucresson.

Glasgow Herald (1994) 'Children's TV Show Dumped in Wake of Playground Killing', 19 October.

Harris, G. (1994) 'Murder Hunt for Twelve Year Old Boy', *Scotsman* November.

Hart, H. L. (1968) *Law, Liberty and Morality*. Oxford: Oxford University Press.

Hengst, H. (1987) 'The Liquidation of Childhood — An Objective Tendency', *International Journal of Sociology* 17: 58–80.

Holt, J. (1974) *Escape from Childhood: The Needs and Rights of Children*. Harmondsworth: Penguin.

Junger-Tas, J. (1991) 'Recent Trends in Juvenile Delinquency and Juvenile Justice', in J. Junger-Tas and L. Bondemaker (eds) *The Future of Juvenile Justice Systems*. Leuven: ACCO.

Kilbrandon Report (1964) 'Report of the Committee on Children and Young Persons (Scotland)', Cmnd 2306.

King, M. (1988) *How to Make Social Crime Prevention Work*. London: NACRO.

Levy, A. (1994) 'The End of Childhood', *The Guardian* 29 November.

McCalpine, J. (1994) 'Caught on Video Nasty', *Scotsman* 2 November.

Murray, K. (1995) *Live Television Link*. Edinburgh: Central Research Unit, The Scottish Office.

NACRO (National Association for the Care and Resettlement of Offenders) (1992) *Crime and Social Policy*. London: NACRO.

Pilkington, E. (1994) 'Killing the Age of Innocence', *The Guardian* 5 May.

Postman, N. (1982) *The Disappearance of Childhood*. New York: Delacourt Press.

Qvortrup, J. (1994) 'Childhood Matters: An Introduction', in J. Qvortrup, M. Bardy, G. Sgritta and H. Wintersberger (eds) *Childhood Matters: Social Theory, Practice and Politics*. Aldershot: Avebury.

Report of the Commission on Social Justice (1994) *Social Justice: Strategies for a National Renewal*. London: Vintage.

Reuters (1994) 'Boys Accused Over Killing', *The Independent* 10 November.

Ryan, W. (1971) *Blaming the Victim*. London: Orbach and Chambers.

Shamgar-Handelman, L. (1994) To Whom Does Childhood Belong?', in J. Qvortrup, M. Bardy, G. Sgritta and H. Wintersberger (eds) *Childhood Matters: Social Theory, Practice and Politics*. Aldershot: Avebury.

Suransky, V. P. (1982) *The Erosion of Childhood*. Chicago: University of Chicago Press.

Walgrave, L. (1994) 'Au dela de la retribution et de la rehabilitation', in J. F. Gazeau and V. Peyre (eds) *La justice reparatrice et les jeunes*, Etudes et Seminaires series. Vaucresson: Centre de Recherche Interdisciplinaire de Vaucresson.

Weithorn, L. and D. Scherer (1994) 'Children's Involvement in Research Participation Decisions: Psychological Considerations', in M. Grodin and L. Glantz (eds) *Children as Research Subjects: Science, Ethics and the Law*. Oxford: Oxford University Press.

55

LOST INNOCENT AND SACRIFICIAL DELEGATE

The JonBenet Ramsey murder

Joann Conrad

Source: *Childhood* 6(3) (1999): 313–315.

How we treat children really tests who we are, fundamentally conveys who we hope to be.[1]

On 26 December 1996, 7 hours after Patsy Ramsey informed the police that her daughter had been kidnapped for ransom, 6-year-old JonBenet Ramsey's beaten body was found by her father in an unused storage room in the basement of their upper middle-class home. JonBenet's case was made more newsworthy by the fact that she had been a successful child beauty queen. With the parents as the police's prime suspects, the persistent speculations of sexual abuse associated with the murder were fueled by the accompanying large portfolio of highly sexualized pageant photos available to the press (Figure 1), merging and blurring the boundaries of news and entertainment. Because of this volatile mix, media attention to the case has been intense and long lived, particularly in the tabloids, which continue to keep the story alive with photos and speculations, nearly 2 years after the murder. The 14 December 1998 edition of *People Weekly*, again devoted its cover story to JonBenet. Across the close-up image of the 6-year-old beauty queen's face is the bold question: 'JonBenet, Unsolved Mystery: Two years after she was murdered, the question is, will there *ever* be an arrest?' (Figure 2).

The media and public fascination with this story, and, in particular, with the visual images of JonBenet Ramsey, serves a point of departure for a discussion of this event and its reception as a signal moment in America's sense of itself. JonBenet's photographic images are the nexus for overlapping and interwoven American narratives on the family, the nation, sexuality,

Figure 1

power and violence, inscribed on the body of the emblematic child. The contradictions embedded in the obsessive coverage of the story are a commentary on the failure of the putative American cultural tradition embedded in the moralistic rhetoric of 'family values'. The interest in, reporting of and management of information concerning the murder of JonBenet Ramsey suggest a shift in attitude toward the archetypal American child and family and the fragile images of reified innocence and deviance which have undergirded a postwar national ideology. The murder of JonBenet not only rocked the notion of the overdetermined 'perfect' family, it perhaps signaled, more than any recent child kidnapping and murder, the erosion of the 'walled garden' of 'Happy, Safe, Protected, Innocent Childhood' (Holt, 1975: 22–3). This article seeks to answer not only why such images of this blonde, blue-eyed, murdered child hold such fascination, but what this fascination means to mainstream America's vision and construction of itself.

Figure 2

The emblematic child – little angels, little monsters[2]

The twentieth century is said to be the 'century of the child' and perhaps at no other time have children been so highly profiled.

(James and Prout, 1997: 1)

Childhood, placed at a tangent to adulthood, perceived as special and magical, precious and dangerous at once, has turned into some volatile stuff – hydrogen, or mercury, which has to be contained. The separate condition of the child has never been so bounded by thinking, so established in law as it is today. This mythology is not fallacious, or merely repressive – myths are not only delusions – chimaeras – but also tell stories which can give shape and substance to practical, social measures. How we treat children really tests who we are, fundamentally conveys who we hope to be.

(Warner, 1995: 46–7)

Such symbolic imagery needs to hold distinct the oppositional categories of child/adult, good/bad, vulnerable/powerful, without slippage or contamination, and, since all these binary pairs contain their own contradiction, the maintenance of tight boundaries is rigorously defended. Thus the symbolic and separate conceptual category of 'childhood' has become increasingly reified and distanced from that of adults. And although it is well attested that symbolic 'childhood' as a conceptual category is a phenomenon of modernity, it cannot be concluded either that the concept of childhood is entirely new (Ariès, 1962), or that the trickle down effect of such a modern concept of 'childhood' into the everyday lives of real, living children is necessarily an improvement. The symbolic 'child' is an epistemological and cultural category and an adult projection that is distinct, and sometimes at odds with, the best interests of real children.

The emblematic child is, in fact, the Janus-faced, good/evil child. These two categories have been typified by Jenks as the 'Dionysian child' and the 'Apollonian child', respectively (Jenks, 1996), and mirror our own fear/fantasy complex toward children (first articulated by Freud, 1959). Through the dual image of the innocent angel/monstrous child, adults attempt to segregate 'good children' from those 'bad children' who dispel the fantasy of the perfect child. As the two visions of the 'child' become more and more essentialized and mutually exclusive, the tension between them increases, while the reified and polarized images of the 'good child' and the 'bad child' that are etched onto public consciousness have real consequences. As a society, we increasingly relate to the 'emblematic child', both good and bad, at the expense of the real child, who is to be seen and not heard, and whose mute and absented body can be easily confused and replaced by photographic or imagined representations. We revel in the images of imagined good kids and in the stories of bad kids, but we increasingly spend less and less time with real kids. Such conceptual children enter the arena of public policy in the rhetoric of policy-makers, placing 'real children at real risk, thereby actualizing or making real the fantasy' (Scheper-Hughes and Stein, 1987: 341).

The modern construction of childhood as separate from adulthood, and as a protected, privileged place of innocence, is a by now naturalized phenomenon. Viviana Zelizer contends that,

> Between the 1870s and the 1930s, the value of American children was transformed. The twentieth-century economically useless but emotionally priceless [child] displaced the nineteenth-century useful child. . . . The new sacred child occupied a special and separate world, regulated by affection and education, not work or profit.
> (Zelizer, 1985: 209; see also Steedman, 1990: 63)

The 'child' became more symbolic and thereby more emblematic; its productive value giving way to a sentimentalized one that was linked to the optimism of early modernism. But this sentimentalized vision of childhood is exaggerated and processed through the emerging technologies of visual media, and marketing and publicity, which require that these children increasingly conform to visual standards and be 'sweet, attractive, and innocent' (Fass, 1997: 259).

The conceptualization of 'childhood' has also included the split and contradictory image of the evil, dangerous child, who coexists in an uneasy relationship with the good, innocent, presexual child (Rose, 1985). In the 1980s and 1990s there has been an increase in 'public awareness' of the 'bad child' (see Hodgson, 1997: 141–50; Holland, 1992: 100–21; Oswell, 1998; Valentine, 1996, for a discussion of the construction of the bad youth) following the ongoing lament for the 'loss of family values' and the heightened moral panic surrounding the 'loss of childhood' (as a site of innocence and goodness, i.e. the good child).[3] The most recent moral panic, encouraged by social experts and the news media, focused on the 'epidemic' of youth murderers. This phenomenon, reported as a new and increasing trend, was jettisoned into the public arena with the highly covered, emotionally charged murder in Britain of 2-year-old James Bulger in February 1993 by two 10-year-old boys, Jon Venables and Robert Thompson.[4] In the essentialized reporting of these cases, not only were these children portrayed as dangerous and evil, but their crimes were seen to warrant individualized, severe, adult punishment.[5] Similarly, at a time that roughly coincided with the coverage of the murder of 'angelic' and 'princess-like' JonBenet, often described as a 'Lost Innocent' (Hewitt, 1997; Mitchard, 1997), was the noticeable rise, beginning in 1997, of media attention to the newly identified social problem of extreme school violence, in which young boys, using controversial and yet glamorized automatic weapons, open fire on their middle and high school mates, resulting in dramatic numbers of dead and injured youth 'at the hands of youth'.[6] The public outrage that such 'Kids that Kill' provoked[7] prompted calls for adult sentences and punishments,[8] measures that not only fail to analyze the phenomenon for its deeper social significance – justifying punishment and incarceration as remedies rather than solutions and ignoring the social chain of violence, aggression and dominance that these boys were reproducing – but also fail to ask why this type of violence was being singled out as a moral panic *at this particular moment in time*.

There is a highly visual system[9] of signification at work in the representation of such emblematic 'good' and 'bad' children, which is dependent on the maintenance of clear binary oppositions, facilitated by the glamorous portfolio photos of JonBenet which glaringly contrast with scenes of bloody school yards and grainy mug shots. Continuing the 19th-century 'Physiognomic Principle' (Sekula, 1986), which itself was linked heavily to the emerging photographic medium, such representations implicitly correlate moral character with specific physical characteristics (i.e. socially defined beauty is equated with 'goodness'; unattractiveness, or 'racial' characteristics are characterized as 'bad'). 'Good' kids are to be protected, 'bad' kids are increasingly and vengefully disallowed into the space of 'childhood'.

Such 'solutions' neatly resolve the nagging tension between our constructed categories of good and bad children: evil children, in this scheme, are no longer allowed within the conceptual space of 'childhood'. The dichotomized, gendered idealization of the 'good child' and the 'bad child' hinges, in fact, on a fluid concept of the application of social constraints: innocence is a state which is without constraints, but which is protected from 'outside' pollution, whereas the lack of constraints that typifies 'dangerous youth' (Oswell, 1998: 38) defines their disruptive capacity. Childhood now is clearly not age dependent,[10] but is defined by a set of qualities – innocence, goodness, dependency. Those who cannot fulfill the demands of such qualities are excluded, and thereby denied the associated social protection.

Also at work in the coding of this solution is the definite gendering of the emblematic child, and all that *she* increasingly stands for. The emblematic child is the 'perfect girl',[11] the ultimate docile body which receives adult protection, whereas the male 'youth', more and more dangerous, less controllable (particularly when gender is combined with race and class), is subject to a growing body of punishments and legal restraints. As the terms of 'childhood' become inextricably associated with innocence and goodness, the markers of such intangibles are linked to a state of presexual purity and ignorance, and also linked to physical markers of goodness – beauty and fairness – the image of JonBenet.

The emblematic child is literalized in the photographic message, itself disingenuously making its own claims to innocence, authenticity and honesty. In the modern context, the public and pervasive photographic image of the child merges with the textually constructed 'image' of childhood, creating and communicating meaning within a broad social context. 'Children – and especially girl children – must learn to present themselves as *an* image' (Holland, 1992: 16), an image that tends to blur the boundaries of fantasy and reality. In the confluence of the symbolic and photographically emblematic child, the 'real' child becomes dematerialized as a corporeal entity, and yet the consequences of such objectification – increased control and overt sexualization – are very real.

With the advent of mass media, advancements in photography and the rise of consumerism and commodity fetishism in this century, the photographic image of the sexualized child has also emerged in the modern enterprise of advertising. Childhood sexuality, ever since it was first articulated by Freud, has been aggressively denied in American culture. Nonetheless, since the first ventures into mass marketing and advertising in the early 20th century, and continuing in the merging entertainment-news business, the sexualized child, in particular the sexualized girl, has been recognized as a potent and persuasive image, and the combination of youth and eroticism have consistently been commercially profitable.

By the early 1920s, advertisers had discovered that they could also 'profit by skilful [*sic*] appeals to sex sentiment in men.' Marketing specialists soon found that 'pretty little girls' as well as attractive women appealed to this sentiment; there was the added bonus that little girls, unlike women in that period, could be shown in various states of undress.[12]

(Coontz, 1992: 170)

Desire is thus displaced onto the image – the 'feminine-as-spectacle' (Solomon-Godeau, 1996: 114). Idealized innocence is now transparently overlain by an overtly sexualized and commodified child. This is most obviously played out corporeally, as in the adult sexualization (in adult controlled terms) of children: photographic images, advertisements and beauty pageants all sharing in the 'spectacularization' (Solomon-Godeau, 1996: 114)[13] of the female child form. In order for the images to register, however, they must paradoxically have no real referent, measuring, instead, the 'distance between ideal beauty and reality' (Peiss, 1996: 321), and, in the case of overtly sexualized girls, the distance between child and adult sensibilities and sexualities.

Such imagined girls are spectacularized versions of the 'perfect girl' which neither represent the masses of kids at risk in their day-to-day lives, nor are they uncompromised in their claims to 'ultimate innocence'. Their knowing looks reflect the unstable boundary between the girl child and the adult woman, a boundary played with both in advertising that portrays girls in adult guise and women playing at being 'little girls'. The blurring of such categories can only result in the conflicted responses of titillation and outrage, provocation and desire (Holland, 1992: 134). Thus the articulated American protection of sexual innocence exists in uneasy tension with our cultural fascination with the sexualized child, made, in fact, more alluring by the taboos that surround her.

JonBenet's photos are simulacra: photographic images of an imagined child parading as an adult that never existed. Hers evoke the beautiful poster child that looks out from the missing children's[14] posters, or from the articles such as the cover story in *Life* (Allen, 1995) (Figure 3). These are the ultimate innocents to be kept safe, in the family, away from strangers. But the girls looking out at us are fascinating and yet troubling in their very beauty. Through the conventions of photography, not only are the images of JonBenet linked with those of the missing children's phenomenon, but also with a whole array of interchangeable, fabricated glamor girls: 'cover girls, poster girls, calendar girls, centerfold pinups . . . Barbies fabricated and propagated throughout all avenues of mass imagery' (Caputi, 1987: 175) all linked in a visually metaphoric chain of associations. The visceral potency of such visual images, all conforming to cultural standards of presenting the female form, confuse and blur the response. We are told, by the

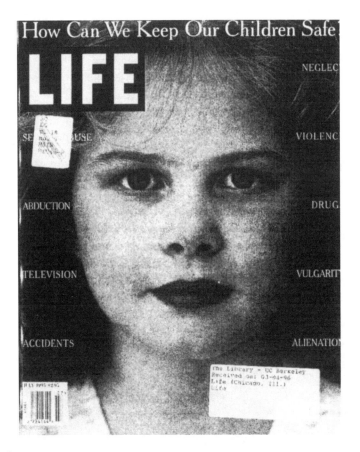

Figure 3

texts that describe the JonBenet murder, of the horrific deeds, and we are told we should be horrified, but when we see the image of her beauty queen face, interchangeable with scores of other such faces used to commercialize and eroticize products or themselves as products, our response cannot but be confused (Figure 4). We react to the murder through these images which never allude to the real child that was murdered. We accept the images of JonBenet as they were originally intended, as fantastic beauty queen photos, not as posthumous testimony to a failed perfect world. The photos of JonBenet are not overtly disruptive, as are the surveillance video tapes of the abduction of James Bulger, but they are quietly unsettling, drawing us in to the voyeuristic pleasure while we protest her innocence.

It is, in fact, the ambiguities, complexities and contradictions that inhere in the meaning of 'innocence' that not only hold us in the grip of such stories, but which threaten to emerge, exposing our darker fantasies and shallow commitments. Innocence, as a defining element of childhood, is a

REPORT:

BEATEN

JonBenet's scalp and brain were badly bruised and her skull was full of blood – all evidence of a savage blow or blows to the head

STRANGLED

Purplish injuries on the neck, inflammation of the windpipe and bleeding in the heart and lungs suggest she was strangled to death

BOUND

JonBenet's right wrist had marks consistent with being bound with a cord

ABUSED

Scars, injuries and blood in the vagina reveal that JonBenet was sexually abused at the time of her murder and had been abused many times before, say experts

BRUISED

JonBenet was severely battered. She had bruises on her right cheek, behind her right shoulder, on the left side of her lower back and the back of her lower left leg

'The killer had to be intimately known to JonBenet – an authority figure who coerced her into a perverse sexual ritual' – Dr. Michael Welner

Figure 4

state of presexuality, with sexual activity constituting a 'loss of innocence'.[15] Sexuality, therefore, inheres in and is essential to, rather than antithetical to, the concept of innocence, and it is in this duality that public fascination lies. Undergirded by the threat of sexual activity (or defilement), innocence, itself, becomes a 'sexual commodity' (Kitzinger, 1997: 167), and is a main source of titillation both for abusers and for a general audience which consumes news stories of abuse and advertisements and entertainment that capitalize on the sexualized images of young children. The reporting of both child abuse and child abduction stories have historically exploited this underlying sexuality, appealing to our collective fears and fantasies, in which the representation of children is itself a form of exploitation. These stories 'do not channel our warm concern for children toward genuine protection and advocacy of their many needs; they substitute thrill for social commitment' (Fass, 1997: 8). Children, in this scheme, not only embody a 'projected (sexual) innocence' but also serve as 'delegate group sacrifices' (Scheper-Hughes and Stein, 1987: 351), entangling projections of endangerment, rescue and fear along with the disavowed *wish* that 'a child is being abused', 'a girl is being molested' (Scheper-Hughes and Stein, 1987: 351). Thus, despite the fact that child abuse and exploitation are very real phenomena, involving real children, public reaction to the issues, mediated though photographic imagery, has been a reaction to the emblematic, imaginary child. This imagined site is inherently vulnerable because such innocence depends on an implicit sexualizing which exposes our own (forbidden, occulted, disavowed and yet condoned) enjoyment. Again, implicit in this vision of childhood innocence is an adult sensibility of how childhood 'really should be' (Kitzinger, 1997: 166) which justifies more surveillance and control over children's lives in order to ensure this image, while punishing all those not contained within it.

> The adult temptation is to swing wildly from notions of childhood innocence to guilt, ignoring all the while the simple fact that children must live in a world that adults create.
>
> (Rodriguez, 1993)

But why is the emblematic child white? Why is she female?[16] How has this image come to be the ultimate delegate for the American child, the American family and, by extension, America itself? The answers to these questions lie in the interwoven strands of the American cultural, social and political scene in the 20th century, and the crisscrossing discourses surrounding the child: stranger danger, child abuse and family values.

The emblematic child in the American construction of itself

The dual image of the good/bad child is fundamental in American society, each part mutually reinforcing and depending on the other. The privileged position of innocence in mainstream American discourse has been increasingly collapsed onto the imagined body of the female child and, as such, the photographic images of JonBenet Ramsey overstate an already defined set of meanings. She represents the 'perfect girl', encapsulating the most fundamental Anglo-American, middle-class, white, heterosexual, conservative values.[17] JonBenet's images mirror those of the emblematic 'good' child: a beautiful, blonde, blue-eyed girl child of an upper-class nuclear family.

As the emblematic child became incrementally sentimentalized, so was it commoditized and commercialized. As a newly identified class of consumers, children 'are the most intensely targeted market segment in the United States today, and the entire spectrum of their embodied desires are overtly managed by capitalist enterprises' (Ivy, 1995: 86), entering children and the child consumer into the complex equation of consumption, sex and gratification. Concurrently, the child increasingly acquired a monetary value. Zelizer points out that, despite the fact that 'the twentieth-century family was defined as a sentimental institution' (Zelizer, 1985: 210), paradoxically, the 'value of its most precious member, the sacred child, was now routinely converted into its monetary equivalent' (Zelizer, 1985: 210–11). Chris Jenks has typified this modern vision of childhood as one of 'futurity', based in the rational and controlled enterprise of capitalism and supported by and embedded in the modern family which 'enabled the modern state to invest in "futures"' where

> [c]hildhood is transformed into a form of human capital, which, through modernity, justifie[s] and [seeks] justification for modernity's expansionist urges in the post-Darwinian conflation of growth and progress.
>
> (Jenks, 1996: 101–2)

As the symbolic value of the child overtook a more practically based value, the insurance business, dealing in compensation for the wrongful or accidental death of children, and adoption agencies flourished: 'Priceless values were being priced, but the pricing process itself was transformed by its association to value' (Zelizer, 1985: 211). The assigning of monetary value to individual children which derived from intangible sentimental evaluation also led to the development of another American institution – child abduction and kidnapping.

The narratives of JonBenet resonate with the phenomenon of the missing/ lost/kidnapped child in modern American tradition, and, because all such stories share in the narrative paradigm, they drive certain cultural expectations and recapitulate cultural truisms. As with all the historical precedents of famous 'lost children', narratives surrounding JonBenet encompass concerns about the family, the child, gender relations, sexuality and power. The mediated narratives of JonBenet Ramsey follow the tendency of emphasizing the victim rather than the perpetrator, the crime rather than the apprehension of its agent, the face of the victim rather than her missing/ dead body which is the underlying, but usually unseen, reason for the media frenzy. It is not the closure, or the apprehension of the perpetrator and his sentencing that are the story in these cases. It is, rather, the mystery,[18] and the spectacle of the girl that are the object of public fascination and titillation. Insomuch as this type of narrative has become an American institution (Fass, 1997), JonBenet's story needs to be read in a historical context which will not only indicate the similarities in the structural elements, but will also suggest shifts in attitudes and social concerns.

The first instance of child kidnapping in America was the ransom abduction of Charley Ross in 1874 (Fass, 1997: 8). Before that, kidnapping 'had no public existence' (Fass, 1997: 9). Although children had been stolen, abducted, forced into slavery and given away by parents to mitigate the economic pressures on the family throughout history,[19] 'before 1874 there was no expectation that children would be kidnapped' (Fass, 1997: 9).

> Child kidnapping emerged at a specific historical moment because it was embedded in the instruments of modern society and culture, both within a specific context of attitudes toward children and toward the obligations of parents, and molded by evolving political institutions like laws and the police and by cultural institutions like psychiatry and the media.
>
> (Fass, 1997: 9)

It was at this historical moment that the sentimentalized child with symbolic value would assume monetary worth in the most exaggerated form, the kidnapper's ransom demand, which implicitly included the expectation that parents would willingly pay huge ransoms to reclaim their child.

In Paula Fass's historical analysis, the social phenomenon of child kidnapping and that of the 'missing child' emerged at a specific moment – one in which the newly envisioned protected space of 'childhood' demanded a particular set of adult beliefs and emotional attachments. These attachments were fed by a newly emerging media which, as a necessary element of recovering such missing children, concentrated on a specific child. Adult concerns thus transformed into personal, parental concerns, and the missing child transformed into the emblematic child – literalized by the mass-mediated photograph and the poster campaign.[20]

Changing discourses on the dangers to children reflect a societal shift: kidnapping, in the period prior to the Second World War, was associated more with ransom and focused on the boy child, presumably with more 'value' that could justify payment of ransom demands. In the postwar period the crime was increasingly sexualized, with the motivation for the crime no longer being ransom but attributed to sexual perversion. This coincided with the growing political psychologizing of America that sought to define the norm in contrast to psychological pathologies and deviants (Freedman, 1987). With a growing awareness of 'perverts' and 'sex offenders' who were increasingly differentiated from the postwar model of the hetero-sexual norm confined within the limits of the marriage union, mainstream America came to narrowly hold its vision of itself in contradistinction to a deviance that contrastively defined the 'norm'. As such, sexualized kidnap-rape-murders by strangers, identified in the Cold War 1950s as a 'social problem', and the media attention to them follow the logic of the time which enshrined the home and family as the sites of the normal American family.

The Cold War rhetoric, in the wake of the Second World War and the uncertainty of the new nuclear age, emphasized domestic 'containment' with its pervasive connections between political and family values. The contained, nuclear family was seen as the bulwark against the dangers of the time. In the identification of the nuclear family as 'American', its defense and that of the country was based, in part, on political containment that doubled as social containment in which 'the vision of the socially fortified, sexually charged, gender-segregated and consumer-oriented home at the heart of American postwar settlement rested on a particular vision of children' (Stephens, 1997: 110).

> Children were to be the defense against the terrors of the age, the hope for the future, the motivation for work, the compensating joy for deprivation in other areas of life, the primary focus of respons-ible suburban consumption and the way for adults to demonstrate their civic values and political loyalties.
>
> (Stephens, 1997: 111)

The defense of these children and of the nuclear family, the concise metonymic expressions of this particular vision of the nation, thus necessitated the containment of a host of threatening, un-American 'deviants': communists, homosexuals, aliens, single or working mothers. The threat to the nation, i.e. the Soviet Union, later dubbed 'The Evil Empire', was translated, at the micro-level, to the threat to the nuclear family by such deviants who came to be amalgamated into the ubiquitous 'stranger danger' (Conrad, 1997; Valentine, 1998) phenomenon – the notion that deviants are lurking 'out there' to kidnap, molest and murder our children at any moment. The threat of stranger danger has followed a historical progression that mirrors signi-ficant shifts in the meaning of childhood, but also highlights how the image of the child has been used and manipulated for other, less obvious and political agendas.

J. Edgar Hoover, head of the FBI during the 1950s, did much to fuel the national hysteria surrounding the newly identified sex crime and deviant and to channel this hysteria into support for stronger law enforcement (Freed-man, 1987: 94). Hoover was also instrumental in shaping the dominant

Figure 5

vision of the normative American family and the national ideology that upheld and protected such an imagined site. In visualizing the sexual deviant and driving the sex crime panic, his foil, the young girl, was increasingly called into service (Figure 5) (Hoover, 1947).[21] The control of the sex deviant became thus linked, not only to the safety and well being of children, but to national security, in that a threat to the emblematic child was seen as a threat to the family and therefore the country. The defense of the icon of the blonde, blue-eyed, female child, and, by extension, the ideal family life, was ultimately the defense of our national destiny; the continuance of the privileged position of the consumerist ideology and the 'meta-narrative of society itself' (Jenks, 1996: 109).

The postwar period saw the expansion of the politically motivated discussion of stranger danger in the rhetoric and folklore concerning the danger to children, despite the fact that researchers at the time had uncovered what was to become 'common knowledge' in the 1980s – that most abuse to children, of a physical, sexual, or psychological nature, occurred within the family and the home.[22] The ideologically motivated containment policy based on the nuclear family largely ignored such research, tending to focus on the constructed sexual deviant as an external threat to the family, defining, thus, the limits of 'the norm' and codifying 'deviance' in the increasingly venacularized psychology that was in vogue. The 'official' reasons for child abuse lay in pathology: from social deviants, often homosexuals, and sociopaths, and, if originating from within the family, from pathological families, again outside the idealized, nuclear family.

The inescapable message that our kids and our families were in danger from evil forces 'out there' would provide the historical framework within which the text and images of the JonBenet Ramsey murder would resonate. In a deliberate reference to the public perception of stranger danger, Patsy Ramsey, shortly after the murder of JonBenet, during an interview on CNN, claimed that, 'There is a killer on the loose. There's somebody out there . . . I don't know who it is. I don't know if it's a he or a she. But if I were a resident of Boulder, I would tell my friends to keep your babies close to you' (Gaines, 1997: 82). The ransom note, which claimed that JonBenet had been kidnapped and which demanded $118,000 for her return, and the explicit linking of JonBenet's death to the random act of a malevolent stranger 'out there', is also a consistent aspect of the narratives of JonBenet's parents. The Ramseys have thus consistently maintained a position that follows the model of parental behavior established by parents of other kidnapped/murdered children (Fass, 1997), a position which stands in contrast both to the general public discussion which sees the parents, themselves, as the most likely suspects, and to national statistics which locate the overwhelming majority of child murders within the family. There is, however, in Patsy Ramsey's rhetorical claims to a 'killer out there' a more subtle resonance with mainstream American ideology: the particular nature of the 'us' and 'family' that is being threatened, and that is presented as normative, generic or generalized, is, in fact, the tightly controlled and shaped middle-class, white, nuclear family.

In fact, in the public presentation of themselves after their daughter's murder, the Ramseys, assisted by their public relations consultants, did much to enhance their image as the 'perfect family'. Press releases during the month after the murder consistently portrayed the Ramsey family as fitting the ideal in almost every way, living 'a life of near-perfect comfort and privilege' (Hewitt, 1997: 41).

'Our family is a loving family, a gentle family,' said John Ramsey to CNN.

(Peyser and Keene-Osborn, 1997: 39)

'We are a Christian, God-fearing family. We love our children. We would do anything for our children,' Mrs. Ramsey said to CNN.

(Peyser and Keene-Osborn, 1997: 39)

Vestra Taylor, who lived across the street from the Ramseys for 10 years said, 'Everyone agreed they were the perfect American family'.

(Wright and Duffy, 1997: 45)

Similarly, media reports of JonBenet described her as the 'perfect girl':

'People who knew JonBenet say she was really a sweet, normal little girl who did well in school and believed in Santa Claus. She was a little angel,' says the parent of one of her school mates. 'I think people have the wrong impression of her since this happened; she was just a normal, happy little girl.'

(Loughrin, 1997: 21)

'She still had an innocence about her' says family pal McReynolds.

(Loughrin, 1997: 21)

The Ramsey family fit the model of the 1950s ideal and symmetrical nuclear family: a working father, a homemaker mother and two children, a boy and a girl, living in a nice house, in a nice suburban neighborhood. The 1950s model was slightly modified to include the affluence and excess of the 1980s: dad was now a billionaire corporate head, mom an ex-beauty queen, and the daughter a current child beauty queen.

The initial furor of stranger danger was to slowly simmer during the instability of the 1960s and 1970s, to emerge with increased vigor during the conservative Reagan era. As much as the kidnapping of Charley Ross in 1874 was a 'defining social experience' (Fass, 1997: 18), so too was the social phenomenon of the 1980s and early 1990s which would become the stranger danger moral panic. This renewed emphasis can be traced in the both the passing, in 1982, of the Missing Children's Act, and the Missing Children's Assistance Act in 1984, and in the establishment of the National Center for Missing and Exploited Children in 1988, as well as in the career of the Attempted Abduction contemporary legend which peaked in 1985–6 (Conrad, 1997). Similarly mediated along ideological lines, the missing children campaign, stranger danger, and the reporting of child kidnappings all relied on images of beautiful, young, white children and the implicit presence of lurking, malevolent deviants in constructing the threat of child abduction as a 'social problem'. The missing children campaign used the most atrocious examples of stranger abduction and murder to typify a missing children situation in which the stranger abduction actually represents only a small fraction of the kids 'missing'. According to the 1990 report on missing children issued by the US Department of Justice, approximately one-half of 1 percent of all missing children are 'stereotypic kidnappings'[23] by strangers, with roughly 70 percent being runaways or throwaways or otherwise missing, and the remainder being 'family abductions' (Finkelhor *et al.*, 1990; Fass, 1997: 202–11). And yet, the missing children movement, at its height, flooded the public view with images of kids endangered by strangers. The movement's tendency to typify the phenomenon by the in-fact rare stranger abduction, was amplified during peak media coverage of certain spectacularly stereotypic kidnap/murder cases in recent years: Etan Patz, Adam Walsh, Megan Kanka, and Polly Klaas.[24]

The late 1970s and 1980s witnessed the emergence and convergence of several discourses concerning the family and the child: stranger danger, the missing children movement, the earlier 'discovery' of the social problem of child abuse (Scheper-Hughes and Stein, 1987), family values and a revamping of Cold War rhetoric. The promise of the American dream, intersected with the implications of the American nuclear family and Cold War policy, had its most exaggerated spokesperson, and its swan song, in Ronald Reagan. His flamboyant use of empty rhetorical icons (Evil Empire, family values) to protect the 'American Way' covered for some of the most aggressively anti-family and anti-children spending cuts in American history (see, for example, Erie *et al.*, 1983; Scheper-Hughes and Stein, 1987: 342–3). Americans had previously bought into the 'Cold War consensus' (Corber, 1993, cited in Stephens, 1997), which accepted the policy of containment, both of outside and inside threats, and of nuclear and military buildup, in exchange for the maintenance of a specific vision of reality – public order, stability and consumption – at the heart of which was the nuclear family. In the Reagan era, this ideal was upheld, and yet, while extolling the values of this idealized family, massive budget cuts and legislation were enacted on the backs of the poor and children, who bore the brunt of the fantastical economic vision of Reaganomics. It was during this period, also, that a heightened public consciousness of child abuse emerged:

> Americans, while giving their consent to abusive social policies, simultaneously expressed renewed horror against child abuse, and exercise[d] a grim moralism toward individuals suspected of harming their children and toward women who have abortions.
>
> (Scheper-Hughes and Stein, 1989: 342)

Feminists in the 1970s had tried, and to a great extent been successful in foregrounding the issue of child abuse as a widespread social phenomenon/problem that was rooted in the privileging of male power and authority, and located, in the majority of cases, in the home. 'Child abuse was realised as an instance of the patriarchal reproduction of oppressive social relations' (Jenks, 1994: 114, citing Herman and Hirschman, 1977) that applied to women and children alike. In the 1980s, however, conservative 'family values' advocates appropriated abuse statistics in their claims that the family was in a state of disarray (Jenks, 1994: 112), and was being corroded by a host of external threats or pathological individuals, disallowing a critical analysis of the existing power structure. Thus, although feminists had successfully raised public awareness of the widespread nature of child abuse, particularly sexual abuse, social response began to mobilize as a result of a discourse that not only focused on the body of the apparently transparent child, but fused such actions with a discourse of personal and family morality that was seated in the emblematic child. In addition, Alcoff and Gray have shown that in eroticizing and individualizing instances of family violence that are actually symptomatic of social problems, the news media are using 'strategies of recuperation' (Alcoff and Gray, 1993: 262) that reproduce national discourses of paternalistic power, with clear gender and race repercussions. The issue which had insistently and persistently been forced onto public awareness in the 1970s was readjusted by press and the media, absorbing and deflecting challenges to mainstream cultural values (Kozol, 1995: 647). Implicit was that abuse was not 'average America's problem' but within the realm of 'bad', individual families. In this move, cases were individualized, maintaining the position of the nuclear family as the site of a particular power relation. It also served to naturalize the eroticization of female children, in that inherent in the presentations of dramatic sex crimes against children was an undercurrent of pornographic, voyeuristic messages which blurred the boundaries between news, crime and entertainment.

The rapid emergence of child abuse as a 'master social problem' and the subsequent expansion of 'high-risk' deviant categories, in parallel with the hysteria surrounding stranger danger, in addition to deflecting common responsibility away from the real endemic threat to large numbers of children in America, i.e. poverty, point to a certain 'unconscious consensus' in America, which lumps together such disparate groups as feminists, right-wing conservatives, family values advocates, beauty pageant sponsors and participants, media, parents, child advocates, and the manufacturers, advertisers and consumers who engage in the commoditization (particularly of childhood sexuality) of the emblematic child. The images of rarefied innocence at risk from sexual deviants were increasingly becoming bluffed with the sexual imagery of young girls in popular culture, media and advertising. The alluring image of the innocent girl staring out from the photo was shared by apologists for child sexual exploitation as well as by child advocates in their respective media campaigns, with the potent allure of sensuality and innocence now so naturalized as to be unremarkable (Figure 3). Discussions of sexual threats to such individual, although emblematic children both eroticized and individualized the victims, serving not only to fascinate and titillate the public in their simultaneous participation, consumption and condemnation of such cases, but also diminishing claims to the widespread nature of such cases, leaving unchallenged and intact the presumed normal family household and reinscribing the tradition of domestic violence (Kozol, 1995).

Our fascination with individual, spectacular cases of child abuse and abduction not only points to our collective fear/fantasy complex, but serves to redirect our attention away from endemic social violence and neglect of children and the redress of such problems. By emphasizing the individualized victim and abuser in such high-profile cases, we perpetuate a social and political system that 'privatizes responsibility for the well-being of children [and] treats families as social adversaries in competition for the polarized rewards of a market society' (O'Neill, 1994: x). This is in keeping with a general national ideology in which the family is inherently asocial, 'family values' absolve social responsibility, and individuals are scapegoats. When the 'family values' advocates pushed for fewer and fewer social programs and more family responsibility, it echoed parental attitude toward children at a macro-level:

> Police and prisons become the new imperatives of public spending, at the same time that fiscal virtue dictates that the provision of national staples such as schools, health care, and social insurances are pruned and privatized.
>
> (O'Neill, 1994: x)

Thus we engage in a vicious cycle that tightens the control of children.

Threats to American children were thus not seen as located within the home but were displaced onto selected scapegoats: evil, perverted strangers; pedophile rings; satanists; single mothers; mothers who abort their babies; pathological child abusers; all of whom were seen to threaten the basic stability of the moral order of society residing in the nucleus of the American family. 'In doing so Americans ignore and deny the institutionalized forms of child abuse which they are supporting in public elections, local and national' (Scheper-Hughes and Stein, 1987: 342).

> National 'guilt' about these hostile policies are displaced by intentifying the 'real abusers' as those poor and unfortunate wretches who beat or molest their own children. In this light, the identified, individualized and *punished* child abusers function as one of our society's official symptom bearers for what is, in fact, a normative pathology.
>
> (Scheper-Hughes and Stein, 1987: 341)

As much as punishing individuals served to displace collective guilt and responsibility, so too did the emphasis and institutional concern over individual abused or missing children deflect attention away from the fact that all children are voiceless, powerless and 'missing' in American policy. Such emphasis on spectacular and individualized abuse and abduction cases also masks the fact that neglect, inextricably connected to poverty, constitutes the greatest threat to child well-being (Scheper-Hughes and Stein, 1987: 352). According to the American Humane Society's (1983) analysis, 'neglect accounts for 60% of all child reporting and for 56% of all related fatalities' (Scheper-Hughes and Stein, 1987: 353), whereas, according to the same report, 'sexual abuse accounts for 7% of all reported cases of child maltreatment and for no fatalities' (Scheper-Hughes and Stein, 1987: 352). Concentration on highly publicized cases of sexual abuse and murder tend to deflect attention away from and thus perpetuate a political and civic system that fosters endemic neglect of its underage citizenry.

The nuclear family, once an idealized model to be aspired to and to be protected, had, in the 1980s, become the terrain of privilege, to be defended and built up at the expense of those not in conformance. The deviant scapegoats of the 1950s and the 1980s, thus, while structurally similar, functioned in vastly different ways. Whereas the 'deviants' of the 1950s were isolated and incarcerated in order to preserve the social order, in the 1980s, punishing 'deviant' individuals served to displace guilt away from institutional and social neglect of children, while, simultaneously, children not fitting the requirements of 'the norm' were increasingly 'sacrificed' for the benefit of those that did.

Ultimately, focusing on child abuse, child abduction and other purported social 'anomalies' serves to mask the fact that all are part of a greater structural oppression of children, which is made possible because our institutionalization of 'childhood' is a function of the persistence of a patriarchal society (Kitzinger, 1997: 185). 'Family values', embraced by many politicians of both parties during the Reagan era, was not only a code for the increased isolation and alienation of the family – ironically and tragically heightening the risks to children at home, the site of most child abuse – but also for a concomitant decrease in social programs and civic responsibility toward children, and the implementation of tougher laws and sentences for criminals – facts which were obscured by the emphasis on 'deviants'.

By the 1980s the perceived and articulated threat to children had become unequivocally sexual and predatory in nature. Fass has suggested that as various social barriers were broken down, including those against premarital sex, homosexuality, adultery, etc., those taboos concerning sexual relations with children became more entrenched, and sex with children came to be perceived as 'more dangerous than ever before' (Fass, 1997: 231). In fact, Fass contends, the sexual revolution of the 1960s and 1970s effected such a general erosion of sexual taboos that 'the taboo against sex with children at once [became] more socially necessary and more *apparently* vulnerable' (Fass, 1997: 230; emphasis in original). Given the fact that the gender of the paradigmatic child at risk from deviants has gradually shifted from male to female in the postwar era, Fass's analysis only partially addresses the many possible social factors at work in the construction of the moral panic of 'stranger danger'.

While statistically girls of puberty age have always comprised the largest category of child rapes and abductions, they have only more recently become the rhetorical focus. The reasons for this shift are manifold, and suggest the complexity of gender and age politics in the late 20th century. Early in the 1950s J. Edgar Hoover had already begun to single out young girls as the preferred emblematic threatened child. By the 1990s, starting perhaps with the abduction and murders of Polly Klaas in 1993 and Megan Kanka in 1994 and culminating in the JonBenet Ramsey murder in 1996, the ultimate emblematic child at risk from sexual molestation/abduction became emphatically and exclusively female, as the issue of the threat to boys from sexual deviants receded from public discourse.

In the 1950s it was the 'deviant' who was overtly pathologized and sexualized: rapists, molesters and homosexuals all inhabiting the same conceptual space. And, although the politically projected image of the innocent child – the ultimate object of paternal protection – was female, public perception held that children of both sexes were vulnerable to molestation, and public attention focused on the protection of children of both sexes from sexual deviants. Mainstream attitudes toward homosexuality in the 1950s ranged from benign ignorance to oppressive and bigoted rhetoric which intentionally stigmatized those not conforming to the stated heterosexual norm as 'deviant'. Political empowerment of gays has made such overt constructionism impossible, and yet, ideologically, gays are, as yet, held apart from 'average America'. When children were seen as being at risk and sexually threatened by the ubiquitous malevolent stranger, who was pathological and outside the family, then it was quite natural that he could be homosexual as well. But, when child advocates and missing children's organizations began to shift their emphasis to the family,[25] to articulate that the danger came, in fact, from *within*, the emphasis focused on girl children, avoiding the issue of homosexuality and reinforcing the ideology of the heterosexual norm.

Neo-conservative family values advocates of the 1980s had ridden the swell of the anti-feminist backlash (Faludi, 1991) that insinuated itself into politics, popular culture and everyday life. This move to reassert the male imperative was evidenced in a host of media: the rise of the slasher/horror movie that inextricably interwove sex and violence against women; graphic, male action movies; the merging of pornographic imagery into mainstream advertising; the increase in commodification and sexualization of the female form in connection with acts of violence, that reached a wider and wider audience; the rise in attention and fascination with the 'serial killer', elevating him to a perverse hero status (Tithecott, 1997); and the age of the 'sex crime' (Caputi, 1987). All of these served not only to naturalize extreme sexualized violence toward women while also naturalizing these acts *as entertainment*, they also reinscribed the 'patriarchal myth'. It is in this sense that, with the focus on the visual images of the girl abuse/murder victim, the fantasy of 'a child is being beaten', 'a girl is being molested' surfaces, breaching the unconscious. As the unconscious projection of the male fantasy, the muted, dependent, violated girl is the ultimate and logical victim – the ultimate recipient of the enactment of fantasies of power and control and masculinity.

> [The child molester], like the rapist . . . is an enforcer of the system
> by which men impose their authority on women and children alike.
> (Goldstein, 17 June 1997: 51)

It is likewise important that the focus of this violence be the white, prepubescent girl, because it is she that has been elevated to the emblematic child, and thus she who best serves as 'sacrificial delegate', and it is perhaps in this that the reason for such extreme media coverage of stories such as JonBenet's lies.

In a country that glorifies violence, incremental increases in such valorized violence, especially toward women, has been accompanied by a concomitant rise in the rhetoric and defence of 'family values', both using gendered images of children to reinforce a system of control and power which is dependent on violence and domination. The more violence becomes, de facto, an American value, the more stridently the cries for the protection of the innocent and the return to family values. It is perhaps a function of the current instability of 'masculinity' in America, on attack from many fronts, that the rhetoric of 'family values', seeking its asocial, patriarchal prerogative, and the images of violence toward women and children, have all become so exaggerated. Or, perhaps it is that a discussion of such violence and abuse, under the cover of revulsion, lets us 'revel in details' (Goldstein, 24 June 1997: 47).[26]

Emblematic delegates vs sacrificial children

> The bodies and minds of children and, indeed, the very space
> of childhood are under assault. This is the message we receive from
> daily news headlines about violence, sexual abuse, exploitation and
> neglect of children; from television dramas about missing children,
> incest victims and organized networks of child molesters; from
> funding appeals for various children's defence organizations.
> (Stephens, 1993: 246)

But the particular media and public attention to individualized, spectacular cases, as has been shown in this article, has tended to deflect attention away from the day-to-day reality of many children in the United States, allowing for the perpetuation of a generalized attitude toward children that has been typified as a 'normative pathology' (Scheper-Hughes and Stein, 1987: 341).

- According to one estimate, almost 2000 children were murdered in the United States during 1996 ('Justice for JonBenet?', 1998), and yet, not only did most receive scant, at best local news coverage, none received the extensive and extended national coverage of JonBenet.

- Sixty-seven newborns die in the United States *every day* (US House of Representatives, 1989), and yet this statistic receives no news coverage and does not generally contribute to our general awareness of child welfare.[27]

- A conservative estimate places the number of children killed each year by their parents or parent surrogates at 1225, and the number of girls aged 5–17 engaged in some sort of sexual activity with their fathers is estimated at 16,000 yearly (Forst and Blomquist, 1991).

- In a 22-month period from 1979 to 1981, the city of Atlanta, Georgia was the site of 28 murders of black youths, ranging in age from 7 to mid-twenties. The public reaction, the police investigation and the media reporting of the crimes all reflect a racial component that works against these murders being included in the stranger danger framework. Pat Turner, in her article on 'The Atlanta Child Murders', suggests that in the folklore that emerged in the black community in the wake of these murders, what is most often reflected is a distrust of the white community, and conspiracy theories that ranged from complicit police involved in cover ups in the investigation to fears that the white, scientific community was using black bodies for experimentation. What is absent in these narratives is the emphasis on the category of the child, as race is the overwhelming determinant. Police attempts to solve these cases often seem to minimize the horror by implying that the events were not as out of the ordinary in this environment (i.e. the black community) as they were in the white community; one FBI agent claiming that 'Some of those kids were killed by their parents', because the kids were a 'nuisance' (Turner, 1991: 80). This is not the world in which kids are the essence of the future and the embodiment of good. These kids are portrayed as already part of a deviant world in which parents are easily capable of killing them. These cases, with their anonymous, generic, dead black children, sparked a fear and anxiety that was localized in the black community and in fact served to underscore the separation between the ideal world of the white, nuclear family and the world of 'deviants', and had few ripples in the general national consciousness or in public policy.

- The day before Thanksgiving, 25 November 1998, nearly 2 years after JonBenet's murdered body was found, Richard Adams beat his 6-year-old daughter, Kayla McKean, to death and disposed of her body in a shallow grave at a remote site approximately 40 miles from their home. Adams called 911 on Thanksgiving morning to report his daughter 'missing', but later confessed to her murder, saying he had an unresolved 'anger problem'. Kayla's body was found on 1 December 1998 (see 'Father Confesses . . .', 1998; and 'Florida Father . . .', 1998). However, this story, although structurally similar to that of JonBenet Ramsey, did not receive wide press coverage, and had disappeared as a news item within a day of the body being found. The quick resolution to the 'mystery' of the missing girl and the identification of her murderer, the lack of spectacular photos and the socioeconomic, familial and racial make-up of those involved, all combined to give the story relatively little sustainable newsworthiness.

• Fourteen days after JonBenet's body was found, on 9 January 1997, Girl X, a nameless, faceless, 9-year-old resident of the Cabrini-Green housing project on Chicago's near North Side,

> . . . was found raped, beaten and poisoned in the seventh-floor stairwell. She was unconscious and foaming at the mouth, her panties shoved down to her knees. Her T shirt had been used to strangle her, and gangster-style graffiti was scrawled on her abdomen in black ink.
>
> (Gleick, 1997: 31)

Initially ignored by the press, local black leaders capitalized on the irony of the timing to call attention to Girl X's plight, and, to the more endemic classist and racist tendencies implicit in editorial decisions:

> 'No one is surprised when an underclass kid is raped or killed,' says Patrick Murphy, the Cook County Public Guardian. 'I think we expect these kids to get killed. It's not that people don't care. It's that they yawn. Whereas if it's a blond-haired, blue-eyed kid, they all go crazy'.
>
> (Gleick, 1997: 31)

But Girl X was an exception to the usual disinterest in such stories in the mainstream press and its readership. Additionally, this article from *Time* which does cover the story is riddled with further traces of the fundamentally different registers of Girl X and JonBenet. The descriptions of Girl X do not attempt to protect her in any way. Her anonymity typifies the perceived generic quality of such crimes, serving to depersonalize and deindividualize her rather than protect her. The lurid, extraneous and intrusive mention of 'her panties shoved around her knees', and the reference to the gang-style graffiti scrawled on her abdomen, serve to join Girl X and her presumed gang attackers together in a world in which such violence is seen as natural and commonplace: they are all living outside the 'walled garden'.

• Similarly, the horrific death of Alisa Izquierdo in November 1995, although making the cover of *Time* magazine (van Biema, 1995), heightened the perception that this type of story was indicative of pathological individuals, in the portrayal of the single mother as unfit and aberrant in her behavior, and the suggestion that Alisa herself was somehow deviant. Press reports conveyed the sense that not only was the family not within the ideal mold, but that it, in fact, was non-human:

> Alisa Izquierdo was brutally killed by her mother after years of abuse. Alisa Izquierdo was six years old. She was killed by her mother who, after burning her with cigarettes, sexually assaulting her with a hair brush, forcing her to eat her own feces and using her hair to mop the floor, crushed her skull against a concrete wall.
>
> From the moment Alisa Izquierdo entered the world . . . she was a child of ill fortune.
>
> Awilda Lopez was a terrible mother. She would leave the kids anywhere and go wherever she pleased.
>
> One police officer said, 'Alisa may have been handicapped in some way, and may have been more difficult to care for than the other [5] kids.'
>
> Alisa's mother called her 'retarded, a Mongoloid . . . a filthy little whore'.
>
> (*The New York Times*, 24 and 25 November 1995)

In the dominant image of the perfect family and its innocent children, these cases are important not only in that they provide a foil, an exaggerated example of deviance and lack of innocence, but also because they help maintain the tight boundary between worlds and serve to justify any attempts at preserving such boundaries. Tellingly, the story and attention to Alisa Izquierdo's life and death fueled the debate going on at the time in Congress concerning the cutting of social services to agencies in charge of such families.

An analysis of why such infrequent and dramatic cases, particularly those involving privileged, white children, receive such high coverage when others do not cannot be dismissed as 'tabloid journalism' – seeking the sensational, the prurient, to boost sales. Likewise, the 'constructionist' analysis – that interest in such cases serves to emphasize the polarity of deviance and innocence and provide the conceptual material for the construction of a menacing stranger 'out there', allowing us to transfer more generalized anxieties and stresses inherent in the times onto a more specific, focused threat – cannot fully explain the particular construction of childhood that these scapegoated deviants are seen to threaten. Such analyses belie the underlying normalized views on childhood and the family, the metanarratives that are shared by the press and the general public. Such discrepancies in news coverage emphasize the dual epistemes of the construction of 'childhood', whose underlying class, gender, race and age biases are encoded in an ideological rhetoric in which the implicit and, indeed hegemonic, image of the 'American child' is that of a white, middle-class, suburban child, embraced within the institutionalized nuclear family – 'purified of toxins [and] fully adapted to the requirements of discipline within an advanced capitalist system' (Ivy, 1995: 97). 'Other' children fall into the other categories – 'poverty', 'Third World', 'inner-city violence' – disallowing such children into the conceptual space of 'childhood' and rendering them deviant and subject to different attitudes and policies. The particular vision of the 'child' and the nuclear family that are the norms, or rather the naturalized ideal, are to be protected from onslaught from the outside. Children not in this mold are seen as needing our help, regimentation, control, and, ultimately, isolation.

The political and social responses to child abductions and murders in different 'communities' are based on an implicit level of 'contamination' and reflect an underlying class and race determinism: 'deviant' victims and their families come under increased surveillance and institutional control, whereas in the case of crimes against children from the 'idealized' families there is increased parental protection and the criminalization of the assailants – the protection of childhood (sexual) innocence being equivalent to the protection of family and political order, and serving to affirm the existing, and arguably patriarchal power structure.

In the book *Children in Danger: Coping with the Consequences of Community Violence* (Garbarino *et al.*, 1992), specifically written to assist those working with child development in inner-cities, we find the implicit ideological premise that the American nuclear family produces model children backed by the establishment, sanctioned by the church and saturated with the ethic of middle-class consumerism, whereas it is 'troubled families' that produce deviant kids. The kids in this case are living violent lives and it is our responsibility as educators, etc., to 'help [kids] cope with their complex feelings about violence in the community – feelings that include fear and terror but also admiration and excitement [to help] anyone who wants to understand what it is like to live in an urban war zone' (Garbarino *et al.*, 1992: xii–xiii). The kids of the 'community' live and are part of their threatening environment and 'community' is a code for inner-city, poor and non-white. For them, the safety that is associated with childhood is replaced by chronic danger (Garbarino *et al.*, 1992: 1), and here community violence and domestic violence are linked in another suggestion: kids that come from 'other' backgrounds than the 'ideal' are more exposed not only to community violence but the parental abuse.

> Some children are blessed with positive, well functioning families *and* strong, healthy constitutions *and* quick minds and supportive communities that provide financial, social, physical, and spiritual resources. Other children contend with troubled families *and* weakened, impaired minds and bodies.
>
> (Garbarino *et al.*, 1992: 2)

This dichotomization has obvious social ramifications and is reflected in the media portrayal of children in public debate and in social consciousness. Idealized American kids are threatened from the outside by deviants, whereas kids from already 'deviant' environments constantly live in danger from within, and need our help for their own development (not, noticeably, to get out). In one case, the 'walled garden' childhood needs constant, vigilant protection and fortification. In the other case, kids of 'others' are deprived of the protected space of 'childhood' and are in the wilderness outside the garden. This is the territory of the street smart kid, the urchin who can take the unsuspecting traveler from the 'other world' unawares. This is the world of childhood prostitution, lost innocence and rapid entry into adulthood.

> In the darkest scenarios . . . unrestrained and undeveloped by the ameliorating institutions of childhood, the innocence of children is perverted and twisted. In these stories, children are represented as malicious predators, the embodiment of dangerous natural forces, unharnessed to social ends.
>
> (Stephens, 1997: 13)

The boundaries between these two spheres are rigorously maintained in many intersecting discourses, and it is because the maintenance of these categories is so fundamental that, on the occasion of penetration or slippage between them, there is a momentary crisis.

JonBenet Ramsey – the 'perfect girl' or sacrificial delegate?

Chris Jenks has suggested that in the postmodern period of the late 20th century, with rapid changes in social relationships, the clearly demarcated, modern and rationally based vision of the child as the site of 'futurity' is being replaced by another vision – of childhood as the site of 'nostalgia' (Jenks, 1996).

> . . . the child has become the site or the relocation of discourses concerning stability, integration and the social bond . . . children are now seen not so much as 'promise' but as primary and unequivocal sources of love, but also as partners in the most fundamental, unchosen, unnegotiated form of relationship . . . our

'nostalgia' for their essence is part of a complex, late-modern, rear-guard attempt at the resolution of the contradictory demands of the constant re-evaluation of value with the pronouncement of social identity.

(Jenks, 1996: 106–8)

But this nostalgia is reflective of an adult self-absorption, and it is only through the image of the child, whose reflected gaze directly meets that of the adult, that the idealized image of the adult's past self or 'inner child' finds a home. The nostalgic vision of the child is even more removed from the real child than Jenks's modern child who was vested with the promise of futurity. With the ever-widening gap between fantasy and reality, between image and substance, with a focus on the former at the expense of the latter, grows a cynical society-wide distancing from a civic responsibility for the needs of real children. As the emblematic child finds itself a site of nostalgia and public concern, real children are made more and more invisible, or pitted in an antagonistic relationship with adults over the limited resources of time and money (Whitman, 1988) and power – a battle that children, in their powerlessness and voicelessness are destined to lose. In this condition of limited good, an increase in children's rights is seen as directly proportional to a decrease in parent rights, which are thus defended.[28]

In the way in which the 'second-wave of feminism' spawned it own 'back-lash' (Faludi, 1991), so too did the children's rights movement, brought about by many of those same feminists, provoke its own form of backlash. Feminists and others, driven by the mounting evidence that the home was often the site of abuses of power on the part of adults, abuses that could manifest in physical and sexual violence, and because of a growing sociological interest in the constructed, analytical category of 'childhood' (James et al., 1998: 3–34), began to demand the consideration and incorporation of the 'rights of the child'. In 1973, Hillary Clinton wrote an article in which she outlined a radically new family system, which would confer both civil and protective rights to children at birth, in an effort to equalize the unequal power relationship that currently exists in family relationships and, ultimately, to reduce paternal authority (Clinton, 1973). But by 1991, the year of her husband, Bill Clinton's, presidential campaign, his conservative opponents were quick to criticize her pro-child position as 'anti-family' (Hodgson, 1997: 11–16). 'Family values' had become a synonym for absolute parental authority, and the family paradoxically became both the foundation on which the democratic nation rests and also one of the least democratic institutions in American society. According to the understanding of Mrs Clinton's opponents, 'family' was the privileged domain of male authority, and such a subversive, if not revolutionary system as the one she had suggested would severely undermine the status quo. Her opponents were upholding a system which individualized, punitive laws serve to enshrine, which places welfare of women and children into in the hands of the fathers, and surrogate fathers – the police, the judicial system and the political and legal system.

A parents' rights backlash began formulating in the 1990s.

> The backlash consists of 'pro-family' groups, religious right groups, and parent groups pushing for legislation that holds, 'The right of parents to direct the upbringing and education of their children shall not be infringed.' The federal version, entitled the Parental Rights and Responsibility Act, prohibits the government from 'interfering with or usurping the right of a parent to govern the upbringing of a child'.
>
> (Hodgson, 1997: 25)

What is at stake in these debates is the protection of the private sphere, the seat of paternal and parental authority, specifically on such matters as parental intervention in matters of sexuality and reproduction (i.e. resistance and opposition to sex education in schools, and mandatory parental consent for teenage abortions, etc.), and a parent's right to use corporal punishment.

The backlash against children not only manifests in the family rights advocates, dooming children in some cases, tragically to the ungovernable private sphere, but also in moral panics about 'bad' children. The violent behavior of kids is seen as epidemic but not related to a general national ideology that valorizes violence and is increasingly repressive and punitive in its policies toward children. And although repressive policies toward children are national in scope, the responsibility has clearly been deflected onto the individual children and their parents. In an article in 1997 entitled 'What's Wrong with Kids?' it is stated that 'adults and parents alike acknowledge that kids face tough social issues, [but] they also think they're spoiled, lazy, and disrespectful'. The same article claims that 'Americans believe that parents are fundamentally responsible for the disappointing state of today's youth' (Russell, 1997: 12). The often proposed solution, the article points out, is for parents to spend more time monitoring and supervising and disciplining their children. But the article is quick to debunk such popular perceptions which scapegoat individual parents: 'Compared with the parents of the 1970s, those of the 1990s are protective and controlling' (Russell, 1997, citing Strauss and Howe, 1991).

Beginning with the 1990s, and concurrent with the backlash, however, a growing cynicism toward the idealized family also began to smoulder, with highly publicized ruptures in the facade: in 1991, presaging the murder of JonBenet, a former Miss America disclosed that her apparent perfection was in fact occulting the fact that she had experienced long-term sexual abuse by her father as a child ('The Darkest Secret', 1991). In that same year (1991) *Ms.* reported on the sexual abuse that haunted such sex goddesses as

210

Rita Hayworth, Marilyn Monroe, Lana Turner and Kim Novak, and asks the question 'How many movie ideals of female sexuality are actually images of female pain?' (Steinem, 1991: 36). Also during this period, David Lynch launched his popular television series *Twin Peaks*, whose main plot was the search for the murderer of teen beauty Laura Palmer, whose homecoming-queen photo provided the background for the opening and closing credits, mirroring the manner in which her sexualized murder provided the background for the accompanying subplots. At the end of the series, Laura's rapist/murderer is determined to be, in fact, the alter-ego of her own father, Leland Palmer, a directorial move that parodies such popularized psychological analyses as multiple personality syndrome, but which, in the apparently enthralling potential that the suggestion of off-screen incest holds, also perhaps has tapped into the 'collective unconscious of the nation's psyche' (George, 1990: 58). In the case of Laura Palmer, *Ms.* has answered its own question.[29] In 1994, the vaulted ideal of mother-love received a severe blow in Susan Smith's drowning of her two young sons (*The New York Times*, 6 November 1994: 1,12; 12 April 1995: A16; see also Grier, 1994: 3). Her initial claims that a black stranger had kidnapped her sons fit the social expectations established by the rhetoric of stranger danger. Her own confession shortly thereafter provoked a sense of betrayal as the public denounced her as a fiend who had done the unthinkable – she had murdered her own children. Rather than asking the more piercing social question, 'Why would a woman be driven to such a dramatic solution?', such a response instead points to the rigid and absolute social categories of good and bad mother that women are held to. But, with the Susan Smith story, the concepts of mother-love and of the mother as the site of emotional stability within the family were severely undermined and echoed a growing cynicism toward the norm of the nuclear family. Thus, concurrent with the image of the scapegoated external enemy, with the remonstrations from right-wing conservatives that the source of the state of moral decay in America is the decline of family values and the call to fortify the American family, is a parallel stream which now sees the 'classic' image of the breadwinner-homemaker, nuclear American family as not only threatened from within, but itself a sham which includes the voices of the postmodern child, the abusive father, the murderous mother, murderous children and the suspicion that control, regulation and manipulation of childhood sexuality by adults is linked to abuse, especially sexual abuse.

Even the National Center for Missing and Exploited Children in 1994 had to reverse itself dramatically and start concentrating on parental abductions over stranger abductions. The inflated charges of the missing children's movement during its initial campaign, coupled with the public saturation with messages of threatened and missing children, had, also, by the 1990s, taken their toll. Sexual abuse and domestic violence had been successfully brought into the public awareness, but, in addition to the gains made (see

Kozol, 1995: 651–2), the public discussion and display of such abuse served to naturalize the sexualized child, and its insistent coverage as a moral social issue served, in the long run, to trivialize it. Similarly the ubiquitous images of missing children, resonant with the emblematic 'perfect girl', ultimately became generic, and invisible. The persistent supply of photographs of children (Ivy, 1996), which originally heightened public awareness of the social problem, in fact contributed to overload, a heightened desensitivity that detached these imaged (and sometimes age-enhanced) children's faces from any physical reality, and perpetuated their 'throw-away' and 'missing' status.

This cynicism is also apparent in the response to the JonBenet story. What would have been unthinkable alternatives in the 1950s and 1960s, with regard to JonBenet's murder, i.e. that her parents had killed her and had sexually molested her prior to the murder, were not only accepted as the obvious conclusion by 1996, they were insisted upon.[30] This cynical public 'knowledge' of family violence contradicts the moralizing and obfuscating rhetoric that expresses horror at individualized and spectacular cases of abuse.

The intense coverage of the JonBenet murder, when coupled with wide-scale fascination with her story, serve to expose the misogynistic and anti-child tendencies in American culture and policy; tendencies reinscribed by the family values movement. In this system of highly reified images, working women and threatening youths are to be punished, and 'traditional homemakers' and 'angelic young girls' are to be protected. But the justification of such control 'in the name of "childhood innocence"' and the assumption of the paternal role as protector, can, ironically place children under virtual house arrest, where they may be most at risk from physical, emotional and sexual abuse. 'The father's role as protector is, on one level, quite compatible with his role as possessor – the notion of ownership lies behind both the duty to protect and to use' (Kitzinger, 1988: 81). Less dramatic but more widespread, what geographer Gill Valentine sees as a general 'othering' of children, resulting in the impositions of 'tight restrictions on children's spatial activities [which] results in children being encouraged to play indoors or being chaperoned to and from organized activities' (Valentine, 1996: 586), derives not only from an articulated sense of danger to children, but from an adult desire to maintain spatial hegemony, and can be extended to simply indicate the exercise of adult authority. In Valentine's assessment, both the 'bad youth' who fill the public space and the 'good child' who may be seen as threatened in those spaces need to be restricted from their access to them, enforcing the barrier between 'us' (adults) and 'them' (others, kids). Paradoxically, the phenomenon of stranger danger, perceived or real, has resulted in the policing of children, and in our growing tendency to see 'childhood' as 'a space to be policed' (Tithecott, 1997: 46).

As the emblematic American child, JonBenet Ramsey was the infantilized citizen (Berlant, 1997), underscoring not only the fact that all children are effectively 'Missing Children' in American policy (O'Neill, 1994), but that the popular representations of 'innocence' are metaphorical links with our infantilized state as political and social citizens, as we retreat deeper into the asocial realm of the family. The repetitious presentation and viewing of JonBenet's photographs tend to negate the usual tendency of the uncontrolled jumble of photographic messages to present a mixed and often contradictory message. In the repetition and isolation of her images, hers became a reified message of American innocence, and innocence lost. JonBenet's perfected image, when contrasted with the stories and speculations surrounding her death, reveal the sham of the paternal protection system, both at the governmental and familial level, a system which engages in wholesale neglect of children and which also participates in the sexualization and exploitation of the young female form.

And yet, the public pretense is maintained. We express public horror at specific, dramatic reports of missing children and the abduction and murder of young, beautiful girls that we have never known except through the posthumous display of their photographic images, while we actively engage in the support of fiscal policies that result in widespread neglect and poor care for children that we may know, and whose lives, at any rate, we might positively affect. JonBenet is a case of having our cake and eating it too. We can mourn the death of a child who has no reality to her audience of mourners other than through her image, and it is the image that fascinates us. At the same time, she can be the poster girl for the abused and missing children, for by focusing on our grief for her, we can pretend to care, while increasing the daily surveillance and socially, sexually, spatially and temporally restrictive policies toward children that we all participate in. The expressions of horror over JonBenet and outrage at the immorality and indecency of society, are disingenuous and contradictory, given the fact that children are increasingly presented with hypersexualized gender models to emulate, and given the enormous expenditure of time and money eroticizing that which we claim to be horrendous.

JonBenet and the feigned horror surrounding her story expose both the public complicity in the sexual fantasy of children and the empty icon of the perfect family and the rhetoric of 'family values'. Her loss, and the loss of kids objectified by adult fantasies, are part of a greater, unspoken national policy that ultimately works against 'the best interest of the child'. The narratives surrounding the murder of JonBenet, both in the fatalistic lack of suspects, and the way in which her parents can so seemingly easily glide back into protected life, and in the way in which her pictures objectify as they eroticize, do much in the way of specifically and generally maintaining the dominant system of power relations. She is our sacrificial victim that we offer up to maintain the status quo. The emblematic good child is thus the delegate who is the object of our concern and commitment to children as idealized, conceptual entities, while she simultaneously serves to obfuscate

LIVERPOOL JOHN MOORES UNIVERSITY
LEARNING SERVICES

social, political, economic and educational trends that are increasingly punitive, repressive and neglectful of real children. Our fantasy violence toward emblematic children distracts from real children and their needs, and yet is part of a spectrum of behavior whose other extreme is the everyday, more 'prosaic' violence that affects 'ordinary kids' – neglect, repression, abuse and restrictive practices and policies.

Incest, child abuse, terror, infanticide, torture and sadism are not new phenomena. What is new is the mutually reinforcing technological capacity and public demand to saturate the public view with descriptions of such events. The motives range from those of child advocates to child exploitation groups, but the result – the naturalization of such individual tragedies – is the same. The blurred contours of fiction and fantasy in the visual convergence of news, entertainment and advertisement tend to anesthetize the horror, lending to its more open enjoyment, and enabling the expressions of projected fantasy on an unprecedented scale. Our expectations negate our horror, or our claims to horror. Now, although partaking in the fantasy, we are immune to its horrors. 'In our creation and consumption of infotainment we have sprung the aesthetics of horror from fiction' (Tithecott, 1997: 130). As if in an ultimate act of violence, children, emblematic children, have become disembodied constructs on which this fantasy is enacted. The fascination with JonBenet Ramsey lies in the voyeuristic pleasure we experience as we simultaneously are revulsed by the distanced, fictionalized reports surrounding her death. There is only a story of JonBenet in her death, and this is the ultimate indictment: JonBenet, tragically, is more precious to us dead.

Notes

1 See Warner (1995: 47).
2 This is a reference to the title of Chapter 3 in Warner (1995).
3 This position, the political darling of the conservative Right in the 1980s, was aggressively appropriated by both parties, all across the political spectrum in the presidential campaign of 1992, and was promoted by social critics, such as Neil Postman, in his discussion of 'the disappearance of childhood' (Postman, 1992).
4 The fact that this murder was outside the United States is, in this case, of little significance. In the hands of the American media, the surveillance video of James Bulger's abduction was decontextualized, and broadcast into homes during nightly news casts, enhancing the perception that this type of crime was, in fact, everywhere.
5 Public opinion and press headlines during the Bulger trial reflected not only a lack of sympathy for the 10-year-old child murderers, but remarkable viciousness toward the boys. Jenks (1996: 128) has shown how the press 'conceptually evicted' the boys from 'childhood', allowing, and in fact, demanding their trial as adults, but this does not include or explain the unconcealed glee with which headlines claimed that the little 'brats' got what they deserved. Following the trial, a series of surveillance techniques were legislated into being (James et al., 1998: 52), in a predictable tightening of control.

6 Since this article was written, this phenomenon has even more graphically and exaggeratedly been thrust into public view with the April 1999 high school shootings at Columbine High School in Littleton, Colorado, in which two male students shot and killed 13 students before killing themselves.

7 For example, replicated in other areas and forums, the Jewish Family and Children's Services of the East Bay, along with the Berkeley Richmond Jewish Community Center and the Parenting Center presented, on 6 May 1998, a community forum entitled 'When Kids Kill: Children and Violence', featuring a 'nationally known authority on child psychiatry' and a 'leading expert on youth violence, the legal system, and social policy'. Such forums involved question-leading discussions with such 'experts' (Herman, 1995) about hypothetical, anticipated problems.

8 A new federal law, effective 1 January 1999, and prompted by public discussions on controlling the phenomenon of 'youth violence', makes the criminal record of anyone 16 years or older permanent, whereas minors, in the past, had started with clean records upon turning 18.

9 It should be noted that some of the most hypnotic and repeated visions of both Jon Benet and the abduction of James Bulger were on video tape: hers of beauty pageant performances, his from surveillance cameras. Both are linked through the medium, which tends to confuse the distinctions between the actual events and their mediated re-production. Both, ultimately, are products, entertainment and spectacles, for the distanced, anesthetized, judgmental gaze of the audience/consumer.

10 Take, for example, a quote from a 'family judge': 'When it comes to kids who rape, maim and kill, their age quickly becomes unimportant' (Sheindlin and Getlin, 1996: 130).

11 The term 'perfect girl' is used in the sense that Gilligan (1991) uses the term to describe how women and girls are taught to conform to social expectations of feminine behavior and presentation.

12 Citing Theresa Leininger (1988).

13 Citing her own previous article (Solomon-Godeau, 1986).

14 Beginning in the late 1970s, a newly effected social awareness of child abuse gradually developed into a generalized perception of an omnipresent, menacing danger to all children's well-being. The foci of such perceptions were the highly sexualized issues of child molestation and sexual abuse, as well as the related phenomenon of child abduction. In the 1980s, with the high media exposure of the sensationalized kidnap/murders of Adam Walsh and Etan Patz and the efforts of child advocates, this awareness grew into moral panic over the threat to children from sexually violent and predatory strangers. Social pressure arising from this moral panic culminated in the creation of the National Center for Missing and Endangered Children (NCMEC). The center continues its campaign to recover 'missing children' through its distribution of fliers, posters, and the posting of photos of such children on the backs of milk containers and in advertisements which ask, 'Have you seen me?'. See Best (1990), Forst and Bloomquist (1991) and Jenkins (1998).

15 For a discussion of childhood innocence in the context of child abuse, see Kitzinger (1997).

16 Whiteness underscores racial hierarchy and the constitutiveness of whiteness in the 'average' or 'normal' American family. The girl child is the ultimate recipient of a systematic gender-based power that is uncontested (whereas it could be by young males) and supports a privileged position of male dominance. Thus boy children are 'guilty' by acts of non-sexual violence – the social problem of kids

killing kids (read: boy kids, youths), whereas the girl child, as innocence incarnate, is defined by her presexual state of 'uncontamination' and purity. 'Childhood' is, thus, a state of 'innocence' that is highly gender dependent: for girls, sexual innocence, for boys, innocence of physical violence. For girls to be sexually active, receptive or defiled means to no longer be a child, childhood being a 'state' of presexual innocence; whereas boys are guilty and bad as a result of violence and murder, but not sexuality, made clear in the public reaction to occasional, although dramatic campus shootings in contrast to the endemic occurrence of campus 'date' rape. Once again, however, these images of childhood are compromised by a contradictory set of social expectations in which the very terms of gender roles that children are bombarded with are defined by sexuality for girls and aggressive and even violent behavior for boys.

17 As if to underscore this association, *People Weekly* dubbed the abducted and murdered Polly Klaas 'America's Child' in its cover story of 20 December 1993 (Gleick *et al.*, 1993). And JonBenet has been referred to as an 'American icon'.

18 Talk show host Geraldo Rivera, dubbing the JonBenet case 'an American Mystery', recycled old bits of information about the case in an attempt to capitalize on the titillation (from Goldstein, 10 June 1997: 39).

19 Fass contends that at the root of American society is the 17th- and 18th-century practice of kidnapping adults and children as indentured servants, recruited to populate and work the new colony (Fass, 1997: 11).

20 The photograph, and, much later, the video camera, are also tools of surveillance and control, 'capturing' the subject in the act. As such, the repeatedly presented still photos and videos of JonBenet Ramsey coexist with the video-taped images of the abduction of James Bulger from a shopping mall – both locked in the uneasy embrace of the adult gaze.

21 The particular magazine, *American Magazine*, 'in the service of the nation', provides an interesting and complementary commentary to Hoover's article, in his identification of the dangers of the sexual deviant, but also in his defining of the American family and its representative, the 'daughter', which set the tone for forthcoming policy and legislation to both incarcerate the deviant and to justify more control over the daughters, as a protective, proactive measure. A brief glance at the advertisements and articles surrounding the Hoover article illustrate the pervasiveness of strictly enforced gender roles and of the smoldering eroticism of the time. The August edition of the same magazine provides an interesting parallel commentary on the commoditization of 'child safety'. In an ad for the Metropolitan Life Insurance Company, which capitalizes on the 'controllability' of 'Childhood diseases' it claims: 'It's up to you to help keep your children safe!', presumably by purchasing insurance (*American Magazine*, August 1947: 69).

22 Fass (1997: 225).

23 The term 'stereotypic kidnapping' is used here to refer to the notion or perception that children are at risk from kidnapping by strangers, that this image constitutes the pervasive 'reality' in American consciousness. Although conceptually stereotypic, however, it is far from typical, representing only a small fraction of missing children. The most typical (as opposed to stereotypically portrayed in the media and in public perception) is the phenomenon of parental abduction.

24 Etan Patz disappeared on 25 May 1979, and was never found, nor were any arrests made in connection to his disappearance. His abduction signals the most recent reawakening of the public hysteria surrounding stranger abduction, the beginning of the intense media campaign concerning missing children, and the beginning of a public consensus that sexual perversion was the only motive for stranger abduction (see Fass, 1997: 213–31, for a more detailed discussion of the case).

Adam Walsh was kidnapped from a shopping mall in Florida and later found murdered in 1981. In 1983, the story was made into the television docudrama *Adam*, bringing the missing children campaign to the attention of politicians and into our everyday reality. John Walsh, Adam's father, has been a high-profile advocate of the missing children's movement ever since the murder of his son. John Walsh has inextricably linked the abduction of Adam to the formation and continuance of the National Center for Missing and Exploited Children in his lobbying in Congress during the 1980s. Additionally, John Walsh is now the host of a nationally syndicated 'info-tainment' series *America's Most Wanted*, in which he has expanded his 'mission' beyond misssing children. Likewise, the father of Kevin Collins, abducted in February 1984, began the Kevin Collins Foundation for Missing Children. Both organizations assist in finding missing children, but also lobby Congress for stiffer laws and harsher punishment for child abduction.

Megan Kanka was abducted, raped and murdered in 1994. A twice-convicted sex offender who lived across the street was eventually sentenced, prompting the establishment of 'Megan's Law', which mandates that previously convicted sex offenders be identified to the community in which they settle. The controversial law not only requires that convicted sex offenders be identified, but also that their entire previous record be made public information, based on their being classified as 'sex offenders', a term that encompasses a whole range of 'deviant' behavior, ranging, in some cases, from consensual but illegal forms of homosexual behavior, to the less frequent pedophile ring or pathological rapist/abductor, who are implicitly the driving force behind the law.

The Polly Klaas abduction, from her bedroom in Petaluma, a small, bucolic suburb of San Francisco, and her subsequent rape and murder in 1993, led to extensive news coverage and public reaction and outcry, including pledges of support from celebrities and from the President himself. Her case was stereotypic, in that it was the normalized public perception of the nature and prevalence of stranger abductions, and the coverage was typical, focusing on the image of Polly Klaas. But the case was hardly typical, and the outcry seems somehow extreme given the number of unpublicized child murders that receive little public acknowledgment. Nonetheless, her case, and a handful of others in 1993–4 that involved the abduction, rape and murders of young, middle-class, white girls, carrying the powerful stereotypic images of innocence and deviance, 'strike fear in the hearts of every parent and have reawakened Americans to the vulnerability of children everywhere' (Allen, 1993: 46).

25 In response to accusations that the National Center for Missing and Exploited Children had inflated and misused statistics, representing stranger danger to be the most pressing risk to children, in 1994 the Center made an abrupt policy switch and 'urged parents to deemphasize "stranger danger". . . . At the same time, he urged an increase in vigilance over the much more widespread problem of parental abductions and the equally frightening problem of child molestation' (Fass, 1997: 245).

26 The contradictory and yet complementary horror/fascination with which the public attends to victims, also occurs with the perpetrators. In the wake of 'Megan's Law' and the public's cry to gain access to information about previous sex offenders, 10 states, numerous counties and cities, and individuals have created web sites with information about local convicted sex offenders. Setting aside the already thorny issues of personal freedom and constitutional rights of rehabilitated criminals, and the loose definition of sex offender, what is remarkable is that the response to such web sites is staggering, and can only be seen as a

form of 'voyeurism' or vicarious titillation. 'Alaska's site has recorded more than 73,000 hits since June [i.e. 7 months]. In Bellingham, Washington, nearly 18,000 people – roughly a third of its population – has visited the city's on line registry, which lists six men' (Ryan, 1999).

27 As Foucault (1974), Armstrong (1983, 1986) and Donzelot (1980) have argued, these types of statistics are the inventions of a particular form of discursive knowledge of the body, and in particular the child's body, and are the result of a medico-sociological gaze which culminated in the relatively new field of pediatrics. Pediatrics provided for child health categories of 'normal' and 'pathological' which justified the intervention of the public and regulatory into the domestic and familial sphere. The purpose here is not to debate this analysis (which the author accepts), nor to debunk this type of statistic on these premises, but to use them because they are by now so naturalized in public discourse and perception as to have their own reality. Given that such numbers are part of our reality and are given validity because of their claims to a scientific base, what is emphasized in this article is that they are, in comparison to the more dramatic individual cases of child murder and kidnap, not given media coverage.

28 Our society, already in an antagonistic relationship with its children, creates a moral panic of degenerate youth, for which the solution is punitive programs. At a Parents' and Teachers' Association (PTA) meeting in 1997 in Berkeley, parents voted unanimously to pay for 'violence mediators' and 'crisis resolution experts' which would take children out of class for workshops in problem solving. This was for kindergarten through third grade level classes! When asked if this was a reaction to 'real' or 'anticipated' violence, I was answered, 'We live in a violent world'. But this same PTA refused even to discuss the physical conditions of bungalow classrooms that housed the kindergarten classes – old, temporary structures, without adequate ventilation, water supply or phones – that were located across the street from the main school building.

29 The entertainment media, simultaneously reflecting and shaping public perception, has firmly grabbed onto the idea of parent infanticide. In the British mystery series *Prime Suspect*, aired in 1996, the prime suspect in a case of a murdered girl is a convicted sex offender, who has been re-established into a community. Public rage against the man is mobilized without any evidence, until, in the final twist of the story line, the mother confesses to the murder of her own child, not out of malice, but because she couldn't cope. In the spring of 1997, the ABC series *NYPD Blue* aired an episode in which a father, after having sodomized and murdered his small son, dumped the boy's body into an abandoned park where homeless took refuge. The father then tried to frame a homeless vagrant who had talked to his son. In both cases, the claims of stranger danger are proven to be hollow, revealing the seat of violence to be located within the family.

30 There have been no police statements or conclusive evidence to determine sexual abuse, but it has been a constant topic of discussion in tabloid and media coverage. Such discussion also lends itself to the sexualized gaze with which the pageant photos of JonBenet are consumed.

References

Alcoff, Linda and Laura Gray (1993) 'Survivor Discourse: Transgression or Recuperation?', *Signs: Journal of Women in Culture and Society* 18(2): 260–90.

Allen, Ernie (1993) 'Missing Children: A Fearful Epidemic', *USA Today* 123(2590): 46.

Allen, Jennifer (1995) 'The Danger Years', *Life*, July: 40–54. (Cover story, with cover caption: 'How Can We Keep Our Children Safe?')

American Humane Society (1983) *Highlights of Official Child Neglect and Abuse Reporting*. Denver, CO: American Humane Society.

Ariès, Phillipe (1962) *Centuries of Childhood: A Social History of Family Life*, trans. R. Baldick. New York: Knopf.

Armstrong, D. (1983) *Political Anatomy of the Body: Medical Knowledge in Britain in the Twentieth Century*. Cambridge: Cambridge University Press.

Armstrong, D. (1986) 'The Invention of Infant Mortality', *Sociology of Health and Illness* 8: 211–32.

Berlant, Lauren (1997) *The Queen of America Goes to Washington City*. Durham, NC and London: Duke University Press.

Best, Joel (1990) *Threatened Children*. Chicago, II: University of Chicago Press.

Caputi, Jane (1987) *The Age of the Sex Crime*. Bowling Green, OH: Bowling Green State University Popular Press.

Chang, Dean, Mark Mooney and Patrice O'Shaughnessy (1997) 'Slain Beauty Queen, 6, Led Storybook Life until the End', *Seattle Times* 5 January. (First printed in *New York Daily News*.)

Clinton, Hillary Rodham (1973) 'Children Under the Law', *Harvard Educational Review* 43: 508.

Conrad, JoAnn (1997) 'Stranger Danger: Defending Innocence, Denying Responsibility', *Contemporary Legend* 6.

Coontz, Stephanie (1992) *The Way We Never Were: American Families and the Nostalgia Trap*. New York: Basic Books.

Cottle, Michelle (1997) 'You've Come a Long Way, Maybe: JonBenet, Diana, the Princess Fantasy, and What it Has Done to Women', *Washington Monthly* 29(11): 20.

Donzelot, J. (1980) *The Policing of Families*. London: Hutchinson.

Erie, Steven P., Martin Rein and Barbara Wiget (1983) 'Women and the Reagan Revolution: Thermidor for the Social Welfare Economy', in Irene Diamond (ed.) *Families, Politics, and Public Policy*, pp. 94–119. New York and London: Longman.

Faludi, Susan (1991) *Backlash: The Undeclared War Against American Women*. New York: Crown.

Fass, Paula (1997) *Kidnapped: Child Abduction in America*. Oxford and New York: Oxford University Press.

'Father Confesses to Killing Daughter' (1998) *San Francisco Examiner* 1 December.

Finkelhor, David, Gerald Hotaling and Andrea Sedlak (1990) 'Missing, Abducted, Runaway, and Thrownaway Children in America', First Report: Numbers and Characteristics, National Incidence Studies. Prepared for the US Department of Justice, Office of Juvenile Justice and Delinquency Prevention.

'Florida Father Says Anger Made Him Kill Daughter' (1998) Reuters News Agency, 1 December.

Forst, Nartin Lyle and Martha-Elin Blomquist (1991) *Missing Children: Rhetoric and Reality*. New York: Lexington Books/Toronto: Macmillan.

Foucault, M. (1974) *The Archaeology of Knowledge*. London: Tavistock.

Freedman, Estelle (1987) '"Uncontrolled Desires": The Response to the Sexual Psychopath, 1920–1960', *The Journal of American History* 74(June): 83–106.

Freud, Sigmund (1959) ' "A Child is Being Beaten": A Contribution to the Study of the Origins of Sexual Perversions', in James Strachey (ed.) *The Standard Edition of the Complete Psychological Works of Sigmund Freud*, Vol. 17. London: Hogarth Press. (Originally published 1919.)

Gaines, James R. (1997) 'This Murder is Ours, Chief: On the Police, the Media and the Death of a Beautiful Young Girl', *Time* 149(3): 82.

Garbarino, James, Nancy Dubrow, Kathleen Kostelny and Carole Pardo (eds) (1992) *Children in Danger*. San Francisco: Jossey-Bass.

George, Diana Hume (1990) 'Lynching Women', *Ms.* 1(3): 58–60.

Gilligan, Carol (1991) 'Joining the Resistance: Psychology, Politics, Girls and Women', in Laurence Goldstein (ed.) *The Female Body: Figures, Styles, Speculations*, pp. 12–47. Ann Arbor: University of Michigan Press.

Gleick, Elizabeth (1997) 'Belated Outrage for Girl X; A Child Raped in a Chicago Housing Project Got None of the Press Lavished on a Rich White Victim', *Time* 149(8): 31.

Gleick, Elizabeth, Tom Dunneff, Johnny Dodd, Lyndon Stambler and Lorenzo Benet (1993) 'America's Child', *People Weekly* 20 December: 84–8.

Goldstein, Richard (1997) A three-part series on JonBenet Ramsey and the 'Culture of Child Abuse', *Village Voice*: 'The Girl in the Fun Bubble: The Mystery of JonBenet' 10 June: 38–41; 'Nymph Mania: Honoring Innocence in the Breach' 17 June: 48–51; and 'The Killer Inside Me: Shirley Temple Meets the Demon Dad' 24 June: 46–48.

Grier, Peter (1994) 'S. Carolina Murders Prompt New Look', *Christian Science Monitor* 8 November: 3.

Herman, Ellen (1995) *The Romance of American Psychology: Political Culture in the Age of Experts*. Berkeley, Los Angeles and London: University of California Press.

Herman, J. and L. Hirschman (1977) 'Father–Daughter Incest', *Signs* 2: 1–22.

Hewitt, Bill (1997) 'Lost Innocent', *People Weekly* 47(2): 38–45.

Hodgson, Lucia (1997) *Raised in Captivity: Why Does America Fail its Children?* St Paul, MN: Gray Wolf Press.

Holland, Patricia (1992) *What is a Child? Popular Images of Childhood*. London: Virago Press.

Holt, John (1975) *Escape from Childhood*. Harmondsworth: Penguin.

Hoover, J. Edgar (1947) 'How Safe is Your Daughter?', *American Magazine* 144(1): 32–3, 102–4.

http://www.fbi.gov/missing/ 'Missing Person' descriptions from 12 January 1998.

Ivy, Marilyn (1995) 'Have You Seen Me? Recovering the Inner Child in Late Twentieth-Century America', in S. Stephens (ed.) *Children and the Politics of Culture*, pp. 79–104. Princeton, NJ: Princeton University Press.

James, Allison and James Prout (1997) *Constructing and Reconstructing Childhood: Contemporary Issues in the Sociological Study of Childhood*. London and Washington, DC: Falmer Press.

James, Allison, Chris Jenks and Alan Prout (1998) *Theorizing Childhood*. New York: Teachers College Press.

Jenkins, Philip (1998) *Moral Panic: Changing Concepts of the Child Molester in Modern America*. New Haven, CT and London: Yale University Press.

Jenks, Chris (1994) 'Child Abuse in the Postmodern Context: An Issue of Social Identity', *Childhood* 2: 111–21.

Jenks, Chris (1996) *Childhood*. New York: Routledge.

'Justice for JonBenet?' (1998) CNN interactive at http://www.cnn.com/us/9712/26/ramsey.year.later/index.html

Kitzinger, Jenny (1988) 'Defending Innocence: Ideologies of Childhood,' *Feminist Review* 28(January): 77–87.

Kitzinger, Jenny (1997) 'Who Are You Kidding? Children, Power, and the Struggle Against Sexual Abuse', in Allison James and Alan Prout (eds) *Constructing and Reconstructing Childhood*, pp. 165–89. London and Washington, DC: Falmer Press.

Kozol, Wendy (1995) 'Fracturing Domesticity: Media, Nationalism, and the Question of Feminist Influence', *Signs: Journal of Women in Culture and Society* 20(3): 646–67.

Leininger, Theresa (1988) 'Type-Cast: An Analysis of the Portrayal of American Women in Business Equipment Advertising, 1917–1929', *University of Cincinnati Forum* 15: 9–10.

Loughrin, Shannon (1997) 'Shocking Secrets Behind Tiny Beauty's Murder', *Star* 21 January: 20–1.

Mitchard, Jacquelyn (1997) 'Two Tales of our Lost Innocence', *Milwaukee Journal Sentinel Online Main Page* (Features), a special to the Journal *Sentinel* 16 February: 1–2.

O'Neill, John (1994) *The Missing Child in Liberal Theory*. Toronto, Buffalo and London: University of Toronto Press.

Oswell, David (1998) 'A Question of Belonging: Television, Youth and the Domestic', in Tracey Skelton and Gill Valentine (eds) *Cool Places*, pp. 35–49. London and New York: Routledge.

Peiss, Kathy (1996) 'Making Up, Making Over: Cosmetics, Consumer Culture, and Women's Identity', in Grazia Furlough (ed.) *The Sex of Things*, pp. 311–36. Berkeley, London and Los Angeles: University of California Press.

Peyser, Marc and Sherry Keene-Osborn (1997) 'A Body in the Basement: Did a Murdered 6-Year-Old Beauty Queen Know her Killer?', *Newsweek* 129(2): 38–9.

Postman, Neil (1992) *The Disappearance of Childhood*. New York: Vintage Books. (Originally published 1984.)

Rodriguez, Richard (1993) 'A Crisis of Intimacy: Who Are Our Children?', *The Los Angeles Times* 19 December: M1.

Rose, N. (1985) *The Psychological Complex*. London: Routledge and Kegan Paul.

Russell, Cheryl (1997) 'What's Wrong with Kids?', *American Demographics* November: 12–16.

Ryan, Joan (1999) 'Molesters, Courtrooms and Kitchens', *San Francisco Chronicle* 10 January (Zone 6): 1.

Scheper-Hughes, Nancy and Howard F. Stein (1987) 'Child Abuse and the Unconscious in American Popular Culture', in Nancy Scheper-Hughes (ed.) *Child Survival*, pp. 339–58. Dordrecht: Reidel.

Sekula, Allan (1986) 'The Body and the Archive', *October* 39(Winter): 3–64.

Sheindlin, Judy and Josh Getlin (1996) 'No Excuses', *Ladies' Home Journal* May: 130.

Solomon-Godeau, Abigail (1986) 'The Legs of the Countess', *October* 39(Winter): 87–105.

Solomon-Godeau, Abigail (1996) 'The Other Side of Venus: The Visual Economy of Feminine Display', in Grazia Furlough (ed.) *The Sex of Things*, pp. 113–50. Berkeley, London, and Los Angeles: University of California Press.

Steedman, C. (1990) *Childhood, Culture and Class in Britain*. London: Virago.

Steinem, Gloria (1991) 'Women in the Dark: of Sex Goddesses, Abuse, and Dreams', *Ms.* 1(4): 35–7.

Stephens, Sharon (1993) 'Children at Risk: Constructing Social Problems and Policies', *Childhood* 1: 246–51.

Stephens, Sharon (ed.) (1995) *Children and the Politics of Culture*. Princeton, NJ: Princeton University Press.

Stephens, Sharon (1997) 'Nationalism, Nuclear Policy and Children in Cold War America', *Childhood* 4(1): 103–23.

Strauss, William and Neil Howe (1991) *Generations.* New York: William Morrow.

'The Darkest Secret' (1991) *People Weekly* 6 July.

'The Strange World of JonBenet' (1997) *Newsweek* 20 January: cover story.

Tithecott, Richard (1997) *Of Men and Monsters: Jeffrey Dahmer and the Construction of the Serial Killer*. Madison: University of Wisconsin Press.

Turner, Patricia A. (1991) 'The Atlanta Child Murders: A Case Study of Folklore in the Black Community', in Stephen Stern and John Allan Cicala (eds) *Creative Ethnicity*, pp. 75–86. Logan: Utah State University Press.

US House of Representatives (1989) 'Fact Sheet' prepared for a hearing before the Select Committee on Children, Youth and Families, 'Caring for New Mothers: Pressing Problems, New Solutions', 24 October.

Valentine, Gill (1996) 'Angels and Devils: Moral Landscapes of Childhood', *Environment and Planning D: Society and Space* 14: 581–99.

Valentine, Gill (1998) *Stranger Danger: Children, Parenting and the Production of Public Space*. London: Cassell (forthcoming).

Van Biema, David (1995) 'Abandoned to her Fate', *Time* 11 December: 32.

Warner, Marina (1995) 'Little Angles, Little Monsters: Keeping Childhood Innocent', *Six Myths of Our Time*, pp. 43–62. New York: Vintage Books.

Whitman, David (1988) 'America's Hidden Poor', *U.S. News and World Report* 11 January: 18–25.

Wright, David and David Duffy (1997) 'How Tiny Beauty Queen Really Died', *National Enquirer* 21 January: 36–7, 45.

Zelizer, Viviana A. (1985) *Pricing the Priceless Child: The Changing Social Value of Children*. New York: Basic Books.

56

THERE'S NO PLACE
LIKE HOME

The public/private distinction in children's theorizing of risk and safety

Jeni Harden

Source: *Childhood* 7(1) (2000): 43–59.

Introduction

Recent sociological work has explored risk as a social construction (Giddens, 1991). It is argued that lay theorizing around risk must be socially situated and contextualized with regards to public discourses and the socioeconomic structures which shape our lives (Green, 1997; Scott *et al.*, 1998). There are several ways in which this is pertinent to the discussion of children and risk. First, public discourses on children and risk are framed by contemporary western ideas about childhood (Jackson and Scott, 1999). Childhood is constructed as a time of innocence, vulnerability and dependence (Jenks, 1996). Second, the discussion of risks to children selectively focuses on particular risks (Roberts *et al.*, 1995). Third, in such discourses the risks that children face are located principally in the public sphere rather than the private sphere of the family.

Recent campaigns by children's organizations have sought to draw attention to the risks children face with regard to domestic violence within the family, yet much public discourse around children continues to focus on risks located in public life. In addition, there tends to be a focus on particular types of risks to children. Considerable media attention is given to cases of child abduction, drug deaths among children and bullying, with less interest being shown about accidents to children in the home. It is argued that this is reflected in parents' own concerns for the safety of their children. It has been estimated that 'stranger danger' was the greatest fear for 98 percent of parents, yet between 1984 and 1994 fewer than six children under 14 were killed by strangers each year in the UK (Moran *et al.*, 1997). This can be contrasted with approximately 600 per year who die in accidents in the home (Harker and Moore, 1996).

Children's participation in public life is perceived to entail specific risks and as a result it is argued this participation is to be controlled and limited by adults. The protection of children involves regulating their participation in public life – where they go, with whom, for how long, for what purpose. In this respect the protection of children is also a source of control over children (Valentine, 1997a). Limits to the scope of children's autonomy, by parents and through legislation, are closely connected to the idea of children as a social group being immature, naive, vulnerable and a danger to themselves (Pilcher, 1996). Yet distinctions are also made concerning children's perceived ability to manage risks and between children in terms of age. For example, the National Society for the Prevention of Cruelty to Children (NSPCC) gives guidelines on the ages when children can be allowed degrees of autonomy: for example, it is noted that children at 8 years old are too young to walk to school (*The Observer, Life* section, 10 March 1996).

In this article, children's own constructions of risk and safety in their everyday lives are explored in relation to the public/private dichotomy. While there has been considerable discussion within feminist research concerning the implications of the public/private distinction for women (Gamarnikow, 1983), less is known about the implications for children or indeed the ways in which children themselves construct their lives around this distinction.

The article first presents the background to the study from which the data presented are drawn. Second, key issues in debates over the public/private distinction within sociology and the pertinence of these issues for the discussion of children and risk are outlined. These issues are then explored further in relation to the data from interviews with children. The children were reflexive in their conceptualizations of risk in public life and did not simply accept official discourses on children and risk. It is argued that children construct their landscapes of risk and safety around concepts of private, local and public. It is shown that while the private sphere of the home was described in terms of safety and security, the children expressed concerns about their vulnerability in public life. The children's accounts also defined an intermediate sphere between private and public – the local sphere – which was identified in terms of proximity to the home and familiarity with places and people.

Background to the study

This article is based on data from a study exploring the ways in which children and parents deal with risk, safety and danger. The focus of the study is on risk and risk anxiety generally and its consequences for children's everyday lives, and specifically on the sexualization of risk in relation to children. In the interviews a topic guide was used, exploring children's everyday fears and concerns, children's attitudes to the boundaries set by parents, children's strategies for managing risks and negotiating parental boundaries. Various task-based work was also developed, including, sentence completion, spider diagrams and grouping exercises.

Individual interviews with 51 children from 30 families were carried out. Of the 51 children, 34 were aged between 9 and 13,[1] and were at primary school when interviewed. To explore the embeddedness of risk within households, where possible, an older sibling was also interviewed: 17 of the children were aged 12–15[2] and at secondary school when interviewed. Across both age groups there are equal numbers of girls and boys.

The sample was generated from one school in an urban area and four schools in rural areas in Scotland, in order to explore the spatial distribution of risk between urban and rural locations (Valentine, 1997b). Using schools to generate the sample enabled the researchers to interview children who potentially shared common networks and local knowledges. The children in this study are from predominantly upper working-class and lower middle-class backgrounds and all but two of the children are white, reflecting the ethnic composition of the areas studied.

While it is recognized that children are not a homogeneous social group and that their experiences and attitudes vary, the focus of this article is not to draw a systematic comparison based on structural differences. Rather, it is noted when significant points of difference were raised between the children, based on age, gender and location.

The public/private distinction and risk

The distinction between public and private has been used by sociologists in many different ways and contexts. Distinctions are drawn between the public and private in terms of: state administration/market economy; collective/individual interests; family/market economy. As Weintraub notes, 'the public/private distinction . . . is not unitary but protean. It comprises not a single paired opposition but a complex family of them, neither mutually reducible nor wholly unrelated' (Weintraub, 1995: 284). Moreover, the way in which such concepts are used can vary. Ribbens McCarthy and Edwards (1999) note the different usages between the identification of the public and private with distinct physical spaces and their identification with particular social practices and experiences. As Slater (1998) notes, the 'public and private are seen as different realms of experience and value, spatially and temporally, separated and epitomised by different sorts of people and roles' (Slater, 1998: 144).

The extent to which there is a sharp distinction between the public and private has also been called into question. New forms of work, for example free-lancing, have blurred the distinction between the public sphere of the workplace and the private sphere of the home (Slater, 1998). As Beck notes:

> The private sphere is not what it appears to be: a sphere separated from the environment. It is the *outside turned inside and made private, of conditions and decisions* made elsewhere, in the television networks, the education system, in firms, or the labour market, or in the transportation system, with general disregard of their private biographical consequences.
>
> (Beck, 1992: 133)

It has been argued that there is an intermediate sphere between the public and the private. Ribbens McCarthy and Edwards (1999) point to the 'sociable' as a sphere of support between the state and the individual, giving the example of friendships. Similarly, Hunter (1995) argues that between the public and the private there is a 'parochial social order' which refers to the communal and the local.

The public/private distinction is central to the theorizing of risk both in terms of physical spaces and modes of experience. First, Goffman argues that there is an increasing vulnerability associated with public life. (Goffman, 1971: 385). Goffman developed the concept of *Umwelt* to refer to 'the sphere around the individual within which potential sources of alarm are found' (Goffman, 1971: 297). Goffman primarily conceptualizes *Umwelt* in spatial terms. Indeed, he refers to the 'critical distance' around the individual from which alarm can be felt (Goffman, 1971: 299). He notes the structures of *Umwelt*, the aspects of our everyday life which can cause alarm – the furnished frame relating to security associated with internal, enclosed spaces; lurk lines and access points to refer to spatial points of vulnerability; and the social net to refer to our concerns about other people, in public spaces (Goffman, 1971: 335–7).

Second, discussions of risk and risk anxiety have centred on individuality and collectivity. Giddens has argued that while anxieties about risk may be shaped by public discussions, it is as individuals that we cope with these uncertainties. Central to this is the individual reflexive monitoring of risk.

> The point ... is not that day to day life is inherently more risky than was the case in prior eras. It is rather that, in conditions of modernity, for lay actors as well as for experts in specific fields, thinking in terms of risk and risk assessment is a more or less ever-present exercise, of a partly imponderable character.
>
> (Giddens, 1991: 123–4)

Nevertheless the significance placed on individual reflexivity in understanding risk and risk anxiety has been criticized. Furlong and Cartmel argue that while individualization is both a real and a rhetorical feature of late modernity, it is constrained by countervailing pressures towards standardization, and individual decisions take place within the context of 'a society characterised by interdependency' (Furlong and Cartmel, 1997: 113). Moreover, it is possible to question, in relation to children, whether all individuals are regarded as being equally reflexive. Public debates on risk rarely include children's own opinions. Rather, risks to children are defined and managed by adults on children's behalf. It appears as though the element of choice, responsibility and reflexivity accredited to adults in relation to risk is denied to children.

Understanding children's theorizing of risk and safety

The data from this study show that children's *Umwelten* are complex and contingent on many different but interrelated factors involving space, time, people and behaviour. A common thread running through these different structures is the externalization of risk and the association made between public life, children and risk. The ways in which children define particular spaces and their experiences of them in terms of risk and safety are explored further in the following sections. In doing so, the extent to which children are engaged in the reflexive monitoring of risk is also addressed.

The home as a safe haven

The idealization of the private sphere of the home has been a central feature of modernity (Slater, 1998). A key element of this has been the segregation of children and childhood into the private sphere: the home is seen as the appropriate place for children to be raised, facilitating their physical and moral protection from the outside world. This is reflected in children's construction of risk and safety. Hood *et al.* (1996) explored the negotiations between children and parents around issues of risk and safety in the home and found that both children and parents tended to externalize risk, that is risk was located as occurring outside the home. In our study, very few of the children interviewed spontaneously mentioned risks in the home. Indeed, many of them specified their family and their home as safe. For example, in the sentence completion exercises one girl wrote: 'I feel safe when I'm sitting in my house at night by the fire with my family' (Jill, 10); an image which portrays the feelings associated with security which the home is seen to represent.

The private physical space of the home was an important element in its association with safety. Goffman argues that 'walls ceiling and floor tend to establish outside limits to a surround, the assumption being that these barriers are stout enough to keep out potential matters for alarm. They establish an "inside" and an "outside"' (Goffman, 1971: 334). The physical space of the home therefore enables control over who occupies and enters that space.

227

This control can, however, be displaced through certain 'access points' (Goffman, 1971: 336). While the children tended to describe the home in terms of safety, they also showed concern that this safety could be breached.

> Me and Caroline have been, come through in our pyjamas on a Saturday morning and watched TV. We couldn't be bothered to get dressed and mum's just gone round to the food shop round the corner. We just feel so unsafe. You don't answer the door. You just sit there and anytime there's a little bit of movement on the gravel like a bird or something then uh oh!
>
> (Christine, 12)

From the children's accounts it seemed that often these feelings of insecurity were felt most keenly at night, as one boy described: 'Well for some reason I only get scared at night when I always feel that someone's gonna break in at night and like kill you or whatever. Just sort of like trash your house or something' (Will, 11).

The displacement of the safety and security the children associated with being at home reflected their belief that people within the home were known – family and friends – and so were safe. One boy explained that he felt safe in his house because: 'there's nobody weird around' (Owen, 10). While it has been argued that we often try to 'escape' from the routine, the known and expected paths of our everyday lives (Cohen and Taylor, 1992), the known and the familiar is also associated with safety. In the private sphere of the home children know everyone around them and how they behave, and they know the location, either their home or their friends' homes. However, as Cheal (1991) argues, the very privacy and closed space of the home and family that these children associated with safety can also serve to hide domestic violence (Cheal, 1991: 82). While for many children the realities of home life are very different than the image reported here, the children in this study constructed their risk landscapes around their own experiences of safety. If homes were risky and unsafe, they chose not to disclose this in the interviews.

While the actual physical space of the home could be breached by the public sphere, perhaps the most obvious way in which the outside world penetrates the private sphere is through the media, in particular television. There has been considerable ongoing academic and public discussion over the impact that watching 'inappropriate' material on television can have on children (Buckingham, 1994). This discourse of risk featured in the children's accounts. Watching programmes that contained violence was described as being dangerous for children's development. One boy noted that such programmes: 'might give the children nightmares, and that might develop them into being quite nasty when they grow up as well' (Lewis, 10).

The children distinguished between different ages of children in terms of their ability to handle swearing or violence on television without being influenced by it (Kelley *et al.*, 1999):

> Well 12 you don't get scared very easily. And 9 and 10 you just like have nightmares for months if you see something like someone being shot or aliens coming out of someone's head. I'm like 'oh no'. You can't get to sleep.
>
> (Caroline, 10)

The older children often contrasted themselves with their younger sibling:

> But film it's not true, it's make believe. But now I'm older, I can tell what's true and what's just, what's not, so it's actually not that bad. But, Jill just thinks everything that's on telly . . . she thinks, oh that's what everybody does, and that's why she's like, why can't I do this?
>
> (Janet, 15)

However, the children's accounts did not simply reproduce the developmentalism inherent in this discourse. Rather, the children constructed their own discourses of risk based on the personality traits of the child. The children referred to such characteristics as being sensible, mature or responsible, in many instances as a key factor in their risk assessments. As a result, distinctions were often drawn between what was regarded as being risky for children in general, and what was regarded by a child as personally risky: 'I wouldn't do it because I'm quite, I'm more sensible to do, I wouldn't go out and take drugs because someone on TV did it. I suppose some people do' (Jill, 10).

In judging what was appropriate for children to watch, they also distinguished between violent and sexual content. Many of them pointed out that swearing and violence was part of their everyday lives, but sex was not. One boy was asked which he saw as being worse for children to see:

> They may have horror, they may have bad language but I couldn't watch anything with heavy sexual and nudity in it. Like that's getting a bit over the top. Well, I mean, what's the fun in seeing two people strip and have sex? I'd rather watch 5 minutes of horror than watch an hour of that.
>
> (Tim, 13)

Children defined risks from television in relation to what is relevant to their lives. They distinguished themselves from other children in terms of age and character and distinguished between different forms of risk in terms of their own experiences.

The discussion of children's attitudes towards risk from television illustrates the way in which the public sphere can intrude on the private sphere of the home. As Hood *et al.* note, 'the boundaries of the private and public are thus crossed inwards; outside dangers come into the home and have to be controlled, managed and generally interacted with' (Hood *et al.*, 1996: 106). Despite this recognition of public risks in the private sphere, the children's accounts showed that overwhelmingly they associated the private sphere of the home with safety. In addition to being located in the public sphere, risks were seen to exist 'outside', as opposed to 'inside' the home.

Between public and private: the local sphere

In contrast to the home, public spaces were frequently defined by the children in terms of risk. However, the children distinguished between their neighbourhoods and those beyond the boundary of their street/village/ network of friends' homes. By doing so, the children described an intermediate 'local' sphere between the public and the private. It is in this sphere that the children, of all ages, tended to spend most of their time and as a result they developed both a familiarity and knowledge of the places and people.

In part the local referred to areas within close proximity to the home: 'Cos it's really a little place so wherever I go . . . I don't have to go very far to see my friends' (Sheryl, 9). In some respects the children's construction of risk and safety was contingent upon the distance from their homes:

> Cos the further away you are, like there's a lot more things could happen to you like on the way. . . . But if you're local, just around this estate and you get hurt you can just go along to your house. But if you're far away you might not know many people.
>
> (Neil, 13)

But the local also referred to the people occupying this intermediate sphere. Hunter describes the intermediate sphere between public and private as 'qualitatively distinct from the public order. It is not a world of citizen strangers' (Hunter, 1995: 216). This was reflected in the comments of one girl about her mother's concerns for her safety: 'Well she doesn't worry as much cos she knows that I can look after myself in a way in this area cos I know lots of people around' (Pam, 10). This was most noticeable in relation to the children from rural areas, where the village was perceived in some respects as an extended family or community with people watching out for each other: 'It's like, well, you never know what's happening down in the city and that. Like in the countryside they could all sort of keep an eye on him, but not in the city' (Steve, 11). However, one girl also described how such watchfulness could also be restrictive:

Especially working in the shop and my mum works in the village and everybody knows who you are. So if I'm seen walking down the street with somebody who's smoking it will go back to my mum that I've been smoking and I'm not.

(Sally, 15)

Nevertheless, the local sphere was not associated with the same level of safety as the private sphere of the home. There were always certain local areas described by the children as risky: 'Well the railway's not as safe as the park cos sometimes weird people go up there' (Liam, 10). Moreover, the local sphere was not physically bounded in the same way and consequently was more open to exposure to risks from the public sphere. The safety associated with local areas, such as parks, was therefore contingent for the children. Particular incidents could alter the children's perceptions of a local area. This was clear from a story told by several of the children from one area, about a man who was said to have been interfering with children in their local park:

If it was Green Park you would need to go with an adult. . . . Cos a boy in my school got put upside down and his trousers pulled down. . . . So I'm not allowed to go there without an adult now till they catch him.

(Jim, 9)

The safety of this park was also described by the younger children as being contingent on the time of day. While the play area was full of children in the daytime, it was occupied by teenagers at night: 'Cos like all the teenagers and that, they all go to drink down there and take drugs and that' (Steve, 11). This changed the nature of the area from the children's perspective from a safe to a risky area.

The children's risk landscapes constructed a local sphere based on proximity to the home, and familiarity with and knowledge of the surroundings and people, within which there were feelings of relative safety. This was contrasted with their attitudes towards the public sphere.

Children and risk in public life

Images of childhood as a time of vulnerability, dependence and incompetence were influential in shaping the children's identities in public life. The children described feelings of vulnerability in public life, in relation to their concerns about unfamiliar spaces and people.

Many of the children described their fears of being lost. This was most apparent when the younger children described the possibilities of going into the city centre with friends for the first time. Often an enclosed out of town shopping centre was described as a stepping stone towards this. Though it may have been expected that the urban children would have expressed more confidence in this matter, being used to living in the city, they in fact expressed the same concerns as the rural children. It appears therefore that children's experiences were firmly situated in the private and local spheres and moving outside these was both challenging and frightening.

The older children, who tended to have greater access to public life, discussed the ways in which they assessed public spaces in terms of risk and safety. One boy described how he defined a particular area as risky: 'Broken glass everywhere, you generally get the idea of a place, I suppose spray painted walls all over' (Peter, 13). Often the physical features associated with risky spaces were based on class differences. For example, the visual images of what was a risky area, tended to be associated with particular forms of housing:

> You look down a street and you can see that you might not want to go down there and it's just by the way it's set out, maybe housing estates and you think it looks a bit rough. So I don't go into places like that because you're asking for it as far as I'm concerned.
>
> (Paul, 14)

Most notably, the children expressed concerns about the people around them in public life. Public space is formed by the bodies within it (Sennett, 1994: 370) and in the children's accounts it seems that public life is dangerous because of the people, the bodies, within it. We exist in a social world often surrounded by other people. To be able to function, we have to trust that these other people have no intention of harming us (Goffman, 1971: 384). Yet trust is often portrayed as a dangerous trait for children because they are regarded as an inherently vulnerable group (Jackson and Scott, 1999). Indeed, given the emphasis in child safety education on strangers, it is no surprise that the children were wary of others in public spaces. One boy spoke about what scared him: 'Other people and everything that I don't know . . . when I'm walking down the road some people just look at you and you think "what's he looking at me for?" and everything' (Drew, 10).

Despite often being surrounded by others, being with known people was often referred to by the children as a form of protection and as an essential form of risk management. One girl discussing the risk of sexual attacks noted that:

> In fact nearly all the kids that have happened, they're always like alone, or there's just a very few of them. I mean if we're going to a disco there'll be a big gang of us and we won't take chances by going up in twos and threes.
>
> (Kerry, 13)

Valentine (1997a) found that girls in particular were given a sense of confidence and invulnerability through the support of their friends. However, this study found that both boys and girls noted the risks of 'being alone' in public space. The reasons for their concerns varied – while for boys support from friends may have been in case of fights, for girls it was seen as a protection against sexual attack.

Children are taught who to trust and who not to, in particular through 'stranger danger' education. As part of the study this education was analysed and it was found that it tends to reinforce the public/private dichotomy in relation to risk – strangers are those who hang about parks, drive by streets where children play, lurk outside school gates. Strangers, by definition, occupy public not private spaces. Indeed, many of the children expressed concerns that as children, they were vulnerable to being 'taken away' by strangers.

> Well a child's more likely to be picked up by a stranger than an adult because . . . an adult's not going to come along and pick up another adult and say 'hey you're coming with me'.
>
> (Rebecca, 11)

Through such forms of safety education, children are given standardized knowledge with which to cope in public life. While the children repeated the official discourse on strangers in their accounts, for example 'don't talk to strangers', it was evident in the interviews that many also interpreted this discourse in their own way. Many of the children presented their own assessment of particular situations involving 'strangers'. They were aware that 'strangers' refer to almost everyone in public life and as such the 'don't speak to strangers' rule was experienced as interactionally problematic:

> Like people in the shop, they're strangers and you maybe have to ask them something. You are a stranger to other people as well and you could ask someone for directions and they could think the same thing about you.
>
> (Amanda, 11)

> If I saw someone that was in trouble, like he'd fallen out of a wheelchair . . . then I'd stop and help him. But I wouldn't stop and help a guy try and pump up his car tyre or clean his car.
>
> (Peter, 13)

Though children are told not to trust strangers, they are also told about 'safe strangers'[3] and thus that the dangers are contingent. The children's accounts indicate that they clearly made judgements about strangers based on criteria including: their appearance; their gender; their manner and actions; the type of questions they asked; and their relative vulnerability.

Furthermore, it is evident from the interviews that while many of the children expressed concerns about 'strangers', it was often older children or teenagers, rather than adult strangers, who were reported as being a source of risk:

> Adults have got more sense. Teenagers just go around with knives and drugs and smash things.
>
> (Caroline, 10)

> Young people, you know 15-year-olds hassling you about stuff, I think they're the kind of people you ought to be worried about . . . if you saw two, like 15- or 16-year-olds, you know, walking down the road I'd feel more worried than two 45-year-olds.
>
> (Darren, 15)

Children of all ages in the study, spoke about teenagers in parks taking drugs, drinking too much and hanging about. Teenagers are perhaps more likely than younger children to challenge the adult monopoly on using public space (Percy-Smith, 1998) and their presence was perceived to be threatening by the children. One girl described how she felt on the bus in the presence of teenagers:

> Me and Rebecca were like sitting on the same seat, and we were just like this because they were, they were like all drunk in the back singing and everything, and it was really scary. You were scared to talk or something.
>
> (Rosemary, 10)

The older children, teenagers themselves, had mixed feelings about this issue. While they, like the younger children expressed concerns about their peers, they also discussed their experiences, as teenagers, in being seen by others, as a source of threat:

> I think of myself as a pretty safe person, it's just the impression, you know, big, I'm a teenager. It's just, it's a stereotyping thing, people sort of seeing me and saying, oh he's bad, he's a teenager and he could be up to anything.
>
> (Darren, 15)

The children's description of their vulnerability and consequent lack of trust towards strangers – both adults and children – related to their perceptions and experiences of their own bodies in public space. Public space is designed primarily for adults, as a result of which children's physical size makes their participation in public life more difficult. This in turn reinforces the sense that public space is adult space. Indeed many of the younger children described themselves as being at risk in public spaces because of their physical size:

> Cos like an adult, if you've got an adult with you, because they've got more chance of fighting a person cos they're big. As long as you've got about seven of your friends that makes up the same as an adult.
>
> (Tom, 12)

Some of the children also described physical differences between boys and girls which made girls appear to be more vulnerable: 'Girls are physically weaker than boys. And boys, women generally don't approach boys, and boys are a bit, wary' (Rebecca, 11). Specific risks were also sometimes seen as gendered. One boy speaking about sexual risk explained why he was not concerned about this:

> I don't think it really worries me . . . girls probably get a bit more worried about it. You're like, OK with men, unless they fancy boys. But like women are hardly going to go out looking for teenage boys or whatever. It's more likely to be men looking for attractive girls.
>
> (John, 13)

While the children were very aware of their physicality in public spaces they also discussed their vulnerability in relation to their lack of knowledge and/or experience. The children tended to describe themselves as less knowledgeable and so less competent in public life than adults:

> Cos sometimes your parents are, they might seem a bit unfair on you, but they're usually right. Like they might tell you that you shouldn't go and do something and then you, then you should probably do that cos they're usually right because they know. Cos they're usually like older, so I suppose they know more about it.
>
> (Josie, 12)

The children seemed to make a direct connection between knowledge and risk management. As such, different forms of knowledge on risks were seen as age appropriate.

> Well we've not been taught about it yet because you get drugs talk in high school. You get all the kiddie things in primary and in high school you get all the drugs. . . . . Cos you could get younger children to get it. But older children are more sensible so they won't do it. . . . Cos they get all the sensible things, like what to do in a fire and that. We just get projects like Vikings.
>
> (Jim, 9)

Therefore from some of the children's accounts, it seemed that to some extent knowledge replaced the need for experiential learning. This relates to the correlation children drew between risk and the unknown and its correlation with risk and danger. However, as Goffman argues, everyday life is not lived in a state of constant alarm, but rather, that we learn to sense alarm and how to cope. We do 'not so much come to know the world around' us as we 'become experienced and practised in coping with it' (Goffman, 1971: 294). Yet, the extent to which children engage in this process of becoming 'experienced and practised' in coping with public life is structured by their subordinate position in adult–child relations.

Limits on children's participation in public life

Cahill argues that, 'the familiar tale of childhood's history in Western societies is a story of the sequestering of the young for what increasing numbers of their elders came to see as the young's own good' (Cahill, 1990: 392). Indeed, public space has come to be defined as adult space in which children are either seen as being at risk, or as being a source of risk (Valentine, 1996). Children's participation in public space is controlled and limited in several ways. First, there are formal, often legal, restrictions on where children are allowed to go. The most extreme example of this is the interest being shown in Britain by the government and the police in the use of curfews for children in the US (Drakeford and Butler, 1998). A curfew for children under 16 was implemented for a trial period between October 1997 and April 1998, in Hamilton, Scotland, thereby legally restricting children's access to public space. Commenting on the curfew in Hamilton, a police superintendent said:

> This is not a case of the heavy hand of the law coming in. It is a case of alerting people to the dangers that children face. Children are at risk from drug dealers and paedophiles and people in some areas complain that they are threatened and harassed by youngsters. The initiative is child safety and the good of the entire community and we dare not lose sight of that.
>
> (*The Observer*, 12 April 1998)

Second, there are parental restrictions on children's participation in and access to public life (Hood *et al.*, 1996). Parents' boundaries limit children's experiences, in terms of the who, what, where, when and why of children's participation in public life. Often such restrictions are based on assumptions about children's lack of competencies in managing risks and so protecting themselves. While this assumption has been challenged (Hutchby and Moran-Ellis, 1997), children's presumed lack of competence is nevertheless influential in shaping parental restrictions on their participation in public life (Valentine, 1997a). For example, road safety advice given in Leeds noted that:

Children of ALL ages are immature, impulsive, unpredictable, lacking in skill and experience, not able to judge speed and distance, not always doing what they're told.... However sensible your child may seem, even at 15 he or she is still a child.

(Hillman *et al.*, 1990)

Third, there are restrictions on children's behaviour in public spaces. It is expected that young children will be accompanied by adults, so much so that children who are alone are often asked by adults where their parents are (Cahill, 1990). Teenagers are perhaps the group most often criticized for their behaviour in public space, most notably 'hanging around' is perceived as a threat to social order (Cahill, 1990). Finally, many public amenities are geared towards adults' use in terms of their physical size, for example, the height of public telephones (Cahill, 1990).

Nevertheless, children do not simply accept the restrictions on their participation in public life. Some of the children were critical of formal restrictions: 'Cos we're small and we're not allowed to go into the shops without an adult, it's quite annoying. You must be accompanied by an adult inside most shops.... It's a bit boring' (Holly, 10). Others complained about the limits that their smaller physical size imposed on their participation:

I like movies, the only thing I hate about it, there's only two things I don't like about the movies, it's the seat, it's the people. I mean if they're tall, I mean I'm primary six and I'm quite small, I'm quite small for my class and if there's usually an adult with a young person, they usually get in my way and I usually have to move seat.

(Lewis, 10)

Furthermore, there were many strategies the children employed for subverting both legal and parental restrictions. One 12-year-old girl described her strategy for gaining entrance to a film for which 15 was the minimum age:

I'm quite small and I'm not, I don't really look 15. So my friends just said, what you just have to do, just put on quite a lot of make up and act like you're 15 and when you go in, like when you're going past the people just pretend to bend down like you've dropped something and they'll think you're just bending down.... I was asking my friend 'how do you act 15?' And they say 'well you just, you don't laugh a lot, like when someone says something you just don't spend the whole time laughing. You don't bite your nails', cos I always bite my nails.... I was just trying to walk in and I was trying to walk as tall as I could cos sometimes people think that if you're taller you look older ... I was wearing like big high heels and trying to look taller.

(Josie, 12)

Similarly, the children were active in their negotiation of boundaries with their parents. There were many different strategies that the children employed in either direct or indirect forms of negotiation: lying; withholding information from parents; breaking rules; collusion with friends or siblings to deceive parents; persistence in asking parents; being moody with parents; earning the right to go out by demonstrating responsibility; playing parents off against each other.

While there were few differences between the children with respect to the strategies used, the issues addressed were often different. For example, while Jill (10) described breaking the rules, by watching a programme on television in her room when she had been told not to, Sally (15) described drinking alcohol with her friends. Furthermore, the older children may be more practised in the art of negotiation with their parents:

> Cos I used to suck up at first and do everything but then I'd realized that they really knew that. So now I just say fine if they want to do it fine. And then I ask again and I don't go all angry . . . and then in the end they do say that I can do it.
>
> (Sally, 15)

Such strategies not only demonstrated children's understandings of the family and their place within it, but also demonstrated competence in the assessment and management of certain risks. However, Kelley *et al.* (1997) found that children were more likely to object to parental restrictions on their activities when the connection between such restrictions and protection was not apparent. This was also evident in our study. In many cases children described parental and legal restrictions as being 'for their own good': 'We've got a good mum. She's over-protective but it's better to have a mum that worries about you a lot than one that lets you run wild and get in trouble' (Peter, 13).

Moreover, the negotiation process between children and parents was limited by children's own perceived limits to their participation in public life:

> I always say to myself, even before I bother asking my mum, it's a bit stupid. Like if I wanted to go to Edinburgh in the middle of the night, I know myself I probably wouldn't want to go if I thought about the danger and stuff.
>
> (John, 13)

Therefore, while the children expected there to be some negotiation with their parents, they also expected their parents to protect them by limiting their access to and participation in public space.

Conclusion

Children's theorizing around risk, safety and danger can be situated within the public/private distinction. Children defined physical locations according to safety and risk. They distinguished between the safety of the private 'inside' sphere of the home and the risky nature of the 'outside' – the local neighbourhood and wider public spaces. The children also described their relations with others in these locations. Most notably, the children expressed concerns about their participation in public life in terms of threats from other people. In particular, this reflected the lack of trust which Giddens (1991) argues is being eroded, as a result of which risk anxiety has become a feature of everyday life.

While the children did therefore seem to reflect public discourses on children and risk, they were also reflexive in their conceptualizations of risk. They did not simply accept official discourses on children and risk. Rather they constructed their own identities within public space, based on their own experiences. In addition, the children negotiated both parental and legal limits placed on their participation in public life. In this respect the children demonstrated their competence in risk assessment and management.

However, the extent to which children engage in the individual reflexive monitoring of risk must be contextualized. First, the extent and nature of children's participation in public life is structured, in the same way as adults by class, gender and so on. For example, social class can determine the extent to which children are exposed to the risk of ill health or accidents (Roberts *et al.*, 1995). Second, children's individualized landscapes of risk occur within the context of discourses on child safety and risk, for example safety education in schools. These standardized discourses present an image of the child at risk which shape their 'individual' risk assessment. Third, children's lives are standardized by their subordinate position in relation to adults (Hood-Williams, 1990). While Büchner *et al.* (1994) argue that children's lives are now increasingly individualized, as a result of their earlier acquisition of independence, parental perceptions of risk are still influential in shaping children's everyday lives (Hood *et al.*, 1996). Therefore, though children reflexively constructed and monitored risk and safety, this must be located within the wider context of the social relations which form children's everyday lives.

Notes

This article is based on a paper, 'What Do You Mean by Risk: Understanding Children's Conceptualisations of Risk', presented at the British Sociological Association conference in Glasgow, April 1999. The research itself derives from a project funded by the ESRC as part of the 'Children 5–16: Growing into the 21st Century' programme. The project, titled 'The Impact of Risk and Parental Risk Anxiety on the Everyday Lives of Children', is based at the University of Stirling and being conducted by Professor Sue Scott of the University of Durham and Dr Jeni Harden, together with Dr Kathryn Backett-Milburn of the University of Edinburgh and Professor Stevi Jackson of the University of York.

1 This age group is referred to in this article as the younger children.
2 This age group is referred to in this article as the older children.
3 Children are advised that 'safe strangers' are police officers, shop keepers and ladies with children.

References

Beck, U. (1992) *Risk Society: Towards a New Modernity.* London: Sage.

Büchner, P., H. H. Krüger and M. du Bois Reymond (1994) 'Growing Up as a "Modern" Child in Western Europe: The Impact of Modernisation and Civilization Processes on the Everyday Lives of Children', *Sociological Studies of Children* 6: 1–23.

Buckingham, D. (1994) 'Television and the Definition of Childhood', in B. Mayall (ed.) *Children's Childhoods Observed and Experienced*, pp. 79–96. London: Falmer Press.

Cahill, S. (1990) 'Childhood and Public Life: Reaffirming Biographical Divisions', *Social Problems* 37: 390–402.

Cheal, D. (1991) *Family and the State of Theory.* New York: Harvester Wheatsheaf.

Cohen, S. and L. Taylor (1992) *Escape Attempts: The Theory and Practice of Resistance to Everyday Life.* London: Routledge.

Drakeford, M. and I. Butler (1998) 'Curfews for Children: Testing a Policy Proposal in Practice', *Youth and Policy* 62: 1–14.

Furlong, A. and F. Cartmel (1997) *Young People and Social Change: Individualisation and Risk in Later Modernity.* Milton Keynes: Open University Press.

Gamarnikow, E. (1983) *The Public and the Private.* London: Heinemann.

Giddens, A. (1991) *Modernity and Self-Identity: Self and Society in the Late Modern Age.* Cambridge: Polity Press.

Goffman, E. (1971) *Relations in Public.* London: Pelican.

Green, J. (1997) *Risk and Misfortune: The Social Construction of Accidents.* London: UCL Press.

Harker, P. and L. Moore (1996) 'Primary Health Care Action to Reduce Child Home Accidents: A Review', *Health Education Journal* 53: 322–31.

Hillman, M., J. Adams and J. Whitelegg (1990) *One False Move: A Study of Children's Independent Mobility.* London: Policy Studies Institute.

Hood, S., P. Kelley, B. Mayall and A. Oakley (1996) *Children Parents and Risk.* London: Social Science Research Unit, Institute of Education.

Hood-Williams, J. (1990) 'Patriarchy for Children: On the Stability of Power Relations in Children's Lives', in L. Chisholm, P. Büchner, H.-H. Krüger and P. Brown (eds) *Children, Youth and Social Change: A Comparative Perspective*, pp. 155–71. London: Falmer Press.

Hunter, A. (1995) 'Private, Parochial and Public Social Orders: The Problem of Crime and Incivility in Urban Communities', in P. Kasinitz (ed.) *Metropolis: Centre and Symbol of Our Times*, pp. 209–22. Basingstoke: Macmillan.

Hutchby, I. and J. Moran-Ellis (1997) *Children and Social Competence: Arenas of Action.* London: Falmer Press.

Jackson, S. and S. Scott (1999) 'Risk Anxiety and the Social Construction of Childhood', in D. Lupton (ed.) *Risk and Sociocultural Theory.* Cambridge: Cambridge University Press.

Jenks, C. (1996) *Childhood.* London: Routledge.

Kelley, P., B. Mayall and S. Hood (1997) 'Children's Accounts of Risk', *Childhood* 4(3): 305–24.

Kelley, P., D. Buckingham and H. Davies (1999) 'Talking Dirty: Children Sexual Knowledge and Television', *Childhood* 6(2): 221–42.

Moran, E., D. Warde, L. Macleod, G. Mayes and J. Gillies (1997) 'Stranger Danger: What Do Children Know?', *Child Abuse Review* 6: 11–23.

Percy-Smith, B. (1998) 'Negotiated Spaces: Exploring the Geography of Adolescents', paper presented at the Institute of British Geographers Conference, Kingston.

Pilcher, J. (1996) 'Gillick and After: Children and Sex in the 1980s and 1990s', in J. Pilcher and S. Wagg (eds) *Thatcher's Children? Politics, Childhood and Society in the 1980s and 1990s*, pp. 77–93. London: Falmer Press.

Ribbens McCarthy, J. and R. Edwards (1999) 'Gendered Lives, Gendered Concepts? The Significance of Children for Theorising "Public" and "Private"', paper presented at the Annual Conference of the British Sociological Association, Glasgow, 6–9 April.

Roberts, H., S. J. Smith and C. Bryce (1995) *Children at Risk?* Milton Keynes: Open University Press.

Scott, S., S. Jackson and K. Backett-Milburn (1998) 'Swings and Roundabouts: Risk Anxiety and the Everyday Worlds of Children', *Sociology* 32: 689–707.

Sennett, R. (1994) *Flesh and Stone: The Body and the City in Western Civilization.* London: Faber and Faber.

Slater, D. (1998) 'Public/Private', in C. Jenks (ed.) *Core Sociological Dichotomies*, pp. 138–50. London: Sage.

Valentine, G. (1996) 'Children Should Be Seen and Not Heard: The Production and Transgression of Adults' Public Space', *Urban Geography* 17: 205–20.

Valentine, G. (1997a) '"Oh Yes I Can." "Oh No You Can't": Children and Parents' Understandings of Kids' Competence to Negotiate Public Space Safely', *Antipode*: 65–89.

Valentine, G. (1997b) 'A Safe Place to Grow Up? Parenting, Perceptions of Children's Safety and the Rural Idyll', *Journal of Rural Studies* 13: 137–48.

Weintraub, J. (1995) 'Varieties and Vicissitudes of Public Space', in P. Kasinitz (ed.) *Metropolis: Centre and Symbol of Our Times*, pp. 280–319. Basingstoke: Macmillan.

57

SPIRITUAL CHALLENGES TO CHILDREN FACING VIOLENT TRAUMA

James Garbarino and Claire Bedard

Source: *Childhood* 3(4) (1996): 467–478.

Religion, sprituality and the psychology of trauma

Religion and spirituality play a central role in the perception and construction of meaning in the lives of many people, including children and youth. Although commonly used interchangeably, 'religion' and 'spirituality', are not synonymous. For instance, while some people seek to infuse practice and theology with spirituality, institutionalized religion can sometimes exist separately from spirituality. Similarly, there are those who live with a profoundly spiritual orientation but operate independently of organized religion. Here, we focus on the spiritual elements of trauma. By 'spiritual', we refer to the inner life of children and adolescents as the cradle for a construction of meaning. (See Helminiak, 1996, for various usages of the term.)

The psychology of religion seeks to link the core human experience of spirituality (especially as it is manifest in institutionalized practices and beliefs) to the principles and models developed to illuminate the non-spiritual (and thus 'secondary') dimensions of human experience. Numerous studies have identified a general link between human well-being and religious foundations (e.g. Ellison *et al.*, 1989; George and McNamara, 1984; Wright *et al.*, 1993). This link includes the role of religious experience as the basis for 'a personal control against problem behavior' in youth (Jessor and Jessor, 1977: 22). The role of religion in conveying a sense of 'meaningfulness' and thereby providing a buffer against depression may well be one source of this effect.

Wright *et al.* (1993) point to the belief that one's life has a spiritual purpose as the source of the 'spiritual support' that buffers against depression. With young people, they have operationalized this concept of spiritual support as church attendance (at least twice a month) and agreement with two statements: 'Religion is especially important to me because it answers many questions about the meaning of my life' and 'I try hard to carry my religion into my other dealings in life because my religious beliefs are what really lie behind my whole approach to life' (Wright *et al.*, 1993: 563). In their study, these measures of spiritual support were correlated with lower depression scores. Of course, this equating of religion and spirituality is not fully adequate, given the less than perfect correlation between the two.

Another important dimension for understanding the role of religious support in human experience is to be found in studies of the *role of religion in coping with stress* (of which our interest in 'trauma' is a crucial subcategory). Shortz and Worthington (1994) have implemented Pargament's (Pargament *et al.*, 1990) idea of translating general stress-coping models to a religious framework in the following formulation:

(a) Stressful events can be religious in nature.
(b) Appraisals are often religious, can take the form of causal attributions, and differ with regard to situational contexts.
(c) Religious activities are often the main coping activities employed by religious individuals.
(d) Finally, outcomes or stressful events are often religious.

(Shortz and Worthington, 1994: 172)

Employing this model with a sample of young adults retrospectively reporting on their adolescent experience of parental divorce, Shortz and Worthington (1994) found that 'spiritually based' coping activities (i.e. 'trusting God for protection and turning to him for guidance') were most significantly related to positive coping behaviors (e.g. 'positive focus' and 'interpersonal support'). As we shall see, the role of trauma in threatening or even shattering an individual's belief in 'divine protective force' and the role of spiritual resources in restoring that link is an issue which deserves the attention of researchers and practitioners.

Carl Jung and Viktor Frankl are two clinical theorists who have explored the role of spiritual support in the larger scheme of life crises encountered by human beings in the modern social environment. For example, Jung (1933) wrote that 'neurosis must be understood as the suffering of a human being who has not discovered what life means for him' (Jung, 1933: 260). Frankl's perspective is evident in the title of his classic work *Man's Search for Meaning* (Frankl, 1963). We can see support for this perspective in the growing body of evidence linking the ability to tell a coherent and *meaningful* account of one's life to the crucial variables of resilience in the face of adversity (Cohler, 1991). Indeed, this evidence offers support for the proposition that the emergence of this ability in children and youth is *the* most important foundation for resilience.

All this provides a backdrop for exploring a central concern with the spiritual challenges of trauma. Trauma has two principal components: overwhelming arousal and overwhelming negative cognitions. This latter facet is captured in Herman's (1992) formulation that to experience trauma is 'to come face to face with human vulnerability in the natural world and with the capacity for evil in human nature'. This is the human core of the term 'overwhelming negative cognitions'. Where do we go with this in practice?

Trauma as a negative religious experience

Religious experience is about enlightenment, coming to know 'the light of the world'. William James (1902) provided the classic formulation of this *positively* overwhelming cognition in his discussion of the core of religion to be found in the partaking of a higher consciousness. James put it this way,

> ... you will undergo so deep an immersion into these exalted states of consciousness as to be wet all over, if I may so express myself, and the cold shiver of doubt ... will have long since passed away. . . . You will then be convinced, I trust, that these states of consciousness, of 'union' form a perfectly definite class of experiences, of which the soul may occasionally partake, and which certain persons may live by in a deeper sense than they live by anything else with which they have acquaintance.
>
> (James, 1902: 101)

These positively overwhelming cognitions provide the basis for religion as

> ... the feelings, acts, and experiences of individual men [*sic*] in their solitude, so far as they apprehend themselves to stand in relation to whatever they may consider the divine.
>
> (James, 1902: 34)

What then is trauma in this scheme of consciousness and expanded under-standing? Initially, we can see trauma is the *reverse* of what could be called a positive spiritual cognition, the experience of darkness rather than enlight-enment, a plunging into the shadows of life, coming face-to-face with the capacity for evil in human nature, with human vulnerability in the natural world, with the reality of the dark side (Herman, 1992). We say 'initially', because upon closer inspection of the great spiritual masters we come to see that these experiences of the dark side need not be spiritual dead-ends, but rather can serve as the beginning of an even deeper spiritual awakening.

Most of the world's major religions contain some awareness of this. Buddhism, for example, builds upon a recognition that 'suffering' is intrinsic to human experience, but that there is an Eightfold Path to the Cessation of Suffering (Sivaraksa, 1992). Likewise, the critical core of Christianity is Christ suffering on the cross and then being reborn. This is where religion and spirituality meet, in the relationship between the experience of the body and mind on the one hand, and the life of the soul, on the other. The issue is always the extent to which religious doctrines, practices and institutions nurture spirituality – as opposed to serving other goals such as socialization, social control, economic and political power, etc.

The core of spirituality is a recognition of oneself as being more than only a physical being, i.e. as a multidimensional person with a physical as well as spiritual identity or existence. This recognition includes awareness of the primacy of spiritual existence. One student of spiritual development describes this as a shift to believing in oneself as a 'spiritual being having a physical experience' (Dyer, 1995). Even for many who see themselves as religious, this recognition requires a fundamental shift: from the western materialist metaphysic of body first, consciousness second, to spirit first, and body second.

What are the requisite elements of this shift? One is a transcendent organizing belief in a coherent spiritual existence (a Higher Power, a spiritual Source, a spiritual Creator, an all-benevolent higher spiritual being). Another is a belief in oneself as being connected in spirit to the Higher Power and to other human beings as other spiritual peers having a physical experience. These elements are deeply implicated in the experience of trauma as well as prospects for recovering from it (even for learning from it).

The challenge of meaning

Bessel van der Kolk (1994) asks incoming psychiatric patients, 'Have you given up all hope of finding meaning in your life?' Among those who experienced major trauma prior to age 5, 74 percent answer 'yes'. Among those who experienced major trauma after age 20 the figure is 'only' 10 percent. We have asked that question of thousands of professionals, students and other adults and find an overall incidence of about 1 percent (asking people to respond anonymously, but in a public setting).

What do we make of this? We think it reflects the fact that trauma represents an enormous challenge to any individual's understanding of the meaning and purpose of life, the metaphysical and spiritual dimensions, and that this crisis is particularly difficult for children. Further, if the crisis of meaning and purpose cannot be acknowledged and mastered, it can result in psychological and physiological symptoms which can become debilitating (to the point of needing psychiatric care).

Spiritual elements of trauma in children and youth

The above data suggest that there is a developmental context for this experience. Just as there are 'critical periods' in the development of many other human attributes (e.g. vision), the initial structures of meaning are most efficiently and effectively established in early childhood. Trauma is a challenge to meaningfulness, and the enormity of this challenge is greatest for the youngest victims. They have less well-developed cognitive skills to be employed in making sense of the world, and they have not had the time to build a solid framework of meaning.

What is more, we can readily acknowledge that children are more open to spirituality than are adults in the sense that their experience of reality is less constricted by social conventions regarding what is real and what is not. Thus, for example, children are generally more ready to believe that there are spirits everywhere around them (as opposed to most adults who have been trained to make clear distinctions between the culturally 'acceptable' spirit world of religion and the 'unacceptable' world of 'fantasy'). Silverman and Worden (1992) offer documentation of this in a study of children of whom a parent had died. Some 57 percent reported speaking to the dead parent; 43 percent of those children felt they received an answer; and 81 percent believed their dead parents were watching them. In contrast, Kalish and Reynolds (1973) reported that 12 percent of adults reported such direct contact with the dead. Barreto and Bermann (1992) proceed from this to explore 'ghosts as transitional objects in clinical work with children coping with bereavement.

As is always the case in comparing children and adults, children are *both* more vulnerable to harm and more open to developmentally enhancing experiences. Thus it is that when spiritual leaders advise us to be 'childlike' they are offering a double-edged sword: to being closer to the spiritual domain and to being less protected by social conventions of belief.

Older individuals have had greater opportunity (i.e. a longer period of experience) to construct a framework of meaning (and thus have the most 'metaphysical momentum' in the sense of the longest period of building up behaviors and beliefs to substantiate and support core belief systems), or are more rooted in the social conventions of meaning (including religion), and possess cognitive skills that enhance their ability to meet the challenge of trauma to meaning successfully. Davidson and Smith (1990) report that when faced with potentially traumatic experiences, children under the age of 10 are three times more likely than teenagers and adults to respond with post-traumatic stress disorder (PTSD) – 56 vs 18 percent.

Where spirituality and religion rely on an intrinsic belief in a higher, all-benevolent power, trauma can temporarily or permanently shatter this belief. It can challenge children's understanding of themselves as spiritual beings having a physical experience because it brings about a perceived threat to or even a severance from their spiritual connection – between them and the Higher Power which they believe exists to protect them. Trauma creates a profound breach which separates the child from a place within where he or she believed in a higher spiritual power, whether referred to as Allah, God, Buddha, Jehovah, the Creator, or whatever language used to reflect their relationship with the larger spiritual dimension of existence. This is a profound form of 'cognitive dissonance', perhaps better termed 'spiritual dissonance'.

That is why we will often hear trauma victims – children, youth and adults – say 'If there is a God, how could He/She allow such atrocities?' Of course, the spiritual dissonance engendered by confronting 'the problem of evil' is itself a fundamental religious issue. 'Solving' that issue is one of the crucial steps in the spiritual path, from Jesus on the cross crying out 'God, why hast thou forsaken me?' to a Bosnian young woman subjected to multiple rape by her Serbian captors (as reported by the psychotherapist who treated her): 'She said that she could no longer make any sense of her life because of the rape, because she had lost everyone she loved, and because she was afraid she was pregnant. Although she was religious, prayer no longer consoled her' (Kozaric-Kovacic *et al.*, 1995: 430).

Even trauma inflicted upon others may trigger this kind of questioning. For example, interviews with teenagers involved in acts of severe violence (e.g. shooting) suggest the possible traumatic dimensions of committing assault (Garbarino, 1995). Those who deal with the most heinous of killers (e.g. sadistic serial killers) outline the nihilism that pervades their metaphysical universe (e.g. Douglas and Olshaker, 1995). Their thinking seems to be thus: 'How could God permit a monster like me to exist?'

Trauma shatters our expectations of divine protection in a fierce psychological confrontation as does the general belief in the existence of evil in a generic theological debate. This is a prime reason why attention to spiritual development issues deserves a central place in efforts to intervene in trauma cases, with the victims *and* with the perpetrators. *Both* are facing dramatic challenges to their very existence as spiritual beings by virtue of their respective experiences with 'the capacity for evil in human nature'.

The eclipse of God and the dawn of spiritual freedom

Children try to understand not only what is happening to them but why; and in doing that, they call upon the religious life they have experienced, the spiritual values they have received, as well as other sources of potential explanation.

(Coles, 1990: 100)

Speaking about children traumatized from having become suddenly crippled due to illness, psychoanalyst Erich Lindemann (cited in Coles, 1990) makes the following observation:

These are young people who suddenly have become quite a bit older; they are facing possible death, or serious limitation of their lives; It would be a mistake . . . to emphasize unduly a psychiatric point of view . . . if those children want to cry with you, and be disappointed with you, and wonder with you where their God is, then you can be there for them.

(Coles, 1990: 101)

If adults imagine the Higher Power as a caring, protective, all-benevolent figure – in short as the ideal parental figure – then it would make sense that children's imagery of a Higher Power also includes a sense of the protective, ideal parent figure. What children may add to this concept of spirituality is that in their cases, God's persona would be magnified by the particular developmental absolute need children have for care, protection and love in addition to their need to believe that a parent is almighty and without flaw, as demonstrated even in the most horrid cases of parental abuses of children.

When this need is absolutely violated, some children will seek out a negative universe on the grounds that anything is better than nothing. This is one of the origins of extreme negative behavior later in life such as exhibited by serial killers – brutal child abuse that leads to a descent into evil to provide *some* structure of meaning for the child (Douglas and Olshaker, 1995). It also has implications for identity in the sense that when faced with the prospect of psychic annihilation, human beings will opt for even negative identities (Gilligan, 1996). A convicted killer once put it this way to a colleague of ours, 'I'd rather be wanted for murder than not be wanted at all.'

Magical thinking is an important feature of early childhood. It forms the basis for fantasy play, which itself is an important resource for children in developing and working through alternative scenarios as solutions for day-to-day issues and problems in their lives. When trauma overwhelms the child's play and constricts it in repetitive unproductive patterns it may be said to be 'captured' (Garbarino and Manley, 1996). Captured play is often linked to traumatic experiences. In captured play children seek unsuccessfully to find a meaningful solution to the crisis of meaning imposed by the shattered assumptions they experience in the wake of trauma. They are often literally looking for God in a world in which God has disappeared.

The origins of these shattered assumptions may be domestic (e.g. child abuse in the family) or community (e.g. living in a war zone or being a street child subject to sexual exploitation and punitive violence). Whatever the specific origins, we believe there are common issues to be found in the challenge to meaningfulness – specifically the eclipse of God in the child's world that flows from the shattered assumptions of trauma. This rendering of trauma as a spiritual challenge finds expression in the work of many thinkers and helpers in the helping tradition who begin their work in the 'psychological' domain, but find their impulse to understand and to help leads them inevitably to the spiritual. We see this evident in the path taken by Carl Jung (1933), Thomas Moore (1992), Robert Coles (1990) and Wayne Dyer (1995), among others. Frankl (1963) followed this path through the Nazi concentration camps to conclude, 'It is this spiritual freedom – which cannot be taken away – that makes life meaningful and purposeful' (Frankl, 1963: 106).

Each of these individuals began seeking answers to the psychological challenges of traumatic experiences in the development of human consciousness, and discovered a path that led to and through the unconscious to the spiritual, and ultimately from the darkness to the light of spiritual freedom. Based upon her work with trauma survivors, Janoff-Bulman puts it this way:

> It may seem remarkable, yet it is not unusual for survivors, over time, to wholly reevaluate their traumatic experience by altering the positive value and meaningfulness of the event itself. The victimization certainly would not have been chosen, but it is ultimately seen by many as a powerful, even to some extent worthwhile, teacher of life's most important lessons.
>
> (Janoff-Bulman, 1992)

We follow the same path to our view of intervention.

Implications for intervention

What does a spiritual analysis imply for intervention? It implies that we embrace psychological even physiological modalities in understanding trauma (and in intervening on behalf of the traumatized individuals and groups), *but only as part of a larger strategy for healing the wounds of trauma.* Thus, we may employ conventional 'psychological first aid' in the form of debriefing and information clarification, and be prepared to offer pharmacological interventions designed to aid the individual in dealing with the sequelae of the overwhelming arousal which is a constituent part of the traumatic experience. But a perspective which is sensitive to the spiritual essence of children and youth tells us to be prepared to go further, to recognize the need to deal with the metaphysical wounds that arise from the overwhelming cognitions, to deal practically with the eclipse of God (or Buddha, or Allah, or Jehovah) itself. To do this we must embrace the spiritual dimensions of traumatized persons and groups and incorporate them into interventions with children and youth (Meyer and Lansell, 1996). We see the following three broad strategies as practical ways to accomplish this goal:

1. Identify culturally appropriate avenues for accessing the spiritual resources of the affected individual or group

For example, working with Khmer traumatized by the barbarism of the Khmer Rouge/Pol Pot regime in Cambodia during the 1970s, Molleca and his colleagues (1985) incorporated Buddhist rituals and spiritual models into the healing process. This permitted the trauma victims to make peace with the physical loss of relatives, and enhanced efforts to intervene psychologically. Central to this intervention strategy is a commitment to meditation.

In North America, American-Indian tribes and Canadian native peoples are slowly returning to traditional healing methods. When dealing with native Indians, a spiritual approach to trauma could include working with the victims by incorporating methods such as healing circles, vision quests, sweat lodges or dialog with elders. In Central and South America, the assistance of religious workers could be integrated into the healing process. The intervention of indigenous spiritual leaders or shamans can provide an essential complement to psychological treatment. Culturally sensitive methods can go a long way in establishing a trust base for non-traditional and traditional healing methods. Since trauma shatters a person's sense of trust in the world, rebuilding trust in this way is an important first step in the therapeutic process. Even the well-known '12 step' programs such as Alcoholics Anonymous make a spiritual connection and incorporate spirituality as a core component.

2. Explore innovative/alternative strategies for accessing spiritual resources in affected individuals and groups

For example, although meditation is 'foreign' to many western populations, it may be useful in assisting trauma victims find spiritual resources otherwise inaccessible for them. This has certainly been testified to by individuals who have found meditation to assist the 'normal' process of personal growth and development. Meditation helps reconnect to a feeling of oneness with all life, helping those who practice it to access a sense of peace.

> Meditation is the most important and distinctive element of Buddhism. Through deepening awareness comes acceptance, and through acceptance comes seemingly miraculous generosity of spirit and empowerment for the work that compassion requires of us.
>
> (Sivaraksa, 1992: 72)

Bell (pers. comm.) has explored the use of the spirituality and discipline of 'eastern' martial arts as a tool for working with traumatized inner-city African-American youth. Once we acknowledge the centrality of spiritual issues in trauma then our eyes are opened to a wide range of possible interventions drawn from 'foreign' cultures, but made relevant by the fact that although people vary dramatically as 'human beings having a physical experience', they are undifferentiated as 'spiritual beings'.

3. Support the spiritual development of those charged with the task of intervention

Many who have been involved in or observed intervention with traumatized individuals and groups have reported a kind of contagious effect, and labeled this phenomenon 'secondary victimization' (Danieli, 1996). To confront horror and evil, even second hand, is itself a spiritual challenge. One implication is the need to support the spiritual development (even remediation) of the helpers themselves. Buddhist activist Sulak Sivaraksa (1992) renders this need thus:

> In the crises of the present day, those of us who work in society, who confront power and injustice on a regular basis, get beaten down and exhausted. At least once a year, we need to visit a retreat center to regain our spiritual strength so that we can continue to confront society. Spiritual masters are like springs of fresh water. We who work in society need to carry that pure water to flood the banks and fertilize the land, the trees, in order to be of use to the plants and animals, so that they can taste something fresh and be revitalized. If we do not go back to the spring, our minds will get polluted, just as water becomes polluted, and we will not be of much use to the plants, the trees, or the earth. At home, we must practice our meditation or prayer at least every morning or evening.
>
> (Sivaraksa, 1992: 71)

Each of these three principles can guide the construction of intervention programs and should be entered into the programing equation each time crises emerge that require professional response to traumatized populations of children and youth, whose special links to the spiritual world coupled with their cognitive functioning create a special vulnerability to the unraveling of meaning implicit in the challenge of trauma. While the full programatic implications of these three principles are yet to be detailed, we see this as important and useful work to be done in accomplishing this goal. Indeed, it is the focal point for our work in the coming years, and it is the rationale for the newly created Half Full Foundation.[1]

Working in collaboration with the Family Life Development Center, the focus of the Half Full Foundation will be to uncover and enhance the spiritual core of violent and troubled youth – who are overwhelmingly kids with a history of traumatic victimization. The first step in this process will be a study of 'Kids Who Kill and Their Brothers Who Don't'. This study is designed to uncover the life histories of young killers, partly to illuminate the path followed, partly to contrast this path with that of a sibling. We believe this study will help document the spiritual development issues faced by traumatized children, and the personal and social costs of leaving these issues unresolved. The second focus of the Half Full Foundation will be to identify and promote spiritual development programs for violent youth – including those in the 'Kids Who Kill' study. The third goal will be to promote educational programs for professionals in the legal system to broaden and deepen their understanding of the inner lives of violent youth – the role of trauma in their background, their potential for healing and the programatic implications of a 'narrative' focus in dealing with them.

Note

1 For further information write to The Half Full Foundation, Box 24, Ithaca, NY 14851–0024, USA.

References

Barreto, S. and E. Bermann (1992) 'Ghosts as Transitional Objects: The Impact of Cultural Belief Systems upon Childhood Mourning', paper presented to the American Orthopsy-chiatric Association, New York, May.

Cohler, B. (1991) 'The Life Story and the Study of Resilience and Response to Adversity', *Journal of Narrative and Life History* 1: 169–200.

Coles, R. (1990) *The Spiritual Life of Children*. Boston, MA: Houghton Mifflin.

Danieli, Y. (1996) 'Who Takes Care of the Caretakers?' in R. Apfel and B. Simon (eds) *Minefields in their Hearts*. New Haven, CT: Yale.

Davidson, J. and R. Smith (1990) 'Traumatic Experiences in Psychiatric Outpatients', *Journal of Traumatic Stress Studies* 3: 459–75.

Douglas, J. and M. Olshaker (1995) *Mindhunter*. New York: Scribner.

Dyer, W. (1995) *Your Sacred Self*. New York: Harper Collins.

Ellison, C., D. Gay and T. Glass (1989) 'Does Religious Commitment Contribute to Individual Life Satisfaction?', *Social Forces* 86: 100–23.

Frankl, V. (1963) *Man's Search for Meaning: An Introduction to Logotherapy*. New York: Washington Square Press.

Garbarino, J. (1995) *Raising Children in a Socially Toxic Environment*. San Francisco: Jossey-Bass.

Garbarino, J. and J. Manley (1996) 'Free and Captured Play', *International Play Journal* 4: 123–32.

George, A. and P. McNamara (1984) 'Religion, Race, and Psychological Well-being', *Journal for Scientific Study of Religion* 23: 351–63.

Gilligan, J. (1996) *Violence*. New York: Putnam.

Helminiak, D. (1996) *The Human Core of Spirituality*. Albany: State University of New York Press.

Herman, J. (1992) *Trauma and Recovery*. New York: Basic Books.

James, W. (1902) *The Varieties of Religious Experience*. Cambridge, MA: Harvard University Press, 1985.

Janoff-Bulman, R. (1992) *Shattered Assumptions: Towards a New Psychology of Trauma*. New York: Free Press.

Jessor, R. and S. Jessor (1977) *Problem Behavior and Psychosocial Development: A Longitudinal Study of Youth*. New York: Academic Press.

Jung, C. (1933) *Modern Man in Search of a Soul*. New York: Harcourt, Brace.

Kalish, R. and D. Reynolds (1973) 'Phenomenological Reality and Post-death Contact', *Journal for the Scientific Study of Religion* 12: 209–21.

Kozaric-Kovacic, D., V. Folnegovic-Smalc, J. Skrinjharic, N. Szajnberg and A. Marusic (1995) 'Rape, Torture, and Traumatization of Bosnian and Croatian Women: Psychological Sequelae', *American Journal of Orthopsychiatry* 65: 428–33.

Moore, T. (1992) *Care of the Soul*. New York: Harper.

Myer, A. and L. Lausell (1996) 'The Value of Including "Higher Powers" in Efforts to Prevent Violence and Promote Optimal Outcomes in Adolescence', in R. Hampton, P. Jenkins and T. Gullotta (eds) *Preventing Violence in America*. London: Sage Publications.

Pargament, K., E. Ensing, K. Falgout, H. Olsen, B. Reilly, K. Van Haitsman and R. Warren (1990) 'God Help Me: (I) Religious Coping Efforts as Predictors of the Outcomes to Significant Negative Life Events', *American Journal of Community Psychology* 18: 793–824.

Shortz, J. and E. Worthington (1994) 'Young Adults' Recall of Religiosity, Attributions, and Coping in Parental Divorce', *Journal for the Scientific Study of Religion* 33: 172–9.

Silverman, P. and J.W. Worden (1992) 'Children's Reactions in the Early Months after the Death of a Parent', *American Journal of Orthopsychiatry* 62: 93–104.

Sivaraksa, S. (1992) *Seeds of Peace: A Buddhist Vision for Renewing Society*. Berkeley, CA: Parallas Press.

Van der Kolk, B. (1994) 'Meaning and Trauma', paper presented at the Rochester Symposium on Developmental Psychopathology, University of Rochester, New York, October.

Wright, S., C. Pratt and V. Schmall (1985) 'Spiritual Support for Caregivers of Dementia Patients', *Journal of Religion and Health* 24: 31–8.

58

Extracts from

RISK SOCIETY: TOWARDS A NEW MODERNITY

Ulrich Beck

Source: *Risk Society: Towards a New Modernity*, London: Sage Publications, 1992, pp. 106–119.

Industrial society is a modern feudal society

The peculiarities of the antagonisms in the life conditions of men and women can be determined theoretically by differentiating them from class conditions. The class antagonisms ignited on the material immiseration of large parts of the working population. They were fought out in public. The antagonisms that emerge with the detraditionalization of the family erupted mainly in private relationships, and they are fought out in the kitchen, the bedroom and the nursery. Their verbal accompaniment and symptoms are the everlasting discussions of relationships or the silent opposition in a marriage, the flight to solitude and back, the loss of trust in the partner one suddenly no longer understands, the pain of divorce, the idolization of children, the struggle for a bit of life to call one's own, to be wrested away from the partner and still shared with him/her, the search for oppression in the trivialities of everyday life, an oppression which one *is* oneself. Call it what you will, 'trench war of the sexes', 'retreat into the subjective', 'the age of narcissism'. This is exactly the way a *social form* – the feudal inner structure of industrial society – implodes into the private sphere.

The class antagonisms that arise with the industrial system are in a way 'inherently modern', grounded in the industrial mode of production itself. The antagonisms between the sexes *neither* bow to the pattern of modern class antagonisms *nor* are a mere relic of tradition. They are a third entity. Just as much as the antagonisms between labor and capital, they are the *product* and the *foundation* of the industrial system, in the sense that wage labor *presupposes* housework, and that the spheres and forms of production

254

and the family are separated and *created* in the nineteenth century. At the same time the resulting conditions of men and women are based on *ascriptions* by birth. In that respect, they are that strange hybrid, *modern estates*. With them, an *industrial society* hierarchy of status is established in modernity. They derive their explosive power and their logic of conflict from the *contradiction* between modernity and counter-modernity *within* industrial society. Correspondingly, the ascribed roles and antagonisms of gender status erupt like class antagonisms not in early modernity, but in *late* industrial modernity, that is, at the point where the social classes have already become detraditionalized and modernity no longer hesitates at the gates of the family, marriage, parenthood and housework.

In the nineteenth century the triumph of industrialism accompanied the shaping of the forms of the nuclear family, which today are in turn becoming detraditionalized. Production and family work are subjected to contrary organizational principles (Rerrich 1986). If the rules and power of the *market* apply to the former, in the latter the *unpaid* performance of everyday work is taken for granted. The *contractual nature* of relationships contrasts with the collective *communality* of marriage and the family. *Individual competition and mobility*, which are required for the realm of production, run up against the contrary demand in the family: *sacrifice* for the other and absorption in the collective communal project of the family. In the shape of familial reproduction and market-dependent production, then, two epochs with contrary organizational principles and value systems – modernity and modern counter-modernity – are welded together in the industrial society, two epochs that complement, condition, and contradict each other.

The life conditions that are created and imposed by the separation of family and production are just as epochally different. There is thus not only a system of inequality that has its basis in production, differences in pay, professions, the position with respect to the means of production, and so forth. There is also a system of inequality located *transversely* to it, which comprises the epochal differences between the 'family situation' in its relative equality, and the variety of production situations. Production work is mediated through the labor market and performed in return for money. Taking it on makes people – no matter how tightly they are bound to dependent work – into *self*-providers. They become the targets of mobility processes, related plans, and the like. Unpaid family work is imposed as a natural dowry through marriage. By nature, taking it on means *dependence* for support. Those who take it on – and we know who they are – run a household with 'second-hand' money and remain dependent on marriage as a link to self-support. The distribution of these jobs – and here lies the feudal foundation of industrial society – remains outside of decision. They are *ascribed* by birth and gender. In principle, one's *fate is already present in the cradle even in industrial society*: lifelong housework or making a living in conformity with the labor market. These feudal 'gender fates' are attenuated, canceled, aggravated or concealed by the love which is also devoted to them. Love is blind. Since love can appear as an escape from its self-created distress, no matter how great that might be, the inequality which it represents cannot be real. It is real, however, and that makes love seem stale and cold.

What appears and is lamented as 'terror of intimacy' are – in terms of social theory and social history – the *contradictions of a modernity bisected by the plan of industrial society*, which has always withheld the indivisible principles of modernity – individual freedom and equality beyond the barriers of birth – from one gender by birth and ascribed them to the other. Industrial society *never* was or can be possible solely as industrial society, but is always only half industrial and half *feudal*. This feudal side is not a relic of tradition, but the *foundation* and *product* of industrial society, built into the institutional plan of work and life.

In the welfare state modernization after the Second World War, a double process takes place: on the one side the requirement for a market-dependent standardized biography is extended to the female life context. Here nothing that is new in principle is occurring, only the application of the principles of developed market societies over and above the gender line. On the other, totally new camps within the family and between men and women in general are created in this way, indeed the feudal foundations of industrial society are being abolished. This is a specific feature of *reflexive modernization*. The *extension* of industrial society beyond its gender-specific division carries out in equal measure the *dissolution* of its family morals, its gender fates, its taboos on marriage, parenthood and sexuality, even the reunification of housework and industrial work.

The status-based hierarchy in industrial society is a building put together from many elements: division of the spheres of labor in production and the family and the contrasting organization of the two, the ascription of the corresponding life conditions by birth, the concealment of the overall conditions through promises of affection and a remedy for loneliness offered by love, marriage and parenthood. Considered retrospectively, this structure had to be constructed, that is, pushed through against resistance.

So people have tended to view modernization too one-sidedly. It actually has a double face. Parallel to the emergence of industrial society in the nineteenth century, the *modern* feudal gender order was constructed. In this sense modernization was accompanied in the nineteenth century by *counter*-modernization. The temporal differences and antagonisms between production and the family were established, justified and transfigured into eternal truths. An alliance of male-inspired philosophy, religion and science ties the whole thing up – for good measure – with the 'essence' of the woman and the 'essence' of the man.

Modernization, then, not only dissolves the feudal conditions of agrarian society but also creates new feudal conditions, and in its reflexive phase dissolves these. The same thing – modernization – has *opposite* consequences under the different overall conditions of the nineteenth and the twentieth centuries. Then the consequences were the *division* of housework and wage labor, today they are the struggle for new forms of *reunification*; then the tying down of women through *marital support*, today their rush into the labor market; there the *establishment* of the stereotypical male and female roles, here the *liberation* of men and women from the feudal dictates of gender.

These are symptoms of how modernity is encroaching today on the counter-modernity it installed in industrial society. The relations of the sexes, which are welded to the separation of production and reproduction and held together with everything the compact tradition of the nuclear family can offer in concentrated communality, role assignments and emotionality, are breaking apart. Suddenly everything becomes uncertain, including the ways of living together, who does what, how and where, or the views of sexuality and love and their connection to marriage and the family. The institution of parenthood splits up into a clash between motherhood and fatherhood, and children with their naturally intense bonding ability become the only partners who do not leave. A general process of struggle and experimentation with 'forms of reunifying' work and life, housework and wage labor is beginning. In short, the private sphere is becoming reflexive and political and this radiates into other areas.

But this only indicates the direction of the development. The salient point of these reflections lies in the following: the problemata of the *established* market society cannot be overcome within the social life forms and institutional structures of the divided market society. Where men *and* women have to and want to lead an economically independent existence, this can occur *neither* in the traditional role assignments of the nuclear family, *nor* in the institutional structures of professional work, social laws, city planning, schools, and so on, which *presuppose* precisely the traditional image of the nuclear family with its gender status foundations.

The 'central conflicts', which discharge themselves in personal guilt feelings and disappointments within the relations of the sexes, also have a basis in the fact that an attempt is still being made to practice the liberation from gender stereotypes (almost) *solely* through the private confrontation of men and women, *within* the framework of the nuclear family, while keeping the institutional structures *constant*. This is tantamount to the attempt to accomplish a change in society with social structures *in* the family remaining the same. What remains is an *exchange of inequalities*. The *liberation* of women from housework and marital support is to be forced by the regression of men into this 'modern feudal existence' which is exactly what women reject for themselves. Historically, that is like an attempt to make the nobility the serfs of the peasants. But men are no more willing than women to follow the call 'back to the kitchen!' (women ought to know that better than anyone else!). But this is only one feature. What remains central is that *the equalization of men and women cannot be created in institutional structures that presuppose their inequality*. We cannot force the new, 'round' person into the 'square' hole required by the labor market, the employment system, city planning, the social security system and so on. If this is attempted, no one ought to be surprised that the private relationship of the sexes becomes the scene for conflicts that can only be inadequately solved by the tug-of-war of 'role swapping' or 'mixed roles' for men and women.

Liberation from male and female roles?

The perspective just sketched out contrasts oddly with the empirical data. They, after all, document impressively the counter-trend to a *renewal* of the gender status hierarchy. In what sense is it at all permissible to speak of a 'liberation' at all? Are women and men freed equally from the dictates of their 'gender fate?' Which conditions bring this about, which work against it?

Essential turning points in the past decades – as the data referred to above attest – have freed women somewhat from the traditional traits ascribed by femininity. Five central conditions are apparent although by no means causally related to one another.

First of all, the biographical structure, the succession of life phases has been shifted by the *increasing of life expectancy*. As has been shown in particular by Arthur E. Imhof in his studies of social history, this has led to a '*demographic* liberation of women'. While in earlier centuries the lifespan of a woman – in statistical terms – was just sufficient to produce and raise the socially 'desirable' number of surviving children, these 'maternal duties' come to an end today at about the age of forty-five. The 'existence-for-children' has become a *passing* life phase for women today. It is succeeded on average by *three decades* of an 'empty nest' – beyond the traditional focus of women's lives. 'Today, in the Federal Republic alone, over five million women in their "best years" are living in post-parental relationships . . . often . . . without any concrete meaningful activity' (Imhof 1981: 181).

Second, modernization, especially in the phase after the Second World War, has *restructured housework*. On the one hand, the *social isolation* of housework is by no means an inherent structural feature as such, but the result of historical developments, to wit the detraditionalization of the lifeworlds. In the wake of individualization processes, the nuclear family sharpens its demarcations, and an 'insular existence' is formed, which autonomizes itself with respect to the remaining commitments (class cultures, neighborhoods, acquaintances). Only in that way does an existence as a housewife become the isolated worker existence *par excellence*. On the other hand, *processes of technical automation* extend into housework. A variety of appliances, machines and consumer goods unburden and empty work in the family. It becomes the invisible and never ending 'left-over work' between industrial production, paid services and technically perfected domestic furnishing of private households. Taken together, isolation and automation bring about a '*de*skilling of housework' (Offe 1984), which also directs women towards work outside the home in search of a 'fulfilled' life.

Third, if it remains true that motherhood is still the strongest tie to the traditional female role, it is difficult to overestimate the importance of *contraceptive and family planning measures*, as well as the *legal possibility of terminating pregnancies* in removing women from the traditional demands. Children and thus motherhood (with all its consequences) no longer constitute a 'natural fate', but, at least in principle, are *wanted* children and *intentional* motherhood. Of course, the data also show that motherhood *without* economic dependence on the husband and responsibility for child care remains a *dream* for many. But the younger generation of women, unlike their mothers, can (co)determine whether, when and how many children to have. At the same time, female sexuality is released from the 'fate of motherhood' and can also be consciously discovered and developed *against* male norms.

Fourth, the growing number of divorces points to the *fragility of marital and family support*. Women are often just 'a husband away from' poverty (Ehrenreich 1983). Almost 70 percent of single mothers must make do with less than DM 1200 per month [1985]. They and female pensioners are the most frequent clients of relief agencies. In this sense too, women are 'freed', i.e. *cut off* from lifelong support by a husband. The statistically documented rush of women into the labor market also shows that many women have understood this historical lesson and seen the consequences.

Fifth, the equalization of educational opportunity, which is among other things also the expression of a strong *career* motivation among young women, tends to work in the same direction.

All these taken together – demographic liberation, deskilling of housework, contraception, divorce, participation in education and occupations – express the degree of *liberation of women from the dictates of their modern, female status fate, which can no longer be altered*. Hence the individualization spiral – labor market, education, mobility, career planning – affects the family with doubled or trebled impact. The family becomes a continuous juggling act with divergent multiple ambitions involving careers and their requirements for mobility, educational constraints, conflicting obligations to children and the monotony of housework.

But these conditions leading towards individualization face others which reconnect women to traditional role assignments. The really *established* labor market society, which would make an independent economic living available to *all* men and women, would multiply the already scandalous unemployment figures. This means that under the conditions of mass unemployment and displacement from the labor market, women are freed *from* marital support, but not free *to* lead an autonomous life through work outside the home. This also means, however, that they continue to be largely *dependent* upon an economic protection from their husbands which *no longer* exists. This intermediate status between 'freedom from' and 'freedom to' in the context of real wage laborer behavior is also further strengthened by their reconnection to *motherhood*. As long as women bear children, nurse them, feel responsible for them, and see them as an essential part of their lives, children remain wished-for 'obstacles' in the occupational competition, as well as temptations to a conscious decision *against* economic autonomy and a career.

In this way, the lives of women are pulled back and forth by this contradiction between liberation from and reconnection to the old ascribed roles. This is also reflected in their consciousness and behavior. They flee from housework to a career and back again, and attempt in different phases of their lives to hold together the diverging conditions of their life 'somehow' through contradictory decisions. The contradictions of the environment amplify their own; for instance, they have to put up with being asked by a divorce court judge why they have neglected their career planning. In family policy they are asked why they have not fulfilled their maternal duties. They are accused of spoiling their husbands' already difficult professional lives with their career ambitions. Divorce law and divorce reality, the lack of social protections, the closed doors of the labor market and the main burden of family work characterize some of the *contradictions* which the individualization process has brought into the female life context.

Men's situations are quite different. While women have to loosen their old ascribed roles of an 'existence for others' and have to search for a new social identity, for reasons of economic security *among others*, for men, making a living *independently* and the *old* role identity *coincide*. In the stereotypical male gender role as 'career man', economic individualization *and* masculine role behavior are joined together. Support by a spouse (the wife) is unknown to men historically, and the 'freedom to' work for a living is taken for granted. The background work that belongs to it traditionally falls upon women. The joys and duties of fatherhood could always be enjoyed *in small doses* as a recreational activity. Fatherhood held no obstacle to practicing a career; on the contrary it was a compulsion to do so. In other words, all the factors that *dislodge* women from their traditional role are *missing* on the male side. In the context of male life, fatherhood *and* career, economic independence *and* familial life are not contradictions that have to be fought for and held together against the conditions in the family and society; instead their compatibility with the traditional male role is prescribed and protected. But this means that individualization (in the sense of making a living through the mediation of the market) *strengthens* masculine role behavior.

If men also turn against the dictates of their gender role, they do so on other grounds. Contradictions are also present in the career fixation of the male role, for instance, sacrificing oneself for something one has neither the leisure, the needs nor the abilities to enjoy, aggressive competition for nothing, exhaustion for professional and organizational goals with which one cannot identify but must anyway, the resulting 'indifference' that really is nothing of the kind, and so on. Nevertheless, essential impulses for liberation from the masculine role are not inherent, but are *externally induced* (through changes in women), and in a double sense. On the one hand, men are freed by the greater participation of women in the labor force from the yoke of being *sole* supporter of the family. That, however, loosens the constraints to subordinate oneself in a career to the will and purposes of others *for* the wife and the children. As a consequence, a different type of commitment to the career *and* the family becomes possible. On the other hand, 'family harmony' is becoming fragile. The female-determined side of male existence is getting out of balance. At the same time men get an inkling of their dependency in everyday matters and their emotional reliance on women. In both areas, essential impulses are found to loosen identification with the dictates of the male role and to try new modes of life.

The conflicts cause the antagonisms between men and women to stand out more sharply. Two 'catalyzing elements' are central: *children* and *economic security*. In both cases conflicts on these themes can be kept hidden during marriage, but they emerge openly in case of divorce. Characteristically, the distribution of burdens and opportunities changes in the transition from the traditional to the two-earner model of marriage. In the marital support model, to put it schematically, the woman is left after divorce *with* children and *without* an income, the man by contrast *with* an income and *without* children. In the two-earner model, little seems to have changed at first glance, other than that the woman has an income *and* she has the children (following prevalent law practice). But to the degree that the economic inequality between men and women is decreased – whether through professional activity of the woman, the support regulations of divorce law, or old-age assistance – *fathers become aware of their disadvantage*, partially naturally and partially legally. The woman has *possession* of the child as a product of her womb, which we all know does belong to her, biologically and legally. The property relations between ovum and sperm become differentiated. The father in the child always remains dependent on the mother and her discretion. This is also true for all questions of terminating a pregnancy. To the extent that the alienation from male *and* female roles progresses, the pendulum tends to swing back. The men who free themselves from the 'fate' of a career and turn to their children come home to an empty nest. This is clearly illustrated by the increasing number of cases (especially in the USA), in which fathers kidnap children not awarded to them in divorce proceedings.

But individualization, which separates the conditions of men and women, conversely also pushes them back to bonding. *As the traditions become progressively diluted*, the promises of relationships grow. Everything that has been lost is suddenly being sought in the other. First God departed (or we displaced him). The word 'belief', which once meant 'having experienced', has taken on the rather shabby tones of 'against our better judgment'. As God disappears, so does the possibility of going to a priest, and thus the guilt grows, and can no longer be thrown off. As the distinctions between right and wrong become blurred, guilt does not grow less significant under keen questioning but only less distinct and less distinguishable. The culture of social class, which at least knew how to interpret built-up suffering, has evaporated from life into a cloud of speeches and statistics. Neighborhoods, grown up with memories and interaction, have melted away due to mobility. Acquaintanceships can be made, but they revolve around their own central point. One can also join clubs. The palette of contacts grows larger, broader and more colorful. But their multiplicity makes them more fleeting, more easily dominated by façades. In the proclaimed interest in each other, any thought of something more is immediately refused. Even intimacies can be exchanged like this, fleetingly, almost like handshakes.

All this might keep things moving and open up 'possibilities', and yet the variety of relationships probably cannot replace the identity-forming power of a stable primary relationship. As studies show, *both* are necessary: a variety of relationships and lasting intimacy. Happily married housewives suffer from contact problems and social isolation. Divorced men who have formed groups to air their problems, cannot overcome the emerging loneliness even by being included in networks.

In the idealizations of modern love the trajectory of modernity is reflected once again. The exaltation is the opposite of the losses modernity leaves behind. Not God, not priests, not class, not neighbors, well at least You. And the size of the You is the inverted emptiness that otherwise prevails.

That also means that it is less material foundation and love than the fear of being alone that holds marriages and the family together. What threatens or is feared beyond marriage and the family is perhaps the most stable foundation of marriage, despite all the crises and conflicts: loneliness.

In all of this, there is first of all a fundamental relativization of the controversy on the family. The bourgeois nuclear family, in whose forms the coexistence of the sexes has been standardized in the highly industrialized democracies of the West, has been sanctified or cursed; people have seen one crisis following the other, or they have seen the family rising again from the nimbus of crisis ascribed to it. All this remains bound to the verdict of the *false alternative*. Anyone who burdens the family with all the good or all the evil is not reaching far enough. The family is only the surface on which the historical conflict situations *between men and women become visible*. In the family, or beyond it, the sexes always encounter each other and thus so do the accumulated contradictions between them.

In what sense can one speak of a *liberation relative to the family*? With the extension of the dynamic of individualization into the family, forms of living together begin to change *radically*. The relationship between family and individual biography loosens. The lifelong standard family, which sublates the parental biographies of men and women summarized in it, becomes a limiting case, and the rule becomes a movement back and forth among various familial and *non*-familial forms of living together, specific to the particular phase of life in question. The family commitment of biography becomes perforated along the time axis between phases of life, *and thus canceled*. Among the family relationships which are becoming interchangeable, the autonomy of the male and female *individual biography* separates inside and outside the family. Each person lives through several family lives as well as non-familial forms of life, depending on the life phase, and *for that very reason* lives more and more his/her *own biography*. Thus it is only in a *longitudinal section* of the biography, and not in a given moment or in family statistics, that the individualization of the family is seen, that is the reversal of priorities between individual biography and family (in and beyond the family). Empirically, the degree of liberation from the family consequently results from the *biographical synopsis* of the data on divorce *and* remarriage, as well as pre-, inter- and extramarital forms of living together, which, taken individually and related to the pro or con of the family, remain contradictory. Placed between the extremes of family or no family, a growing number of people begin to 'decide' on a third way: a contradictory, *pluralistic overall biography in transition*. This biographical pluralism of forms of life, i.e. the alternation between families, mixed with and interrupted by other forms of living together or alone, is becoming the (paradoxical) 'norm' for the cooperation and opposition of men and women under conditions of individualization.

Considered over their entire life, the majority of people have thus entered a painful and fearful *historically prescribed test phase of their forms of living together*. They have begun a *reflexive way of loosening and coordinating* male and female biographies, whose outcome cannot be predicted at all today. But all the suffered 'mistakes' cannot deter anyone from renewed 'attempts'.

Becoming conscious of inequalities: chances for and constraints on choice

Differences and antagonisms in the situations of men and women did not just come into existence yesterday. And yet until the sixties they were accepted as 'self-evident' by the overwhelming majority of women. For two decades attention to them has been growing and there have been political efforts targeted at obtaining equal rights for women. With the first successes the consciousness of the inequalities is *heightened*. The *actual* inequalities, their conditions and causes must be distinguished from the *awareness* of them. The antagonisms between men and women have two sides, which can vary quite independently of one another, the objectivity of the situations *and* their delegitimation and the awareness of this. If one compares the long period of acceptance of inequality to the short period when it has been problematized and simultaneously sees that the removal of some inequalities has only really opened people's eyes to them, one should not underestimate the independent significance of awareness. We shall now inquire into the conditions for this awareness.

As modernization proceeds, the decisions and constraints to decide multiply in all fields of social action. With a bit of exaggeration, one could say: 'anything goes'. Who does the dishes and when, who changes the screaming baby's diaper, who takes care of the shopping and pushes the vacuum cleaner around the house is becoming just as unclear as who brings home the bacon, who decides whether to move, and why the nocturnal pleasures in bed must be enjoyed only with the daily companion duly appointed and wed by the registrar's office. Marriage can be subtracted from sexuality, and that in turn from parenthood; parenthood can be multiplied by divorce; and the whole thing can be divided by living together or apart, and raised to a higher power by the possibility of multiple residences and the ever-present potentiality of taking back decisions. This mathematical operation yields a rather large, though fluctuating, sum on the right side of the equation, and gives some idea of the variety of direct and multiply nested shadow existences that are more and more often concealed today behind the unchanged and so upright words 'marriage' and 'family'.

In all biographical dimensions, *opportunities* for and *constraints* on choice open up, as if forced upon us. A whole apparatus of planning and agreements becomes necessary, which in principle is revocable and dependent on legitimation in its assignment of unequal burdens. In discussion and agreements, in mistakes and conflicts related to these choices, the differing risks and consequences for men and women become clearer. Transforming givens into decisions has a double meaning if considered systematically. The *option of not deciding is tending to become impossible.* First, the opportunity to decide acquires a compulsive character which one cannot readily retreat behind. It is necessary to go through the mills of the private relationship, the problems and thus the balancing of the differing consequences. But this also means, secondly, that the decisions being thought through become *consciousness raisers of the emerging inequalities as well as the conflicts and efforts at solution they ignite.*

This already begins with the rather conventional decision on mobility. On the one hand, the labor market demands mobility without regard to personal circumstances. Marriage and the family require the opposite.

Thought through to its ultimate consequence, the market model of modernity implies a society *without* families and children. Everyone must be independent, free for the demands of the market in order to guarantee his/her economic existence. The market subject is ultimately the single individual, 'unhindered' by a relationship, marriage or family. Correspondingly, the ultimate market society is a *childless* society – unless the children grow up with mobile, single, fathers and mothers.

This contradiction between the requirements of a relationship and those of the labor market could only remain hidden so long as it was taken for granted that marriage meant renunciation of a career for women, responsibility for the children and 'comobility' according to the professional destiny of the husband. The contradiction bursts open where *both* spouses must or want to be free to earn a living as a salary earner. *Institutional* solutions to or ameliorations of this contradiction are quite conceivable (for instance, a minimum income for all citizens, or social protections not linked to professional work; the removal of all impediments to the joint employment of married couples; corresponding 'acceptability criteria', etc.). These, however, are neither present nor in any way contemplated. Accordingly the couple must search for *private* solutions, which under the options available to them amount to an internal distribution of *risks*. The question is: who will *give up* economic independence and security, the very things that are the unquestioned prerequisites for leading a life in modern society? Anyone who moves with a spouse, after all, must (usually) accept considerable professional disadvantages, if *she* is not in fact thrown completely off her career path. The level of conflict rises accordingly. Marriage, family and relationships become places where the personalized contradictions of a thoroughly modernized market society are compensated, but no longer completely.

The decisive question of professional mobility is joined by other, equally vital ones: the timing, number and support of children, the ever-present issue of dividing everyday chores equally, the 'one-sidedness' of contraceptive methods, the nightmarish issue of terminating a pregnancy, differences in type and frequency of sexual urges, not forgetting the irritation of an attitude that senses sexism even in margarine advertisements. In all these conflict-igniting central issues of how men and women live together, the *dissociation of positions* becomes conscious: the *timing* of parenthood encounters quite different presuppositions and impediments in the male than in the female life context, and so on.

If marriage is then finally conducted 'subject to recall' – 'suitable for divorce', so to speak (as the marriage counseling books flooding the market demand through contractual agreements covering everything from splitting property to extramarital sexuality) – then the split which was to be avoided is simply anticipated, and the unequal consequences of all the decisions and regulations emerge more and more openly. If one thinks of the new technical possibilities and the breakdown of taboos – the possibilities of shaping children's psyches as demonstrated by psychology and pedagogy, the possibilities of intervening in the gestation process, not to mention the science fiction realities of human genetics – then what is besetting the family divides the positions once united in it, piece by piece: woman against man, mother against child, child against father. The traditional unity of the family breaks apart in the face of decisions demanded of it. It is not that people bring many of these problems into the family, as they may believe and accuse themselves. Almost all the issues of conflict also have an institutional side (the children issue, for instance, is essentially based on the institutionally well protected impossibility of uniting caring for children with professional commitment). But this insight of course, does not support the children! In this way, everything that strikes the family from outside – the labor market, the employment system or the law – is distorted and foreshortened with a certain inevitability into the personal sphere. In the family (and in all its alternatives) there arises the systematically conditioned delusion that it contains the strings and the levers required to change the newly evident central fate of the inequality of the sexes within the concrete relationship.

Even the core of the family, the sanctuary of parenthood, is beginning to disintegrate into its components, the positions of motherhood and fatherhood. In Germany today, compared with the United States and Sweden, 'only' every tenth child is growing up under the care of single men and women. The number of single-parent families is rising as the number of two-parent families diminishes. Being a single mother is no longer just a consequence of 'abandonment', but rather an option that is chosen. Given the conflicts with fathers (who in truth are needed merely *to father* and no longer for anything else), lone parenthood is seen by many women as the only way to the child now desired more than ever.

The relationship and quality of the commitment to the child varies along with the intrafamilial individualization process, as Elisabeth Beck-Gernsheim (1988) and Maria Rerrich (1986) show. On the one hand, the child is viewed as an *impediment* in the individualization process. It costs money and work, is unpredictable, ties one up and throws carefully drawn up daily plans and life plans into a hopeless confusion. As soon as it appears the child develops and perfects its 'dictatorship of neediness' and forces its biological rhythm of life on its parents through the naked power of its vocal cords and the warmth of its smile. And, on the other hand, that very thing makes it irreplaceable.

The child is the source of the last *remaining, irrevocable, unexchangeable primary relationship*. Partners come and go. The child stays. Everything that is desired, but not realizable in the relationship, is directed to the child. With the increasing fragility of the relationships between the sexes the child acquires a monopoly on practical companionship, on an expression of feelings in a biological give and take that otherwise is becoming increasingly

266

uncommon and doubtful. Here an anachronistic social experience is celebrated and cultivated which has become improbable *and* longed for precisely because of the individualization process. The excessive affection for children, the 'staging of childhood' which is granted to them – the poor, overloved creatures – and the nasty struggle for the children during and after divorce are some symptoms of this. The child becomes the *final alternative to loneliness* that can be built up against the vanishing possibilities of love. It is the *private type of re-enchantment*, which arises with, and derives its meaning from, disenchantment. The number of births is declining, but the importance of the child is *rising*. Usually one child is all. The expense makes any more than that hardly affordable. But those who believe that the (economic) costs deter people from bringing children into the world, are simply falling into their own entrapment in cost–benefit thinking.

The bit of the Middle Ages that industrial society has not just preserved but produced, is melting away. People are being freed from the feudal bonds of gender, which have been transfigured into nature. It is important to recognize this in its historic dimensions, *because* this sociohistorical change takes place as a private, personal conflict. Psychology (and psychotherapy), which trace the suffering now being referred to them *en masse* back to the individual history of early childhood socialization, are becoming *short-circuited*. Where conflicts confront people from the forms of living that are dictated to them, where they lose an example of how to live, their ills can no longer be traced back to mistakes and decisions of their individual biographical history. Under the conditions of a liberation from the modern feudal gender fates of men and women, sexuality, marriage, eroticism, and parenthood have a great deal to do with inequality, career, the labor market, politics, the family and the forms of living embedded in them that have lost their relevance for the future. Psychology has yet to undertake this historization and sociohistorical revision of its forms of thinking, necessary if it is not to run aground on the appearance of individuality from which it profits by displacing the causes for problems into the very people who have them.

References

Allerbeck, K., W. Hoag (1984) *Jugend ohne Zukunft*. Munich.

Ariès, P. (1984) 'Liebe in der Ehe', in P. Ariès, A. Béjin, M. Foucault *et al.* (eds), *Die Masken des Begehrens und die Metamorphosen der Sinnlichkeit – Zur Geschichte der Sexualität im Abendland*. Frankfurt.

Beck, U., E. Beck-Gernsheim (1990) *Das ganz normale Chaos der Liebe*. Frankfurt. In English (1993). Cambridge.

Beck-Gernsheim, E. (1983) 'Vom "Dasein für andere" zum Anspruch auf ein Stuck "eigenes Leben"', *Soziale Welt*, 34: 307–340.

Beck-Gernsheim, E. (1984) *Vom Geburtenrückgang zur Neuen Mütterlichkeit? Über private und politische Interessen am Kind*. Frankfurt.

Beck-Gernsheim, E. (1985) *Das halbierte Leben. Männerwelt Beruf, Frauenwelt Familie*, 2nd edn. Frankfurt.

Beck-Gernsheim, E. (1986) 'Von der Liebe zur Beziehung? Veränderungen im Verhältnis von Mann und Frau in der individualisierten Gesellschaft', in J. Berger (ed.), *Moderne oder Postmoderne*. Special issue 4 of *Soziale Welt*. Göttingen.

Beck-Gernsheim, E. (1988) *Die Kinderfrage: Frauen zwischen Kindern und Unabhängigkeit*. Munich.

Béjin, A. (1984) 'Ehen ohne Trauschein heute', in P. Ariès, A. Béjin, M. Foucault *et al.* (eds), *Die Masken des Begehrens und die Metamorphosen der Sinnlichkeit – Zur Geschichte der Sexualität im Abendland*. Frankfurt.

Berger, B., P. L. Berger (1983) *The War over the Family*. New York. In German (1984) Reinbek.

Berger, P., H. Kellner (1965) 'Die Ehe und die Konstruktion der Wirklichkeit', *Soziale Welt*, 16: 220–241.

Bernardoni, C., V. Werner (eds) (1983) *Der vergeudete Reichtum – Über die Partizipation von Frauen im öffentlichen Leben*. Bonn.

Beyer, J. *et al.* (eds) (1983) *Frauenlexikon – Stichworte zur Selbstbestimmung*. Munich.

Biermann, I., C. Schmerl, L. Ziebell (1985) *Leben mit kurzfristigem Denken – Eine Untersuchung zur Situation arbeitsloser Akademikerinnen*. Weilheim und Basel.

Brose, H.-G., M. Wohlrab-Sahr (1986) 'Formen individualisierter Lebensführung von Frauen – ein neues Arrangement zwischen Familie und Beruf', in H.-G. Brose (ed.), *Berufsbiographien im Wandel*. Opladen.

Buchholz, W. *et al.* (1984) *Lebenswelt und Familienwirklichkeit*. Frankfurt.

Bundesminister für Bildung und Wissenschaft (1982/83, 1984/85) *Grund- und Struktur- daten*. Bonn.

Bundesminister für Jugend, Familie und Gesundheit (1981) *Frauen 80*. Cologne.

Bundesminister für Jugend, Familie und Gesundheit (1985) *Nichteheliche Lebensgemeinschaften in der Bundesrepublik Deutschland*. Cologne.

Degler, C. N. (1980) *At Odds – Women and the Family in America from the Revolution to the Present*. New York.

Demos, J., S. S. Boocock (eds) (1978) *Turning Points – Historical and Sociological Essays on the Family*. Chicago.

Diezinger, A., R. Marquardt, H. Bilden (1982) *Zukunft mit beschränkten Mögli- chkeiten, Projektbericht*. Munich.

Ehrenreich, B. (1983) *The Hearts of Men*. New York. In German (1985) Reinbek.

Erler, G. A. (1985) 'Erdöl und Mutterliebe – von der Knappheit einiger Rohstoffe', in T. Schmid (ed.), *Das pfeifende Schwein*. Berlin.

Frauenlexikon (1983). Munich.

Gensior, S. (1983) 'Moderne Frauenarbeit', in *Karriere oder Kochtopf: Jahrbuch für Sozialökonomie und Gesellschaftstheorie*. Opladen.

Gilligan, C. (1984) *Die andere Stimme. Lebenskonflikte und Moral der Frau*. Munich.

Glick, P. C. (1984) 'Marriage, divorce, and living arrangements', *Journal of Family Issues*, 5, no. 1: 7–26.

Hoff, A., J. Scholz (1985) *Neue Männer in Beruf und Familie: Forschungsbericht*. Berlin.

Imhof, A. E. (1981) *Die gewonnenen Jahre*. Munich.

Imhof, A. E. (1984) *Die verlorenen Welten*. Munich.

Institut für Demoskopie Allensbach (1985) *Einstellungen zu Ehe und Familie im Wandel der Zeit.* Stuttgart.

Jurreit, M.-L. (ed.) (1979) *Frauenprogramm. Gegen Diskriminierung. Ein Handbuch.* Reinbek.

Kamerman, S. B. (1984) 'Women, children poverty: public policies and female-headed families in industrialized countries', in *Signs: Journal of Women in Culture and Society.* Special issue *Women and Poverty.* Chicago.

Kommission (1983) *Zukunftsperspektiven gesellschaftlicher Entwicklungen, Bericht (erstellt im Auftrage der Landesregierung von Baden-Württemberg).* Stuttgart.

Lasch, C. (1977) *Haven in Heartless World: the Family Besieged.* New York.

Metz-Gockel, S., U. Müller (1985) 'Der Mann', *Brigitte-Untersuchung*, ms. Hamburg.

Müller, W., A. Willms, J. Handl (1983) *Strukturwandel der Frauenarbeit.* Frankfurt.

Muschg, G. (1976) 'Bericht von einer falschen Front', in H. P. Piwitt (ed.), *Literaturmagazin 5.* Reinbek.

Offe, C. (1984) Arbeitsgesellschaft. Frankfurt.

Olerup, A., L. Schneider, E. Monod (1985) *Women, Work and Computerization – Opportunities and Disadvantages.* New York.

Ostner, J., B. Piper (eds) (1986) *Arbeitsbereich Familie.* Frankfurt.

Pearce, D., H. McAdoo (1981) *Women and Children: Alone and in Poverty.* Washington.

Pross, H. (1978) *Der deutsche Mann.* Reinbek.

Quintessenzen (1984) *Frauen und Arbeitsmarkt.* IAB. Nürnberg.

Rerrich, M. S. (1983) 'Veränderte Elternschaft', *Soziale Welt*, 34: 420–449.

Rerrich, M. S. (1986) *Balanceakt Familie.* Freiburg.

Rilke, R. M. (1980) *Briefe.* Frankfurt.

Rubin, I. B. (1983) *Intimate Strangers. Men and Women Together.* New York.

Schulz, W. (1983) 'Von der Institution "Familie" zu den Teilbeziehungen zwischen Mann, Frau und Kind', *Soziale Welt*, 34: 401–419.

Seidenspinner, G., A. Burger (1982) *Mädchen 82, Brigitte-Untersuchung.* Hamburg.

Sennett, R. (1976) *The Fall of Public Man.* London. In German (1983) Frankfurt.

Statistisches Bundesamt (1983) *Datenreport.* Bonn.

Wahl, K. *et al.* (1980) *Familien sind anders!* Reinbek.

Weber-Kellermann, I. (1975) *Die deutsche Familie. Versuch einer Sozialgeschichte.* Frankfurt.

Wiegmann, B. (1979) 'Frauen und Justiz', in M.-L. Jurreit (ed.), *Frauenprogramm. Gegen Diskriminierung. Ein Handbuch.* Reinbek.

Willms, A. (1983) 'Grundzüge der Entwicklung der Frauenarbeit von 1800 bis 1980', in W. Müller, A. Willms, J. Handl (eds), *Strukturwandel der Frauenarbeit.* Frankfurt.

Part 9

CHILDHOOD AS A SOCIAL AND EDUCATIONAL CATEGORY

59

THE PROBLEM OF GENERATIONS

Karl Mannheim

Source: *Essays in the Sociology of Knowledge*, London: RKP, 1927, pp. 98–110.

The problem of generations is important enough to merit serious consideration. It is one of the indispensable guides to an understanding of the structure
of social and intellectual movements. Its practical importance becomes clear
as soon as one tries to obtain a more exact understanding of the accelerated
pace of social change characteristic of our time. It would be regrettable
if extra-scientific methods were permanently to conceal elements of the
problem capable of immediate investigation.

It is clear from the foregoing survey of the problem as it stands today that
a commonly accepted approach to it does not exist. The social sciences
in various countries only sporadically take account of the achievements
of their neighbours. In particular, German research into the problem of
generations has ignored results obtained abroad. Moreover, the problem
has been tackled by specialists in many different sciences in succession; thus,
we possess a number of interesting sidelights on the problem as well as
contributions to an overall solution, but no consciously directed research
on the basis of a clear formulation of the problem as a whole.

The multiplicity of points of view, resulting both from the peculiarities
of the intellectual traditions of various nations and from those of the
individual sciences, is both attractive and fruitful; and there can be no doubt
that such a wide problem can only be solved as a result of co-operation
between the most diverse disciplines and nationalities. However, the
co-operation must somehow be planned and directed from an organic
centre. The present status of the problem of generations thus affords a
striking illustration of the anarchy in the social and cultural sciences, where
everyone starts out afresh from his own point of view (to a certain extent, of
course, this is both necessary and fruitful), never pausing to consider the
various aspects as part of a single general problem, so that the contributions
of the various disciplines to the collective solution could be planned.

Any attempt at over-organization of the social and cultural sciences is naturally undesirable: but it is at least worth considering whether there is not perhaps one discipline – according to the nature of the problem in question – which could act as the organizing centre for work on it by all the others. As far as generations are concerned, the task of sketching the layout of the problem undoubtedly falls to sociology. It seems to be the task of *Formal Sociology* to work out the simplest, but at the same time the most fundamental facts relating to the phenomenon of generations. Within the sphere of formal sociology, however, the problem lies on the borderline between the static and the dynamic types of investigation. Whereas formal sociology up to now has tended for the most part to study the social existence of man exclusively *statically*, this particular problem seems to be one of those which have to do with the ascertainment of the origin of social dynamism and of the laws governing the action of the dynamic components of the social process. Accordingly, this is the point where we have to make the transition from the formal static to the formal dynamic and from thence to applied historical sociology – all three together comprising the complete field of sociological research.

In the succeeding pages we shall attempt to work out in formal sociological terms all the most elementary facts regarding the phenomenon of generations, without the elucidation of which historical research into the problem cannot even begin. We shall try to incorporate any results of past investigations, which have proved themselves relevant, ignoring those which do not seem to be sufficiently well founded.

A. Concrete group – social location (Lagerung)

To obtain a clear idea of the basic structure of the phenomenon of generations, we must clarify the specific inter-relations of the individuals comprising a single generation-unit.

The unity of a generation does not consist primarily in a social bond of the kind that leads to the formation of a concrete group, although it may sometimes happen that a feeling for the unity of a generation is consciously developed into a basis for the formation of concrete groups, as in the case of the modern German Youth Movement. But in this case, the groups are most often mere cliques, with the one distinguishing characteristic that group-formation is based upon the consciousness of belonging to one generation, rather than upon definite objectives.

Apart from such a particular case, however, it is possible in general to draw a distinction between generations as mere collective facts on the one hand, and *concrete social groups* on the other.

Organizations for specific purposes, the family, tribe, sect, are all examples of such *concrete groups*. Their common characteristic is that the individuals of which they are composed do actually *in concrete* form a group, whether the entity is based on vital, existential ties of 'proximity' or on the conscious application of the rational will. All 'community' groups (*Gemeinschaftsgebilde*), such as the family and the tribe, come under the former heading, while the latter comprises 'association' groups (*Gesellschaftsgebilde*).

The generation is not a concrete group in the sense of a community, i.e. a group which cannot exist without its members having concrete knowledge of each other, and which ceases to exist as a mental and spiritual unit as soon as physical proximity is destroyed. On the other hand, it is in no way comparable to associations such as organizations formed for a specific purpose, for the latter are characterized by a deliberate act of foundation, written statutes, and a machinery for dissolving the organization – features serving to hold the group together, even though it lacks the ties of spatial proximity and of community of life.

By a concrete group, then, we mean the union of a number of individuals through naturally developed or consciously willed ties. Although the members of a generation are undoubtedly bound together in certain ways, the ties between them have not resulted in a concrete group. How, then, can we define and understand the nature of the generation as a social phenomenon?

An answer may perhaps be found if we reflect upon the character of a different sort of social category, materially quite unlike the generation but bearing a certain structural resemblance to it – namely, the class position (*Klassenlage*) of an individual in society.

In its wider sense class-position can be defined as the common 'location' (*Lagerung*) certain individuals hold in the economic and power structure of a given society as their 'lot'. One is proletarian, *entrepreneur*, or *rentier*, and he is what he is because he is constantly aware of the nature of his specific 'location' in the social structure, i.e. of the pressures or possibilities of gain resulting from that position. This place in society does not resemble membership of an organization terminable by a conscious act of will. Nor is it at all binding in the same way as membership of a community (*Gemeinschaft*) which means that a concrete group affects every aspect of an individual's existence.

It is possible to abandon one's class position through an individual or collective rise or fall in the social scale, irrespective for the moment whether this is due to personal merit, personal effort, social upheaval, or mere chance.

Membership of an organization lapses as soon as we give notice of our intention to leave it; the cohesion of the community group *ceases to exist* if the mental and spiritual dispositions on which its existence has been based cease to operate in us or in our partners; and our previous class position loses its relevance for us as soon as we acquire a new position as a result of a change in our economic and power status.

Class position is an objective fact, whether the individual in question knows his class position or not, and whether he acknowledges it or not.

LIVERPOOL
JOHN MOORES UNIVERSITY
AVRIL ROBARTS LRC
TEL. 0151 231 4022

Class-consciousness does not necessarily accompany a class position, although in certain social conditions the latter can give rise to the former, lending it certain features, and resulting in the formation of a 'conscious class'. At the moment, however, we are only interested in the general phenomenon of social *location* as such. Besides the concrete social group, there is also the phenomenon of similar location of a number of individuals in a social structure – under which heading both classes and generations fall.

We have now taken the first step towards an analysis of the 'location' phenomenon as distinct from the phenomenon *'concrete group'*, and this much at any rate is clear – *viz.* the unity of generations is constituted essentially by a similarity of location of a number of individuals within a social whole.

B. The biological and sociological formulation of the problem of generations

Similarity of location can be defined only by specifying the structure within which and through which location groups emerge in historical-social reality. Class-position was based upon the existence of a changing economic and power structure in society. Generation location is based on the existence of biological rhythm in human existence – the factors of life and death, a limited span of life, and ageing. Individuals who belong to the same generation, who share the same year of birth, are endowed, to that extent, with a common location in the historical dimension of the social process.

Now, one might assume that the sociological phenomenon of location can be explained by, and deduced from, these basic biological factors. But this would be to make the mistake of all naturalistic theories which try to deduce sociological phenomena directly from natural facts, or lose sight of the social phenomenon altogether in a mass of primarily anthropological data. Anthropology and biology only help us explain the phenomena of life and death, the limited span of life, and the mental, spiritual, and physical changes accompanying ageing as such; they offer no explanation of the relevance these primary factors have for the shaping of social interrelationships in their historic flux.

The sociological phenomenon of generations is ultimately based on the biological rhythm of birth and death. But to be *based* on a factor does not necessarily mean to be *deducible* from it, or to be implied in it. If a phenomenon is *based* on another, it could not exist without the latter; however, it possesses certain characteristics peculiar to itself, characteristics in no way borrowed from the basic phenomenon. Were it not for the existence of social interaction between human beings – were there no definable social structure, no history based on a particular sort of continuity, the generation would not exist as a social location phenomenon; there would merely be birth, ageing, and death. The *sociological* problem of generations therefore begins at that point where the sociological relevance of these biological factors is discovered. Starting with the elementary phenomenon itself, then, we must first of all try to understand the generation as a particular type of social location.

C. The tendency 'inherent in' a social location

The fact of belonging to the same class, and that of belonging to the same generation or age group, have this in common, that both endow the individuals sharing in them with a common location in the social and historical process, and thereby limit them to a specific range of potential experience, predisposing them for a certain characteristic mode of thought and experience, and a characteristic type of historically relevant action. Any given location, then, excludes a large number of possible modes of thought, experience, feeling, and action, and restricts the range of self-expression open to the individual to certain circumscribed possibilities. This *negative* delimitation, however, does not exhaust the matter. Inherent in a *positive* sense in every location is a tendency pointing towards certain definite modes of behaviour, feeling, and thought.

We shall therefore speak in this sense of a tendency 'inherent in' every social location; a tendency which can be determined from the particular nature of the location as such.

For any group of individuals sharing the same class position, society always appears under the same aspect, familiarized by constantly repeated experience. It may be said in general that the experiential, intellectual, and emotional data which are available to the members of a certain society are not uniformly 'given' to all of them; the fact is rather that each class has access to only one set of those data, restricted to one particular 'aspect'. Thus, the proletarian most probably appropriates only a fraction of the cultural heritage of his society, and that in the manner of his group. Even a mental climate as rigorously uniform as that of the Catholic Middle Ages presented itself differently according to whether one were a theologizing cleric, a knight, or a monk. But even where the intellectual material is more or less uniform or at least uniformly accessible to all, the *approach* to the material, the way in which it is assimilated and applied, is determined in its direction by social factors. We usually say in such cases that the approach is determined by the special traditions of the social stratum concerned. But these traditions themselves are explicable and understandable not only in terms of the history of the stratum but above all in terms of the location relationships of its members within the society. Traditions bearing in a particular direction only persist so long as the location relationships of the group acknowledging them remain more or less unchanged. The concrete form of an existing behaviour pattern or of a cultural product does not derive from the history of a particular tradition but ultimately from the history of the location relationships in which it originally arose and hardened itself into a tradition.

D. Fundamental facts in relation to generations

According to what we have said so far, the social phenomenon 'generation' represents nothing more than a particular kind of identity of location, embracing related 'age groups' embedded in a historical-social process. While the nature of class location can be explained in terms of economic and social conditions, generation location is determined by the way in which certain patterns of experience and thought tend to be brought into existence by the *natural data* of the transition from one generation to another.

The best way to appreciate which features of social life result from the existence of generations is to make the experiment of imagining what the social life of man would be like if one generation lived on for ever and none followed to replace it. In contrast to such a utopian, imaginary society, our own has the following characteristics:

(a) new participants in the cultural process are emerging, whilst
(b) former participants in that process are continually disappearing;
(c) members of any one generation can participate only in a temporally limited section of the historical process, and
(d) it is therefore necessary continually to transmit the accumulated cultural heritage;
(e) the transition from generation to generation is a continuous process.

These are the basic phenomena implied by the mere fact of the existence of generations, apart from one specific phenomenon we choose to ignore for the moment, that of physical and mental ageing. With this as a beginning, let us then investigate the bearing of these elementary facts upon formal sociology.

(a) The continuous emergence of
new participants in the cultural process

In contrast to the imaginary society with no generations, our own – in which generation follows generation – is principally characterized by the fact that cultural creation and cultural accumulation are not accomplished by the same individuals – instead, we have the continuous emergence of new age groups.

This means, in the first place, that our culture is developed by individuals who come into contact anew with the accumulated heritage. In the nature of our psychical make-up, a fresh contact (meeting something anew) always means a changed relationship of distance from the object and a novel approach in assimilating, using, and developing the proffered material. The phenomenon of 'fresh contact' is, incidentally, of great significance in many social contexts; the problem of generations is only one among those upon which it has a bearing. Fresh contacts play an important part in the life of the individual when he is forced by events to leave his own social group and enter a new one – when, for example, an adolescent leaves home, or a peasant the countryside for the town, or when an emigrant changes his home, or a social climber his social status or class. It is well known that in all these cases a quite visible and striking transformation of the consciousness of the individual in question takes place: a change, not merely in the content of experience, but in the individual's mental and spiritual adjustment to it. In all these cases, however, the fresh contact is an event in one individual biography, whereas in the case of generations, we may speak of 'fresh contacts' in the sense of the addition of new psychophysical units who are in the literal sense beginning a 'new life'. Whereas the adolescent, peasant, emigrant, and social climber can only in a more or less restricted sense be said to begin a 'new life', in the case of generations, the 'fresh contact' with the social and cultural heritage is determined not by mere social change, but by fundamental biological factors. We can accordingly differentiate between two types of 'fresh contact': one based on a shift in social relations, and the other on vital factors (the change from one generation to another). The latter type is *potentially* much more radical, since with the advent of the new participant in the process of culture, the change of attitude takes place in a different individual whose attitude towards the heritage handed down by his predecessors is a novel one.

Were there no change of generation, there would be no 'fresh contact' of this biological type. If the cultural process were always carried on and developed by the same individuals, then, to be sure, 'fresh contacts' might still result from shifts in social relationships, but the more radical form of 'fresh contact' would be missing. Once established, any fundamental social pattern (attitude or intellectual trend) would probably be perpetuated – in itself an advantage, but not if we consider the dangers resulting from onesidedness. There might be a certain compensation for the loss of fresh generations in such a utopian society only if the people living in it were possessed, as befits the denizens of a Utopia, of perfectly universal minds – minds capable of experiencing all that there was to experience and of knowing all there was to know, and enjoying an elasticity such as to make it possible at any time to start afresh. 'Fresh contacts' resulting from shifts in the historical and social situation could suffice to bring about the changes in thought and practice necessitated by changed conditions only if the individuals experiencing these fresh contacts had such a perfect 'elasticity of mind'. Thus the continuous emergence of new human beings in our own society acts as compensation for the restricted and partial nature of the individual consciousness. The continuous emergence of new human beings certainly results

279

in some loss of accumulated cultural possessions; but, on the other hand, it alone makes a fresh selection possible when it becomes necessary; it facilitates reevaluation of our inventory and teaches us both to forget that which is no longer useful and to covet that which has yet to be won.

(b) The continuous withdrawal of previous participants in the process of culture

The function of this second factor is implied in what has already been said. It serves the necessary social purpose of enabling us to forget. If society is to continue, social remembering is just as important as forgetting and action starting from scratch.

At this point we must make clear in what social form remembering manifests itself and how the cultural heritage is actually accumulated. All psychic and cultural data only really exist in so far as they are produced and reproduced in the present: hence past experience is only relevant when it exists concretely incorporated in the present. In our present context, we have to consider two ways in which past experience can be incorporated in the present:

(i) as consciously recognized models on which men pattern their behaviour (for example, the majority of subsequent revolutions tended to model themselves more or less consciously on the French Revolution); or

(ii) as unconsciously 'condensed', merely 'implicit' or 'virtual' patterns; consider, for instance, how past experiences are 'virtually' contained in such specific manifestations as that of sentimentality. Every present performance operates a certain selection among handed-down data, for the most part unconsciously. That is, the traditional material is transformed to fit a prevailing new situation, or hitherto unnoticed or neglected potentialities inherent in that material are discovered in the course of developing new patterns of action.

At the more primitive levels of social life, we mostly encounter unconscious selection. There the past tends to be present in a 'condensed', 'implicit', and 'virtual' form only. Even at the present level of social reality, we see this unconscious selection at work in the deeper regions of our intellectual and spiritual lives, where the tempo of transformation is of less significance. A conscious and reflective selection becomes necessary only when a semi-conscious transformation, such as can be effected by the traditionalist mind, is no longer sufficent. In general, rational elucidation and reflectiveness invade only those realms of experience which become problematic as a result of a change in the historical and social situation; where that is the case, the necessary transformation can no longer be effected without conscious reflection and its technique of de-stabilization.

We are directly aware primarily of those aspects of our culture which have become subject to reflection; and these contain only those elements which in the course of development have somehow, at some point, become problematical. This is not to say, however, that once having become conscious and reflective, they cannot again sink back into the a-problematical, untouched region of vegetative life. In any case, that form of memory which contains the past in the form of reflection is much less significant – e.g. it extends over a much more restricted range of experience – than that in which the past is only 'implicitly', 'virtually' present; and reflective elements are more often dependent on unreflective elements than *vice versa.*

Here we must make a fundamental distinction between *appropriated* memories and *personally acquired* memories (a distinction applicable both to reflective and unreflective elements). It makes a great difference whether I acquire memories for myself in the process of personal development, or whether I simply take them over from someone else. I only really possess those 'memories' which I have created directly for myself, only that 'knowledge' I have personally gained in real situations. This is the only sort of knowledge which really 'sticks' and it alone has real binding power. Hence, although it would appear desirable that man's spiritual and intellectual possessions should consist of nothing but individually acquired memories, this would also involve the danger that the earlier ways of possession and acquisition will inhibit the new acquisition of knowledge. That experience goes with age is in many ways an advantage. That, on the other hand, youth lacks experience means a lightening of the ballast for the young; it facilitates their living on in a changing world. One is old primarily in so far as he comes to live within a specific, individually acquired, framework of useable past experience, so that every new experience has its form and its place largely marked out for it in advance. In youth, on the other hand, where life is new, formative forces are just coming into being, and basic attitudes in the process of development can take advantage of the moulding power of new situations. Thus a human race living on for ever would have to learn to forget to compensate for the lack of new generations.

(c) Members of any one generation can only participate in a temporally limited section of the historical process

The implications of this basic fact can also be worked out in the light of what has been said so far. The first two factors, (a) and (b), were only concerned with the aspects of constant 'rejuvenation' of society. To be able to start afresh with a new life, to build a new destiny, a new framework of anticipations, upon a new set of experiences, are things which can come into the world only through the fact of new birth. All this is implied by the factor of social rejuvenation. The factor we are dealing with now, however, can be adequately analysed only in terms of the category of 'similarity of location' which we have mentioned but not discussed in detail above.

Members of a generation are 'similarly located', first of all, in so far as they all are exposed to the same phase of the collective process. This, however, is a merely mechanical and external criterion of the phenomenon of 'similar location'. For a deeper understanding, we must turn to the phenomenon of the 'stratification' of experience (*Erlebnisschichtung*), just as before we turned to 'memory'. The fact that people are born at the same time, or that their youth, adulthood, and old age coincide, does not in itself involve similarity of location; what does create a similar location is that they are in a position to experience the same events and data, etc., and especially that these experiences impinge upon a similarly 'stratified' consciousness. It is not difficult to see why mere chronological contemporaneity cannot of itself produce a common generation location. No one, for example, would assert that there was community of location between the young people of China and Germany about 1800. Only where contemporaries definitely are in a position to participate as an integrated group in certain common experiences can we rightly speak of community of location of a generation. Mere contemporaneity becomes sociologically significant only when it also involves participation in the same historical and social circumstances. Further, we have to take into consideration at this point the phenomenon of 'stratification', mentioned above. Some older generation groups experience certain historical processes together with the young generation and yet we cannot say that they have the same generation location. The fact that their location is a different one, however, can be explained primarily by the different 'stratification' of their lives. The human consciousness, structurally speaking, is characterized by a particular inner 'dialectic'. It is of considerable importance for the formation of the consciousness which experiences happen to make those all-important 'first impressions', 'childhood experiences' – and which follow to form the second, third, and other 'strata'. Conversely, in estimating the biographical significance of a particular experience, it is important to know whether it is undergone by an individual as a decisive childhood experience, or later in life, superimposed upon other basic and early impressions. Early impressions tend to coalesce into a *natural view* of the world. All later experiences then tend to receive their meaning from this original set, whether they appear as that set's verification and fulfilment or as its negation and antithesis. Experiences are not accumulated in the course of a lifetime through a process of summation or agglomeration, but are 'dialectically' articulated in the way described. We cannot here analyse the specific forms of this dialectical articulation, which is potentially present whenever we act, think, or feel, in more detail (the relationship of 'antithesis' is only one way in which new experiences may graft themselves upon old ones). This much, however, is certain, that even if the rest of one's life consisted in one long process of negation and destruction of the natural world view acquired in youth, the determining influence of these early impressions would still be predominant. For even in negation our orientation is fundamentally centred upon that which is being negated, and we are thus still unwittingly determined by it. If we bear in mind that every concrete experience acquires its particular face and form from its relation to this primary stratum of experiences from which all others receive their meaning, we can appreciate its importance for the further development of the human consciousness. Another fact, closely related to the phenomenon just described, is that any two generations following one another always fight different opponents, both within and without. While the older people may still be combating something in themselves or in the external world in such fashion that all their feelings and efforts and even their concepts and categories of thought are determined by that adversary, for the younger people this adversary may be simply non-existent: their primary orientation is an entirely different one. That historical development does not proceed in a straight line – a feature frequently observed particularly in the cultural sphere – is largely attributed to this shifting of the 'polar' components of life, that is, to the fact that internal or external adversaries constantly disappear and are replaced by others. Now this particular dialectic, of changing generations, would be absent from our imaginary society. The only dialectical features of such a society would be those which would arise from social polarities – provided such polarities were present. The primary experiential stratum of the members of this imaginary society would simply consist of the earliest experiences of mankind; all later experience would receive its meaning from that stratum.

(d) The necessity for constant transmission of the cultural heritage

Some structural facts which follow from this must at least be indicated here. To mention one problem only: a utopian, immortal society would not have to face this necessity of cultural transmission, the most important aspect of which is the automatic passing on to the new generations of the traditional ways of life, feelings, and attitudes. The data transmitted by conscious teaching are of more limited importance, both quantitatively and qualitatively. All those attitudes and ideas which go on functioning satisfactorily in the new situation and serve as the basic inventory of group life are unconsciously and unwittingly handed on and transmitted: they seep in without either the teacher or pupil knowing anything about it. What is consciously learned or inculcated belongs to those things which in the course of time have somehow, somewhere, become problematic and therefore invited conscious reflection. This is why that inventory of experience which is absorbed by infiltration from the environment in early youth often becomes the historically oldest stratum of consciousness, which tends to stabilize itself as the natural view of the world.

But in early childhood even many reflective elements are assimilated in the same 'a-problematical' fashion as those elements of the basic inventory had been. The new germ of an original intellectual and spiritual life which is latent in the new human being has by no means as yet come into its own. The possibility of really questioning and reflecting on things only emerges at the point where personal experimentation with life begins – round about the age of 17, sometimes a little earlier and sometimes a little later. It is only then that life's problems begin to be located in a 'present' and are experienced as such. That level of data and attitudes which social change has rendered problematical, and which therefore requires reflection, has now been reached; for the first time, one lives 'in the present'. Combative juvenile groups struggle to clarify these issues, but never realise that, however radical they are, they are merely out to transform the uppermost stratum of consciousness which is open to conscious reflection. For it seems that the deeper strata are not easily destabilized and that when this becomes necessary, the process must start out from the level of reflection and work down to the stratum of habits. The 'up-to-dateness' of youth therefore consists in their being closer to the 'present' problems (as a result of their 'potentially fresh contact'), and in the fact that they are dramatically aware of a process of de-stabilization and take sides in it. All this while, the older generation cling to the re-orientation that had been the drama of *their* youth.

From this angle, we can see that an adequate education or instruction of the young (in the sense of the complete transmission of all experiential stimuli which underlie pragmatic knowledge) would encounter a formidable difficulty in the fact that the experiential problems of the young are defined by a different set of adversaries from those of their teachers. Thus (apart from the exact sciences), the teacher-pupil relationship is not as between one representative of 'consciousness in general' and another, but as between one possible subjective centre of vital orientation and another subsequent one. This tension appears incapable of solution except for one compensating factor: not only does the teacher educate his pupil, but the pupil educates his teacher too. Generations are in a state of constant interaction.

This leads us to our next point:

(e) The uninterrupted generation series

The fact that the transition from one generation to another takes place continuously tends to render this interaction smoother; in the process of this interaction, it is not the oldest who meet the youngest at once; the first contacts are made by other 'intermediary' generations, less removed from each other.

Fortunately, it is not as most students of the generation problem suggest – the thirty-year interval is not solely decisive. Actually, all intermediary groups play their part; although they cannot wipe out the biological difference between generations, they can at least mitigate its consequences. The extent to which the problems of younger generations are reflected back upon the older one becomes greater in the measure that the dynamism of society increases. Static conditions make for attitudes of piety – the younger generation tends to adapt itself to the older, even to the point of making itself appear older. With the strengthening of the social dynamic, however, the older generation becomes increasingly receptive to influences from the younger. This process can be so intensified that, with an elasticity of mind won in the course of experience, the older generation may even achieve greater adaptability in certain spheres than the intermediary generations, who may not yet be in a position to relinquish their original approach.

Thus, the continuous shift in objective conditions has its counterpart in a continuous shift in the oncoming new generations which are first to incorporate the changes in their behaviour system. As the tempo of change becomes faster, smaller and smaller modifications are experienced by young people as significant ones, and more and more intermediary shades of novel impulses become interpolated between the oldest and newest re-orientation systems. The underlying inventory of vital responses, which remains unaffected by the change, acts in itself as a unifying factor; constant inter-action, on the other hand, mitigates the differences in the top layer where the change takes place, while the continuous nature of the transition in normal times lessens the frictions involved. To sum up: if the social process involved no change of generations, the new impulses that can originate only in new organisms could not be reflected back upon the representatives of the tradition; and if the transition between generations were not continu-ous, this reciprocal action could not take place without friction.

60

CHILDHOOD AS GENERATIONAL CONDITION

Towards a relational theory of childhood[1]

Leena Alanen

Source: *Research in Childhood: Sociology, Culture and History*, Denmark: University of Southern Denmark, 2000, pp. 11–30.

The sociology of childhood is a project still very much in its beginning. It started some 10–15 years ago as a kind of 'meeting place' for individual and groups of researchers who shared a discontent with the existing state of childhood knowledge, and interests in bringing to the study of childhood a range of perspectives already applied in other, more established fields of social science. The field has grown, and as it has grown it also has become more diversified. One of the fruits of this development is that we now can more readily see also some important differences and divisions existing between the approaches that are used in researching childhood. Choices of focus and the concrete research methods vary, of course, but more important are the metatheoretical, methodological commitments with which researchers have come to the field, as they work to produce sociological understandings of childhood.

My paper starts by identifying three different methodologies in use by sociologists researching children and childhood. Two of them – I have named them the 'sociology of children' and the 'sociology of childhood' – are particularly relevant for the topic of this paper as they both are approaches that claim to focus on the empirical realities of actual children and their childhoods. (The third sociology is a deconstructive one, and does not aim to produce knowledge about childhood's reality.) They do this in different ways: one focusing on the micro-'level' and the other one on the 'macro-level'. Both of these methodologies commit to a social constructionism at the meta-theoretical level but I want to argue that both show a remarkable, and consequential, 'constructionism deficit' at the moment of conceptualizing children: the understanding and definition of children is, and remains in them, an empiricist one. Such a lingering empiricism is unhelpful when the aim is to proceed towards theorizing childhood as a genuinely social phenomenon. A more consistent and comprehensive constructionist sociology of childhood would need, the paper argues, a methodology that is relational from the very beginning.

The latter part of the paper presents a small-scale, data-intensive study on children and their everyday lives, as an attempt to develop a relational sociology of childhood, grounded in empirical work on children's childhoods.

1. Introduction

The sociology of childhood is a project still very much in its beginning. It was started some 10–15 years ago as a kind of meeting place for individual and groups of researchers who shared a discontent with the existing state of childhood knowledge, and an interest in bringing to the study of children's lives a range of perspectives already applied in other, more established fields of social science. Since then the field has grown, and as it has grown also some important differences and divisions among the different approaches taken in researching childhood are becoming visible. Choices of focus and concrete research methods vary, of course, but so do the metatheoretical and methodological commitments with which researchers have come to the field. These commitments, I would argue, are also far more significant and consequential for the understandings of childhood resulting from sociological work, than the particular topics that are studied or the research methods that are used.

The focus of this paper is childhood as an essentially generationally defined social condition and the aim is to develop a methodology for the study of childhoods that respects this startingpoint. The central argument in the paper is that the sociology of childhood lacks a methodology that would correspond to this relational nature of the childhood phenomenon. The problem can be seen to be in the 'constructionism deficit' in current approaches in the empirical study of children and childhood. This helps to sustain a lingering empiricism in them, leading to the unfortunate consequence that the generational nature of childhood is lost out of analytical sight. Therefore, a consistently constructionist sociology of childhood is in need of a methodology that is relational from the very beginning.

In this paper, an attempt is made to develop such an approach, and to study empirically how children, in their daily lives, actively participate in the construction of a generational order which defines them as 'children'.

2. Methodologies in researching children and childhood

Considering the original reasons for the emergence of the sociological study of children and childhood, it is understandable that most of the new empirical research has focused directly on 'real' children, their activities and experiences, understandings, knowledges and meanings. Children are seen to act in the social world, and to participate in ongoing social life, and are centrally involved in the construction of their own childhoods, through their negotiations with the adult world and among themselves. Children's childhoods (cf. Mayall 1994) is the immediate focus in this strand of sociological childhood research, and quantitatively probably the dominant approach in the field so far.

A second important approach also focuses on the socially constructed nature of the childhood phenomenon (cf. James & Jenks & Prout 1998, 26–28). Discussions around postpositivist philosophies of science and their implications for social research ground this approach. Now childhood is viewed as a discursive, or culturally constructed, phenomenon and therefore always context-dependent. To investigate the childhood(s) of today is to 'deconstruct' the cultural ideas, images, models and practices through which children and childhood are presently 'known' and acted on.

A third perspective on childhood presents childhood as a (relatively) permanent element in the life of modern societies, even when for individual children it means a temporary period of life. In this view, 'childhood' is a structural category (e.g. Qvortrup 1994), comparable and parallel to the proto-sociological 'class', as well as the more recent 'gender', and also in continuous interplay with these and other categories of social structure, while also being constructed and reconstructed within their interplay. Here actual living children, each with their different childhoods, are not the immediate focus; they are of course there, but assembled under the socially formed structural category of childhood.

These three different perspectives, or approaches in the sociological study of childhood are informed by three different methodologies:

{1} a micro-oriented sociology of children, in which the focus remains on the local level of actual, active children and their childhoods,
{2} a deconstructive sociology in which the focus is on the discursive formation(s) of childhood and the aim is to deconstruct (contextualize) them, and
{3} a structural sociology of childhood that aims to link empirical manifestations on the level of children's childhoods with their macro-level contexts, social structures and mechanisms which 'determine' these manifestations.

Despite the shared investment in the agency of children in each of these methodologies, their combined effect across the field is that the very notion of childhood remains unstable, conceptually polysemantic and even ambiguous. In the first two methodologies, childhoods are always diverse and plural, whereas in the structural perspective childhood is seen as a singular phenomenon, as a structural 'form' to which actual living children relate as its 'incumbents' (Qvortrup 1994, 6). In postmodernist times, such a plurality of meanings might be regarded as the 'normal' case, and for some even nothing to deplore, but the ambiguities involved actually only help to contrast micro- and macroperspectives with each other – in a true manner of modernist sociology – instead of pointing to ways towards overcoming them.

However, building on the strengths contained in each of the three methodologies, a more comprehensive (and 'past-modern': Stones 1996) methodology can be developed for explaining the formation of children's childhoods while preserving them as agents in this formation. Such a methodology will also be a structural one, in that it will link the actor-centred observations on children and empirical aspects of their childhoods to the social 'structures' that make possible those particular childhoods to actualize, to become experienced as well as observed. This time, the relevant structures will be explicitly generational.

3. Childhood as generationally structured relations

Most children of the world are born into families and spend varying proportions and lengths of their daily lives within these generationally structured 'units' in which some members are 'parents' while others are 'children'. This is the normal assumption of most (Western) sociology, long ago crystallized in notions such as the family and socialization. Mostly sociologists take this generational structuredness for granted, accepting it as a (social) fact and as the basis for formulating research questions.

In this paper, this 'fact' will be scrutinized in an empirical study on the specifically generational structuring of children's social relationships, in the case of a small sample of Finnish children. Generational structuring – or 'generationing' (2) – refers to processes through which some individuals become ('are constructed as') 'children' while others become ('are constructed as') 'adults', having consequences for the activities and identities of inhabitants of each category as well as for their interrelationships.

The (at this point merely theoretical) assumption of ongoing generationing processes need not be restricted to the familial domain, for schools, day-care centres and other institutionalized domains for children are further obvious sites in which generationing takes place. Like gendering and 'classing', perhaps even 'racing', generationing can be assumed to take place also outside such child-marked institutions, in fact in every domain of social life – in working life and in politics just as much as in the cultural field – and quite irrespective of whether real, concrete children are actually 'seen' to be present and acting in them. Therefore, in the empirical study to follow, generationing processes are explored across all the arenas of children's daily lives.

One of the grounding axioms of Childhood Studies is that childhood is to be understood a social and historical 'construction'. There is, however, somewhat paradoxically, often a grave 'deficit' of constructionism in researchers' own approaches to studying children, in that the condition of being a child is simply assumed as a startingpoint without giving attention to the complexity of material, social and discursive processes and their interplay through which childhood is daily reproduced as a specifically generational condition. After all, not everything in the lives of the little beings who in everyday parlance are called 'children', follows from their being children and being related to other generational categories (such as adults). Children are also boys and girls, so that their childhoods are also gender ordered. And the same case can be argued also for class, 'race' or ethnicity: these are also social conditions that structure children's lives while also being structured through their activities. The problematization of generation, or the generational order (comparable to gender order; e.g. Connell 1987), lags far behind the level and quantity of work given by researchers to analyzing gender, class, 'race' or ethnicity, and its equally (but differently) constructed nature and the material, social and discursive processes of its construction remain unilluminated. The natural attitude (Garfinkel) still prevails in the social study of childhood.

In order to start 'deconstructing' also generation, a conceptual distinction is needed between

{1}   child as the socially constructed sign for a concrete individual – generally a person who is small and young, but such designations vary from context to context – and
{2}   'child' as the conceptual presentation of a position within a generational structure.

Consistently constructionist thinking also needs the conceptual distinction between

{1}   childhood as referring to a concrete, undifferentiated social phenomenon – such as the childhood of an individual child, or the childhoods of a group of children – and
{2}   'childhood' (in the singular) as a theoretical concept referring to a specific, socially constructed generational condition.

These distinctions are in terms of level of abstraction, but they are not just analytical distinctions, made by the researcher for the purpose of analysis. On the contrary, I want to argue that they are abstractions that represents a real social condition, in as much as we do have clear and unambiguous evidence of the fact that childhood is a distinct category in our kind of societies with several and often dramatic social consequences for those who are categorized as children, as well as those others positioned into the countercategory of adults (e.g. Qvortrup 1997). Consequently, to theorize childhood would mean to arrive at a conceptual understanding of childhood as a generational condition.

The aim of the empirical study to follow is to proceed towards a sociological theory of childhood as a socially constructed position defined by its relations within a generationally structured social world.

A specific interest in exploring the generational structures within which children live their daily lives concerns the understanding of children's agency. In a relational framework, 'agency' need not be restricted to a microconstructionist understanding of 'being a social actor', as in the sociology of children. Rather, it refers now to the 'powers' of those in 'child' positions to influence, organize, coordinate and control events taking place in their everyday worlds. Such powers are best understood as possibilities of action and as determined by the structures within which children are positioned as 'children'. Therefore, in order to detect the range and nature of children's agency the exploration needs to be oriented towards the generational structures from which children's powers (or lack of them) derive: the source of their agency as 'children' is to be found in the social organization of generational relations. Present structural positioning and the agency that the position makes possible for its incumbents – here: children – also determine how and to what extent they may gain access to new empowering resources, and to further control (power) over the conditions of their lives, and to expansion of agency.

In summary, a relational methodology as I have started to sketch above, will need to [1] begin from children's childhoods – their daily lives as enacted and experienced by them. It is then a clear case of a standpoint methodology (3). And as childhood is a relational (generational) concept, the analytical strategy therefore is to proceed towards [2] identifying the social practices within which children in their everyday lives relate to objects in their environment (both people and 'things') in relatively enduring ways. Some of these patterns can be identified as the everyday practices of generationing, as the practices through which one first becomes a 'child', in relation to non-children. This 'becoming' is by no means a natural or automatical process: it involves active construction, therefore agency, at every step.

After identifying one or more generationing practices, [3] their structuredness are analyzed: these are the dynamic generational structures which are reproduced, and occasionally transformed, by the agents positioned and acting within the practice in question (4). At the end of this analytical journey the gaze may be turned back to the empirical childhoods that were the startingpoint for the analysis; now they can be seen as outcomes of structures and processes, in which children, at every 'level', from everyday activities to generationing practices and structures, are involved as agents sustaining a set of (possibly several) generational, generationing practices.

4. The study: data and methodology

This is the route I have followed also in my empirical study. The data for the study was collected with twenty 9–10-year old children living in a typical suburb of a middle-sized Finnish town. The children and their parents were first contacted in spring 1998 when they all were in the third grade of the suburban primary school and went to the same class. The main part of the data was collected through interviews, first in pairs and later individually. Before interviews, I spent a lot of time in school, being present in the classroom, getting to know the children, going out with them during breaks, walking on the yard with them, talking and skipping rope (after being invited to do so), having lunch together with them at the school cafeteria, and walking home with them after school. Pair interviews conducted in their school during school time and mostly in the school library area and lasted from 45 minutes to one hour. For these sessions, children chose a friend from the class with whom she or he wanted to be interviewed. All the children in the class volunteered eagerly for these discussions.

The next phase of data collection was during the autumn of the same year when the children went to the fourth grade of the same school. Now they were in a larger class, as the three third-grade classes from last spring were put into two fourth-grade classes. During the autumn data collection continued by individual interviews with eight of the original twenty children, the sessions being combined with walks home from school or they took place in the evening at the child's home (5). In the latter cases, interviewing was mixed with talks also with the parent(s) and siblings. The afternoon interviews took between 1.5–2 hours while these evening sessions took longer times to complete.

Analysis of the data was started by constructing 'inventories' of the daily life for each of the participating children; these inventories were then compared with each other to find similarities and differences in ways in which children related to people and things. Based on comparisons, a number of domains of daily life were identified which were 'typical' in the studied group of children and also relatively separate from each other, also in the subjective sense of the children themselves: the domains are part of their everyday knowledge and discourse. Four such childhood domains were found in the data and common-sensically named as Family, Friendships, School, and Personal Interests.

A relational analysis of each of the domain followed from this first stage of analysis. Here the aim was to explore the generational positions existing within each of these four domains. Within the scope of this paper, only the positions within the Family domain can only be described; the other domains are presented in terms of the difference of each from Family. Indicators for the positioning of the ('empirical') children as expressly 'children' within the domain in question – i.e. within its particular generational structure – consist of the various rules by which children's action on the domain are organized, coordinated and controlled, as well as the responsibilities which they assume (or are made to assume) within domains. The justifications given to the rules and responsibilities and known to them, whether they accepted and followed them or not, contribute to the 'input' side of children's positioning within the domains. The reverse, or 'outcome' side of children's positioning is looked at from the standpoint of dependence and independence as experienced and practiced by the children. The degree of (in)dependency in occupying a position within a generational structure, and in maintaining (or expanding) a specific structural practice, is indicated by children's experiences and feelings about self-care and of times being away from home or from family, of feelings raised by times spent alone, and of experiences of having a say in matters important to and affecting oneself. Finally, children's own understandings of what it is to be a child also indicate differences in the four practices of 'childing' (as a specification of 'generationing') in the four domains, confirming the view that there are indeed several different ways of being (and becoming) 'children'.

Third, a closer look at these practices is needed to identify some of the structuring 'mechanisms' responsible for producing each generationing practice. This is done by asking 'retroductive' questions about what makes the different practices possible, which kinds of resources (or 'capitals', cf. Bourdieu), or 'powers', need to be available for the person (agent) to reproduce the practice in question, and even to strengthen and elaborate his or her position within it, and in which ways is access to such resources provided or not, in the normal course of daily (or weekly) life. Other structures and mechanisms may also help to sustain the position-holding and the practice, whereas the absence of some resources may predispose children to one practice rather than another.

Based on such a resource analysis, some of the social trajectories of childhood can be sketched, in terms of the transitions children have already made, or are in the process of making, from the domain and its practice to a new one, but of course two or even three practices can also be maintained simultaneously. Such trajectories suggest some of the possible routes that children traveled within the overall generational order. Observing such trajectories also helps to focus the analysis also towards asking further questions about the resources necessary for generationing practices to be sustained, as well as about the mechanisms of moving children from one practice to another.

This opens a final stage in the logic of this study in which we can begin to collect pieces for an explanation for the daily lives of the children participating in the study. If the possibility of practicing a particular childhood will depend on the availability of and access to specific material, social and cultural (semiotic) resources, then it is relevant to ask how the resources necessary for the practice in question are socially distributed and made available (or not) for children in general to deploy. Resource distributions are socially constructed facts within a historically existing society, and so are the mechanisms of distribution, of which there are many: through markets or through families, directly targeted on children, built into public services and made accessible on an equal basis, or made dependent on purchasing, or readily available in the everyday environment. The present analysis does not go beyond this stage, where it merely points to the large-scale contextual enablements and constraints on the regional, national and even transnational level that exist also for the childhoods studied here. Other kinds of data – historical and statistical – would be needed in order to link these suburban childhoods to such global structures and mechanisms.

5. Analysis

Childhood domains

Most children in the Minority world start their 'career' as children by being born into a 'family' and becoming members of such a unit, and are dependent on it for the material, social and cultural resources that they deploy in their becoming particular kinds of children. The degree of this kind of formative dependency on a family of one's own does, of course, vary transnationally but even among children living in the same region or locality, such as the home suburb of the children studied here. Most of the twenty children have lived in the same suburb since they were born, perhaps having only moved house within the area. But there are also other features of life history which the children share: all of them have been in day-care outside home before starting school, many of them all through their preschool years – a direct consequence of the fact that most of their parents – as most Finnish parents in general – work full-time outside home.

But such shared experiences of extra-familial worlds notwithstanding, family – or home at least – continues to be a significant site for children's daily activities. Other sites, or domains of everyday life, were identified by reading analytically children's descriptions of [1] their daily activities, hobbies and pursuits, to find patterns in their initiation, planning and coordination, [2] the web of people with whom children do things together, such as parents (both own and other children's parents), siblings, friends and mates, other kids in the neighbourhood, club members and leaders, coaches, members and directors of choir, people at the college for music, at dance school or riding school, and [3] their understandings of what these activities are pursued for, and why they prefer some activities to others, and

participate in them on a regular basis. Four bounded domains were identified from these accounts, and named as Family, School, Friendships and
Personal Interests.

All the children in the study moved (almost) daily within all of these
domains; they were to a greater or lesser extent part of every child's life.
However, some children moved more on one domain than another, and
related to the other three domains in a patterned way. These patterns,
and the domains themselves are described below as the domains of children
who appeared to be 'strong' on the particular domain, i.e. 'empowered' in
terms of having access and knowing how to use the material, social and/or
cultural resources relevant for the domain specific activities. There is, of
course, variation among the children 'strong' in each domain; the descriptions
here attempt to catch their typicalities.

Family

Inka is one of the altogether seven children (out of twenty), whose daily life
takes place predominantly within the Family domain: her daily activities
outside school take place mainly indoors, either at her own home or at the
home of a 'best friend' living, in her case living downstairs in the same block
of apartments. She also spends many weekends with her mother at their
summer cottage, near grandmother's house, and her mother (a lone parent)
also takes her every week to enjoy an hour of riding, or swimming at the
city swimming hall. Often a friend of Inka's is invited also to come with
along. Inka enjoys doing housework and making things pretty and tidy in
their household their is not much to do as her mother takes care of most
things, from shopping and cooking; however, Inka is expected to manage
her own room. The weekly rotation of activities and going to places is
largely managed by parents in agreement: Hers is a bi-nuclear family situation and she spends every second weekend, and some holiday time, at her
father's new family. Also there, with her two 'social siblings', her life is filled
with activities and relationships of the familial kind: TV-watching and
playing games together, going to sauna, shopping and making outings with
the new family.

Friendships

Inka, of course, has friends and they are important to her, but in contrast to
her fairly small circle of play mates, the number of friends *Maija* is able
to list, and the frequency with which she sees them is far beyond Inka's
circle of friends as well as her idea of what friendships are for. Maija meets
her friends – or friends of her friends, for there is going on a constant
weaving of new children into the network – mostly out-of-doors, as she
moves with other children in the yards between the blocks or the little parks

and woods of which there are many in the suburb. They are often in large groups, and Maija is particularly interested (as well as good at) getting to know new characters, preferably older than she is. Friendships, Maija herself pointed out, are the most important thing in her life: without friends her daily life would be gray and dull. In the world of friendships, she asserts, she is learning all kinds of new things and competencies all the time, and the experience of becoming and being competent is paramount to her and best secured for her within this domain – not, for instance, in the School domain.

School

Names here an activity domain which does not refer simply to school as the obligatory place for children to go for purposes of learning. For *Sami*, the concrete school where he goes to, with its schedules of learning, is at times a dull place and some days really boring, but then some school subjects and events can be very interesting, too. The (rare) moments of fascination in school are of the kind as when 'one learns to use the pencil [in art classes] in a different way, so as to produce a thick or a slim stroke' (Sami). Perpetually learning new things, getting to know how to do things by oneself, the experience that one grows in knowledge – all of this is significant for him, and they are also the kinds of experiences he is perpetually hunting for outside school. Sami is on the look for such possibilities by joining the school choir, the scouts and even the cooking club which meets once a week in the school. He goes often to the local library and reads a lot, he also eagerly tries new programs on his parents' computer at home, and contemplates on starting to play some instrument, dreaming of joining the school brass band. Having a lot of friends is not something to look forward to in itself; much more important is what kind of people they are and what you can do with them. It therefore also does not matter if they are girls or babies or adults, and in fact Sami confesses (lowering his voice) that he in fact enjoys being with both babies and girls, and he particularly likes to be around and participate in discussions when colleagues and friends of his parents are visiting his home. Being alone is also no problem, and he in fact often keeps himself to himself, likes to be in peace, without therefore feeling lonely.

Personal interests

For Pauliina, having to go to school, and everything that this implies, is the least interesting thing in her life. It is of course essential to cope with the demands of school, but 'real' life waits elsewhere, and this is where she can freely follow her personal interests. In her case at the moment, they are musical: she travels every week to the college of music downtown, for lessons in playing as well as in theory of music, and she also practices playing at home. She also recently looked up for the entrance examination of the city children's choir and went and passed the test, now travelling by bus also to choir rehearsals once or twice a week. The exact number of friends is hard for her to specify, for friends are those who currently share her interests, with whom she can talk about them and who enjoy doing the same kind of things, even though she may see them just once or twice a week. Pilvi is another child whose daily life is significantly dominated by activities in the Personal Interests domain. Differently from Pauliina, her personal interests are in the sports, but as for Pauliina, for her, too, the experience of feeling successful in her favourite activity and being among people who share her personal interest is the driving motive for continuing, even competitively, her (burgeoning) career in sports.

When asked, all the children talk easily about their families, friends, school and what they like to do in their free time; also their accounts of daily activities show that they all move in and about all of the four domains distinguished here and exemplified by individual cases of children. Although no domain is completely cut from each other, for any one child, there are clear indications of an order existing between the domains in (nearly) each case. As for the few children presented above, also the rest of the children can be categorized according to the main activity domain in their lives; we therefore have a relatively large group of 'Family (domain)' children, and smaller groups of 'Friendships' children, 'School' children and finally 'Personal Interests' children (6):

'Family' children	Anni, Ari, Elina, Esa, Inka, Oona, Otto (4 girls, 3 boys)
'Friendships' children	Maija, Meri, Minna (3 girls)
'School' children	Sami, Satu (1 girl, 1 boy)
'Personal Interests' children	Pauliina, Pilvi (2 girls)

'Childing' practices

The evidence of some children being both objectively and subjectively 'strong' in one domain, others on the other domains, give sufficient reason to ask; what separates the domains from each other in the sense of constituting them as different kinds of power bases (7) for children? Possible answers to such questions are sought in the data first by looking at differences in the rules and responsibilities that children identify as regulators of their daily activities. There were rules that in fact all the children could recount, the most notable one being about coming on schooldays straight home, first sitting down to do the homework (Friday being the exception), and having a snack before watching TV, or going out, or playing with friends. From the data it appears that the 'Family children' were able to list many more as well as more exact rules and responsibilities compared to the other children:

'Family' children	– time schedules: mealtime, coming in from out-doors, bedtimes (at 21)
	– call the parent(s) when at home from school
	– not allowed to watch 'certain kinds' of movies or TV programs
	– friends that may come to child's home while parents are away, and number of them at a time
	– not to use bad language
	– to obey parents
	– not to mess up places when at home after school
	– to help in housework by keeping own room tidy
	– not to use cutting knives, electric stove or other electric appliances when alone at home

The lack of clear rules in the case of children of the other domains does not mean that they would be allowed to behave as they pleased. Most of the children confirmed that they currently have no such rules to obey, but that they in many cases nevertheless tended to act in similar ways. The same went for responsibilities: they would 'help with the housework anyway', even liked to do specific task such baking or cooking a meal for the family; they also 'often called their parents after school and had a chat over the phone' or left a note on the table to tell homecoming parents where they were and when they would be coming back. Such 'habits' of children, in the absence of clearly stated rules and responsibilities, inform about the degree of self-care practiced by children. Even further indications of self-care by non-'Family children' were found:

'Friendships' children	– travels downtown (e.g. to swimming hall) with friends
	– makes snacks for oneself, also evening snacks
	– arranges often to stay overnight at friends' homes
'School' children	– wakes up on school mornings by oneself (alarm clock)
	– takes care of leaving in time for school
	– travels by bus downtown alone

298

	– spends a lot of time alone, doing one's own things
'Personal Interests' children	– wakes up in the mornings by oneself (alarm clock) – takes care of leaving in time for school – travels by bus downtown alone – takes care of matters related to personal interests (music lessons, training sessions, choir rehearsals – homework from school autonomously (also on Fridays, to have the weekend free for personal interests)

Based on this evidence from the data, there seems to be some clear differences between the domains in the extent of routinely practiced self-care and also the confidence with which children say they take care of their everyday matters: the 'Family' children display least of self-care while the 'Personal Interests' children display more than the other groups, the two other groups being somewhere in-between.

The differences between domains allow the conclusion that being a child means different things for children strong in different domains. The routines of everyday life as given by the kinds and numbers of familial rules and responsibilities as well as the extent of children's self-care practices highlight the material and social aspects of 'childness' (Wartofsky 1983; Cook-Gumperz 1991). The pattern of differences shown above is confirmed also by children's self-positioning of themselves as 'children' (or perhaps something else) and generally their own discourse an childhood: Only the 'Family' children would present extensive lists of the advantages of their (still) being a child, as well as disadvantages connected to the position of the child. And each of them confirmed that at present they preferred being a child. Children of the other three domains were very much more vague about such topics. Either they wished to detach themselves from the category of 'children' by using finer distinctions than just child vs. adult, as when defining themselves as young persons (in the case of 'Friendships' children), or they were plainly disinterested in having conversations on the topic at all, and found it difficult or irrelevant to position themselves on some generational scale ('School' and 'Personal Interests' children). 'School' children preferred instead to give long narratives about the many skills and competencies they already have, emphasizing the personal significance of continuously learning to do and understand new things, and linking this to their own growing (but not to growing up!). This simply made irrelevant for them a hierarchy such as the child vs. adult. In the case of the 'Personal Interests' children, childness was mentioned merely as a common – and annoying – attribution to small-sized people, as Pilvi felt she was herself, with her less than 140 cm, which she felt to prevent her from progress in her gymnastics career as quickly as she would like. For Pauliina – the other 'Personal Interests' child – being a child meant the equally annoying situation that one had to live in a family, which brought about a number of limitations to her personal projects. But 'there are not many alternatives, are there, as somebody has to provide you with food and housing and clothes and that kinds of things, so you just have to tolerate the situation . . .' (Pauliina).

One further conclusion to be drawn from this section is that there exist a number of different generationing practices in which also children actively participate, and are in fact constrained to participate through their necessary dependence on adult-led households. One of the generating practices found in the study seems to be, more solidly than the others, a 'childing practice', in that children's participation in this practice tended to (re)produced a distinct 'child' position for children to occupy, with rules and responsibilities prescribing the position and bringing for the children following the prescription, as well as subjectively experienced advantages and disadvantages, and a self-identification and a (mainly positive) self-image of childness. This is the practice that is most clearly dependent, firstly, on the quasi-autonomous family-household as its material basis, secondly, on close connections between members of the family, also the larger family of grandparents, cousins, aunts, uncles and godparents as its social basis and, thirdly, a particular discourse of 'the (nuclear) family' as its cultural (semiotic) basis.

The other generationing practices have their material, social and cultural bases mainly elsewhere, partly, it seems, in other non-familial institutions (educational institutions) and organizations (sports organizations, youth organizations, public/welfare state services, such as libraries or children's clubs). The social relationships which incorporate children to these non-familial practices, and their semiosis (meaning-making), bring within the reach of children a variety of resources, and therefore opportunities for negotiating their own position, also in relation to their family lives. The always provisional result of such negotiations is an unstable position, therefore one that also the children in the study were unwilling to describe in the terms of any popular discourse of childhood, as they were known to them. Interpreted within a developmental discourse, the childhoods of the non-'Family' children certainly would soon begin to look risky and dangerous, and more supervision, guidance and control (by adults) would be recommended to save the children from the looming dangers. The interpretation that presents itself when the very same childhoods are approached from children's standpoint is very different, and the risks and dangers that children may well meet are to be looked for elsewhere: in changes of societal distributions of material, social and cultural resources and children's possibilities to access them alone, with other children or with sympathetic and supportive adults. In times of recess, with high rates of parental unemployment also among the children living in the suburb studied here, and the simultaneous dismantling of welfare state provisions and public services, the programmatics of child-friendly politics is clear enough.

Generational structures

Why is the generationing practice a familial, 'childing' practice in the case of some children, while in the case if others it may be of the 'Friendships' type, the 'School' type, or the 'Personal Interests' type? Mainstream sociology would probably suggest as explanatory 'variables' such as the beliefs that parents have about children, their ideas about the family, their education or socio-economic status, size of family, gender. The material organization of childhood, in Western societies, is basically through children's household membership, and while some resources needed for the construction of childhoods exist in the household, the household also to a great extent mediates children's access to material, social and cultural resources outside the family/household. Other mediators exist, too. Above, the provision made by public services, institutions and organizations was mentioned. The suburb – as the physical and social environment of children's daily life – in itself provides resources: space and things (playgrounds, woods and forests, parks, clubhouses, school buildings and school yards, library, the mall, sporting grounds, ice rinks, . . .) and, of course, people in all of these places. The suburb is large and consists of five neighbourhoods, different from each other in terms of spatial planning, type of housing, and distance from the centre of the suburb (where the school as well as public and commercial services are).

The number of resources that make possible particular generationing practices (such as the ones identified above), is potentially huge and their coming together a complex process of interplay, in which also the children's active negotiations are a constitutive factor. To account for a total 'generational structure' consisting of all existing childhood practices would require the investigation of a large number of such processes, which in the case of the studied children span over their own life-time, and even longer, as some of the structural elements (such as the planning and building of suburbs) was there, constructed, before they arrived there, sometimes by 'people long dead' (Archer).

Although the generational structures involved in producing the four generationing practices can only crudely be sketched, in a small-scale study like this, the information below indicates that there are real differences also between the structures: the 'Family' children seem to have lived in circumstances of more limited access to resources, and the resources are predominantly provided by the neighbourhood, the child's own family as well as the larger family, whereas the 'Friendships children' and the 'School children' seem to have had access to 'social capital' (cf. Bourdieu) through relationships with other people (children and adults) and through experiences of other places (they have lived also outside suburb or do a lot of traveling):

'Family' children	– have lived all their lives in suburb – half of them are only children – live in block houses (both low rise and high rise) – before school start: a mixture of home care and day-care – summer cottage (in a few cases) – domestic travels to visit larger family
'Friendships' children	– have lived all their lives in suburb – largest families/several siblings – binuclear or reconstituted families (social siblings) – live in block houses or one-family house – summers spent at summer cottage (with cousins) or at home
'School' children	– have moved to suburb from other town – smallest families – live in row-house – summer trips abroad with family – a lot of domestic traveling (also alone) – parents are professionals
'Personal Interests' children	– have lived all their lives in suburb – live in row house and (low rise) block house – nuclear families

Trajectories

Finally, it would be far too deterministic to assume that children are born to, and stay within the confines of just one dominant domain – in which they are presently 'strong' – one generationing practice and one (although very complex) generational structure. Children can and do display strength and powers in more than one domain. And as the scheme below shows, many of the children are beginning to move to a new domain and even two domains.

From 'Family'	to	–	(Anni)
	to	'Friendships'	(Inka, Oona, Jussi)
	to	'Friendships' to 'Personal Interests'	(Otto)
	to	'Personal Interests'	(Elina)
	to	'Personal to 'School'	(Esa)
From 'Friendships'	to	'Personal Interests'	(Maija, Meri)
	to	–	(Minna)
From 'School'	to	'Personal Interests'	(Satu, Sami)
From 'Personal Interests'	to	'Friendships'	(Pauliina, Pilvi)

A summarizing conclusion from the patterns in these movements presented in the above scheme would be in terms of the generational structures which 'determine' the four activity domains on the left side of the scheme: the question then is, what is in the structures, in their combining of material, social and cultural resources that make possible, if not constrain, a movement to another domain. The data suggests that the strengths, or the powers, which children gain by participating in the 'childing' mode of generationing, are conducive to their movement both to a 'Friendships' mode and a 'Personal Interests' mode, while the 'School' domain seems to provide resources for acquiring 'Personal Interests'. However the numbers of the children in this study is small and the nature of data such as to merely raise the question – now, however, on the structural level, and not on the level of individual capacities and their development.

6. Conclusion

The theme running through this paper is 'generation'. The paper has explored empirically the daily lives and relationships of a group of 9-10-year-old children living in a particular (Finnish, suburban) context, with the aim of finding out, what it is in that context that tends to give those social relationships a specifically generational shape, thus making them into particular kinds of childhoods and identifying 'little beings' as expressly children. Methodologically, this approach assumes relational thinking, this in turn being based on a view (an ontology) of the social world as consisting basically of relations, and relations between relations (or structures) (8). The childhoods and the differences among them that were detected in the empirical study now also become explicable, but this time not in terms of the social, class, ethnic etc. background, culture or the local circumstances of the children in the study (as conventionally done in substantialist analyses), but by detecting the both direct and indirect, invisible relations through which children are firmly embedded in structured sets of relations larger than their very immediate local relations and potentially extending as far as the global social system. A small-scale study, such as the one presented here, is a beginning can be made to show the containment of children's childhoods within larger structures, on the condition that a relational notion of the socially constructed essence of (any) childhood is accepted as a methodological startingpoint.

Notes

1 This paper is based on a chapter written for the book Conceptualizing child-adult relations (Working title), edited by Leena Alanen and Berry Mayall. Parts of the paper were presented at the 94th Annual Meeting of the American Sociological Association (ASA), August 6–10, 1999, Chicago (USA). Special Session: Childhoods in International Perspective.

2 In making the noun into a verb I am following the parallel move from 'gender' to 'gendering' in feminist research. Cf. also Morgan (1999, 16) who argues that 'family' is best seen as 'less of a noun and more of an adjective or, possibly, a verb'.

3 For standpoint methodology in sociology, see e.g. Smith (1987, 105–147: on women's stand point); Alanen (1992: on children's standpoint). Cf. feminist 'standpoint epistemologies' (e.g. Alcoff & Potter 1993; Henwood & als 1998).

4 A structure is given in the set of material, social and discursive limitations and enablements for possible action for the agents (such as 'children') to take.

5 In half of the interviews, when both the child and the parent(s) preferred the afternoon walking home interview, I met the child at the end of the schoolday. On the way home, we talked about the day at school, the part of the suburb where they were living, their preferred routes to school and their favourite places as well as places they would avoid. Coming to the child's home, interviewing took place in the child's room, the kitchen, or the living room, with no other family members present than perhaps other siblings also arriving home. In the other half of the interview cases, walks were taken together home after school, but the interview sessions were in the evening at the child's home.

6 In this list, fourteen of the original twenty children are included. Two of the remaining six are hard to categorize because of the scant information they chose to share with me during the pair interview (they were interviewed together). Four other children were also not listed, as they proved not to be 'strong' in any of the four domains. Their cases will be analyzed elsewhere.

7 Cf. Bourdieu's notion of fields (e.g. Bourdieu & Wacquant 1992, 94–115), and of power as resources or 'capitals', each form of them specific to field (ibid, 115–120; Swartz 1997, 65–94).

8 On relational thinking in sociology, see e.g. Bhaskar (1979), Bourdieu (1990, 123–139); Bourdieu & Wacquant (1992, 94–98), Swartz (1997, Ch. 6), Manicas (1998) and Scott (1998). Pierre Bourdieu argues strongly for relationalism and constrasts it with a mode of thought he (following Cassirer) calls 'substantialism' which 'leads people to recognize no realities except those that are available to direct intuition in ordinary experience, individuals and groups'. Relationalism, or relationism (Scott 1998), identifies the real not with substances but with relations, and sociology, according to this view, is the analysis of 'relative positions and relations between positions' (Bourdieu 1990, 126).

References

Alanen, Leena (1994) Gender and generation. Feminism and the 'child question'. In Qvortrup, Jens et als. (eds) *Childhood matters*. Aldershot: Avebury.

Bhaskar, Roy (1999) *The possibility of naturalism*. Hemel Hempstead: Harvester Wheatsheaf.

Bourdieu, Pierre (1990) *In other words*. Cambridge: Polity Press.

Bourdieu, Pierre & Wacquant, Loic J. D. (1992) *An invitation to reflexive sociology*. Cambridge: Polity Press.

Connell. R. W. (1987) *Gender & power*. Cambridge: Polity Press.

Henwood, Karen & Griffin Christine & Phoenix, Ann (eds) (1998) *Standpoints and differences: essays in the practice of feminist psychology*. London: Sage.

James, Allison & Jenks, Chris & Prout, Alan (1998) *Theorizing childhood*. Cambridge: Polity Press.

Alcoff, Linda & Potter, Elizabeth (eds) (1993) *Feminist epistemologies*. New York and London: Routledge.

Manicas, Peter (1998) A realist social science. In Archer, Margaret et als. (eds) *Critical realism*. London: Routledge.

Mayall, Berry (ed.) (1994) *Children's childhoods: Observed and experienced*. London: Falmer Press.

Morgan, David H. J. (1999) *Family connections*. Cambridge: Polity Press.

Qvortrup, Jens (1994) Introduction. In Qvortrup, Jens et als. (eds) *Childhood matters*. Aldershot: Avebury.

Scott, John (1998) Relationism, cubism, and reality: beyond relativism. In May, Tim & Williams, Malcolm (eds) *Knowing the social worlds*. Buckingham: Open University Press.

Smith, Dorothy E. (1987) *The everyday world as problematic*. Milton Keynes: Open University Press.

Stones, Rob (1996) *Sociological reasoning. Towards a past-modern sociology*. Houndsmill: Macmillan.

Swartz, David (1997) *Culture & power. The sociology of Pierre Bourdieu*. Chicago: The University of Chicago Press.

Cook-Gumperz, Jenny (1991) Children's construction of 'childness'. In Scales, Barbara & als (eds) *Play and the social context of development in early care and education*. New York: Teachers College Press.

Wartofsky, Marx (1983) The child's construction of the world and the world's construction of the child: from historical epistemology to historical psychology. In Kessel, Frank S. & Siegel, Alexander W. (eds) *The child and other cultural inventions*. New York: Praeger.

61

CHILDREN'S CONSTRUCTIONS OF FAMILY AND KINSHIP

Margaret O'Brien, Pam Alldred and Deborah Jones

Source: J. Brannan and M. O'Brien, eds, *Children and Families: Research and Policy*, London: Falmer Press, 1996, pp. 84–100.

Although most adults may have a common-sense understanding of 'the family' there is much debate in social science about the meaning and indeed usefulness of the term itself (Bernardes, 1985; Trost, 1990). Radical changes in how adults live together and raise children have shaken received wisdom concerning definitions of the family. Humpty Dumpty has fallen off the wall and his fragments cannot be reassembled in quite the same way (Laslett, 1991). In the latter part of the twentieth century new words have been created to describe the diversity of families that are emerging — one-parent family, bi-nuclear family, network family, reconstituted family, blended family — leading some to call for more precision in the use of 'family words'.

Typically the word family is used to refer to a heterosexual married couple and their dependent children who reside in one household sharing resources. In the 1980s family sociologists in particular, notably Bernardes (1985), began to reappraise the term family, to disentangle its various meanings. Most writers about the family now make a clear distinction between household and family pointing out that the two are not always coincidental. Families exist within and between households and not all households contain families. Demographic analysis shows that in the UK the proportion of households containing a married couple with dependent children has declined from 38 per cent in 1961 to 24 per cent in 1991 (Utting, 1995). There is an increasing number of households containing individuals living alone and an expansion of households with lone parents and their children. At an individual level it is clear that the experience of family life is complex and fluid. Over the life course individuals enter into, exit from, and redefine a range of relationships although, for many, a significant amount of time is spent in nuclear family households. Culturally too family life is represented by a wider range of signifiers: for instance media images of dyads in locations outside of the home (mother and child alone, father and child on the move in cars or in aeroplanes) coexist alongside the more conventional static home-based group images of two parents and two children eating together around a table. The word family prefixes many hitherto stand-alone objects and activities: the family car, the family disco, the family holiday. Not surprisingly therefore research shows that adults hold contradictory beliefs or 'multiple personal realities' about the family (Morgan, 1985; Trost, 1990).

What is still relatively unexplored is how children make sense of discourses and patterns of family life. Recent estimates suggest that only just over one half (53 per cent) of current UK children can expect to spend their whole childhood living with their married, biological parents (Clarke, 1992). Clarke (this volume) predicts that there will be increasing diversity in children's life-time family experiences. She suggests that, in comparison to previous cohorts, UK children born from the 1980s onwards will experience less time in their life span with two natural parents and more movements into and out of household types. Over relatively brief periods of time more children will experience significant restructuring of kin networks and household circumstances: transition from a two-parent household to a one-parent household and back again is now a common pathway for a growing proportion of children. Such transitions involve simultaneous expansion and contraction of kin networks, typically the loss of a co-resident natural father but the gain of a step-father, half-sibling and a further set of grandparents. Increasingly, the narratives of stories for children are grappling with fluidity and change in family and kinship ties (Cox, 1995).

The main academic discipline to examine children's experience of family life has been developmental psychology although the research has had a rather narrow focus (e.g., Gilby and Pederson, 1982). Typically developmental psychologists have traced an age-related sequence in children's acquisition of the concept family and have shown that as children enter their second decade they are more likely to demonstrate understanding of complex kinship arrangements (for instance, that consanguinity continues between biologically related individuals irrespective of changes in the emotional and legal aspect of their relationship). Psychologists traditionally locate maturation in cognitive processes as the explanatory mechanism for this age patterning although some have suggested that personal experience plays a part since, for example, children from divorced families tend to have more sophisticated understanding at all age levels (McGurk and Glachan, 1987). Unfortunately, the developmental paradigm has often rested on the assumption that there is one, correct definition of the family, typically the nuclear family, against which children's knowledge is judged, and so tends to exclude detailed exploration of non-nuclear family forms.

The adequacy of cognitivist explanations has been contested by those psychologists and sociologists concerned to move beyond a view of children

LIVERPOOL JOHN MOORES UNIVERSITY
LEARNING SERVICES

as being only adults in the making (e.g., Richards and Light, 1986; Dunn, 1988; Alanen, 1990; James and Prout, 1990). These writers have begun the process of setting children's relationships and development within the context of the social institution of childhood. As James and Prout have argued:

> the social institution of childhood [is] an actively negotiated set of social relationships within which the early years of human life are constituted.
>
> (James and Prout, 1990, p. 7)

It appears that the early years of human life, at least in western societies, are increasingly taking place in a familial context of flux and change, created in recent generations by parental separation and not parental death. In order to understand how children make sense of contemporary family and kin relationships we argue in this chapter that it is important to give space to their own experiences, representations and language. As James and Prout suggest in this volume 'the family represents a social context within which children discover their identities as 'children' and 'selves'. Giving voice to children's perspectives and conceptualizing them as active in the making of their own lives is implicit in the emergent paradigm of childhood studies. Research data collected within this frame of reference can allow comparisons to begin to be made between adult and child accounts and experiences of family life.

Studying children's constructions of family life

In this chapter we will draw on two empirical studies of children living in East London. Project 1 was designed to examine young children's accounts of their own families and to elicit their beliefs about 'the family'. Seventy-nine children from one inner East London borough were investigated. Our intention was to focus on children in their first five years at school; when UK children are for the first time spending significant amounts of time with other children and non-kin carers in institutional contexts. The average age of the children was 9 years, but the group consisted of three different school classes: 7-year-olds, 9-year-olds and 10-year-olds. Since age grading has been such a central concern of previous research on children's views of family life the research was designed to allow variation by age to be explored although not to govern fieldwork and interpretation.

Project 2 was conducted with older children (average age 14 years) and was also designed to give a profile of their views on, and constructions of, contemporary family life, as well as capture accounts of their daily lives at home, at school, at work and in leisure. The children lived in an outer East London locality and are part of a larger investigation of inter-generational perceptions of family life in East London. 600 children in six of the eight state secondary schools in the borough were surveyed.

Whilst the two studies were carried out in schools, research strategies were very different. In Project 1 a more ethnographic style was adopted with one of the investigators spending at least two weeks in each class group, getting to know the children before involving them more explicitly in the concerns of the research. Fieldwork was carried out over a three month period in each class group. As well as examining children's views on family life through participant observation and interviews, the research was set up to cover the naturally occurring daily activities of children in school contexts: writing, drawing, and conversation about topics introduced by adults. Data from the older children in Project 2 was collected through a more brief encounter of about one hour where children completed a questionnaire in the classroom and then took away a diary to complete at home over the subsequent week.[1] Project 2 was designed in this way so that specific subsamples of children living in differing household types could be identified and followed up to be investigated in the context of their own families. In both projects consent to participate in the research was requested of each individual child as well as the head teachers. A minority of children were withdrawn from Project 1 because of teachers' concerns about the children's personal difficulties at home. In addition a number of the children in Project 1 did not consent to having their interview tape-recorded. Whilst this chapter describes children's constructions of family and kinship through a mix of methodologies, it must be remembered that the research setting was the public forum of a school and variations in representation across setting, for instance between the school and the home, have not yet been explored (Mayall, 1995).

As the children in our studies went to school each morning they left a range of families behind (Table 1). Significant proportions of the children in both samples no longer lived with both birth parents. For instance 37 per cent of children from the oldest class group in Project 1 had experienced parental separation or divorce and were living with only one of their parents. Children in the youngest class group in Project 1 were more likely to be

Table 1 Children's households by school class (Project 1).

	School Class		
Type of Household *n =*	*7 Yrs* *(21)*	*9 Yrs* *(28)*	*10 Yrs* *(30)*
Two parents and children only	76	68	63
Two parents, children and other	10	14	7
One parent and children only	14	11	13
One parent, children and other	0	4	13
Grandparent and children only	0	0	4
Grandparent, children and others	0	4	0

still living with their natural parents. In the second Project many of the children had also personally experienced changes in household and family structures in their first fourteen years of life. Whilst a majority currently lived with both birth parents (68 per cent), 14 per cent lived in stepfamily households (12 per cent with their mothers and step-fathers, 2 per cent with their fathers and step-mothers) and 14 per cent in lone parent households (10 per cent lone mothers, 4 per cent lone fathers). 4 per cent co-resided with just grandparents, other kin or foster parents.[2]

'A proper family'

Fieldwork in Project 1 indicated that children often had considerable knowledge of each other's background and family circumstances. It was not uncommon for children to make asides to each other in the classroom about another child's father 'running away' or the arrival of a mother's 'new boyfriend'. Their accounts suggested that school records were often out-of-date. Children's own personal experiences, both from school and home, were drawn on when they were explicitly asked about their views on family life.

A vignette methodology was adopted to examine children's beliefs about the family. This method has been used with adults and has provided an illuminating window on their normative views of family life (Finch and Mason, 1993). Our research vignettes, or short stories, were developed to include a range of contemporary lifestyles (adapted from Trost, 1990). The stories were skeletal in content and acted as prompts for children to elaborate their views. Whilst ostensibly about the different ways adults and children live together, the vignettes also covered the gendered positions of parents, the permanence of marriage, the legitimacy of non-marital child-rearing, single parenthood, the nuclear family; all important issues in debates about contemporary family life. As Finch and Mason (1993, p. 12) show, hypothetical questions about third parties enable individuals to articulate publicly expressed norms about what is 'right and proper' for others:

> This type of research can tap beliefs at one level — the level at which people acknowledge publicly what is right and proper for third parties. But it does not tell us whether or how such beliefs get translated into relationships within families, or how far they are reflected in the responsibilities which people acknowledge for their own relatives.

The five vignettes were:

1 Married couple without child
   Bill and Betty are a married couple without any children. Are they a family?

2 Married couple with child
  Jenny and Dave are a married couple with a 6-year-old son called Ben.
  Are they a family?
3 Cohabiting couple with child
  Jim and Sue live together with their 6-year-old son called Paul. They
  are not married. Are they a family?
4 Lone mother with child
  Sally is divorced with a 10-year-old daughter Karin. Karin lives with
  Sally. Are these two a family?
5 Non-residential divorced father and child
  Karin's father, Tom, lives at the other end of the city. Are Karin and
  Tom a family?

Project 1 children were asked, in the context of an individual interview, whether they felt the people in the story were a family or not and then to give justifications for their opinion (for Project 2 the vignettes were included in the survey questionnaire). Children were left to use their understanding about what a family might be and were told that there was no right or wrong response.[3] A summary of children's views on whether each scenario constituted a family are outlined in Table 2.

Table 2 Children defining a vignette as a family, by age of child (Project 1 and 2): percentages.

		Vignette				
		1	*2*	*3*	*4*	*5*
7-year-olds						
n = 21	Yes	33	86	20	33	38
	No/Unsure	67	14	80	67	62
9-year-olds						
n = 25	Yes	52	96	35	64	52
	No/Unsure	48	4	65	36	48
10-year-olds						
n = 30	Yes	27	100	40	40	33
	No/Unsure	73	0	60	60	67
Project 1 Total						
n = 76	Yes	37	95	33	46	41
	No/Unsure	63	5	67	54	59
Project 2 Total						
n = 384	Yes	52	98	74	72	47
	No	48	2	26	28	53

Of all the lifestyles presented a married couple with a child was the most frequently affirmed by children as being a family. Nearly all children in both projects clearly felt that this way of living constituted a family. Presence of a child was cited as the major justification for a married couple with a child being a family ('because they've got a child'). Children were described as 'holding' and 'keeping' a couple together. Some felt that adults would be miserable if they did not have children to live with. A smaller number of children invoked close emotional feelings between the adults and child in the story as making the group a family: 'They like each other and get on together. They are a good family' (10-year-old). Clearly for children, couples without children, even married couples without children, are not a family. 63 per cent of children in Project 1 and 48 per cent of those in Project 2 thought that a married couple did not constitute a family: the main reason being the absence of children 'you need children to make a family' (9-year-old). Irrespective of age, children as a group appeared concerned about household size when discussing the nature of families. No vignette included more than one child, which often provoked responses such as 'it's half a family' (10-year-old); 'just the two of them' (10-year-old), not a 'full-up family' (7-year-old discussing a divorced mother and daughter), 'a teeny, weeny family' (7-year-old talking about a divorced mother and child). Despite the growth of dyadic family images in popular culture these results show the continuing importance of the nuclear four person family grouping and residual potency of cultural norms about ideal numbers of children in families. For children families are meant to be groups of people and should not be 'too small'.[4]

However, when responses to the vignettes were taken as a whole it appeared that the principle of the presence of children 'making' a family came into conflict with another principle, voiced particularly by younger respondents, that parents living with children should be married. 54 per cent of children in Project 1 and 26 per cent of children in Project 2 felt that a cohabiting couple with a child was not a family, mainly because the parents were not married. Younger children seemed most unsure about the nature of cohabitation as one child put it 'that's a complicated one' (9-year-old); 'you need to be married if you're going to be a family' (7-year-old); 'before you have a child you should get married' (9-year-old); it's not a proper family yet' (9-year-old). Some children were unsure of the child's status or permanence of the living arrangement, for others it appeared to provoke feelings of vulnerability: 'It's not really a family because they are not married . . . being married is more secure. She could run off with another man.' (10-year-old); 'what would happen if they love each other but don't look after the child?' (7-year-old).

The minority of younger children who described a cohabiting couple and child as a family justified their decision on the grounds of co-residence 'they live together' (7-year-old) or emotional closeness 'you don't need a piece of paper to show you love somebody' (9-year-old). As can be seen from Table 7.2 a majority of the older children were more accepting of cohabitational lifestyles, also invoking the principle of love and emotional closeness.

In many of these responses children were showing awareness of the continued higher status and legitimacy of marriage in British culture and perhaps the real structural fragility of living with parents who are not married. Recent research indicates that relationship breakdown is higher amongst cohabiting couples with children than for married couples with children (Kiernan and Estaugh, 1993). Moreover, despite the dramatic recent increase in births outside marriage, living in cohabitational households is not yet legally affirmed, celebrated or socially sanctioned in the same way as marriage. Currently the language used to describe non-married emotional relationships is clumsy and vague; the most common adult term to describe the couple is 'partner', a loan from the world of employment and business. A further indication of the marginality of the lifestyle is the formal legal nature of cohabiting child–father relationships. Under English law if a cohabiting couple separate a child has no immediate right of access to the father (under *The Children Act 1989*, unmarried fathers have no formal parental reponsibilities, either during their relationship or after a separation, unless special application is made).[5]

Responses to vignettes of lifestyles including parental divorce showed that lone mother and child households were generally endorsed as being a legitimate family form, particularly by older children: 72 per cent of the 14-year-olds felt lone mother and child households were families, as did 46 per cent of the younger children. The main reason offered by children in both projects was a view that a divorce did not alter the continuity of the mother–child tie, 'They're still a family, even if mum and dad split up, whatever' (10-year-old). Biological and emotional closeness between mothers and children were referred to by children 'they have the same blood' (9-year-old). The fact that mother and daughter still lived together was the second most commonly mentioned reason.

Those that felt a lone mother and child household was not a familial life-style generally invoked the absence of a father figure: It's only got a mum, hasn't got a dad' (10-year-old). 'You need mother, father and children to make a family' (10-year-old). The tenuous nature of relationships between fathers and children after divorce is shown by the relatively low proportion of children, in both projects, who felt that non-residential fathers and their children constituted a family: less than half the children in both samples responded positively to this idea. The majority of children thought that because the two no longer co-resided they were no longer a family. These children appeared to assume that when fathers lived apart from children they had little contact with them: 'Not really no, because she couldn't see him very often, because they are not living together'

(10-year-old). A minority of children implied that divorced fathers had committed some misdemeanour: 'he's naughty' (7-year-old) or that families needed mothers 'it's not complete without mum' (9-year-old). Those that felt otherwise stressed the continuity of biological and emotional closeness 'he's still Karin's Dad' (9-year-old), 'she might still love him, and him her' (10-year-old).

There was a complex association between expressed beliefs about vignettes and the actual family circumstances of children. For instance, in the 14-year-old sample, when compared to children who had always lived with their birth parents, those who had experienced parental separation in their lives were more likely to say that non-residential fathers and children did not constitute a family. This was especially the case for children living in stepfather households, a significant proportion of whom had irregular contact with their biological fathers.

The material suggests that with respect to the fifth vignette children, like adults, are drawing on lived experience and cultural discourses concerning the peripherality of divorced fathers. A majority of children still live with their mothers after marital separation and the decline in contact between non-residential divorced fathers and their children has been well documented (e.g., Bertaux and Delcroix, 1992). In this context it is understandable that for some children a father is central to family life only when he is co-resident. However, further research is needed to clarify the relative importance of parental gender and co-residence in shaping children's perceptions of the stability of family relationships after divorce, for it may well be that children have similar perceptions of non-residential mothers.

Children talking together about family life

In order to explore the negotiation of norms about family life small group discussions were held with some of the children in Project 1. These took place after they had been individually interviewed. Children were selected from a range of family backgrounds and cultures and were asked to discuss the vignettes again and if possible come to a group consensus. The purpose of this agenda was to encourage an exchange of views in the group. Group composition was carefully discussed with class teachers to ensure that it did not include children who had unharmonious relationships with each other, so as not to upset a particular child. The discussions took place in a quiet room away from the classroom, lasted on average three-quarters of an hour and were tape-recorded. We found that the children were very keen to participate in group discussion. An extract from one of the discussions is presented in some detail below to examine some of the issues in more depth. All the children were 9 years old. The children's names are self-chosen pseudonyms.

Veronica: Girl. Lives with mother and father and two older brothers. Youngest child in family. White British. Non-religious.

James: Boy. Lives with grandparents, aunt and his cousin aged 6. His mother and stepfather live nearby, with younger stepbrother. Parents separated when he was 6 years. No regular contact with father (although has had phone calls). White British. Non-religious.

Zain: Boy. Lives with mother and younger brother. Born in Poland. Parents separated. Father from Pakistan, mother from Poland. Catholic.

Thahera: Girl. Lives with mother, father, two brothers and two sisters (she is the second child). Born in UK, parents from India. Muslim.

Alan: Boy. Lives with mother, her new boyfriend and sister. Another older sister lives nearby. Mother white British. Parents separated when he was 5/6 years old. No contact with father, born in the West Indies. Non-religious.

In this group most of the discussion centred around the vignettes about lifestyles after parental divorce. A predominant dynamic was an attempt by the two girls who lived in nuclear family households, Veronica and Thahera, to convince the others that both lone mother and child households and non-residential fathers and children were legitimate family forms. The children who had experienced some form of parental separation in their lives argued that parents, particularly fathers, needed to show caring contact with children before they could be considered part of a family. It was notable that each of these children had little or no contact with their own non-residential father, which clearly influenced their feelings about this issue. Both Veronica and Thahera initially invoked the principle of consanguinity in their argument:

Thahera: Miss, I think that Sally and Karin are family and Sally and her father are family because they've all got the same flesh of blood, but I don't think Sally and her husband [Karin's father] are family because they've got nothing to do with each other anymore and they haven't got the same blood of flesh.

(Interchange follows with Veronica supporting Thahera's position)

Alan: I don't think all three of them are a family, because the little girl, I don't think she's a family with him because she don't live with him or nothing and he might have forgotten everything about her and might even have gone and had another child or something.

Veronica: But, Alan, her dad's still got the same flesh of blood.

Alan: Yes, but I don't think it counts, right. I think it counts on what he does, like. She might not even know where he is. My mum and dad split up three or four years ago. I don't know where he is. He ain't sent us no money or nothing. I don't know where he is.

Researcher: So what you feel is, the contact or whatever is more important than the actual blood relation?

Alan: Yes.

(Discussion continues for some time mainly between Veronica and Alan, without much change in position. Alan offers more examples of negligent paternal behaviour 'just say if he started nicking your money, taking things, getting you into trouble you wouldn't count him as family would you?')

Researcher: Right. It sounds as if you two have got as far as you're going to get. There's two distinct positions on that and James and Thahera are desperate to talk. Which one of you wants to go first?

James: Thahera can go first.

Thahera: Miss, but . . .

Researcher: Go on, Thahera.

Thahera: But just say that you knew where your father was, right.

James: I don't.

Thahera: Just say that your mum was very ill. She was really badly sick, she was critical and you knew where your father was. Who would you phone? You'd, I would phone my father.

Veronica: Would you phone your uncle or would you phone your aunt or would you phone your . . .

Thahera: Yes, but you don't always know your aunt's phone number.

Zain: I would phone for an ambulance.

(The children start talking simultaneously and Thahera and Veronica attempt to ascertain who James would phone if his mother was seriously ill, and then if his mother and father died. He eventually says he would phone for an ambulance and go to his big sister's house. After this is established Thahera introduces a further traumatic scenario for Alan to consider.)

Thahera: If your mother and father were both dead you'd probably go to an orphanage or you'd probably just live on the street or something.

Alan: Yes, I didn't want to go to an orphanage.

Thahera: You'd probably go to your grandmother's uncle.
Alan: All my grandmothers and my great-grandmothers are dead.
Zaid: Alright, you'd probably live on the street.

(Thahera then turns her attention to James and asks)

Thahera: Do you meet your dad?

(James relates that he does not see his father, although he has phoned and he knows where he lives. He points out that his father does not send him cards 'or nothing', a point which is taken up later by Alan).

James: I don't want to see my dad. I want to see my mum.
Alan: I don't want to see my dad either. He knows our address, he knows my birthday, he cannot forget my birthday, it's Christmas day [event changed by authors], right and they're just getting a divorce through sort of thing . . . she (mother) phoned and said you can send the kids birthday cards, I'll let 'em have 'em. Right. And she said like, sometime, right, would you like to have the children, for half-term? And he said yes. And you know what? He never turned up for months. And we found out he's hired a car and he's gone to Brighton for a holiday like.

(After further elaboration by Alan, Veronica and Thahera announce to the group that they have changed their positions).

Veronica: I just want to say that . . . Alan's convinced me . . . about Karin and his dad aren't family with Karin.
Researcher: Right I see.
Thahera: I think Alan's convinced me, miss, because, oh God, what he said because I just think he convinced me.

These discussions show that individual opinions were not totally fixed. Children could persuade each other to change position, particularly after listening to accounts where others had relevant experience and had been upset by parents. The discussions enabled more specific conditional aspects of family life to be unpicked and explored in depth by the children. For these children talking about divorce spontaneously generated consideration of parental departure, abandonment and even death. Children used the group to examine the boundaries of acceptable parenting for them as children and particularly the deserving and undeserving father after divorce. A father who forgot his child's birthday did not deserve to be included in a family grouping. It appeared that children, like adults, can hold contradictory principles of what makes a family: whilst being aware of the formal relevance of consanguinity in defining a family this principle becomes a secondary one in the face of parental disregard.

In addition, the dialogue shows that opinions expressed about the vignettes were not just the products of individual children's understandings and emotional coping strategies but were also themselves social products constructed in this particular research context. When Alan had been interviewed on his own before the group discussion he had endorsed both post-divorce lifestyles as legitimate family groups, as did all the other children, except Zain. It may well be that children test out their own positions about a topic through constructing different accounts or what Hallden (1995, p. 78) calls 'narrative fictions' in response to different research contexts.

Children's drawings of their families

Whilst children's accounts of their own family lives emerged when they talked about other children's families, in both projects attempts were made to focus more directly on respondents' own families through diaries, stories, drawings as well as interviews (because of length constraints only drawings are discussed here).

Drawing is an important everyday activity in which younger children engage. We wanted to explore what children came up with when they were asked to draw their own family (see Issacs and Levin, 1984) (Project 1). A further motivation for using drawings came from a comment in Young and Willmott's introduction to *Family and Kinship in East London*. One of the authors lived in the area during fieldwork and described his child returning from school and saying:

> The teacher asked us to draw pictures of our family. I did one of you and Mummy and Mikey and me, but isn't it funny, the others were putting in their Nannas and aunties and uncles and all sorts of people like that.
>
> (Young and Willmott, 1962, p. 14)

On the basis of previous research we anticipated that children would draw those who were emotionally significant to them and wondered how this might vary across different family types (Klepsh and Logie, 1982). Children were asked to draw a picture of their whole family and then write a story about their drawing. After receiving this somewhat general request several asked for more guidance on what exactly they should draw. Here are fieldnotes of classroom interaction in the first minutes after a class of 10-year-olds was asked to draw their family (Project 1):

> First question: 'all your family or just your house?' Talking amongst themselves, showing each other, reluctance, 'cos not good drawer'

— 'This is rubbish' etc — 'All my cousins?' 'cos I've got eighteen cousins and I'm just going to draw my mum and dad and me' — 'Do you draw yourself?' — 'Do you draw your mum and dad?' — 'Miss, can I draw my pets?' — 'Miss can you draw your grand-parents, nan and granddad?' . . . — It's up to you.

[said many times]

In a very short period children articulated the key issue: whether or not their representation should go beyond the co-residential unit. Our response was to convey to the children that their drawing could be of whatever they wanted. In general it appeared that the 7- and 9-year-olds felt more at ease with drawing in a classroom setting, whilst the 10-year-olds were more self-conscious and concerned about creating realistic images 'I wish I could draw.' (10-year-old) 'I can't do my dad [right]' (10-year-old). We wondered whether this pattern was an indicator of how children themselves age-graded their own activities; for 10-year-olds this sort of drawing may be perceived as a 'childish' activity.

The largest group of children (40 per cent of the total sample of Project 1), eventually drew the individuals they lived with, indicating that in this particular context a family was the household unit. For the remaining children there was not a direct match between the co-residential unit and the number and composition of human figures in their family drawing. Some did not include all the members of their household (27 per cent), whilst others added individuals outside the household (29 per cent). In 4 per cent of cases it was not clear who was depicted in the drawing. There were no significant age differences to this general patterning which contests a tradi-tional psychological prediction that younger children would produce a less accurate or household-matched drawing.

Those who drew their co-residential group adopted a conventional style: parents to the left of the paper (usually indicating that they were drawn first), often father before mother, then the children, biggest to smallest (Figure 1). This drawing was created by Adress, a 9-year-old boy who lives with his parents and three siblings — two older brothers and younger sister. He was born in the UK, of Pakistani parents. Dad is drawn to the left followed by mum and an age-graded set of children. All the male figures have hats and there are brand names printed on some of the hats and shoes; it was not uncommon for boys particularly to indicate brand names on clothes.

Children's accounts about why they included the people they did in their drawings indicated that several principles guided the activity. All the human figures had a consanguineal, affinal or adoptive relationship to the child (no child included a friend or an unrelated adult in their drawing although several included a household pet). In the main children included those with whom they lived, but not always everyone in the house. Non-co-resident kin

Figure 1 Drawing of the family by 'Adress'.

appeared to be included either when they were seen regularly or if they were emotionally and/or practically important to the respondent.

Moreover, household type rather than age emerged as significant in trying to make sense of the way children drew their families. As Table 3 shows, children living in non-nuclear households were more likely to produce family drawings which did not match the household membership. The most common pattern was to include in the family drawing individuals who were not co-resident (in addition to drawing either the whole or part of

Table 3 Composition of children's family drawing by household type (percentages).

	Type of household		
	Two parent *n = 60*	*One parent* *n = 15*	*Other* *n = 2*
Identical composition to household	48	13	0
Fewer figures than in household	32	13	0
More figures than in household	18	60	100
Unclear	2	13	0

the co-residential unit). 60 per cent of children living in one-parent house-holds drew in this way in comparison to 18 per cent of children living in two-parent households. These additional figures drawn were not in the main biological fathers but were primary and secondary kin (grandparents, cousins, older siblings, aunts and uncles and so on). This finding suggests that markers in addition to co-residence are especially important when some children in one-parent households depict their family; extended kin networks may be particularly significant.[6]

In turn, it is possible that for children in conventional nuclear families more significant and emotionally important figures are those with whom they live. It must be remembered also that children's representations are part of a social world where the nuclear family model is strongly valued, indeed as seen in previous sections the respondents themselves adhered to the view that the nuclear family was the 'proper family'. Accordingly, in the context of this research, children in nuclear families may have been trying 'to get it right' (in relation to wider cultural norms) and children in lone mother families may have drawn more figures in order to achieve a rep-resentation that resembled a two-parent family in size.

Figure 2 is a drawing produced by Alan, one of the children who took part in the group discussion described above. His family drawing consists of four figures: mother, self and two sisters. His mother is surrounded by her children. Alan is on one side and two sisters on the other.

The non-residential sister who is included in the family drawing is 18 years old and has only recently left home. During the small group discussion Alan talks about his sister's house as a place he would go to if his mother was ill. In his story he writes of his father 'I don't count him as family because he can't even remember our birthdays.' He also mentions this issue in the group discussion. Whilst drawing Alan asked whether he could include his

Figure 2 Drawing of the family by 'Alan'.

mother's new boyfriend (a 'nice' man who had made him a go-cart) but decided not to although it was indicated he could. In the individual interview the mother's boyfriend was cited as a main source of instrumental support (for instance, helping to fix toys) and his mother as the main provider of emotional support (the person he would go to when he felt sad). Alan's biological father, with whom he had no contact, was not included in the drawing.

Conclusion

These studies suggest that, as with adults, children's concepts of family are complex, fluid and sometimes contradictory. What counts as family for young children is not straightforward although consanguinity, co-residence, consistent care, size, the presence of married parents and other children are important. Whilst a diversity of family models are available for children in their conceptualizations of family life, the nuclear family remains a potent image. When children examined contemporary lifestyles the vignette they most strongly endorsed as being a proper family was the married couple and child living together. Several children, notably the younger respondents were especially uncertain about the status of cohabiting parents and of post-divorce lifestyles. Perhaps this uncertainty reflects the continuing structural fragility of these household forms and the lack of clarity of children's position within them. Whilst there has been a growth in cohabitation and one parent households through the 1980s in the UK many children in these research projects continued to place great significance on marriage and the nuclear family. For some children, particularly those who had experienced parental separation, the idea of family went beyond the household or conjugal pair. Such children drew on primary and secondary kin as important figures and resources in their lives, but excluded non-resident fathers. This finding gives some support to Boyden's (1990, p. 201) suggestion that 'new alliances and innovative survival strategies' may be adopted by children and adults in the wake of breakdown in traditional networks.

Notes

1 We would like to thank Julia Brannen for her help with the design of the questionnaire.
2 Whilst over 90 per cent of the children in both projects were born in the UK, children in Project 1 were much more likely to have had parents who had been born outside of the UK particularly from the Asian subcontinent. Inner East London is much more ethnically diverse than outer East London, which has an ethnically homogeneous profile dominated by those whose parents originate in the UK. Both localities are traditionally working class, which was reflected in the project samples (O'Brien and Jones, in press, 1996). Older children were more likely to have had mothers who worked outside the home (48 per cent of 7-year-olds' mothers worked in contrast to 62 per cent of the mothers of 14-year-olds).

3 As Solberg argues elsewhere in this volume, in a school environment it is important to emphasize to children that a research procedure is not some sort of test. But inevitably such a view must have been present, for instance, the children in Project 1 despite protestations to the contrary called the researcher 'Miss' (an English child's description of a female teacher).

4 Any future researcher using this methodology would be advised to construct vignettes including more than one child. The proportion of one-child families was low in both project samples (less than 10 per cent in both projects) and even rarer for ethnic minority children.

5 However, under the UN Convention on the Rights of the Child, all children have a right of access to both parents.

6 The relationship of children to their non-residential biological father is complex: whilst he may not be drawn as a separate figure there may be other references to him. For instance, one child who had not seen her father, who was living in the USA, for over five years had USA written on her drawn T-shirt. Further research needs to be carried out with children of divorce who have regular contact with the non-residential parent. In Project 1 most of the children in lone mother households had little or no contact with their fathers.

References

ALANEN, L. (1990) 'Rethinking socialization, the family and childhood', in ADLER, P., ADLER, P., MANDELL, N. and CAHILL, S. (Eds) *Sociological Studies of Child Development: A Research Annual*, 3, Greenwich, CT.

BERNARDES, J. (1985) 'Do we really know what "the family" is?', in CLOSE, P. and COLLINS, R. (Eds) *Family and Economy*, London, Macmillan.

BERTAUX, D. and DELCROIX, C. (1992) 'Where have all the daddies gone?', in BJORNBERG, U. (Ed) *European Parents in the 1990s: Contradictions and Comparisons*, New York, Transaction Books.

BOYDEN, J. (1990) 'Childhood and the policy makers: A comparative perspective on the globalization of childhood', in JAMES, A. and PROUT, A. (Eds) *Constructing and Reconstructing Childhood*, London, Falmer Press.

CLARKE, L. (1992) 'Children's family circumstances: Recent trends in Great Britain', *European Journal of Population*, 8, pp. 309–40.

COX, R. (1995) 'Reading about the family in contemporary children's fiction: Modes of representation', in BRANNEN, J. and O'BRIEN, M. (Eds) *Childhood and Parenthood*, London, Institute of Education.

DUNN, J. (1988) *The Beginnings of Social Understanding*, Oxford, Basil Blackwell.

FINCH, J. and MASON, J. (1993) *Negotiating Family Responsibilities*, London, Routledge.

GILBY, R. and PEDERSON, D. (1982) 'The development of the child's concept of the family', *Canadian Journal of Behaviourial, Sciences*, 14, 2, pp. 110–21.

HALLDEN, G. (1995) 'The family — A refuge from demands or an arena for the exercise of power and control — children's fictions on their future families', in MAYALL, B. (Ed) *Children's Worlds Observed and Experienced*, London, Falmer Press.

ISSACS, M. and LEVIN, I. (1984) 'Who's in my family?: A longitudinal study of drawings of children of divorce', *Journal of Divorce*, 7, 4, pp. 1–21.

JAMES, A. and PROUT, A. (1990) (Eds) *Constructing and Reconstructing Childhood: Contemporary Issues in the Sociological Study of Childhood*, London, Falmer Press.

KIERNAN, K. and ESTAUGH, V. (1993) 'Cohabitation: Extra marital child-bearing and social policy', Occasional Paper 17, London, Family Policy Studies Centre.

KLEPSH, M. and LOGIE, L. (1982) Children Draw and Tell: An Introduction to the Projective Uses of Children's Human Figure Drawings, New York, Bruner Mazel.

LASLETT, P. (1991) 'Opening address', Child, Family and Society, European Commission Conference, Luxembourg.

MAYALL, B. (1995) 'Children in action at home and school', in MAYALL, B. (Ed) Children's Childhoods Observed and Experienced, London, Falmer Press.

McGURK, H. and GLACHAN, M. (1987) 'Children's conception of parenthood following divorce', Journal of Child Psychology and Psychiatry, **28**, 3, pp. 427–35.

MORGAN, D. (1985) The Family, Politics and Social Theory, London, Routledge and Kegan Paul.

O'BRIEN, M. and JONES, D. (in press, 1996) 'Family and kinship in an outer London borough: Continuity and change', in RUSTIN, M., BUTLER, T. and CHAMBERLAYNE, P. (Eds) The Regeneration of East London, London, Lawrence and Wishart.

RICHARDS, M. P. M. and LIGHT, P. (1986) Children of Social Worlds: Development in a Social Context, Cambridge, Polity.

TROST, J. (1990) 'Do we mean the same by the concept of family?', Communication Research, **17**, 4, pp. 431–43.

UTTING, D. (1995) Family and Parenthood: Supporting Families, Preventing Breakdown, York, Joseph Rowntree Foundation.

YOUNG, M. and WILLMOTT, P. (1962) Family and Kinship in East London, Middlesex, Penguin Books.

62

MODERN CHILDHOOD

Ivar Frones

Source: *Among Peers: On the Meaning of Peers in the Process of Socialization*, Oslo: Scandanavian University Press, 1995, pp. 132–151.

The development of modern childhood

According to Ariés, childhood is a relatively new cultural invention linked to the development of the modern bourgeois family, of educational institutions, and the art of reading. The child was plucked out of a common existence and placed in its own protected cultural reservation. If, under feudalism, children were regarded as small adults, this did not mean that people were not aware that they were children, or that no terms for children existed. What Ariés and others purport to demonstrate is that new ideas about children and about what pertained to them were developed in a particular historical period, and that the idea of childhood as a cultural sphere of its own was developed and underscored during that period. The creation of modern childhood meant, as mentioned earlier, not that children became more oriented toward one another, but, on the contrary, that the children of the new bourgeoisie were taken from the village and into the family. It also meant that children became separated from adults other than the family and educators as well as also from the servants, among whom the children of the nobility had formerly grown up. Finally, it also meant that they, to some degree, were taken away from the company of peers which, as we have claimed, existed in the rural village, and placed more under the control of the family. Community control gave way to increased private family control, exercised in part through the new institutions of education.

We shall distinguish five dimensions for an understanding of childhood. Children as an *age group*, i.e., their position with regard to *power and the economy*; children in *the family*; children seen *generationally*; the shaping of *peer relations*; and the *institutional or organizational framework* within which children grow up. The evolution of childhood will display different profiles

325

seen from these different dimensions, and which dimension is emphasized sets the premises for how childhood is understood, and for the conclusions drawn about it.

Children as an age group

Age groups are distinct from social classes and generations, but have characteristics in common with both. Unlike the members of a social class, an age group continuously loses old members and gains new ones. Most members of a generation are lifelong members, even if, within certain limits, some persons are able to redefine their affiliation to different historical generations. The members of an age group, unlike social classes and generations, do not have stable interests, since for the individual an age group is a life phase he or she must pass through. Thus an age group's interests may be of essential importance for the society as such, yet still not be realized, since such a group seldom has active actors that view the group's interests as their own.

In an agrarian society, and in early industrial society, children had a direct significance for production. This did not mean that their parents always benefited from them; often the children of the poor were an expense for their parents until they were old enough to begin to work. They then had to move to the homes of richer, large farmers where they were useful not primarily to their parents, but to others. This is not so important for our present purposes, but it does show that children's position in production did not necessarily mean that their position in their own family was of any definite value.

The trajectory from the working child to the educated child is part of an all-embracing process, whose historical pace differed considerably for different social classes and spheres. Although educational institutions serve other purposes than the education of children, we will define modern childhood and youth as a phase for the acquisition of competences or qualifications. It follows that during this time, children are of no direct economic benefit to parents (or to others), and indeed are for them even a burden economically. Any future benefit from this education will accrue to the society at large. The political and economic contract between the generations is different at the other end of the age scale, where a family's private responsibility for its elderly was diminished in favour of a generational contract on the societal level, which is only partly based on an insurance system. The elderly became the economic responsibility of the society at large, not of the family. Children, on the other hand, are largely a private expense, even if in most societies some of the expenses of qualification have been taken over by the public domain.

A relatively small proportion of public budgets go to children; most is allocated to the running of educational institutions (Frønes, Jenssen, and

Solberg 1990). On the other hand, it is reasonable to believe that children have seen a considerable material improvement in their lives as a consequence of the general economic improvement on the private level. At the same time developments over the past few years indicate that poverty has changed from being dominated by the elderly to being dominated by often single parents and small children. Demographic developments also influence the situation and position for children. Children comprise a declining proportion of the population in industrial countries. Few children has conflicting implications for socialization. In one sense it enhances the value of children, while, for example, parents may see their political influence diminished because the proportion of adults in the parent phase declines. Following Easterlin (1980), we can say that small generations are allocated the most resources, and that is especially true for children and young people in that educational institutions for them are better, they have easier access to the labour market, etc. Large generations, on the other hand, have the greatest numerical strength.

Although children's position as producers has declined in importance, quite a number of children and young people are nonetheless involved in production nonetheless. Brusdal and Lavik (1991) claim that their position as producers may often be rooted in their position as consumers. Part-time work by children and adolescents is a function of their consumer desires. Commercial consumption by children and adolescents has gradually developed into an age-specific consumption. Consumption by smaller children as well has become subject to fashion: the rate of replacement in this consumption is probably increasing. Such a pattern has consequences for socialization: children encounter consumer morality and the consumer role before they encounter the morality of duty and production morality. Commercialization makes children visible through their role as consumers, and contributes to the trend toward individuation and individualization within childhood.

Demographic changes in the family

The demographic changes are well known, but their consequences have not always been fully recognized. From the standpoint of socialization, it is important that the declining number of children means fewer children in the families. At the same time, in families with two children of about the same age, a specially close relationship will probably develop between siblings. Historically, changes in relations between siblings have most probably been along the same lines as changes in relations otherwise in the family, from obligations and responsibility to the emotional dimensions.

An age gap between siblings makes for different family functions for them, and sib relations are then also experienced differently by younger and older sibs, respectively. In Norway, one third of all children born in the 1930s had siblings who were fifteen years older or younger than themselves

(Frønes 1985). Several historical generations were thus often represented in the same group of offspring. In the 1950s, the kind of family now viewed as "natural" became dominant: two children usually born close together. Thus biological generations in the family have come to overlap with historical generations, so that now the relation between historical generations is readily regarded as a relation between children and parents. Divorces and remarriages alter these patterns again, and half-sibs and social sibs are again widening the age gap between children in many families.

The age of parents influences the cultural and social distance between parents and children. Young parents mean young grandparents, a higher longevity means several generations in a lifetime, and the different age levels for bearing children in the different social groups creates cultural and social differences. Varying cultural and political conditions influence demographic profiles: for example, the number of teenage mothers is high in the USA but low and declining in Scandinavia. A prosperous society with few children also means that family ties will have an increasing influence on economic conditions; inheritance and support from parents is very important for children in such a demographic and economic context. Few children together with a relative prosperity means that many parents can shoulder the economic responsibility for their children longer, which is something an "education society" often requires. The modern landscape of socialization reveals a structure marked by early social maturation and late economic independence.

The changing tasks of the family

The feudal family was an organization with responsibility for production, for family members during illness, age, etc. It was the key unit in society's organization of power, and it had responsibility for those aspects of socialization concerned with food, clothing, and economic and social control. It also exercised affective functions in relation to children, but to what extent is uncertain. Sibs probably had a central place in many families because of the high mortality among parents. Spouses often spent little time together, and the family was not an interaction community either ideologically or practically.

The bourgeois family took the woman out of production and placed her in the private sphere. The bourgeois family was no longer a joint production unit, although, in contrast to the upper stratum of feudal society, it was extremely industrious. The bourgeois family disposed over its manufacturing, commercial, or other properties from which it lived and with which it died, without the security net or security systems of modern society.

In the bourgeois family, children and women were segregated, and were seen ideologically as belonging to the private sphere. Ideally, conjugal union was viewed as a matter of free choice governed by feelings. The union and complementarity between men and women in large measure followed a particular conception of the nature of the two sexes. The bourgeois family further developed the mother's role ideologically as well as concretely. But the bourgeois mother often ran her house and governed her children's upbringing through servants and special institutions for that purpose. The mother and father figures had clear roles, the one being the expressive, the other the instrumental pole. The father was in fact rarely present, but he was there as the dominating shadow that Freud made part of his theory.

The housewife family is in a sense the democratic variant of the bourgeois family, with a place in the welfare society and within that society's broader framework. The housewife family has lost the more economic dimensions earlier types of family had. A marriage based on love and structured both practically and ideologically as a social interaction unit that lives life together is a different type of social unit from the feudal family, and indeed from the bourgeois family as well.

The *symmetric family* differs from the bourgeois family and housewife family in that both spouses are gainfully employed and economically autonomous. In the ideal model of the symmetric family the woman has a professional career outside the home; her professional work, moreover, is not subordinate to the family's needs. The modern symmetric family typically consists of an educated couple with separate careers outside the home; it is no longer the working class family of early industrial society, in which both spouses worked. The symmetric family is an affective project: the providing and provider dimension that defined a complementarity of roles is gone. Children continue to be an emotional undertaking and the common project of both the spouses, but they no longer provide legitimation of the woman's role, and no longer define the woman's purpose. Separate professional careers also give both spouses not merely a certain economic independence, but also a certain social autonomy.

Divorces have also changed along with the basic content of a marriage. In a marriage where love and the ability to live together are the main pillars – the foundation of the marriage – dissolution will be more likely than in a marriage based on a set of obligations of a non-emotional nature. Divorces as such are not the same phenomenon from one marriage type to another, aside from the fact that the spouses separate. In the housewife family it was often the man who took the initiative to divorce. This was often to marry a younger woman, at the same time as the man retained economic responsibility for his previous wife until she became the responsibility of a new husband, if that should occur. There is some resemblance here to forms of marriage in other traditions which allow a man takes a new wife provided that he retains economic responsibility for the old one. Scandinavian divorces in the '70s and '80s were often initiated by the woman, and only in some cases directly precipitated by the establishment of a new love relation. The relations between the former spouses after divorce will also be economically and culturally different when the partners are economically autonomous and social autonomy is part of the dominant ideology.

The problem of divorce illustrates differences in the various forms of the nuclear family. The nuclear family has changed even if the categories of members are the same. Although socialization has always been one of the family's tasks, the content of the tasks, and the ways they are accomplished, have changed. The family has changed from being an institutional contract with its basis in a patriarchal social order to being a private contract between two individuals. It has evolved from being the central social arrangement for those functions that are now the domain of public authorities (such as social security, formal social control, etc.) into a relationship between two individuals for the purpose of self-realization, to which of course children are central. The evolution of the family is a typical illustration of the evolution of individuation and individualization in general.

That a private conjugal and affective contract between equal individuals is more unstable than earlier forms of the family is hardly surprising. What is surprising perhaps is the stability that does exist.

The family as the landscape and agency of socialization

Though the evolution of the family in modern society has strong universal features, there are also important variations. The housewife family in Norway was in large measure a combination of the always-present mother and an active children's culture with a large measure of freedom for children in the local surroundings (Frønes 1994a). The idealization of this type of children's culture is also evident in many other countries, e.g., as in Mark Twain's stories and in films such as *The Little Rascals*, a new version of which was released in the USA in 1994. The childhood depicted in these works is very different from the modern child's organized life.

As regards children, the symmetric family implies an ideology which lays emphasis on independence and the capacity for participation on different levels. Historically, this ideology probably has its roots not only in the family, but also in modern everyday and working life as they have evolved over the last few decades. Independence, the ability to express oneself, the ability to work together with others, etc., are ideals promoted both in school and in industry.

The fact that we can often identify the family unit as consisting of mother, father and children in West European history may have overshadowed the enormous changes the family has gone through, even where mother, father and children have invariably been present. Indeed, not only are the feudal and the modern family very different from each other, but the housewife family and the symmetric family also represent very different social and institutional arrangements, and not merely different private solutions. The disparities have probably also been underestimated in that the transition from one type of family to another was gradual and in the fact that many families have varied between, for instance, being a housewife family and a more symmetric family for some periods. This made it seem that these were simply different private solutions rather than quite different types of family. The term nuclear family refers to very different social and institutional arrangements, even if the same persons fill the family portraits.

The implications for children of the changes that have taken place within the modern family may be studied by an analysis of the way in which children's social and physical world is structured. Where mother and father are away from the home in the symmetric family, the children often move in (Solberg and Danielsen 1988). Children often have their own private area in their own room, and the whole house becomes their territory when the parents are at work. The children of a modern symmetric family are more in the home than are the children in a traditional housewife family, which did not regard the home as an area for the children to use. The "latchkey children" who marked the family debate in many countries of the '50s and '60s is no longer a topic in the media or in the debate in Scandinavia, owing in large measure to broader transformations at the cultural level: gainfully employed mothers are in the majority and culturally dominant, and the cultural critique has died down. But the latchkey children have also retreated into the home, which is one of the new social patterns observable among children.

The symmetric family with its ideals of democracy and children's rights, with its demands for autonomous and reflexive children, and children who spend a large portion of the day elsewhere than in the family and its immediate surroundings, is developing its own special ideology of upbringing, and its own ways of resolving social conflicts and exercising social control (Frønes 1994b; du Bois-Reymond 1993). Relations between children and parents may be described as representing a *negotiation-based family*, where negotiation is understood as being based on a contract in which it is agreed that the force of argument decides, and that a mutual solution must be achieved. This protects both the parties' autonomy, and the parents' need for social control, at the same time as the children are assured that illegitimate arguments may not be used. The logic of negotiation also opens the way to solutions based on compromises, and the negotiation model ensures reason, autonomy, and control. Research indicates that where this model has been dominant, families also avoid the typical "teenage conflicts" that can often be found both in the authoritarian family and in laissez-faire families (Coleman and Hendry 1990).

Changes in the family, structure children's everyday life in a new way and create new relations between children and parents. The guidelines according to which the family operates also change: the family becomes a different organization.

Children and generations

The relation between the generations in modern society is marked by trends toward individuation and individualization, where the symbolic dividing lines between the adult domain and children's domain become blurred and are replaced by more complicated and individualized codes. Indicators of adult status are becoming unclear and embrace a broader age range. The social age is partly culturally determined, and does not automatically follow biological age, as the history of childhood illustrates. In modern society cultural age is in part a result of individual effort. This is especially the case in certain age phases such as early teenage or late childhood, so that many at the age of twelve or thirteen may have a say in determining whether they are children or young teenagers. Child and adult roles and the simple boundary lines between the generations have broken down and have been replaced by differential criteria based on indicators of social maturity (Frønes 1994b). The boundaries between children and youth and adults are becoming more complex at the same time as the meeting points between the generations have changed. Children and adolescents have been barred from working life and all that that implied as a meeting place between the generations. For girls the household has more or less vanished as the locus of socialization.

The idea that there is a "natural" adulthood probably corresponds to certain periods in industrial society where young men were able to provide for themselves and a family at about the age of twenty. The relatively strict social control meant that the initiation of sexual life (the furtive forays of teenagers aside), work, marriage, and a completed education all occurred at about the same time. To what extent this created the idea that these various conditions naturally coincided, remains hypothetical. The key point is that these indicators later part company.

Institutionalization and organization

The modern symmetric family of course creates an increased need for organized supervision of children, in the form of both day-care and kindergarten facilities and expanded school time. The development of leisure-time organizations is rooted in the development of the modern neighborhood as less suitable environment for children, in parents' wish to give their children useful skills and an educated upbringing, in the intrinsic dynamic of organizations and their drive to expand, and in the differentiation of leisure time in the modern world. Organizations providing structured activities for children range from non-profit organizations to commercial ones, from sports to politics, from art to hobbies. Some organizations are important social institutions, others are limited to leisure-time activities and are often run on a purely commercial basis.

332

In modern childhood, a child's day is increasingly spent in specific institutions and activities from school and day-care centres to leisure-time organizations. But the term *institutionalization* is often misleading since it covers an range of disparate activities from a rigorously organized training to free play in recreational facilities. The term *pedagogization* implies that young people are increasingly surrounded by people with pedagogical qualifications, motives, and goals. It refers both to the growing scope of educational institutions, and to a stronger pedagogical culture in these institutions as well as quite generally. To that extent it is not unreasonable to say that popular psychology has contributed to an increasing pedagogization of the home as well. Some aspects of organized life, as for example sports, have also undergone a similar development toward an increasing professionalization, in regard to children and youth as well.

Nor is it far-fetched to say that the sector of the educational system directed toward children has undergone a *feminization* in that the adults in children's educational landscape are almost exclusively women. Whether this means in general an increased feminine influence is a complicated question: the housewife landscape was also feminine. But the fact is that the personnel landscape in educational systems has become largely dominated by women.

Organizations structure a child's day and influence its cultural and social landscape. Because organizations are specialized, it is claimed that they undermine the local children's culture: children can no longer go out into the fields or the streets and participate in local culture. But organizations can also contribute to local integration: the school team or the football club can be an important local meeting point, both for the local environment generally and as a place where children can establish social roots.

Our interest here is primarily the way in which the organization of childhood influences children's social culture and physical landscape. Organized childhood makes for new pressures on the family: active children demand active parents.

Organized childhood creates different recreational profiles, and also quite different lifestyles, for different environments, groups, and individuals. Different children move along different cultural and social paths and meet on common grounds. The fact that children increasingly use the home as a meeting place and a place to be will also strengthen the tendency toward fewer and fewer children crossing one another's paths. Common playgrounds are divided up into different organized meeting places and private territories.

Peers

The influence of peers and the form assumed by peer groups vary with social class, local culture, and the general national and cultural background.

In general, research from various Western countries indicates that working-class children are more outside the home, more together with friends outside the home, and more oriented toward groups of the same age than middle-class children. Working-class children and young people seem to be more closely tied to their local territory while middle-class children have broader networks, are more frequently organized, use the home more as a meeting place, and are under strictly family control (see, for example, Bjurman 1981). But, although the middle class dominates organized childhood, the general tendency is toward an increased participation in various activities and organizations open to all social groups (see, for example, Grue 1984; Qvortrup 1994).

Social class is usually reflected in housing and living conditions. But cultural variations also follow lines other than social class as class is usually identified. Studies in the early 1970s in Norway indicate that in a suburban satellite town near the capital Oslo young people more often met in one another's homes than they did in a small town in the southwest of the country, despite the fact that there was more room in the homes in the smaller town (Frønes 1975). Time-budget analyses and qualitative analyses from Oslo's working-class suburbs indicate a high degree of organization and social contact among peers, as well as a fluctuating social network rather than very stable and well-defined groups or gangs (Frønes 1987, Gulbransen 1978). As showed in *Peer Environment, Socialization, and the Local Community* (Frønes 1987), peer contact and the manner of contact varied with material and cultural conditions. Differences between local communities, and between groups within local surroundings, indicate social patterns embedded in a complex interplay of different factors.

A number of studies indicate that children and young people structure their organizational lives in accordance with their social relations. Social life and activity are intermingled. The effect of organized childhood as regards peers is on many levels. Organization represents increased adult control, and increased regulation of activities. But at the same time organizations tend to group children of the same age together, so that children tend to spend more of the day together with others of the same age.

The general movement toward modernity is a movement from a landscape based on clear social dividing lines, and broad similarity within the different social and cultural spaces, to a breakdown of the classic dividing lines as differentiation grows. Different choices of recreational activities also indicate differences in lifestyle. Ballet, football, ice hockey, or ecological interests often become a component of lifestyle. A study from three Norwegian environments (Frønes 1975) indicate that musical preferences, viewed as indicators of cultural identification correlated most strongly (in particular, more than social background) with attitudes and actions in other areas.

If way of life refers to a more general situation, and lifestyle to a personal or a group-related pattern, we can say that the way of life has become more homogeneous, with the growth of educational institutions, day-care centres, common media, etc., but that below the general level we also find an increasing variation in what we mean by lifestyle. Whenever day-care centres, recreation clubs, sports teams, nurseries, and piano lessons are invoked to demonstrate the "institutionalization" of childhood, it camouflages the heterogenous composition of modern childhood.

The modern trend toward social and cultural differences is represented by marginalization, where groups of the population end up in social positions that construct ways of life that diverge from the majority's. The American middle-class child and the ghetto child represent extremely disparate ways of life, despite the same TV programs, formal rights and educational systems, and the same nation. Similar tendencies are visible in all Europe.

Childhood in the modern industrial countries varies considerably as regards play and being in the company of other children. Japanese childhood, for example, is dominated to a much greater extent than Norwegian and American childhood by the education system; American children spend much more time than Norwegian children watching TV. These variations are a reflection not merely of clear differences in TV habits, but of differences in the social organization of childhood as well.

Social integration and socialization's modern landscape

A central theme of sociology is social integration. In Durkheim, integration refers to integration at the societal level, i.e., the social system's capacity to integrate. But in modern society social integration is most often seen from a different standpoint, as a relation between an actor or group of actors and a broader system, or its specific institutions, expressed as the actor's "degree of integration". An example is a schoolchild's integration in the school system, or his or her failure to integrate, as illustrated by the term "dropout". Whereas the opposite to societal integration is disintegration and dissolution, when integration refers to the quality of a relation the opposite term is then segregation or marginalization. Integration in the first sense refers to the social system as a whole, and in the second to a relationship between the system and the individual.

There are a number of ways that children are bonded with the broader society: the mechanism for social integration varies over the course of history. We will distinguish between *task-related integration, territorial integration,* and *institutional integration. Task-related integration* refers social tasks assigned to children and adolescents as individuals, groups, or as a "generation". *Territorial integration* refers simply to social integration on common terrains, i.e., social life in areas in common. Participation in work can thus both have a territorial aspect, if the work is linked to a territory shared with several others, and be task-related. In the simple societies we described earlier, the culture, norms, and values are conveyed by an information-open society existing on a common territory where the central mechanism for the transmission of norms and learning was play. The anthropological literature shows that the clearest examples of task-related integration are when young men are assigned their own specified military tasks; such societies also have segregated subcultures of young men.

Institutional integration refers to social integration of children as exercised through specific institutional arrangements, ranging from feudalism or the organization of youth in Sparta to modern pedagogical institutions. Institutional integration is associated with what is often claimed to be the modern organization of childhood: children are brought into society by tying them to different institutions. While archaic institutions like kinship, villages, religious institutions, or patriarchal society generally operated as mechanisms for social integration in Durkheim's sense, modern institution-alization is structured as a series of relations between individuals and organizations, such as school and the workplace.

Whereas pre-industrial society featured both the territorial and task-related forms of integration, territorial integration is the dominant form in later industrial society, and tasks are less evident. Mark Twain's world, childhood at play in small towns, close to work and social life and to a large gallery of adults at work or at leisure, testifies that territorial integration was alive. Through physical proximity to adult models and social life in areas in common, territorial integration also provides for a normative control. In contrast, task-related integration is relatively modest for Mark Twain's characters compared to what it was for working youth of the Middle Ages or the subsocieties we have mentioned. Territorial integration involves familiarity with a common social world. Children and youth have their own life and their own places to be alone in, but their world is still ringed by older generations.

In Durkheim's sociology, integrative rituals refer to situations capable of mobilizing whole groups; such rituals are institutionally key. But ritual-ized procedures may also entail individuals performing specific every-day actions in specific ways. For socialization, this form of social ritualization is important for several reasons. The rituals of everyday life set the pace for children's social routines and shape the landscape in which they grow up. At the same time they are themselves susceptible to social change, and contribute to change in the child's world as well.

By the *ritualization of everyday life* we mean that certain situations are con-fronted in prescribed ways, that specified action sequences are performed at specified times, etc. Family meals and bath time, the ritualization of certain situations by the youth culture, etc. – all these things may be classified as the ritualization of everyday life. The term covers both public situations and private, but here we shall be interested in ritualistic patterns played out in the public arena. If, for example, many people do the same thing at the same time, the private sphere will thereby acquire a public character, even if the mechanisms that explain the phenomenon have nothing to do with the public sphere. If everyone eats dinner at the same time, it is because of conditions such as working hours, etc., which have a public character. But one can also construe this to mean that wherever one finds everyone adapting privately, new public patterns will emerge later on: for children there is a "time to eat" which is a time when no one is outside. For children the phenomenon of "dinner", i.e., dinner time, may be a public phenomenon, not a private "choice". For children, the ways and patterns of everyday life constitute their common cosmology.

Jeremy Seabrook (1982) gives a clear illustration of this way of thinking in his description of an English working-class neighbourhood. The lack of hot water and bathrooms not only mean that baths are infrequent, it means that people take baths when they need most to be freshly washed, i.e., before holidays is a time to bathe. Several children bathe in the same water; there is one bath day for all the children. This is not only a private ritual, it is common to all, and it is also reflected in the public space in that at certain times the children are not outside, i.e., it is bath time.

A monthly wage deposited directly in one's bank account is not simply a different method of payment from receiving one's weekly wage cash in hand. A weekly wage, especially when it is relatively meager, gives the week a rhythm that in a sense revolves around the pocket book and stretches from payday, which means better meals and nice clothes, to the scraps still remaining by the time the next Thursday arrives. Money in the hand implies "payday"; by contrast, a bank account is timeless and without end, there is nothing cyclic about it.

Holidays and common festive rituals, shopping days, and days for sweets, bath days, and wash days punctuated by the vision of clothes hung out to dry, give the public sphere their special rhythms. Such everyday ritualizations may be attributed to certain social routines. These ritualized behaviors are partly private, but their common rhythm gives them a public character. In many instances, ritualization is also a way to economize on resources. Triple marriages were arranged not simply because they were especially festive, but also because they permitted a concentration of resources; time, competence, and money. Variation has its costs, mentally, socially, and economically. Mealtime, with everyone eating at the same time, is not merely a social phenomenon; it is also a question of resources of time and money, which, however, microwave ovens have in large measure resolved.

The ritualization of everyday life emphasizes the social dimension, in the same way as do "heavier" ritual acts; society acquires a manifest form through the existence of supra-individual behaviours. Everyday rituals also create a predictable world, provide a social mooring, and allow for social control.

Historical changes in socialization's landscape

Simple hunter-gatherer societies probably had a kind of social integration based in part on a certain division of tasks, and in part on family ties and group membership. The social control of children was based on a territorial integration in everyday life, aside from the fact that the general openness to information and the modest size of these societies simply made the problem of "not being socially integrated", in the modern sense of the term, for the most part irrelevant to the extent it signified being outside the society, not integrated into society's fundamental organizations.

From the perspective of socialization, the classical rural village reflects a general social integration which also reached children through their common life on public territory. There was strong social control in a life lived before everyone's eyes. On top of all was a patriarchal structure with its hierarchies and systems of duties and power. For children, social integration was secured in a normative framework of hierarchy and duties, as well as in informal public life. The changes in socialization's landscape are obvious if we compare this against the modern world. Even allowing for the variations between regions and cultures, Western society bears clear witness to a movement from *public to private mechanisms of social integration.*

Privatization is evident in the evolution of the physical environment, with the separation of functions and the disappearance of a common local public sphere. The separation of functions goes beyond just having different areas for dwelling, work, and recreation. Tennis players, restaurant guests, chess players, and hikers share in common the fact that they are not on their own local territory, but they are also not on any common recreational territory. Two-income families have made the suburbs no longer a common territory for local children and women.

The modern landscape also generally tacks the openness to children many local environments used to have. In the world of Tom Sawyer or *The Little Rascals,* or in Astrid Lindgren's books, children's social life created its own local public sphere surrounded by adults, in a kind of territorial integration. The arena where socialization takes place in a complex society is shifting progressively from the common public territory children made their own in the past to various circumscribed institutions and organizations. At the system level these provide the machinery for social integration, but integration takes place along other lines than a common social life on common territory.

The school provides a good example of the modern mechanisms for social integration. Everyone is required to go to school, but successful school integration requires achievement and proficiency, and for some the school is an arena for marginalization. That applies as well to central aspects of organizational life: integration demands engagement and active effort. When mobile persons make a choice of friends, friendship and social contact become something that is to be achieved, rather than something that in large measure follows family ties or is a natural consequence of being neighbours. The schoolchild's environment is an illustration: it does not follow from being a pupil that one is an integral part of the pupil environment. Integration must be achieved, and requires competence. Modern friendship illustrates the same: it opens the way to deeper social relations and commitment, but it also demands social competence, i.e., that one contributes something to the relation.

Social integration can also be undermined in that prosperity undermines the ritualization of everyday life that scarcity, primitive technological solutions, few opportunities and little mobility produce. Private actions no longer coalesce into a common rhythm, which children would experience as a common cosmology.

The possibility of making private choices, which is a key benefit of a modern affluent society, enables privatized active and prosperous persons to range over different social arenas and to have different interests, such as is expressed in the concept of *lifestyle*. The kind of social integration that was premised on a common pace of life and common territories breaks down in such a landscape. The modern mechanisms for social integration rely more on individual and family resources, which thus increase in their importance. The lines along which integration takes place in the modern world, situate, in general, the individual in a landscape with many possible way stations, each of which must be achieved in its own right. Individual characteristics and resources determine the degree of integration, or, seen from another perspective, the degree of marginalization. At the same time, marginal environments are characterized by general disintegration.

References

Bjurman, E. L. *Barn och barn: om barns olika vardag.* Lund: Liber, 1981.

Brusdal, R., and Lavik, R. *Hva gjør barn og unge i fritiden?* Lysaker, SIFO-Rapport No. 6, 1991.

Coleman, J. C., and Hendry, L. *The Nature of Adolescence.* London: Routledge, 1990.

du Bois-Reymond, M., Büchner, P., and Krüger, H. H. "Modern Families as Everyday Negotiation: Continuities and Discontinuities in Parent–Child Relationships". *Childhood* 1(2), 1993.

Easterlin, R. A. *Birth and Fortune.* New York: Basic Books, 1980.

Frønes, I. *Ungdomskultur og sosial endring.* Oslo: Department of Sociology, University of Oslo, 1975.

Frønes, I. "Generasjoner og Livsløp i Norge". In Alldén L., *et al.: Det norske samfunn.* Oslo: Gyldendal, 1985.

Frønes, I. *Jevnaldermiljø, sosialisering og lokalsamfunn.* [Peer Environment, Socialization, and Local Community.] Oslo, INAS-rapport 87:9, 1987.

Frønes, I. *Den norske barndommen.* Oslo: Cappelen, 1994a.

Frønes, I. "Dimensions of Childhood". In Qvortrup, J., *et al.* (eds.): *Childhood Matters*. Vienna: Avebury, 1994b.

Frønes, I., Jensen, A. M., and Solberg, A. *Childhood as a Social Phenomenon*. National Report Norway. European Centre Eurosocial Report 36/1, 1990.

Grue, L. *Bedre enn sitt rykte*. Oslo: STUI, 1984.

Gulbrandsen, L. M. *En funksjonell analyse av barns sosiale relasjoner*. Oslo, INAS-rapport, 1978.

Qvortrup, J. "Childhood Matters: An Introduction". In Qvortrup, J., *et al.* (eds.): *Childhood Matters*. Vienna: Avebury, 1994.

Seabrook, J. *Working Class Childhood*. London: Victor Gollancz, 1982.

Solberg, A., and Danielsen, K. *Dagligliv i familier med store barn*. Oslo, NIBR Rapport No. 22, 1988.

63

EDUCATION

Its nature and its role

Emile Durkheim

Source: *Education and Sociology*, Glencoe: Free Press, 1956, pp. 61–90.

1. Definitions of education. Critical examination

The word "education" has sometimes been used in a very broad sense to designate the totality of influences that nature or other men are able to exercise either on our intelligence or on our will. It includes, says John Stuart Mill, "all that we ourselves do and all that others do for us to the end of bringing us closer to the perfection of our nature. In its most widely accepted sense, it includes even indirect effects on the character and faculties of men produced by things having quite a different objective: by laws, by forms of government, the industrial arts, and even by physical phenomena, independent of human will, such as climate, soil, and locality." But this definition includes elements that are quite disparate, and that one cannot combine under a single heading without confusion. The influence of things on men is very different, in their processes and effects, from that which comes from men themselves; and the influence of peers on peers differs from that which adults exercise on youth. It is only the latter that concerns us here, and, therefore, it is this meaning that it is convenient to reserve for the word "education."

But what is the specific nature of this influence? Various answers have been given to this question; they can be divided into two main types.

Following Kant, "the end of education is to develop, in each individual, all the perfection of which he is capable." But what is meant by perfection? It is, as has often been said, the harmonious development of all the human faculties. To carry to the highest point that can be reached all the capacities that are in us, to realize them as completely as possible, without their interfering with one another, is not this an ideal beyond which there can be no other?

But if, to a degree, this harmonious development is indeed necessary and desirable, it is not wholly attainable; for it is in contradiction to another rule of human behavior which is no less cogent: that which has us concentrate on a specific, limited task. We cannot and we must not all be devoted to the same kind of life; we have, according to our aptitudes, different functions to fulfill, and we must adapt ourselves to what we must do. We are not all made for reflection; there is need for men of feeling and of action. Conversely, there is need of those whose job is thinking. Now, thought can develop only in detachment from action, only by turning in upon itself, only by turning its object entirely away from overt action. From this comes a first differentiation which is accompanied by a break of equilibrium. And behavior, in turn, as thought, can take a variety of different and specialized forms. Doubtless this specialization does not exclude a certain common base and, consequently, a certain balance of functions, organic and psychic alike, without which the health of the individual would be endangered, as well as social cohesion. We see, thus, that perfect harmony cannot be presented as the final end of conduct and of education.

Still less satisfactory is the utilitarian definition, according to which the objective of education would be to "make the individual an instrument of happiness for himself and for his fellows" (James Mill); for happiness is an essentially subjective thing that each person appreciates in his own way. Such a formula, then, leaves the end of education undetermined and, therefore, education itself, since it is left to individual fancy. Spencer, to be sure, tried to define happiness objectively. For him, the conditions of happiness are those of life. Complete happiness is the complete life. But what is meant by life? If it is a matter of physical existence alone, one may well say: that without which it would be impossible; it implies, in effect, a certain equilibrium between the organism and its environment, and, since the two terms in relation are definable data, it must be the same with their relation. But one can express, in this way, only the most immediate vital necessities. Now, for man, and above all for the man of today, such a life is not life. We ask more of life than normal enough functioning of our organs. A cultivated mind prefers not to live rather than give up the joys of the intellect. Even from the material point of view alone, everything over and above what is strictly necessary cannot be exactly determined. The "standard of life," as the English say, the minimum below which it does not seem to us that we can consent to descend, varies infinitely according to conditions, milieux, and the times. What we found sufficient yesterday, today seems to us to be beneath the dignity of man, as we define it now, and everything leads us to believe that our needs in this connection grow increasingly.

We come here to the general criticism that all these definitions face. They assume that there is an ideal, perfect education, which applies to all men indiscriminately; and it is this education, universal and unique, that the theorist tries to define. But first, if history is taken into consideration, one finds in it nothing to confirm such an hypothesis. Education has varied infinitely in time and place. In the cities of Greece and Rome, education trained the individual to subordinate himself blindly to the collectivity, to become the creature of society. Today, it tries to make of the individual an autonomous personality. In Athens, they sought to form cultivated souls, informed, subtle, full of measure and harmony, capable of enjoying beauty and the joys of pure speculation; in Rome, they wanted above all for children to become men of action, devoted to military glory, indifferent to letters and the arts. In the Middle Ages, education was above all Christian; in the Renaissance, it assumes a more lay and literary character; today science tends to assume the place in education formerly occupied by the arts. Can it be said, then, that the fact is not the ideal; that if education has varied, it is because men have mistaken what it should be? But if Roman education had been infused with an individualism comparable to ours, the Roman city would not have been able to maintain itself; Latin civilization would not have developed, nor, furthermore, our modern civilization, which is in part descended from it. The Christian societies of the Middle Ages would not have been able to survive if they had given to free inquiry the place that we give it today. There are, then, ineluctable necessities which it is impossible to disregard. Of what use is it to imagine a kind of education that would be fatal for the society that put it into practice?

This assumption, so doubtful, in itself rests on a more general mistake. If one begins by asking, thus, what an ideal education must be, abstracted from conditions of time and place, it is to admit implicitly that a system of education has no reality in itself. One does not see in education a collection of practices and institutions that have been organized slowly in the course of time, which are comparable with all the other social institutions and which express them, and which, therefore, can no more be changed at will than the structure of the society itself. But it seems that this would be a pure system of *a priori* concepts; under this heading it appears to be a logical construct. One imagines that men of each age organize it voluntarily to realize a determined end; that, if this organization is not everywhere the same, it is because mistakes have been made concerning either the end that it is to pursue or the means of attaining it. From this point of view, educational systems of the past appear as so many errors, total or partial. No attention need be paid to them, therefore; we do not have to associate ourselves with the faulty observation or logic of our predecessors; but we can and must pose the question without concerning ourselves with solutions that have been given, that is to say, leaving aside everything that has been, we have only to ask ourselves what should be. The lessons of history can, moreover, serve to prevent us from repeating the errors that have been committed.

In fact, however, each society, considered at a given stage of development, has a system of education which exercises an irresistible influence on individuals. It is idle to think that we can rear our children as we wish.

There are customs to which we are bound to conform; if we flout them too severely, they take their vengeance on our children. The children, when they are adults, are unable to live with their peers, with whom they are not in accord. Whether they had been raised in accordance with ideas that were either obsolete or premature does not matter; in the one case as in the other, they are not of their time and, therefore, they are outside the conditions of normal life. There is, then, in each period, a prevailing type of education from which we cannot deviate without encountering that lively resistance which restrains the fancies of dissent.

Now, it is not we as individuals who have created the customs and ideas that determine this type. They are the product of a common life, and they express its needs. They are, moreover, in large part the work of preceding generations. The entire human past has contributed to the formation of this totality of maxims that guide education today; our entire history has left its traces in it, and even the history of the peoples who have come before. It is thus that the higher organisms carry in themselves the reflection of the whole biological evolution of which they are the end product. Historical investigation of the formation and development of systems of education reveals that they depend upon religion, political organization, the degree of development of science, the state of industry, etc. If they are considered apart from all these historic causes, they become incomprehensible. Thus, how can the individual pretend to reconstruct, through his own private reflection, what is not a work of individual thought? He is not confronted with a *tabula rasa* on which he can write what he wants, but with existing realities which he cannot create, or destroy, or transform, at will. He can act on them only to the extent that he has learned to understand them, to know their nature and the conditions on which they depend; and he can understand them only if he studies them, only if he starts by observing them, as the physicist observes inanimate matter and the biologist, living bodies.

Besides, how else to proceed? When one wants to determine by dialectics alone what education should be, it is necessary to begin by asking what objectives it must have. But what is it that allows us to say that education has certain ends rather than others? We do not know *a priori* what is the function of respiration or of circulation in a living being. By what right would we be more well informed concerning the educational function? It will be said in reply that from all the evidence, its object is the training of children. But this is posing the problem in slightly different terms; it does not resolve it. It would be necessary to say of what this training consists, what its direction is, what human needs it satisfies. Now, one can answer these questions only by beginning with observation of what it has consisted of, what needs it has satisfied in the past. Thus, it appears that to establish the preliminary notion of education, to determine what is so called, historical observation is indispensable.

2. Definition of education

To define education we must, then, consider, educational systems, present and past, put them together, and abstract the characteristics which are common to them. These characteristics will constitute the definition that we seek.

We have already determined, along the way, two elements. In order that there be education, there must be a generation of adults and one of youth, in interaction, and an influence exercised by the first on the second. It remains for us to define the nature of this influence.

There is, so to speak, no society in which the system of education does not present a twofold aspect: it is at the same time one and manifold.

It is manifold. Indeed, in one sense, it can be said that there are as many different kinds of education as there are different milieux in a given society. Is such a society formed of castes? Education varies from one caste to another; that of the patricians was not that of the plebeians; that of the Brahman was not that of the Sudra. Similarly, in the Middle Ages, what a difference between the culture that the young page received, instructed in all the arts of chivalry, and that of the villein, who learned in his parish school a smattering of arithmetic, song and grammar! Even today, do we not see education vary with social class, or even with locality? That of the city is not that of the country, that of the middle class is not that of the worker. Would one say that this organization is not morally justifiable, that one can see in it only a survival destined to disappear? This proposition is easy to defend. It is evident that the education of our children should not depend upon the chance of their having been born here or there, of some parents rather than others. But even though the moral conscience of our time would have received, on this point, the satisfaction that it expects, education would not, for all that, become more uniform. Even though the career of each child would, in large part, no longer be predetermined by a blind heredity, occupational specialization would not fail to result in a great pedagogical diversity. Each occupation, indeed, constitutes a milieu *sui generis* which requires particular aptitudes and specialized knowledge, in which certain ideas, certain practices, certain modes of viewing things, prevail; and as the child must be prepared for the function that he will be called upon to fulfill, education, beyond a certain age, can no longer remain the same for all those to whom it applies. That is why we see it, in all civilized countries, tending more and more to become diversified and specialized; and this specialization becomes more advanced daily. The heterogeneity which is thus created does not rest, as does that which we were just discussing, on unjust inequalities; but it is not less. To find an absolutely homogeneous and egalitarian education, it would be necessary to go back to prehistoric societies, in the structure of which there is no differentiation; and yet these kinds of societies represent hardly more than one logical stage in the history of humanity.

345

But, whatever may be the importance of these special educations, they are not all of education. It may even be said that they are not sufficient unto themselves; everywhere that one observes them, they vary from one another only beyond a certain point, up to which they are not differentiated. They all rest upon a common base. There is no people among whom there is not a certain number of ideas, sentiments and practices which education must inculcate in all children indiscriminately, to whatever social category they belong. Even in a society which is divided into closed castes, there is always a religion common to all, and, consequently, the principles of the religious culture, which is, then, fundamental, are the same throughout the population. If each caste, each family, has its special gods, there are general divinities that are recognized by everyone and which all children learn to worship. And as these divinities symbolize and personify certain sentiments, certain ways of conceiving the world and life, one cannot be initiated into their cult without acquiring, at the same time, all sorts of thought patterns which go beyond the sphere of the purely religious life. Similarly, in the Middle Ages, serfs, villeins, burgers and nobles received, equally, a common Christian education. If it is thus in societies where intellectual and moral diversity reach this degree of contrast, with how much more reason is it so among more advanced peoples where classes, while remaining distinct, are, however, separated by a less profound cleavage! Where these common elements of all education are not expressed in the form of religious symbols, they do not, however, cease to exist. In the course of our history, there has been established a whole set of ideas on human nature, on the respective importance of our different faculties, on right and duty, on society, on the individual, on progress, on science, on art, etc., which are the very basis of our national spirit; all education, that of the rich as well as that of the poor, that which leads to professional careers as well as that which prepares for industrial functions, has as its object to fix them in our minds.

From these facts it follows that each society sets up a certain ideal of man, of what he should be, as much from the intellectual point of view as the physical and moral; that this ideal is, to a degree, the same for all the citizens; that beyond a certain point it becomes differentiated according to the particular milieux that every society contains in its structure. It is this ideal, at the same time one and various, that is the focus of education. Its function, then, is to arouse in the child: (1) a certain number of physical and mental states that the society to which he belongs considers should not be lacking in any of its members; (2) certain physical and mental states that the particular social group (caste, class, family, profession) considers, equally, ought to be found among all those who make it up. Thus, it is society as a whole and each particular social milieu that determine the ideal that education realizes. Society can survive only if there exists among its members a sufficient degree of homogeneity; education perpetuates and reinforces this homogeneity by fixing in the child, from the beginning, the essential similarities that collective life demands. But on the other hand, without a certain diversity all co-operation would be impossible; education assures the persistence of this necessary diversity by being itself diversified and specialized. If the society has reached a degree of development such that the old divisions into castes and classes can no longer be maintained, it will prescribe an education more uniform at its base. If at the same time there is more division of labor, it will arouse among children, on the underlying basic set of common ideas and sentiments, a richer diversity of occupational aptitudes. If it lives in a state of war with the surrounding societies, it tries to shape people according to a strongly nationalistic model; if international competition takes a more peaceful form, the type that it tries to realize is more general and more humanistic. Education is, then, only the means by which society prepares, within the children, the essential conditions of its very existence. We shall see later how the individual himself has an interest in submitting to these requirements.

We come, then, to the following formula: *Education is the influence exercised by adult generations on those that are not yet ready for social life. Its object is to arouse and to develop in the child a certain number of physical, intellectual and moral states which are demanded of him by both the political society as a whole and the special milieu for which he is specifically destined.*

3. Consequences of the preceding definition: the social character of education

It follows from the definition that precedes, that education consists of a methodical socialization of the young generation. In each of us, it may be said, there exist two beings which, while inseparable except by abstraction, remain distinct. One is made up of all the mental states that apply only to ourselves and to the events of our personal lives: this is what might be called the individual being. The other is a system of ideas, sentiments and practices which express in us, not our personality, but the group or different groups of which we are part; these are religious beliefs, moral beliefs and practices, national or professional traditions, collective opinions of every kind. Their totality forms the social being. To constitute this being in each of us is the end of education.

It is here, moreover, that are best shown the importance of its role and the fruitfulness of its influence. Indeed, not only is this social being not given, fully formed, in the primitive constitution of man; but it has not resulted from it through a spontaneous development. Spontaneously, man was not inclined to submit to a political authority, to respect a moral discipline, to dedicate himself, to be self-sacrificing. There was nothing in our congenital nature that predisposed us necessarily to become servants of divinities, symbolic emblems of society, to render them worship, to deprive ourselves in order to do them honor. It is society itself which, to the degree that it is firmly established, has drawn from within itself those great moral forces in the face of which man has felt his inferiority. Now, if one leaves aside the vague and indefinite tendencies which can be attributed to heredity, the child, on entering life, brings to it only his nature as an individual. Society finds itself, with each new generation, faced with a *tabula rasa*, very nearly, on which it must build anew. To the egoistic and asocial being that has just been born it must, as rapidly as possible, add another, capable of leading a moral and social life. Such is the work of education, and you can readily see its great importance. It is not limited to developing the individual organism in the direction indicated by its nature, to elicit the hidden potentialities that need only be manifested. It creates in man a new being.

This creative quality is, moreover, a special prerogative of human education. Anything else is what animals receive, if one can apply this name to the progressive training to which they are subjected by their parents. It can, indeed, foster the development of certain instincts that lie dormant in the animal, but such training does not initiate it into a new life. It facilitates the play of natural functions, but it creates nothing. Taught by its mother, the young animal learns more quickly how to fly or build its nest; but it learns almost nothing that it could not have been able to discover through its own individual experience. This is because animals either do not live under social conditions or form rather simple societies, which function through instinctive mechanisms that each individual carries within himself, fully formed, from birth. Education, then, can add nothing essential to nature, since the latter is adequate for everything, for the life of the group as well as that of the individual. By contrast, among men the aptitudes of every kind that social life presupposes are much too complex to be able to be contained, somehow, in our tissues, and to take the form of organic predispositions. It follows that they cannot be transmitted from one generation to another by way of heredity. It is through education that the transmission is effected.

However, it will be said, if one can indeed conceive that the distinctively moral qualities, because they impose privations on the individual, because they inhibit his natural impulses, can be developed in us only under an outside influence, are there not others which every man wishes to acquire and seeks spontaneously? Such are the divers qualities of the intelligence which allow him better to adapt his behavior to the nature of things. Such, too, are the physical qualities, and everything that contributes to the vigor and health of the organism. For the former, at least, it seems that education, in developing them, may only assist the development of nature itself, may only lead the individual to a state of relative perfection toward which he tends by himself, although he may be able to achieve it more rapidly thanks to the co-operation of society.

But what demonstrates, despite appearances, that here as elsewhere education answers social necessities above all, is that there are societies in which these qualities have not been cultivated at all, and that in every case they have been understood very differently in different societies. The advantages of a solid intellectual culture have been far from recognized by all peoples. Science and the critical mind, that we rank so high today, were for a long time held in suspicion. Do we not know a great doctrine that proclaims happy the poor in spirit? We must guard against believing that this indifference to knowledge had been artificially imposed on men in violation of their nature. They do not have, by themselves, the instinctive appetite for science that has often and arbitrarily been attributed to them. They desire science only to the extent that experience has taught them that they cannot do without it. Now, in connection with the ordering of their individual lives they had no use for it. As Rousseau has already said, to satisfy the vital necessities, sensation, experience and instinct would suffice as they suffice for the animal. If man had not known other needs than these, very simple ones, which have their roots in his individual constitution, he would not have undertaken the pursuit of science, all the more because it has not been acquired without laborious and painful efforts. He has known the thirst for knowledge only when society has awakened it in him, and society has done this only when it has felt the need of it. This moment came when social life, in all its forms, had become too complex to be able to function otherwise than through the co-operation of reflective thought, that is to say, thought enlightened by science. Then scientific culture became indispensable, and that is why society requires it of its members and imposes it upon them as a duty. But in the beginning, as long as social organization is very simple and undifferentiated, always self-sufficient, blind tradition suffices, as does instinct in the animal. Therefore thought and free inquiry are useless and even dangerous, since they can only threaten tradition. That is why they are proscribed.

It is not otherwise with physical qualities. Where the state of the social milieu inclines public sentiment toward asceticism, physical education will be relegated to a secondary place. Something of this sort took place in the schools of the Middle Ages; and this asceticism was necessary, for the only manner of adapting to the harshness of those difficult times was to like it. Similarly, following the current of opinion, this same education will be understood very differently. In Sparta its object above all was to harden the limbs to fatigue; in Athens, it was a means of making bodies beautiful to the sight; in the time of chivalry it was required to form agile and supple warriors; today it no longer has any but a hygienic end, and is concerned, above all, with limiting the dangerous effects of a too intense intellectual culture. Thus, even the qualities which appear at first glance so spontaneously desirable, the individual seeks only when society invites him to, and he seeks them in the fashion that it prescribes for him.

We are now in a position to answer a question raised by all that precedes. Whereas we showed society fashioning individuals according to its needs, it could seem, from this fact, that the individuals were submitting to an insupportable tyranny. But in reality they are themselves interested in this submission; for the new being that collective influence, through education, thus builds up in each of us, represents what is best in us. Man is man, in fact, only because he lives in society. It is difficult, in the course of an article, to demonstrate rigorously a proposition so general and so important, and one which sums up the works of contemporary sociology. But first, one can say that it is less and less disputed. And more, it is not impossible to call to mind, summarily, the most essential facts that justify it.

First, if there is today an historically established fact, it is that morality stands in close relationship to the nature of societies, since, as we have shown along the way, it changes when societies change. This is because it results from life in common. It is society, indeed, that draws us out of ourselves, that obliges us to reckon with other interests than our own, it is society that has taught us to control our passions, our instincts, to prescribe law for them, to restrain ourselves, to deprive ourselves, to sacrifice ourselves, to subordinate our personal ends to higher ends. As for the whole system of representation which maintains in us the idea and the sentiment of rule, of discipline, internal as well as external—it is society that has established it in our consciences. It is thus that we have acquired this power to control ourselves, this control over our inclinations which is one of the distinctive traits of the human being and which is the more developed to the extent that we are more fully human.

We do not owe society less from the intellectual point of view. It is science that elaborates the cardinal notions that govern our thought: notions of cause, of laws, of space, of number, notions of bodies, of life, of conscience, of society, and so on. All these fundamental ideas are perpetually evolving, because they are the recapitulation, the resultant of all scientific work, far from being its point of departure as Pestalozzi believed. We do not conceive of man, nature, cause, even space, as they were conceived in the Middle Ages; this is because our knowledge and our scientific methods are no longer the same. Now, science is a collective work, since it presupposes a vast co-operation of all scientists, not only of the same time, but of all the successive epochs of history. Before the sciences were established, religion filled the same office; for every mythology consists of a conception, already well elaborated, of man and of the universe. Science, moreover, was the heir of religion. Now, a religion is a social institution.

In learning a language, we learn a whole system of ideas, distinguished and classified, and we inherit from all the work from which have come these classifications that sum up centuries of experiences. There is more: without language, we would not have, so to speak, general ideas; for it is the word which, in fixing them, gives to concepts a consistency sufficient for them to be able to be handled conveniently by the mind. It is language, then, that has allowed us to raise ourselves above pure sensation; and it is not necessary to demonstrate that language is, in the first degree, a social thing.

One sees, through these few examples, to what man would be reduced if there were withdrawn from him all that he has derived from society: he would fall to the level of an animal. If he has been able to surpass the stage at which animals have stopped, it is primarily because he is not reduced to the fruit only of his personal efforts, but cooperates regularly with his fellow-creatures; and this makes the activity of each more productive. It is chiefly as a result of this that the products of the work of one generation are not lost for that which follows. Of what an animal has been able to learn in the course of his individual existence, almost nothing can survive him. By contrast, the results of human experience are preserved almost entirely and in detail, thanks to books, sculptures, tools, instruments of every kind that are transmitted from generation to generation, oral tradition, etc. The soil of nature is thus covered with a rich deposit that continues to grow constantly. Instead of dissipating each time that a generation dies out and is replaced by another, human wisdom accumulates without limit, and it is this unlimited accumulation that raises man above the beast and above himself. But, just as in the case of the cooperation which was discussed first, this accumulation is possible only in and through society. For in order that the legacy of each generation may be able to be preserved and added to others, it is necessary that there be a moral personality which lasts beyond the generations that pass, which binds them to one another: it is society. Thus the antagonism that has too often been admitted between society and individual corresponds to nothing in the facts. Indeed, far from these two terms being in opposition and being able to develop only each at the expense of the other, they imply each other. The individual, in willing society, wills himself. The influence that it exerts on him, notably through education, does not at all have as its object and its effect to repress him, to diminish him, to denature him, but, on the contrary, to make him grow and to make of him a truly human being. No doubt, he can grow thus only by making an effort. But this is precisely because this power to put forth voluntary effort is one of the most essential characteristics of man.

4. The role of the State in education

This definition of education provides for a ready solution of the controversial question of the duties and the rights of the State with respect to education.

The rights of the family are opposed to them. The child, it is said, belongs first to his parents; it is, then, their responsibility to direct, as they understand it, his intellectual and moral development. Education is then conceived as an essentially private and domestic affair. When one takes this point of view, one tends naturally to reduce to a minimum the intervention of the State in the matter. The State should, it is said, be limited to serving as an auxiliary to, and as a substitute for, families. When they are unable to discharge their duties, it is natural that the State should take charge. It is natural, too, that it make their task as easy as possible, by placing at their disposal schools to which they can, if they wish, send their children. But it must be kept strictly within these limits, and forbidden any positive action designed to impress a given orientation on the mind of the youth.

But its role need hardly remain so negative. If, as we have tried to establish, education has a collective function above all, if its object is to adapt the child to the social milieu in which he is destined to live, it is impossible that society should be uninterested in such a procedure. How could society not have a part in it, since it is the reference point by which education must direct its action? It is, then, up to the State to remind the teacher constantly of the ideas, the sentiments that must be impressed upon the child to adjust him to the milieu in which he must live. If it were not always there to guarantee that pedagogical influence be exercised in a social way, the latter would necessarily be put to the service of private beliefs, and the whole nation would be divided and would break down into an incoherent multitude of little fragments in conflict with one another. One could not contradict more completely the fundamental end of all education. Choice is necessary: if one attaches some value to the existence of society—and we have just seen what it means to us—education must assure, among the citizens, a sufficient community of ideas and of sentiments, without which any society is impossible; and in order that it may be able to produce this result, it is also necessary that education not be completely abandoned to the arbitrariness of private individuals.

Since education is an essentially social function, the State cannot be indifferent to it. On the contrary, everything that pertains to education must in some degree be submitted to its influence. This is not to say, therefore, that it must necessarily monopolize instruction. The question is too complex to be able to be treated thus in passing; we shall discuss it later. One can believe that scholastic progress is easier and quicker where a certain margin is left for individual initiative; for the individual makes innovations more readily than the State. But from the fact that the State, in the public interest, must allow other schools to be opened than those for which it has a more direct responsibility, it does not follow that it must remain aloof from what is going on in them. On the contrary, the education given in them must remain under its control. It is not even admissible that the function of the educator can be fulfilled by anyone who does not offer special guarantees of which the State alone can be the judge. No doubt, the limits within which its intervention should be kept may be rather difficult to determine once and for all, but the principle of intervention could not be disputed. There is no school which can claim the right to give, with full freedom, an antisocial education.

It is nevertheless necessary to recognize that the state of division in which we now find ourselves, in our country, makes this duty of the State particularly delicate and at the same time more important. It is not, indeed, up to the State to create this community of ideas and sentiments without which there is no society; it must be established by itself, and the State can only consecrate it, maintain it, make individuals more aware of it. Now, it is unfortunately indisputable that among us, this moral unity is not at all points what it should be. We are divided by divergent and even sometimes contradictory conceptions. There is in these divergences a fact which it is impossible to deny, and which must be reckoned with. It is not a question of recognizing the right of the majority to impose its ideas on the children of the minority. The school should not be the thing of one party, and the teacher is remiss in his duties when he uses the authority at his disposal to influence his pupils in accordance with his own preconceived opinions, however justified they may appear to him. But in spite of all the differences of opinion, there are at present, at the basis of our civilization, a certain number of principles which, implicitly or explicitly, are common to all, that few indeed, in any case, dare to deny overtly and openly: respect for reason, for science, for ideas and sentiments which are at the base of democratic morality. The role of the State is to outline these essential principles, to have them taught in its schools, to see to it that nowhere are children left ignorant of them, that everywhere they should be spoken of with the respect which is due them. There is in this connection an influence to exert which will perhaps be all the more efficacious when it will be less aggressive and less violent, and will know better how to be contained within wise limits.

5. The power of education. The means of influence

After having determined the end of education, we must seek to determine how and to what extent it is possible to attain this end, that is to say, how and to what extent education can be efficacious.

This question has always been very controversial. For Fontenelle, "neither does good education make good character, nor does bad education destroy it." By contrast, for Locke, for Helvetius, education is all-powerful. According to the latter, "all men are born equal and with equal aptitudes; education alone makes for differences." The theory of Jacotot resembles the preceding.

The solution that one gives to the problem depends on the idea that one has of the importance and of the nature of the innate predispositions, on the one hand, and, on the other, of the means of influence at the disposal of the educator.

Education does not make a man out of nothing, as Locke and Helvetius believed; it is applied to predispositions that it finds already made. From another point of view, one can concede, in a general way, that these congenital tendencies are very strong, very difficult to destroy or to transform radically; for they depend upon organic conditions on which the educator has little influence. Consequently, to the degree that they have a definite object, that they incline the mind and the character toward narrowly determined ways of acting and thinking, the whole future of the individual finds itself fixed in advance, and there does not remain much for education to do.

But fortunately one of the characteristics of man is that the innate predispositions in him are very general and very vague. Indeed, the type of predisposition that is fixed, rigid, invariable, which hardly leaves room for the influence of external causes, is instinct. Now, one can ask if there is a single instinct, properly speaking, in man. One speaks, sometimes, of the instinct of preservation; but the word is inappropriate. For an instinct is a system of given actions, always the same, which, once they are set in motion by sensation, are automatically linked up with one another until they reach their natural limit, without reflection having to intervene anywhere; now, the movements that we make when our life is in danger do not at all have any such fixity or automatic invariability. They change with the situation; we adapt them to circumstances: this is because they do not operate without a certain conscious choice, however rapid. What is called the instinct of preservation is, after all, only a general impulse to flee death, without the means by which we seek to avoid it being predetermined once and for all. One can say as much concerning what is sometimes called, not less inexactly, the maternal instinct, the paternal instinct, and even the sexual instinct. These are drives in a given direction; but the means by which these drives are expressed vary from one individual to another, from one occasion to another. A large area remains reserved, then, for trial and error, for personal accommodations, and, consequently, for the effect of causes which can make their influence felt only after birth. Now, education is one of these causes.

It has been claimed, to be sure, that the child sometimes inherits a very strong tendency toward a given act, such, as suicide, theft, murder, fraud, etc. But these assertions are not at all in accord with the facts. Whatever may have been said about it, one is not born criminal; still less is one destined from birth for this or that type of crime; the paradox of the Italian criminologists no longer counts many defenders today. What is inherited is a certain lack of mental equilibrium, which makes the individual refractory to coherent and disciplined behavior. But such a temperament does not predestine a man to be a criminal any more than to be an explorer seeking adventures, a prophet, a political innovator, an inventor, etc. As much can be said of any occupational aptitudes. As Bain remarked, "the son of a great philologist does not inherit a single word; the son of a great traveler can, at school, be surpassed in geography by the son of a miner." What the child receives from his parents are very general faculties: some force of attention, a certain amount of perseverance, a sound judgment, imagination, etc. But each of these faculties can serve all sorts of different ends. A child endowed with a rather lively imagination will be able, depending on circumstances, on the influences that will be brought to bear upon him, to become a painter or a poet, or an engineer with an inventive mind, or a daring financier. There is, then, a considerable difference between natural qualities and the special forms that they must take to be utilized in life. This means that the future is not strictly predetermined by our congenital constitution. The reason for this is easy to understand. The only forms of activity that can be transmitted by heredity are those which are always repeated in a sufficiently identical manner to be able to be fixed, in a rigid form, in the tissues of the organism. Now, human life depends on conditions that are manifold, complex, and, consequently, changing; it must itself, then, change and be modified continuously. Thus it is impossible for it to become crystallized in a definite and positive form. But only very general, very vague dispositions, expressing the characteristics common to all individual experiences, can survive and pass from one generation to another.

To say that innate characteristics are for the most part very general, is to say that they are very malleable, very flexible, since they can assume very different forms. Between the vague potentialities which constitute man at the moment of birth and the well-defined character that he must become in order to play a useful role in society, the distance is, then, considerable. It is this distance that education has to make the child travel. One sees that a vast field is open to its influence.

But, to exert this influence, does it have adequate means?

In order to give an idea of what constitutes the educational influence, and to show its power, a contemporary psychologist, Guyau, has compared it to hypnotic suggestion; and the comparison is not without foundation.

Hypnotic suggestion presupposes, indeed, the following two conditions: (1) The state in which the hypnotized subject is found is characterized by its exceptional passivity. The mind is almost reduced to the state of a *tabula rasa*; a sort of void has been achieved in his consciousness; the will is as though paralyzed. Thus, the idea suggested, meeting no contrary idea at all, can be established with a minimum of resistance; (2) however, as the void is never complete, it is necessary, further, that the idea take from the suggestion itself some power of specific action. For that, it is necessary that the hypnotizer speak in a commanding tone, with authority. He must say: *I wish*; he must indicate that refusal to obey is not even conceivable, that the act must be accomplished, that the thing must be seen as he shows it, that it cannot be otherwise. If he weakens, one sees the subject hesitate, resist, sometimes even refuse to obey. If he so much as enters into discussion, that is the end of his power. The more suggestion goes against the natural temperament of the subject, the more will the imperative tone be indispensable.

Now, these two conditions are present in the relationships that the educator has with the child subjected to his influence: (1) The child is naturally in a state of passivity quite comparable to that in which the hypnotic subject is found artificially placed. His mind yet contains only a small number of conceptions able to fight against those which are suggested to him; his will is still rudimentary. Therefore he is very suggestible. For the same reason he is very susceptible to the force of example, very much inclined to imitation. (2) The ascendancy that the teacher naturally has over his pupil, because of the superiority of his experience and of his culture, will naturally give to his influence the efficacious force that he needs.

This comparison shows how far from helpless the educator is; for the great power of hypnotic suggestion is known. If, then, educational influence has, even in a lesser degree, an analogous efficacy, much may be expected of it, provided that one knows how to use it. Far from being discouraged by our impotence, we might well, rather, be frightened by the scope of our power. If teachers and parents were more consistently aware that nothing can happen in the child's presence which does not leave some trace in him, that the form of his mind and of his character depends on these thousands of little unconscious influences that take place at every moment and to which we pay no attention because of their apparent insignificance, how much more would they watch their language and their behavior! Surely, education cannot be very effective when it functions inconsistently. As Herbart says, it is not by reprimanding the child violently from time to time that one can influence him very much. But when education is patient and continuous, when it does not look for immediate and obvious successes, but proceeds slowly in a well-defined direction, without letting itself be diverted by external incidents and adventitious circumstances, it has at its disposal all the means necessary to affect minds profoundly.

At the same time, one sees what is the essential means of educational influence. What makes for the influence of the hypnotist is the authority which he holds under the circumstances. By analogy, then, one can say that education must be essentially a matter of authority. This important proposition can, moreover, be established directly. Indeed, we have seen that the object of education is to superimpose, on the individual and asocial being that we are at birth, an entirely new being. It must bring us to overcome our initial nature; it is on this condition that the child will become a man. Now, we can raise ourselves above ourselves only by a more or less difficult effort. Nothing is so false and deceptive as the Epicurean conception of education, the conception of a Montaigne, for example, according to which man can be formed while enjoying himself and without any other spur than the attraction of pleasure. If there is nothing somber in life and if it is criminal artificially to make it so in the eyes of the child, it is, however, serious and important; and education, which prepares for life, should share this seriousness. To learn to contain his natural egoism, to subordinate himself to higher ends, to submit his desires to the control of his will, to confine them within proper limits, the child must exercise strong self-control. Now, we restrain ourselves, we limit ourselves, only for one or the other of the following two reasons: because it is necessary through some physical necessity, or because we must do it on moral grounds. But the child cannot feel the necessity that imposes these efforts on us physically, for he is not faced directly with the hard realities of life which make this attitude indispensable. He is not yet engaged in the struggle; whatever Spencer may have said about it, we cannot leave him exposed to these too harsh realities. It is necessary, then, that he be already formed, in large part, when he really encounters them. One cannot, then, depend on their influence to make him bow his will and acquire the necessary mastery over himself.

Duty remains. The sense of duty is, indeed, for the child and even for the adult, the stimulus *par excellence* of effort. Self-respect itself presupposes it. For, to be properly affected by reward and punishment, one must already have a sense of his dignity and, consequently, of his duty. But the child can know his duty only through his teachers or his parents; he can know what it is only through the manner in which they reveal it to him through their language and through their conduct. They must be, then, for him, duty incarnate and personified. Thus moral authority is the dominant quality of the educator. For it is through the authority that is in him that duty is duty. What is his own special quality is the imperative tone with which he addresses consciences, the respect that he inspires in wills and which makes them yield to his judgment. Thus it is indispensable that such an impression emanate from the person of the teacher.

It is not necessary to show that authority, thus understood, is neither violent nor repressive; it consists entirely of a certain moral ascendancy. It presupposes the presence in the teacher of two principal conditions. First, he must have will. For authority implies confidence, and the child cannot have confidence in anyone whom he sees hesitating, shifting, going back on his decisions. But this first condition is not the most essential. What is important above all is that the teacher really feels in himself the authority the feeling for which he is to transmit. It constitutes a force which he can manifest only if he possesses it effectively. Now, where does he get it from? Would it be from the power which he does have, from his right to reward and punish? But fear of chastisement is quite different from respect for authority. It has moral value only if chastisement is recognized as just even by him who suffers it, which implies that the authority which punishes is already recognized as legitimate. And this is the question. It is not from the outside that the teacher can hold his authority, it is from himself; it can come to him only from an inner faith. He must believe, not in himself, no doubt, not in the superior qualities of his intelligence or of his soul, but in his task and in the importance of his task. What makes for the authority which is so readily attached to the word of the priest, is the high idea that he has of his calling; for he speaks in the name of a god in whom he believes, to whom he feels himself closer than the crowd of the uninitiated. The lay teacher can and should have something of this feeling. He too is the agent of a great moral person who surpasses him: it is society. Just as the priest is the interpreter of his god, the teacher is the interpreter of the great moral ideas of his time and of his country. Let him be attached to these ideas, let him feel all their grandeur, and the authority which is in them, and of which he is aware, cannot fail to be communicated to his person and to everything that emanates from him. Into an authority which flows from such an impersonal source there could enter no pride, no vanity, no pedantry. It is made up entirely of the respect which he has for his functions and, if one may say so, for his office. It is this respect which, through word and gesture, passes from him to the child.

Liberty and authority have sometimes been opposed, as if these two factors of education contradicted and limited each other. But this opposition is factitious. In reality these two terms imply, rather than exclude, each other. Liberty is the daughter of authority properly understood. For to be free is not to do what one pleases; it is to be master of oneself, it is to know how to act with reason and to do one's duty. Now, it is precisely to endow the child with this self-mastery that the authority of the teacher should be employed. The authority of the teacher is only one aspect of the authority of duty and of reason. The child should, then, be trained to recognize it in the speech of the educator and to submit to its ascendancy; it is on this condition that he will know later how to find it again in his own conscience and to defer to it.

64

THE FUTILITY OF SCHOOLING

Ivan Illich

Source: *Celebration of Awareness: A Call for Institutional Revolution*, London: Calder & Boyars, 1971, pp. 105–120.

To provide every citizen in the United States with a level of schooling now enjoyed by the well-off one-third would require the addition of forty billion dollars per year to the present cost of elementary and secondary education in the United States, which is about thirty-seven billion. This sum exceeds the present expenditure for the war in Vietnam. Evidently the United States is too poor to provide compensatory education on this scale. And yet it is politically inexpedient and intellectually disreputable to question the elusive goal of providing equal educational opportunities for all citizens by giving them access to an equal number of years in school.

One man's illusions are often best recognized in the light of another man's delusions. My discussion of the futility of schooling in the Third World—published as a magazine article in 1968—may help to demonstrate the general futility of world-wide educational institutions.

For the past two decades, demographic considerations have colored all discussion about development in Latin America. In 1950 some 200 million people occupied the area extending from Mexico to Chile. Of these, 120 million lived directly or indirectly on primitive agriculture. Assuming both effective population controls and the most favorable possible results from programs aimed at the increase of agriculture, by 1985 forty million people will produce most of the food for a total population of 360 million. The remaining 320 million will be either marginal to the economy or will have to be incorporated somehow into urban living and industrial production.

During these same past twenty years, both Latin American governments and foreign technical assistance agencies have come to rely increasingly on the capacity of grammar, trade, and high schools to lead the non-rural majority out of its marginality in shanty towns and subsistence farms into the type of factory, market, and public forum which corresponds to modern technology. It was assumed that schooling would eventually produce a broad middle class with values resembling those of highly industrialized nations, despite the economy of continued scarcity.

Accumulating evidence now indicates that schooling does not and cannot produce the expected results. Some years ago the governments of the Americas joined in an Alliance for Progress, which has, in practice, served mainly the progress of the middle classes in the Latin nations. In most countries the Alliance has encouraged the replacement of a closed, feudal, hereditary elite by one which is supposedly "meritocratic" and open to the few who manage to finish school. Concomitantly, the urban service proletariat has grown at several times the rate of the traditional landless rural mass and has replaced it in importance. The marginal majority and the schooled minority grow ever further apart. One old feudal society has brought forth two classes, separate and unequal.

This development has led to educational research focused on the improvement of the learning process in schools and on the adaptations of schools themselves to the special circumstances prevailing in under-developed societies. But logic would seem to require that we do not stop with an effort to improve schools; rather that we question the assumption on which the school system itself is based. We must not exclude the possibility that the emerging nations cannot be schooled, that schooling is not a viable answer to their need for universal education. Perhaps this type of insight is needed to clear the way for a futuristic scenario in which schools as we know them today would disappear.

The social distance between the growing urban mass and the new elite is a new phenomenon, unlike the traditional forms of discrimination known in Latin America. This new discrimination is not a transitory thing which can be overcome by schooling. On the contrary: I submit that one of the reasons for the awakening frustration in the majorities is the progressive acceptance of the "liberal myth," the assumption that schooling is an assurance of social integration.

The solidarity of all citizens based on their common graduation from school has been an inalienable part of the modern, Western self-image. Colonization has not succeeded in implanting this myth equally in all countries, but everywhere schooling has become the prerequisite for membership in a managerial middle class. The constitutional history of Latin America since its independence has made the masses of this continent particularly susceptible to the conviction that all citizens have a right to enter—and, therefore, have some possibility of entering—their society through the door of a school.

More than elsewhere, in Latin America the teacher as missionary for the school-gospel has found adherents at the grassroots. Only a few years ago many of us were happy when finally the Latin American school system was singled out as the area of privileged investment for international assistance funds. In fact, during the past years, both national budgets and private investment have been stimulated to increase educational allocations. But a second look reveals that this school system has built a narrow bridge across a widening social gap. As the only legitimate passage to the middle class, the school restricts all unconventional crossings and leaves the underachiever to bear the blame for his marginality.

This statement is difficult for Americans to understand. In the United States, the nineteenth-century persuasion that free schooling ensures all citizens equality in the economy and effective participation in the society survives. It is by no means certain that the result of schooling ever measured up to this expectation, but the schools certainly played a more prominent role in this process some hundred years ago.

In the United States of the mid-nineteenth century, six years of schooling frequently made a young man the educational superior of his book. In a society largely dominated by unschooled achievers, the little red schoolhouse was an effective road to social equality. A few years in school for all brought most extremes together. Those who achieved power and money without schooling had to accept a degree of equality with those who achieved literacy and did not strike it rich. Computers, television, and airplanes have changed this. Today in Latin America, in the midst of modern technology, three times as many years of schooling and twenty times as much money as was then spent on grammar schools will not produce the same social result. The dropout from the sixth grade is unable to find a job even as a punch card operator or a railroad hand.

Contemporary Latin America needs school systems no more than it needs railroad tracks. Both—spanning continents—served to speed the now-rich and established nations into the industrial age. Both, if now handled with care, are harmless heirlooms from the Victorian period. But neither is relevant to countries emerging from primitive agriculture directly into the jet age. Latin America cannot afford to maintain outmoded social institutions amid modern technological processes.

By "school," of course, I do not mean all organized formal education. I use the term "school" and "schooling" here to designate a form of child care and a *rite de passage* which we take for granted. We forget that this institution and the corresponding creed appeared on the scene only with the growth of the industrial state. Comprehensive schooling today involves year-round, obligatory, and universal classroom attendance in small groups for several hours each day. It is imposed on all citizens for a period of ten to eighteen years. School divides life into two segments, which are increasingly of comparable length. As much as anything else, schooling implies custodial care for persons who are declared undesirable elsewhere by the simple fact that a school has been built to serve them. The school is supposed to take the excess population from the street, the family, or the labor force. Teachers are given the power to invent new criteria according to which new segments of the population may be committed to a school. This restraint on healthy, productive, and potentially independent human beings is performed by schools with an economy which only labor camps could rival.

Schooling also involves a process of accepted ritual certification for all members of a "schooled" society. Schools select those who are bound to succeed and send them on their way with a badge marking them fit. Once universal schooling has been accepted as the hallmark for the in-members of a society, fitness is measured by the amount of time and money spent on formal education in youth rather than ability acquired independently from an "accredited" curriculum.

A first important step toward radical educational reform in Latin America will be taken when the educational system of the United States is accepted for what it is: a recent, imaginative social invention perfected since World War II and historically rooted in the American frontier. The creation of the all-pervasive school establishment, tied into industry, government, and the military, is an invention no less original than the guild-centered apprenticeship of the Middle Ages, or the *doctrina de los indios* and the *reducción* of Spanish missionaries in Mexico and Paraguay, respectively, or the *lycée* and *les grandes écoles* in France. Each one of these systems was produced by its society to give stability to an achievement; each has been heavily pervaded by ritual to which society bowed; and each has been rationalized into an all-embracing persuasion, religion, or ideology. The United States is not the first nation that has been willing to pay a high price to have its educational system exported by missionaries to all corners of the world. The colonization of Latin America by the catechism is certainly a noteworthy precedent.

It is difficult now to challenge the school as a system because we are so used to it. Our industrial categories tend to define results as products of specialized institutions and instruments. Armies produce defense for countries. Churches procure salvation in an afterlife. Binet defined intelligence as that which his tests test. Why not, then, conceive of education as the product of schools? Once this tag has been accepted, unschooled education gives the impression of something spurious, illegitimate, and certainly unaccredited.

For some generations, education has been based on massive schooling, just as security was based on massive retaliation and, at least in the United States, transportation on the family car. The United States, because it industrialized earlier, is rich enough to afford schools, the Strategic Air Command, and the car—no matter what the toll. Most nations of the world are not that rich; they behave, however, as if they were. The example of nations which "made it" leads Brazilians to pursue the ideal of the family car—just for a few. It compels Peruvians to squander on Mirage bombers— just for a show. And it drives every government in Latin America to spend up to two-fifths of its total budget on schools, and to do so unchallenged.

362

Let us insist, for a moment, on this analogy between the school system and the system of transportation based on the family car. Ownership of a car is now rapidly becoming the ideal in Latin America—at least among those who have a voice in formulating national goals. During the past twenty years, roads, parking facilities, and services for private automobiles have been immensely improved. These improvements benefit overwhelmingly those who have their own cars—that is, a tiny percentage. The bias of the budget allocated for transportation thus discriminates against the best transportation for the greatest number—and the huge capital investments in this area ensure that this bias is here to stay. In some countries, articulate minorities now challenge the family car as the fundamental unit of transportation in emerging societies. But everywhere in Latin America it would be political suicide to advocate radical limitations on the multiplication of schools. Opposition parties may challenge at times the need for superhighways or the need for weapons which will see active duty only in a parade. But what man in his right mind would challenge the need to provide every child with a chance to go to high school?

Before poor nations could reach this point of universal schooling, however, their ability to educate would be exhausted. Even ten or twelve years of schooling are beyond 85 per cent of all men of our century if they happen to live outside the tiny islands where capital accumulates. Nowhere in Latin America do 27 per cent of any age group get beyond the sixth grade, nor do more than 1 per cent graduate from a university. Yet no government spends less than 18 per cent of its budget on schools, and many spend more than 30 per cent. Universal schooling, as this concept has been defined recently in industrial societies, is obviously beyond their means. The annual cost of schooling a United States citizen between the ages of twelve and twenty-four equals as much as most Latin Americans earn in two or three years.

Schools will stay beyond the means of the developing nations: neither radical population control nor maximum reallocations of government budgets nor unprecedented foreign aid would end the present unfeasibility of school systems aimed at twelve years of schooling for all. Population control needs time to become effective when the total population is as young as that of tropical America. The percentage of the world's resources invested in schooling cannot be raised beyond certain levels, nor can this budget grow beyond foreseeable maximal rates. Finally, foreign aid would have to increase to 30 per cent of the receiving nation's national budget to provide effectively for schooling, a goal not to be anticipated.

Furthermore, the per capita cost of schooling itself is rising everywhere as schools accept those who are difficult to teach, as retention rates rise, and as the quality of schooling itself improves. This rise in cost neutralizes much of the new investments. Schools do not come cheaper by the dozen.

In view of all these factors, increases in school budgets must usually be defended by arguments which imply default. In fact, however, schools are untouchable because they are vital to the status quo. Schools have the effect of tempering the subversive potential of education in an alienated society because, if education is confined to schools, only those who have been schooled into compliance on a lower grade are admitted to its higher reaches. In capital-starved societies not rich enough to purchase unlimited schooling, the majority is schooled not only into compliance but also into subservience.

Since Latin American constitutions were written with an eye on the United States, the ideal of universal schooling was a creative utopia. It was a condition necessary to create the Latin American nineteenth-century bourgeoisie. Without the pretense that every citizen has a right to go to school, the liberal bourgeoisie could never have developed; neither could the middle-class masses of present-day Europe, the United States, and Russia, nor the managerial middle elite of their cultural colonies in South America. But the same school which worked in the last century to overcome feudalism has now become an oppressive idol which protects those who are already schooled. Schools grade and, therefore, they degrade. They make the degraded accept his own submission. Social seniority is bestowed according to the level of schooling achieved. Everywhere in Latin America more money for schools means more privilege for a few at the cost of most, and this patronage of an elite is explained as a political ideal. This ideal is written into laws which state the patently impossible: equal scholastic opportunities for all.

The number of satisfied clients who graduate from schools every year is much smaller than the number of frustrated dropouts who are conveniently graded by their failure for use in a marginal labor pool. The resulting steep educational pyramid defines a rationale for the corresponding levels of social status. Citizens are "schooled" into their places. This results in politically acceptable forms of discrimination which benefit the relatively few achievers.

The move from the farm to the city in Latin America still frequently means a move from a world where status is explained as a result of inheritance into a world where it is explained as a result of schooling. Schools allow a head start to be rationalized as an achievement. They give to privilege not only the appearance of equality but also of generosity: should somebody who missed out on early schooling be dissatisfied with the status he holds, he can always be referred to a night or trade school. If he does not take advantage of such recognized remedies, his exclusion from privilege can be explained as his own fault. Schools temper the frustrations they provoke.

The school system also inculcates its own universal acceptance. Some schooling is not necessarily more education than none, especially in a country where every year a few more people can get all the schooling they want while most people never complete the sixth grade. But much less than six years seems to be sufficient to inculcate in the child the acceptance of the ideology which goes with the school grade. The child learns only about the superior status and unquestioned authority of those who have more schooling than he has.

Any discussion of radical alternatives to school-centered formal education upsets our notions of society. No matter how inefficient schools are in educating a majority, no matter how effective schools are in limiting the access to the elite, no matter how liberally schools shower their non-educational benefits on the members of this elite, schools do increase the national income. They qualify their graduates for more economic production. In an economy on the lower rungs of development toward United States-type industrialization, a school graduate is enormously more productive than a dropout. Schools are part and parcel of a society in which a minority is on the way to becoming so productive that the majority must be schooled into disciplined consumption. Schooling therefore—under the best of circumstances—helps to divide society into two groups: those so productive that their expectation of annual rise in personal income lies far beyond the national average, and the overwhelming majority whose income also rises, but at a rate clearly below the former's. These rates, of course, are compounded and lead the two groups further apart.

Radical innovation in formal education presupposes radical political changes, radical changes in the organization of production, and radical changes in man's image of himself as an animal which needs school. This is often forgotten when sweeping reforms of the schools are proposed and fail because of the societal framework we accept. For instance, the trade school is sometimes advocated as a cure-all for mass schooling. Yet it is doubtful that the products of trade schools would find employment in a continuously changing, ever more automated economy. Moreover the capital and operating costs of trade schools, as we know them today, are several times as high as those for a standard school of the same grade. Also, trade schools usually take in sixth graders, who, as we have seen, are already the exception. Trade schools pretend to educate by creating a spurious facsimile of the factory within a school building.

Instead of the trade school, we should think of a subsidized transformation of the industrial plant. It should be possible to obligate factories to serve as training centers during off-hours, for managers to spend part of their time planning and supervising this training, and for the industrial process to be so redesigned that it has educational value. If the expenditures for present schools were partly allocated to sponsor this kind of educational exploitation of existing resources, then the final results—both economic and educational—might be incomparably greater. If, further, such subsidized apprenticeship were offered to all who ask for it, irrespective of age, and not only to those who are destined to be employees in the particular plant, industry would have begun to assume an important role now played by school. We would be on the way to disabuse ourselves of the idea that manpower qualification must precede employment, that schooling must precede productive work. There is no reason for us to continue the medieval tradition in which men are prepared for the "secular world" by incarceration in a sacred precinct, be it monastery, synagogue, or school.

A second, frequently discussed, remedy for the failure of schools is fundamental, or adult, education. It has been proved by Paulo Freire in Brazil that those adults who can be interested in political issues of their community can be made literate within six weeks of evening classes. The program teaching such reading and writing skills, of course, must be built around the emotion-loaded key words of the adults' political vocabulary. Understandably this fact has gotten Freire's program into trouble. It has also been suggested that the dollar-cost of ten separate months of adult education is equal that of one year of early schooling, and can be incomparably more effective than schooling at its best.

Unfortunately, "adult education" now is conceived principally as a device to give the "underprivileged" a palliative for the schooling he lacks. The situation would have to be reversed if we wanted to conceive of all education as an exercise in adulthood. We should consider a radical reduction of the length of the formal, obligatory school sessions to only two months each year—but spread this type of formal schooling over the first twenty or thirty years of a man's life.

While various forms of in-service apprenticeship in factories and programmed math and language teaching could assume a large proportion of what we have previously called "instruction," two months a year of formal schooling should be considered ample time for what the Greeks meant by *scholē*—leisure for the pursuit of insight. No wonder we find it nearly impossible to conceive of comprehensive social changes in which the educational functions of schools would thus be redistributed in new patterns among institutions we do not now envisage. We find it equally difficult to indicate concrete ways in which the non-educational functions of a vanishing school system would be redistributed. We do not know what to do with those whom we now label "children" or "students" and commit to school.

It is difficult to foresee the political consequences of changes as fundamental as those proposed, not to mention the international consequences. How should a school-reared society coexist with one which has gone "off the school standard," and whose industry, commerce, advertising, and participation in politics is different as a matter of principle? Areas which develop outside the universal school standard would lack the common language and criteria for respectful coexistence with the schooled. Two such worlds, such as China and the United States, might almost have to seal themselves off from each other.

Rashly, the school-bred mind abhors the educational devices available to these worlds. It is difficult mentally to "accredit" Mao's party as an educational institution which might prove more effective than the schools are at their best—at least when it comes to inculcating citizenship. Guerrilla warfare in Latin America is another education device much more frequently misused or misunderstood than applied. Che Guevara, for instance, clearly saw it as a last educational resort to teach a people about the illegitimacy of their political system. Especially in unschooled countries, where the transistor radio has come to every village, we must never underrate the educational functions of great charismatic dissidents like Dom Helder Camara in Brazil or Camilo Torres in Colombia. Castro described his early charismatic harangues as "teaching sessions."

The schooled mind perceives these processes exclusively as political indoctrination, and their educational purpose eludes its grasp. The legitimation of education by schools tends to render all non-school education an accident, if not an outright misdemeanor. And yet it is surprising with what difficulty the school-bred mind perceives the rigor with which schools inculcate their own presumed necessity, and with it the supposed inevitability of the system they sponsor. Schools indoctrinate the child into the acceptance of the political system his teachers represent, despite the claim that teaching is non-political.

Ultimately the cult of schooling will lead to violence, as the establishment of *any* religion has led to it. If the gospel of universal schooling is permitted to spread in Latin America, the military's ability to repress insurgency must grow. Only force will ultimately control the insurgency inspired by the frustrated expectation that the propagation of the school-myth enkindles. The maintenance of the present school system may turn out to be an important step on the way to Latin American fascism. Only fanaticism inspired by idolatry of a system can ultimately rationalize the massive discrimination which will result from another twenty years of grading a capital-starved society by school marks.

The time has come to recognize the real burden of the schools in the emerging nations, so that we may become free to envisage change in the social structure which now makes schools a necessity. I do not advocate a sweeping utopia like the Chinese commune for Latin America. But I do suggest that we plunge our imagination into the construction of scenarios which would allow a bold reallocation of educational functions among industry, politics, short scholastic retreats, and intensive preparation of parents for providing early childhood education. The cost of schools must be measured not only in economic, social, and educational terms, but in political terms as well. Schools, in an economy of scarcity invaded by automation, accentuate and rationalize the coexistence of two societies, one a colony of the other.

Once it is understood that the cost of schooling is not inferior to the cost of chaos, we might be on the brink of courageously costly compromise. Today it is as dangerous in Latin America to question the myth of social salvation through schooling as it was three hundred years ago to question the divine rights of the Catholic kings.

INDEX

abandonment **II** 81–93; as a catch-all
term **II** 82; children's perspectives
II 91–2; context of non-Western
childhood **II** 86–8; context of proper
Western childhood **II** 84–6; dreams
II 102; evoking the child **II** 103–5;
idea of dependent child **II** 87; literary
characters **II** 83–4; mode **I** 334; as a
moral discourse **II** 88–9; positive
defiance **II** 91; remedial action
II 89–90, 91; as a social constraint
II 84; typologies **II** 82–4
abortion **III** 265; moral dispute **I** 85;
teenage **III** 210
abstraction **III** 11; reflective **III** 12
abuse **I** 112; media/political campaigns
I 395–6; *see also* child sexual abuse
acrobats: trade **I** 289–90
Actionaid **I** 209, 210–11
actions: additive coordination **III** 12;
individual **III** 12
actor network theory **III** 23
adolescence: love **I** 322; mind **I** 322
Adorno, T. **I** 111
adult duty **I** 90–2
adult society and childhood **I** 112,
113–14, 114–17
adult-child relationship **I** 129–30; and
generation **I** 135; studying **I** 131, 133
adulthood: Judaism **III** 27; preparation
for **I** 84
adults and children **II** 245–7; class
analysis **II** 247–9; formation of
stratification system **II** 243–4;
generational mode of human capital
production **II** 250–5
advice literature: significance **III** 35–7
aesthetic of childhood **I** 293

affective individualism **I** 353, 364
age: of consent **I** 86; market
segmentation **II** 211–12; stratification
principle **I** 66
age group: children as **III** 326–7
agrarian society **III** 326
Aid agencies: women's organizations
III 50
Ainsworth, M.: and Crittenden, P. **II** 5,
6, 7
Aitken, C. S. **I** 169, 175–6
Alanen, L. **I** 71
Alaska **II** 86
Alice Green **I** 297
Altaible (Huidobro) **I** 99
Althusser, L. **I** 15
altruism **I** 13–14; main expression **I** 426
Ambert, A. M. **I** 13, 14, 70, 110
ambivalent mode **I** 334
ambulatory stage **I** 318
America: 17th century **I** 343; 18th
century **I** 344–6, 351–2
American Geographers, Association of
I 170
American Humane Society **III** 201
American States, Organization of **I** 213
analysis: aims **I** 370–1; fundamental
categories **I** 382
anarchist: child as **I** 28
anarchistic tendencies **I** 140
Annie **III** 155–6
anorexia **II** 62
Ansell, N. **I** 176
Anthony, K. H. **I** 256–7, 259–60
anthropology **I** 144, 155; age systems
I 66
anti-social behaviour: root causes **I** 394
Anton Reiser (Moritz) **I** 105

368